Conversations with **Maida Springer**

YEVETTE RICHARDS

Conversations with **Maida Springer**

A Personal History of Labor, Race, and International Relations

University of Pittsburgh Press

Published by the University of Pittsburgh Press, Pittsburgh, Pa., 15260
Copyright © 2004, University of Pittsburgh Press
Manufactured in the United States of America
Printed on acid-free paper
10 9 8 7 6 5 4 3 2 1

Library of Congress Cataloging-in-Publication Data

Richards, Yevette.
  Conversations with Maida Springer : a personal history of labor, race, and
international relations / Yevette Richards.
      p. cm.
  Includes bibliographical references and index.
  ISBN 0-8229-4231-3 (cloth (hardcover) : alk. paper)
  1. Springer, Maida. 2. Women labor leaders—United States—Biography.
3. Women labor union members—United States—Biography. 4. African
American women—Biography. 5. International labor activities—History.
6. Pan-Africanism—History. I. Title.
  HD8073.S84R53 2004
  331.88'092—dc22

                              2004003484

To my mother
Bobbie Jean Richards

And in memory of my father
Louis Thurman Richards

Contents

Acknowledgments

First on my list of those to thank is Maida Springer Kemp for graciously allowing me to conduct countless hours of interviews with her. For over a decade she has provided me the opportunity to research her private collection of papers and to meet with her family, friends, and colleagues, both in the United States and in East Africa. All attest to what I have come to know: Her activism on behalf of labor, civil rights, and women reflects an extraordinary generosity of spirit and a selfless devotion to improving the lives of others.

Many of the people I thanked in *Maida Springer, Pan-Africanist and International Labor Leader,* I also thank in this companion book of interviews. The many archivists who aided me in my research efforts include M. Lee Sayrs, George Meany Memorial Archives; Brenda Square, Amistad Research Center; Patrizia Sione, Kheel Center for Labor-Management Documentation and Archives; Sylvia McDowell, Schlesinger Library; and Carol Leadenham, the Hoover Institution. The sources of funding that enabled me to pursue this project included a George Mason University Mathy Junior Faculty Award in the Arts and Humanities, a Ford Foundation postdoctoral fellowship, a grant from Carnegie Mellon's Center for African American Urban Studies and the Urban Economy (CAUSE), a University of Pittsburgh postdoctoral fellowship, a Swarthmore College research grant, and a Yale University John F. Enders special research assistance grant.

I am deeply indebted to many friends, family members, colleagues, and mentors who helped sustain me while I compiled these interviews. I thank Hazel Carby, David Montgomery, Joe William Trotter Jr., Diana Wylie, and two anonymous reviewers who read most of these interviews and provided me with ideas for other avenues of inquiry. A host of others I thank either for their valuable discussions about the process of interviewing or for their views on the activism or personality of Maida Springer. These include: Kanyama Chiume, Sharon Ghamari, Lynn Hudson, Barbara Lazarus, Jan and Melvin McCray, Bibi Titi Mohamed, Martin Morand, Maynard Mpangala, Sabiyha Prince, Marcus Rediker, Jackie Mullins, Vernell Lillie, and Jennie Silverman. I am grateful to Dawn Virtue for her excellent transcriptions of a number of taped interviews. The debt I owe my family is eternal. My mother and husband Paul

Jordan gave infinitely of their time to help me complete this project. Paul's humor, support, and love are among my many blessings. I thank our young daughter Amara for sometimes allowing me to go without her to "Aunt Maida's" house to work. Finally, I am grateful for our newborn son Kayin, whose smiles helped sustain me through the last months of manuscript preparation.

Acknowledgments

Conversations with **Maida Springer**

Introduction

When I first met Maida Springer in 1989, I marveled at the wonderful array of clowns decorating her house. From many parts of the world, they were exquisite in detail and vibrant in color. Springer explained that the presence of clowns kept her humble and served as a reminder to not take herself too seriously. She also identified with the dilemma of the protagonist Canio, a theater troupe leader who plays a clown in the opera *I Pagliacci*. Although heartbroken after discovering that his wife is having an affair, Canio attempts to act in a professional manner symbolized by the saying "the show must go on." He has to put on his makeup, hide his great pain, and give his best to the audience. As I became better acquainted with Springer, I began to appreciate why this story resonated with her. As an activist on the domestic and international stage she often sublimated her feelings of bitterness and disappointment in order to obtain minimal support for the labor programs she designed to foster improved living conditions for others. Although the diplomatic tightrope she walked as a labor activist entailed heartbreak and stress, she never sacrificed her self-respect.

Born in Panama in 1910, Springer came to the United States when she was seven years old. Her activist spirit was kindled at a young age as she listened to black leaders of Harlem pay homage to Africa, condemn colonialism, and decry their own treatment in the United States. After she joined the International Ladies' Garment Workers' Union (ILGWU) in 1933, her work for civil rights and the labor movement became intertwined and inseparable as she forged a friendship with A. Philip Randolph, who would later become an AFL-CIO vice president. A 1945 meeting with George Padmore, the premier pan-African network builder, took her down the path of international labor activism. She formally joined the AFL-CIO Department of International Affairs in 1960 and served as an expert in African labor affairs and a confidante of many African labor and political leaders. Springer also dedicated herself to women's advancement both nationally and internationally, particularly in Turkey, Indonesia, and various African countries.

Through her work she gained a reputation as a skilled organizer and a tireless activist for social change.

Springer's status as a black woman working in the white and male-dominated field of organized labor meant that she was alternately celebrated as a pioneer, subject to use as a token, or attacked because of her representation. In the following interviews, she states, "When I was told that I was different, my blood pressure would rise, and I would become angry and illogical. It's pointless to give you examples. It was on so many levels and so trivial sometimes that it made you want to scratch." As an ILGWU officer she became adept at confronting the prejudices of both union leaders and members without jeopardizing the larger goal of labor solidarity. Without minimizing the racism present in organized labor, she tried to bridge the gap between labor and black workers and the black community. As an international labor representative, she faced paternalistic and racist treatment from officials of the British Trade Union Congress and the International Confederation of Free Trade Unions (ICFTU), a world body composed of non-Communist national labor centers. She learned to tailor her responses to these insults in a way that was least damaging to relations between the ICFTU and its African affiliates. However, the stress Springer experienced working in international affairs was not inconsequential. It led to serious illness, including ulcers and bouts of depression.

The AFL-CIO's strong anticolonial stance and Springer's obvious empathy with African labor combined to make her anathema to colonial governments as well. Colonial officials and European labor leaders accused her and other supporters of pan-Africanism of being Communists or unwittingly aiding the Communists through their adoption of a strident anticolonial position. Some officials of U.S. consulates, particularly in the Congo and Southern Rhodesia, also showed a veiled hostility toward Springer's presence in Africa. In contrast, many African labor and independence leaders viewed her as a valuable ally because of her ability to publicize the oppression they faced outside the continent. Procolonialists took note. Springer remarked, "Nothing was secret. Maida Springer arrived somewhere. The grapevine works. Both politically and in government circles. . . . The news spread that this Maida Springer would come here trying to start trouble, also to encourage people, to talk to the Africans."

The complexities of cold war politics undermined Springer's efforts to bring about closer relations between the West and Africa. With the purpose of marshaling their countries' resources for economic development, most African governments became one-party states, forced the labor centers to disaffiliate from the ICFTU, and then incorporated the labor centers into the political parties. The AFL-CIO charged that these labor centers were no longer workers' organizations but government entities, and the organization strongly opposed moves to open relations with unions from Communist countries. Although Springer had opposed the disaffiliation of African labor centers, she resisted efforts of U.S. labor leaders to have her speak against the new African government structures. In reference to Western labor's denunciation of the new labor structures as antidemocratic and comparable to the ones in Communist countries, Springer commented, "All the Africans had dealt with were the wrong things from the colonial powers or whoever was trying to purify them." Her empathy for the enormous tasks facing these new governments, however, was tempered by the realization that ordinary African workers would pay a high price as the governments reined in the labor movements in the name of nation building. She had directed her efforts in Africa to raising the skill levels of ordinary workers and educating workers' representatives in the skills necessary to secure the greatest benefits for workers. To her dismay the acrimonious struggle over affiliation negatively affected some of her relationships: "I thought foolishly that I had enough credit that I would not be affected by it."

By and large, however, the disagreements Springer had with her African labor colleagues over the affiliation issue did not diminish the esteem in which she was held, and many continued to view her as family. (She was widely known on the Continent as Mama Maida.) Not only did she share in some of their criticisms of the ICFTU, but her faith in the democratic West was also always ambivalent. The egregious policies of the U.S. government in Africa, the recalcitrant unions upholding formal discrimination within the AFL-CIO, and the slow pace of civil rights reform in the United States placed her in contradictory positions. She once remarked that some of her experiences with racism within the U.S. labor movement "ate her up inside." Until 1963 she considered moving permanently to Africa. With the passage of the 1965 Voting Rights Act, Springer told her ILGWU colleague Martin Morand that she had some hope that the United States might move closer to the ideal of equality.

Despite Springer's many disappointments, a marvelous sense of humor, humility, and a wellspring of hope have combined to produce a regenerative effect on her outlook. She has survived to give testimony to a singular life of a black woman's remarkable journey from an industrial worker to a leader in international labor affairs during a revolutionary period of change. Not only is she honored for her efforts on behalf of African independence and labor development, but she is also remembered by ordinary people, both domestically and internationally, as one who gave hope and encouragement and many times committed her own personal resources to improving their lives. For these reasons she affirms her life as one lived with few regrets.

After first becoming aware of Maida Springer in 1985, I was astounded by her absence from the established histories of women, labor, and African Americans. In 1989, as an American Studies graduate student at Yale University, I learned of an unpublished oral history she had done under the auspices of the Twentieth-

Century Trade Union Woman: Vehicle for Social Change, Oral History Project.[1] I was captivated by these interviews, but they left me with many unanswered questions. The interviewer's primary interest and expertise lay in the U.S. labor movement; information about Springer's international work got only cursory coverage. I then determined to find Springer in hopes that she would allow me to record a more full life history.

After weeks of effort and finally with the help of the AFL-CIO, I was able to locate Springer in Pittsburgh. She agreed to my request for a weekend visit and insisted that I stay at her house and not a hotel. At the time I was surprised that she would trust a stranger to come into her home. I would later learn that hospitality was a hallmark of her personality. During our conversation that weekend, she asked with straightforward ease what I wanted of her. I replied by telling her I wanted to do a series of oral history interviews with her and shape them into a narrative for my dissertation. Her initial response was to gently decline.

I believed there were at least three reasons informing this decision. First, as I later learned during the interview process, many aspects of her past were painful to recall. Second, she is by nature unassuming and balks at the prospect of appearing self-promoting. Finally, her explanation to me then was that she did not think she had the stamina to endure going over her life's work and that she had declined previous requests of people wanting to write about her work. She believed that they had preconceived and incorrect notions about the roles she had played. In response, I accepted that she might not want to record her story with me or at this time, but insisted that she document her story in the near future. Her subsequent comments reflected her awareness of the special role she saw herself as privileged to have played in the shaping of social movements. Then, to my surprise, she changed her mind about the collaboration offer, telling me that she thought whatever I wrote would be fair.

Maida Springer's lyricism, humorous twists of phrases, and insightful analysis of her character and those of others convinced me of the intrinsic value and appeal that her life history narrative would convey. I resolved to write the biography *Maida Springer, Pan-Africanist and International Labor Leader* as a social history and as a

---

1. The oral history of Maida Springer Kemp conducted by Elizabeth Balanoff was a joint project of the Twentieth-Century Trade Union Woman: Vehicle for Social Change, Oral History Project (Ann Arbor: University of Michigan; Detroit: Wayne State University, 1970s) and the Schlesinger Library's Black Women Oral History Project, Interviews, 1976–1981. It is now published as "Maida Springer Kemp Interview," in *The Black Women Oral History Project*, from the Arthur and Elizabeth Schlesinger Library on the History of Women in America, Radcliffe College, vol. 7, ed. Ruth Edmonds Hill (New Providence, NJ: K. G. Saur Verlag, 1991), 39–127. See http://www.reuther.wayne.edu/use/ohistory.html#20th.

companion book, her oral narrative. Springer's inspirational voice provides a personal view of the connections among labor, civil rights, and international relations.

The history profession has shifted toward acceptance of oral history as a legitimate tool of historical analysis. Sherna Berger Gluck attributes this change to the work of past presidents of the Oral History Association and the increased use of oral history by graduate students in their doctoral research. Oral historians are more critically scrutinizing life histories and are no longer viewing them as unmediated representations of experience. A whole host of factors, they now theorize, have an impact on the way a life is represented, including subjectivity, the power dynamics of the interview process, the construction of memory, the performative aspects of oral history, and gendered speech patterns.[2]

Proponents of oral history include feminists seeking to uncover the role of women in histories dominated by the experiences of prominent white men. They argue that oral histories of nonelite people who did not have the benefit of institutional resources to document their experiences are essential to the recovery of marginalized voices and may lead to new interpretations of established history. In the absence of documentary sources, oral history may represent the only resource that can be used to reconstruct the experiences of these groups.[3] Although Springer's story comes out of the ranks of marginalized groups whose experiences change our conception of history, her story is not bereft of corroborating documentary evidence. Springer's story, therefore, is less vulnerable to traditional academia's criticism that oral history does not represent objective history.

In response to the objectivity argument, oral historians and feminist scholars have rejoined that objective history is itself an illusory concept; all history is mediated. Historians and the authors of documents that historians study are not free from the social, cultural, economic, and political constructs that shape their experiences, perceptions, and interpretations. Alice Hoffman notes that "Archives are replete with self-serving documents, with edited and doctored diaries and memoranda written 'for the record.'"[4] Springer, too, has reflected on this issue: "Very few people in the world are [objective]. They are objective to what suits their purposes."

Oral history proponents have recognized that the fallibility and malleability of memory raise concerns about representations of past events. The narrators' present-

2. Sherna Berger Gluck, "Reflections on Oral History in the New Millennium: Roundtable Comments," *Oral History Review* 26 (Summer–Fall 1999): 6.

3. Selma Leydesdorff, Luisa Passerini, and Paul Thompson, eds., *International Yearbook of Oral History and Life Stories*, vol. 4, *Gender and Memory* (New York: Oxford University Press, 1996), 4.

4. Alice Hoffman, "Reliability and Validity in Oral History," in *Oral History: An Interdisciplinary Anthology*, 2nd ed., ed. David K. Dunaway and Willa K. Baum, 87–93 (Walnut Creek, CA: AltaMira Press, 1996), 92.

Introduction

day political, cultural, and economic contexts are reflected in how they remember the past. Over time memory undergoes new constructions as people forget, omit, add, distort, reorganize, and combine details from the past to fit their present-day orientation. Nevertheless, oral historians see value in subjective remembrances. How people remember, what they remember, and how consciousness changes over time are important points of inquiry for understanding social forces.[5]

In place of objectivity, oral historians have adopted "intersubjectivity," a term scientist Marcia Westkott has used to describe her relationship to those she has researched. Intersubjectivity defines a process in which the interviewer compares her own experiences with her research and then shares her ideas and perceptions about the project with the narrator. The narrator may then offer suggestions that might lead to a new conceptual vision of how to proceed with the research. Thus, oral history is recognized as a collaborative project involving two subjectivities, that of the narrator and the interviewer. Alessandro Portelli notes that the interviewer and narrator come to the oral history process with their own agendas, which then undergo constant renegotiation.[6]

Maida Springer and I engaged in an interview process that represented an evolutionary endeavor. The quality of the interviews improved as I learned from my mistakes during reviews of the taped sessions. I recognized the need to ask open-ended questions, follow her leads on issues of importance to her, allow her to speak to issues and events that she associated together, and question my preconceptions. The anthropologist Lawrence Watson has remarked that although interpreters can never completely disassociate themselves from the mental constructs that sift information for them, they can attempt to suspend prejudices in order to be prepared to hear a new story.[7] While my research gave me a familiarity with the people and events that touched Springer's life, I often found that her evaluations and stories of personal encounters and interactions imparted a new perspective to my view of historical events.

To decrease the potential of misrepresenting or ignoring Springer's narrative constructions and to give her the opportunity to expand upon the topics of the interview, I involved her in every phase of the project. I often gave her the questions

5. See Katherine Borland, "That's Not What I Said": Interpretive Conflict in Oral Narrative Research," in *Women's Words: The Feminist Practice of Oral History*, ed. Sherna Berger Gluck and Daphne Patai (New York: Routledge, 1991), 64; David Thelen, ed., *Memory and American History* (Bloomington: Indiana University Press, 1990), viii–x.

6. Sondra Hale, "Feminist Method, Process, and Self-Criticism: Interviewing Sudanese Women," in Gluck and Patai, *Women's Words*, 125; Alessandro Portelli, "Oral History as Genre," in *Narrative and Genre*, ed. Mary Chamberlain and Paul Thompson (New York: Routledge, 1998), 23, 29.

7. Lawrence C. Watson, "Understanding Life History as a Subjective Document: Hermeneutical and Phenomenological Perspectives," *Ethos* 4 (Spring 1976): 98–101, 118.

beforehand and shared with her the transcripts of our conversations. Discussing some of the topics before taping them allowed time for her to reflect on the meaning of her experiences and raise other issues that concerned her. In order to avoid interrupting the narrative flow, I learned to resist the urge to ask questions of clarification. Instead, I wrote notes on questions that her narration elicited and pursued them after she finished her thoughts. If in response to my question Springer recalled other experiences or demonstrated that she misconstrued my question, I again tried to resist the impulse to redirect. My aim in following this procedure was to hear another story that might participate in shaping a new historical context.

The dialogic process in oral history interviewing does not necessarily negate the presence of an unequal relationship of power and privilege between the interviewer and narrator. In relation to this question of power imbalance, Michael Frisch has asked how issues of race, sex, class, ethnicity, voice, and dress may produce distortions in the interview process. He has noted that the oral history approach raises "important issues of culture, communication, and politics—not only in the material they engage, but in the very processes of engagement."[8] The relationship that Springer and I forged based on cultural experiences emanating from our shared race, gender, and class positions served as mitigating factors in the power dynamics of the interview process. Springer later informed me that her decision to collaborate with me was based on her assessment that my experiences as a black woman imparted to me an underlying basis with which to interpret the history that the interviews would unfold. As Sherna Gluck notes, "the subtle cues to which culturally similar women can respond" not only build trust but "might mean the difference between a good and bad interview."[9]

Fortuitously, the University of Pittsburgh recruited me for a teaching position. My subsequent move closer to Springer enabled us to forge a stronger relationship as I began the process of revising my dissertation for publication. During that period she attended my wedding, became an "aunt" to my child, and introduced me to friends and associates both in the United States and Africa. Sharing our family histories also helped to build trust and friendship. Springer admired my parents who married as teenagers without high school degrees and rose from a position of poverty and segregation in the South to lead successful lives. My father received his doctorate in mathematics as the last of their five children was born, and my mother earned her college degree as a grandmother of eight.

8. Michael Frisch, "Dialogue I," in *Memory and History: Essays on Recalling and Interpreting Experience*, ed. Jaclyn Jeffrey and Glenace Edwall (Lanham, MD: University Press of America, 1994), 64–65, 68; quote in Michael Frisch, *A Shared Authority: Essays on the Craft and Meaning of Oral and Public History* (Albany: State University of New York, 1990), xvi.
9. Gluck, "What's So Special about Women? Women's Oral History," in Dunaway and Baum, *Oral History*, 221.

My higher level of formal education did not automatically confer upon me greater power over the shaping of the story. A determined will and a sophisticated awareness of human behavior and motivation buttress Springer's compassionate nature. While she evinced respect for me as a scholar interested in working-class history, she often served as my teacher, educating me about facets of global and national movements that were not part of documented history. Springer's greater age and more complex life experiences and challenges she had faced easily overcame our imbalance in levels of education.

My power in helping to create this version of Springer's life stemmed from decisions I made concerning lines of inquiry, editing, presentation, and interpretation. My decisions on editing were made in consideration of the divergent views of oral historians concerning how to present an oral history narrative.[10] I have removed many of the false starts because I judged that they did not add anything of consequence to the narrative. At times I have indicated the tone of Springer's voice, particularly to indicate soft or whimsical moods. I have italicized words that she stridently pronounces and occasionally comment on her body language. I often have indicated when she is laughing when I think it is necessary to show the mood in which she gave statements. Her laughter does not always indicate amusement; sometimes it indicates irony, incredulity, and derision, particularly when she speaks of experiences with racism. For example, she laughs on occasion while telling the story of a shop chairman who spat on her office floor after seeing that his new educational director was black. Springer also laughs in derisive bemusement at those who had wrong assumptions about her or who underestimated her ability and intelligence. Laughter is also a signature of her modesty whenever she tells stories that reflect on her high stature. Such nonverbal cues enhance the performative aspects of the narrative.

The process of refashioning the transcripts into the finished interviews made apparent Carl Wilmsen's statement that the finished product represents a "jointly produced set of meanings."[11] Springer and I discussed the parts of the transcripts that concerned her. Sometimes her motivation for wanting to make a change was to give tribute to the work of someone she had inadvertently left out. Other times

10. Rhonda Y. Williams, "'I'm a Keeper of Information': History-Telling and Voice," *Oral History Review* 28 (Winter–Spring 2001): 41–63; Debra J. Blake, "Reading Dynamics of Power through Mexican-Origin Women's Oral Histories," *Frontiers* 19 (September–December 1998): 24–41; Carl Wilmsen, "For the Record: Editing and the Production of Meaning in Oral History," *Oral History Review* 28 (Winter–Spring 2001): 65–85; Kathryn L. Nasstrom, *Everybody's Grandmother and Nobody's Fool: Frances Freeborn Pauley and the Struggle for Social Justice* (Ithaca, NY: Cornell University Press, 2000), 195–204.
11. Wilmsen, "For the Record," 66.

she was concerned that her language might leave the impression that Africans she knew who were struggling economically were desperate and without dignity. I negotiated these changes with her, trying to be sensitive to her feelings. On those occasions when I spoke against a change, remarking that the meaning that she had conveyed would lose its striking appeal, she relented, saying that she would trust my judgment.

In preparing the document for publication I was guided by my research, preliminary discussions with Springer, and a desire to present her story in a roughly chronological order except when it would have harmed her construction of a story. To improve the narrative flow, I removed many of my questions concerned with clarification or identification of subjects or events and combined separate versions of stories when new information was given. I have occasionally rearranged sentences, edited out words, or added a sentence in the place of my question, particularly to help with transition. Due to Springer's gift as a storyteller, the finished interview does not represent a radical departure from her spoken word. The questions I preserve in the text are necessary to understand narrative transitions and to clarify why Springer responds in particular ways. They also serve to reinforce the nature of the interview as a dialogic discourse, by providing some clues to the relationship between the interviewer and the narrator. The removal of most of my questions hides the fact that this oral history represents one of several possible versions of Springer's life story. A different interviewer, a different approach, and a different temporal context would have resulted in a different performance and presentation.[12]

Although I conducted some of these interviews as late as 2003, the political present out of which the bulk of these interviews were conducted was the early 1990s. Many of the momentous world changes that were happening largely as a result of the cold war's demise are reflected in Springer's construction of memory and the questions I asked. In 1990 the Berlin Wall had fallen and Eastern European governments were being overturned. Just before the break-up of the Soviet Union, President Mikhail Gorbachev was pursuing his reform movement perestroika (economic restructuring) and glasnost (openness). The long struggle against the vicious system of apartheid in South Africa was bearing fruit with Nelson Mandela's release from prison. Namibia finally won independence from South Africa. And the Persian Gulf War was beginning to unfold. With the cold war ending, popular movements in Africa were rising against the one-party states and military dictatorships in favor of multiparty democracy and trade union independence from government.

12. Emily Honig, "Getting to the Source: Striking Lives: Oral History and the Politics of Memory," *Journal of Women's History* 9 (Spring 1997): 140.

The changes brought about as a result of the cold war meant that corrupt dictatorships that had been on the side of the West no longer could count automatically on Western support.

Overtones of the domestic racial politics also resonate in the interviews. Springer's comments reflect a sense of the clock being turned back on racial progress in the wake of the Reagan-Bush presidential administrations. The interviews took place when George H. W. Bush, in nominating Clarence Thomas to the Supreme Court, made the dubious assertion that he was the most qualified person for the position. The charges that Thomas sexually harassed Anita Hill and others while heading the Equal Employment Opportunity Commission in the 1980s under both Reagan and Bush had not yet emerged. Springer's views were aligned with those of the majority of black leaders who asserted that the nomination of Thomas was a cynical ploy to establish a beneficiary of the civil rights movement to a position where he could rule against the very policies that had contributed to his rise. Also in the news was the debate over racial nomenclature. Jesse Jackson was leading the call for black Americans to adopt the designation "African American." Having experienced a number of such debates in her lifetime, Springer saw them as a distraction from more pertinent issues affecting the lives of blacks, such as unequal opportunity and income inequality.

Access to archival material was a tremendous boost to my work as interviewer. In addition to the documents in Springer's possession, I researched her papers at both Tulane University's Amistad Center and Radcliffe University's Schlesinger Library. I also researched documents about her work in the Jay Lovestone Papers at Stanford University's Hoover Institution, in the ILGWU Archives at Cornell University's Kheel Center, and in the AFL-CIO papers at the George Meany Memorial Archives. The letters, reports, memorandums, diaries, speeches, newspapers, photographs, labor publications, and pamphlets documenting Springer's activism demonstrate that she had played a fundamental role in building relationships between the AFL-CIO and African labor.

The documentation served as a source for formulating questions and prodding her to talk about events she would rather leave out, as an aid in learning the context of her activism, and as a tool to trigger recall and establish the chronology of events. For example, after I showed Springer a photograph of Julius Nyerere addressing a mass rally of thousands that she had attended in Tanganyika in 1957, she was mentally transported back to that time, remembering how she felt and the spirit of hope and excitement that was palpable in the crowd. Generally, I found a high correlation between the documented evidence and Springer's interpretation and memory of past events. Her voluminous letter writing over the years helped to commit experiences to memory and thus made them stable.

Occasionally, the review of documentation did not help Springer recall the event. Her "lost" memories fall into the category of "episodic memory," a term coined by Endel Tulving to distinguish from "semantic memory." Semantic memory involves retention of factual or conceptual knowledge about the world, whereas episodic memories involve the ability to remember and reexperience personal memories in a highly subjective manner.[13] For example, Springer did not remember a play called *New Phase* that she had mentioned in a 1957 letter to Nyerere. She had written that the play, which was free and had capacity audiences, was disparaging toward Africans. Springer remarked, laughing, "Some of the things that you were exercised about and that you went to see and you supported, and you marched and you protested I don't remember . . . because I was always marching and I was always protesting and I was always writing letters."

Not only was Springer quick to point out when she thought her memory was fallible, but she also was careful to distinguish between what was told to her and what she witnessed. Occasionally, however, I found areas in which she exercised intended forgetfulness. For example, in the documentation concerning her African activism, I twice came across material in which she stated that white officials in colonial governments secretly came to the aid of her or Africans. In order to protect their identity, she did not write down their names at the time. Although she has not forgotten their deeds and speaks of them, she remarks that she has perhaps intentionally forgotten their names. Even if she did remember, she believes that they should have control over whether they want it to be known that they acted against the interests of the British Empire.

The recollections of her immigration experience to the United States demonstrate the important role of rehearsal to the retention of memory and the value of corroborative evidence to substantiate memory. Springer remembers with no hesitation the name of the ship she traveled on from Panama because her mother with pride constantly reminded her that they were able to pay for a full passage on the S.S. *Alianza*. Having the name of the ship helped me to obtain the ship's manifest, from which I was able to glean other information about her family members and their voyage.

Many of the humorous stories about Springer's grandmother belong to a repertoire of family stories that are well rehearsed and were passed on to her by her mother as a form of entertainment. Like the family stories of Kathryn Morgan in her book *Children of Strangers*, they also carry lessons about how strength and ability can overcome adversity. The immediate recall of these stories and Springer's

---

13. Donald A. Ritchie, "Foreword," viii; Kim Lacy Rogers, "Comment," 85–86; and Alice M. Hoffman and Howard S. Hoffman, "Reliability and Validity in Oral History: The Case for Memory," 120; all in Jeffrey and Edwall, *Memory and History*.

evident joy in telling them confirmed the workings of the Pollyanna principle, which holds that people more easily recall good events than bad, and that most events become more neutral with passage of time.[14]

Springer's easy recall of pleasant events, however, did not mean that she had a difficult time recalling painful experiences when my questions elicited them. Neither did her response indicate a mellowing of feelings. Her silence on some issues of great pain in her life demonstrate that a "catharsis associated with telling" was an unreasonable expectation. For example, because her father was not kind to her or her mother, she speaks sparingly of his brief influence in her early life before her parents separated. Respecting the "conventions of social discourse," I accepted the boundaries she placed on these discussions.[15] I had agreed at the beginning of this endeavor that this would be a biography covering her public and not her private life. Still, she has provided evocative portraits of some family members.

The interview process as a whole I believe had the power to help heal some very painful experiences for Springer. My not pursuing areas she clearly did not want to discuss publicly was a factor in her later decision to open up for discussion other areas that I would not have known to address. Nine years after our initial series of interviews, Springer decided to speak about a painful experience with Kenyan labor and political leader Tom Mboya, hoping that through the act of telling she would relieve the distress she had carried since his assassination in 1969. This particular experience with Mboya also demonstrates how highly negative events can lead people to reevaluate the meaning of their life or work.[16]

Information I shared with Springer from her files sometimes gave rise to distress. For example, the deteriorating relationship between Africa nations and Israel and its effect on her work was one such case. After I questioned her about a series of letters she wrote, including one that indicated that the UN resolution equating Zionism with racism had led to the termination of plans for U.S. union participation in building a child care center in Bamako, Mali, Springer and I had this exchange:

Ooh. Lord, these letters are coming to haunt me. Maybe those letters should have been thrown away.

14. Kathryn Morgan, *Children of Strangers: The Stories of a Black Family* (Temple University Press, 1980); Marigole Linton, "Phoenix and Chimera: The Changing Face of Memory," in Jeffrey and Edwall, *Memory and History*, 78, 80.

15. First quote from Gleance E. Edwall, "Comment," in Jeffrey and Edwall, *Memory and History*, 15; second quote from Kathryn Anderson and Dana C. Jack, "Learning to Listen: Interview Techniques and Analyses," in Gluck and Patai, *Women's Words*, 13.

16. Thompson, "Believe It or Not: Rethinking the Historical Interpretation of Memory," 10; Kim Lacy Rogers, "Comment," 87; both in Jeffrey and Edwall, *Memory and History*.

Introduction

(*Laughing.*) No. It's nothing.

(*Laughing.*) You may learn more about me by those letters than I want you to know.

Although Springer here is evoking humor, her anxiety at times was palpable and often limited her response to questions about conflicts. Occasionally during our discussions Springer would pause, shake her head from side to side, and with a contemplative, far-off gaze, she would say to me that there were experiences she would never reveal to anyone. Her silence, abbreviated responses, or vagueness on some issues reveal her performance as a diplomat in the world of organized labor and in this oral history project. She sought at times to remove emotion from the process by stating what she tried to do given the limitations under which she worked. Speaking sometimes in the third person was another way she may have tried to distance herself emotionally from painful events.

Other events about which she showed obvious distress and reticence included the assassination of Congolese leader Patrice Lumumba and her experiences with white oppression and factional conflicts among Africans in Southern Rhodesia (Zimbabwe) and South Africa. Springer stated how she felt at the time of Lumumba's death: "I could not accept assertions of U.S. complicity. If I had, I would have raised questions within myself about my role in Africa." Once, when she stated that the experiences of apartheid got under her skin, she was literally moved to scratch her arm. Her other responses also included expressions of sorrow for the ways in which colonialism and white minority rule destroyed people's lives and of regret that she had not been more effective.

In general, Springer was circumspect about sharing experiences that she believed others might use in malicious and narrow ways to discredit organized labor and the struggles for African independence. She did not want to discuss publicly some of the documentation I found within her voluminous collection in her home that revealed that a few high-ranking people in the United States and Africa had acted in self-serving ways at her expense. After I showed her these papers, she asked that I not use them and promptly tore them up. I agreed I would only cite the material for the biography I wrote on her if I found the same papers in public archives.

Whatever the shortcomings of the organized labor or the independence struggles, Springer never lost faith in the wider implications of these movements. For example, only in our private conversations did she stridently criticize some of the more egregious dictators of independent Africa. Having been personally acquainted with some of these heads of state before independence, she wondered about the effects of power on those whom she deemed to have had good intentions but who turned into oppressors. When she does comment on repressive regimes or inequality, she often does so within the larger context of similar situations in other organizations or parts of the world.

Similarly, Springer sometimes resisted revealing the full extent of the tensions among Western and African labor leaders. In her initial recollection of the 1957 American Trade Union Scholarship Program for Africa, Springer downplayed the damage that ICFTU policy caused in the confederation's relations with African labor. Pressure from European labor leaders and particularly the British resulted in the curtailment of this program and a ban on AFL-CIO independent activity in Africa. In exchange, the ICFTU agreed to accede to the long-standing African request for a labor school in Africa. Springer at first indicated that she had no quarrel with the compromise because the labor school was built. The archival material, however, told a different story. Although Springer's correspondence demonstrates that she was very supportive of the school, it also indicates that she and her African colleagues were bitterly disappointed with the ICFTU policy. After becoming aware of this documentation, Springer talked more openly about her feelings about the conflict over the program. Complicated cold war political alliances and antagonisms among Western labor leaders help to explain Springer's earlier, more diplomatic rendition of this story.

Another area in which Springer shows sensitivity is in discussions of the status of women in Africa. In her relations with the male-dominated African labor movements, she acknowledged that her older age, nationality, and ability to lessen the isolation of their struggles helped to militate against any negative responses to her as an authority figure. Yet Springer rarely speaks in specific terms about the nature of the inequalities she witnessed. Her reluctance to speak except in generalities is not an indication of complacency. She often spoke stridently to labor and nationalist leaders about their failure to focus on women in the project of nation building. And with some she had a close enough relationship that she could talk to them about their personal practices. For example, on a trip to East Africa I undertook while Springer was there in 1991, I encountered her and a former labor colleague after they had just finished a conversation regarding his female relationships. She was looking peeved, and he was looking like a child who had been scolded. Springer's reluctance to talk about gender inequality in Africa except in the context of worldwide inequalities women experience reflects her concern with protecting Africans from the double standards that they sometimes face from the Western world. Similarly, despite my prodding, she resisted speaking on the record of incidents in which her work was imperiled in part by sexual harassment.

In Sondra Hale's interview with the famed Sudanese political leader Fatma Ahmed Ibrahim, she discovered a similar dynamic at work. Although as the leader of the Women's Union Ibrahim was concerned with improving the status of women, Hale was unable to get her to define what she meant by women's issues or to talk about the elements in Islamic culture that might liberate or those that might oppress women. Hale concluded that Ibrahim was not "unaware of the complexities of the role of women in Islam," but that she "apparently deems it strategically sound to argue an uncritical position in public."[17]

Springer's narration of her experiences with African American communities also has strategic omissions. The role of the black community as a source of strength and identity in the face of unremitting oppression sometimes held her back from talking about her perceptions of color and class distinctions among specific prominent blacks. She, however, did not hesitate to discuss intraracial conflicts as a community phenomenon. Springer may not have wanted to make negative statements that might diminish the importance of the contributions of these noted personalities. Gwendolyn Etter-Lewis's assessment that a critical component of black female oral histories is the creation of a black female self strongly linked to the black community certainly holds true for Springer.[18]

Springer's awareness that some of her undocumented experiences could be discredited by others, coupled with an impulse to protect me by minimizing the challenges to my scholarship, form another component of her strategic omissions. For example, in Springer's presence, her friend Martin Morand told me that high-ranking people in the first independent Ghana government considered her for an important position dealing with development. She refused the position in part because she asserted she did not have the expertise needed. Soon after this offer was made, the vicissitudes of the cold war negatively affected Springer's status in some Ghana circles. The relationship between Ghana and Western labor movements deteriorated rapidly after 1959 when Ghana led the movement for African labor centers to leave the ICFTU. Springer refrained from repeating this undocumented story involving people who might challenge its validity because of wider political concerns that developed. Yet this story helps to illustrate the high level of esteem in which she was held in Ghana government circles.

Springer's strong loyalty to the U.S. labor movement and the leaders who supported her Africa projects explain her occasional reticence to reflect critically on AFL-CIO policies with which she was in disagreement or to pass judgment on the more unsavory aspects of leadership conduct. Instead, she tends to give the reasons various groups objected to a policy, and seldom attempts to disassociate from the policy. After our initial conversations about the detrimental policy of the AFL-CIO in South Africa, I found documentation that demonstrated that she

17. Hale, "Feminist Method, Process, and Self-Criticism," 125, 128–30 (quote is on p. 130).
18. Gwendolyn Etter-Lewis, "Black Women's Life Stories: Reclaiming Self in Narrative Texts," in Gluck and Patai, *Women's Words*, 53–54.

and her colleague Lester Trachtman had tried to steer the AFL-CIO in a different direction. Only after I brought to her attention the information in these documents did she talk more broadly about her feelings about AFL-CIO policy.

One of the more controversial aspects of Springer's international activism was her association with the preeminent cold warrior Jay Lovestone. Lovestone, who served as one of the primary architects of AFL and later AFL-CIO foreign policy and as a speechwriter for AFL-CIO president George Meany, had a longtime secret relationship with CIA official Jim Angleton. Lovestone's overarching anti-Communist agenda, combined with his CIA connections, raises important questions about the extent to which the AFL-CIO may have undermined democratic processes that they considered as consciously or unconsciously aiding Communists. Moreover, Lovestone's CIA connection taints all of those whose work fell under his purview.

Lovestone served as head of the International Affairs Department during part of Springer's tenure. She was among the many international labor representatives whose reports were either addressed to Lovestone or copies of which ended up in his voluminous files. For this reason, perhaps, Lovestone biographer Ted Morgan dubs Springer "Lovestone's Africa agent."[19] Yet archival records and the personal reminiscences of Springer's labor colleagues portray her as primarily an agent of African leaders.

Springer was always aware of the cloud of suspicion surrounding Lovestone's activities. When she learned of documentary evidence of his CIA connections after the completion of our initial set of interviews, she was disturbed but did not radically reconstruct her relationship with him. The three African American labor leaders most active on the African continent during the 1950s—Springer, Randolph, and George McCray—all had positive relationships with Lovestone. In the context of the sometimes hostile or indifferent attitude that some AFL-CIO and European labor officials had toward African labor development, these black leaders valued him for his strong anticolonialism. Unlike Lovestone, however, their anticolonialism was not fueled by an overriding obsession with eliminating Communism. Among these African Americans and their African colleagues, Communism was rarely broached in letters to one another. The documentation

19. In Morgan's account of Springer's life and activism, there are many mistakes and incorrect statements, including Springer's timeline in Africa and her activities. Some of the mistakes are due to a misreading of my dissertation on Springer, Yevette Richards, "My Passionate Feeling About Africa": Maida Springer Kemp and the American Labor Movement (Ph.D. diss., Yale University, 1994). For example, a story I told about Mabel Keaton Stauper's childhood he attributed as Springer's experience. See Ted Morgan, A Covert Life: Jay Lovestone, Communist, Anti-Communist, and Spymaster (New York: Random House, 1999), 304.

also indicates that Springer and McCray disagreed with the scope of AFL-CIO anti-Communist policies in Africa. Whatever goals Lovestone may have had in supporting Springer's activism, she viewed her work as having been done at the behest of Africans.

In the narrative, Springer presents herself as a participant in extraordinary times rather than as an extraordinary person. However, she was both. Her single-minded commitment to social justice set her on a course of involvement in some of the most significant social and political movements of the twentieth century. She walked in the circles of people who led Africa to independence and those who placed the civil rights movement in the United States on a firm foundation before the explosion of the nonviolent protests of the 1960s. She had a special concern for the women and children of Africa, often paying school fees through her modest means.

Although Springer recognized that she served as a symbol of hope and a re-source for Africans, she has a desire not to appear boastful. Some of her statements such as, "all I was, was an international labor representative," "I was only one small person getting the backing of the union," and "not that I was anything special," demonstrate her unassuming nature. Moreover, her presentation conforms to the findings of the limited studies that have been done on gendered differences in sto-rytelling. Women tend to understate their accomplishments and their power. They are more passive and often use "we" or "one" to show their activism as part of a group, whereas men tend to put themselves in the center of action and more read-ily view themselves as individual actors by using "I."[20] Springer's presentation of herself reveals that she takes seriously the advice she has offered to others: Don't be arrogant about successes or bitter about defeats, because both can limit you.[21]

Due to the multifaceted nature of Maida Springer's activism, her oral history provides new insights into the fields of United States and international labor history, African American history, women's history, and pan-Africanism. As the historian David Thelen remarks, using memory allows the historian to ask new questions of traditional sources and topics and gives rise to points of fresh syn-thesis.[22] Springer's story opens up a new understanding of how gender and race operate in the labor movement. Her story of activism in the ILGWU relates the role a black woman played in a union dominated by white ethnic women in mem-bership and white ethnic men in the leadership. In the international arena, her activism runs counter to the usual male-centered approach to pan-Africanism and

20. Thompson, "Believe It or Not," 10; Etter-Lewis, "Black Women's Life Stories," 48.
21. Balanoff, "Maida Springer Kemp Interview," in Hill, *The Black Women Oral History Project*, 145.
22. Thelen, *Memory and American History*, vii.

international labor relations. Springer's constructions also allow the reader to view the AFL-CIO's foreign policy operations from the vantage of the Africans and African Americans who attempted to shape that policy. Moreover, her rich and vivid reflections, passionate advocacy of social justice, and palpable sense of humor combine together in this oral history to give a riveting and inspirational portrait of a black woman whose activism embraced some of the most powerful social movements of the twentieth century.

I

A Panamanian Immigrant in Harlem

Maida Springer's humorous stories about her strong-willed grandmother and her moving portraits of other family members provide evocative glimpses of her childhood in Panama and in New York. The stories reveal the genesis of her family's deep attachment to Africa and the ways they negotiated class, ethnic, and racial hierarchies. The cultural and ethnic conflicts between Caribbean migrants and Panamanians were played out on a personal level between young Maida's Barbadian father and Panamanian mother. And the discriminatory employment practices that her father and other blacks experienced while working on the Panama Canal construction project under U.S. rule served as a prelude to her own experiences with racist employment practices in the United States.

Springer describes the nature of racism, intraracial conflict, and anti-immigrant sentiment that flourished in Harlem. With the great influx of blacks to Harlem throughout the 1920s and the restrictions on their settlement in other areas of New York City, tensions arose between blacks and the older immigrant communities of Germans, German Jews, Irish, and others. As Springer testifies, among the bitter experiences for Harlem blacks was their treatment at the hands of white business owners in the main shopping thoroughfare of 125th Street. H. C. F. Koch and his family followed up their discourteous treatment of black customers by selling Koch Department Store in 1930 rather than accede to demands for equal opportunity and treatment. That same year, L. M. Blumstein, who had long refused to hire blacks in any position at Blumstein's Department Store, allowed for their employment only as elevator operators. As an adult, Springer joined with an alliance of diverse organizations that in 1934 successfully used the strategies of picket and boycott to force these large department stores and other Harlem businesses to open up sales, clerk, and cashier positions to blacks.[1]

1. Gilbert Osofsky, *Harlem: The Making of a Ghetto, Negro New York, 1890–1930*, 2nd ed. (New York: Harper & Row, 1971), 121.

During Springer's childhood, Jamaican-born Marcus Garvey (1887–1940), leader of the Universal Negro Improvement Association (UNIA), championed the "don't buy where you can't work" campaign. Springer talks about her mother's activism in the UNIA and the indelible impression the movement left on her. Garvey came to the United States in 1916 and settled in Harlem where he built the UNIA into the largest organized black movement of its kind. With wonder Springer recalls the breathtaking oratory of UNIA officer Henrietta Vinton Davis (1860–1941). A famous elocutionist before joining with Garvey as one of the thirteen founding members of the UNIA in New York, Davis was very effective with recruitment drives because of her name recognition and her powerful oratorical skills.[2]

The various political movements for black rights that flourished during Springer's childhood demonstrate that people of African descent were eager to mobilize against the rampant discrimination they faced in employment, housing, health care, and education. However, the leaders of these movements were often in discord, inveighing against each other over issues of policy, personality, and nationality, and over color and class differences. The U.S. government had a policy of disrupting these organizations, deeming their demands for equal rights and African liberation a threat to domestic tranquility and the war effort. With the UNIA targeted by the FBI, Garvey was indicted on the dubious charge of mail fraud in 1922. His final conviction three years later and his acrimonious struggles with black leaders within and outside the UNIA led to the decimation and splintering of the organization. Davis eventually left Garvey's organization. The strong disagreements that black leaders had with Garvey's policies did not necessarily gain them the animus of Garvey adherents, however. Springer relates how her mother and others took consolation in the messages they delivered, for these leaders shared with Garvey a keen ability to express the black community's outrage and bitter disappointment over the continuation and intensification of racist treatment following World War I.

Springer discusses the activism of two such leaders, Asa Philip Randolph (1889–1979) and Frank Crosswaith (1892–1965). Both served as her mentors after she joined the garment workers. Randolph, who migrated to New York from Florida in 1911, became the head of the Brotherhood of Sleeping Car Porters in 1925, and an AFL-CIO vice president in 1955. Crosswaith, who was from Frederickstad, St. Croix, the Virgin Islands, worked as an organizer for both the porters' union and the International Ladies' Garment Workers' Union (ILGWU). Early

2. See William Seraile, "Henrietta Vinton Davis and the Garvey Movement," *Afro-Americans in New York Life and History* (July 1983): 7–24.

Panamanian Immigrant in Harlem

advocates of interracial unionism, Randolph and Crosswaith showed courage in labor organizing efforts and civil rights activism. Randolph's impassioned indictments of the government led the U.S. Justice Department to label him "the most dangerous Negro in America," and his magazine, *The Messenger*, "the most dangerous of all Negro publications." The Lusk committee, appointed by the New York State legislature to investigate radicalism and sedition, also paid special attention to Randolph's activities.[3]

Although the experience of racial oppression sometimes deepened the chasms among people of African descent, this experience also brought about a sense of community and pride. Springer's descriptions of her community life in Harlem are of a close-knit neighborhood where everyone, including her future husband, Owen Springer, looked after the younger children. The lyrical portraits she draws of her community life are spiced with flavors of Caribbean culture. Institutions like the church and segregated schools served as unifying forces for all blacks.

For part of her teenage years, Springer attended the Manual Training and Industrial School for Colored Youth, a boarding school in Bordentown, New Jersey. She reflects on the dynamic black teachers and black visitors who served as role models, such as William Edward Burghardt Du Bois (1868–1963), Paul Leroy Bustill Robeson (1898–1976), and Lester Blackwell Granger (1896–1976). Du Bois was one of the United States' foremost intellectuals and the leading propagandist for civil rights. A cofounder of the NAACP in 1909, he founded and edited the NAACP's *Crisis* magazine until 1934. Deemed the father of pan-Africanism he always linked the struggle for equality in the United States to the anticolonial struggle in Africa. The U.S. government persecuted him in the 1950s for his radicalism. In 1961, he joined the Communist Party and moved to Ghana, where he died the day before the historic 1963 March on Washington.

Like Du Bois, Paul Robeson was persecuted by the U.S. government for his pro-Soviet views, defense of Communists arrested under the Smith Act, and unstinting criticisms of the treatment of blacks in the United States. The son of a runaway slave and a woman from a prominent Pennsylvania family that dated back to the colonial times, Robeson was multitalented, exceptional, and internationally renowned. He was valedictorian of his class at Rutgers University, a law school graduate, athlete, actor, singer, and activist. He devoted his talents to work against racism and in support of African liberation and trade unionism worldwide. As a promoter of international solidarity, he sang songs in a couple of dozen languages.

At Bordentown, Granger served as extension agent for the school and comman-

<hr>

3. Jervis Anderson, A. *Philip Randolph: A Biographical Portrait* (Berkeley and Los Angeles: University of California Press, 1972), 118–19.

dant over the boys from 1922 to 1934. His job included questioning applicants to the school and then following up on the progress of graduates as they settled in urban areas.[4] Later, as a labor activist, Springer worked closely with Granger when he became the executive director of the National Urban League, a position he held from 1941 to 1961.

The strongest influence on Springer's early life was her mother, Adina Stewart Carrington. Having separated from her husband soon after they settled in Harlem, Stewart struggled as a single mother to make a secure home for her child and served as her fearless protector against unfair employment practices and discriminatory treatment. Envisioning a mother-daughter business, Adina Stewart sent the reluctant young Maida to Poro College, one of the beauty schools of Annie Minerva Turnbo Malone (1869–1957), a philanthropist and entrepreneur in the hair care business.

After declining an employment position with Madame Malone in favor of marriage, Springer held her wedding reception in the townhouse built by the other major hair care entrepreneur of the period, Madame C. J. Walker (1867–1919). Born Sarah Breedlove, Walker took her name from her third husband, newspaperman Charles Joseph Walker. Both Malone and Walker are credited with being the first black female millionaires. Walker had studied under Malone and served briefly as a Malone agent in 1905 before starting her own hair care business. Her daughter A'Lelia Walker operated the townhouse as a café/salon until 1928.[5]

In Springer's reconstruction of her early years of marriage, she portrays Owen Springer as patient, intelligent, and meticulous. Four years after their son was born, she was forced to find employment because the Depression lessened her husband's earning power. The unemployment rate for Harlem blacks during much of the Depression was between one and a half to three times that of whites in New York City. By 1932, more than 60 percent of Harlemites were unemployed.[6] The dressmaking skills Springer learned as a teenager attending Bordentown and her brief job experiences as a preteen and teenager led her during these difficult times to find employment in the garment industry.

4. *The Ironsides Echo*, June 1955.
5. The home at 108–110 West 136 Street was built by renowned black architect Vertner Tandy for Madame C. J. Walker. See A'Lelia Bundles, "Madam C. J. Walker, 1867–1919, Entrepreneur, Philanthropist, Social Activist," 1998–2001, the Lewaro Corporation®, http://www.madamcjwalker.com/; Anthony L. Williams, "Annie Turnbo Malone," Black Heritage Day II, www.isomedia.com/homes/bhd2/annie_malone.htm (both retrieved March 18, 2003).
6. Mark Naison, *Communists in Harlem during the Depression* (New York: Grove Press Inc., 1984), 31, 116.

I was born at home in Panama City, Panama. I am told that the woman who acted as a great-grandmother figure in my life, Nana Sterling, brought me into this world. I didn't know her. She was a local midwife. My father thought I was a cripple because I was born with my legs under me and my arms folded.[7] My great-grandmother and my grandmother massaged my folded limbs and pulled them out. It took them a week.

I'm told that my great-grandmother was born in Africa. They say she knew that she came from Africa when by her figures she was a teenager. She knew that she was from the west in Africa because the stories she told my grandmother and which were passed down to my mother and to me were West African folktales. As a small child, *I* grew up on West African folktales — Brother [A]nansi the wily spider, and all of the animals in the forest, the lion who was intelligent but could be outwitted by this wily spider. When I went to Ghana for the first time and heard some of these stories, it made my hair stand on end. They said, "Oh yes, yes, yes! You're West African!" (*Laughter.*)

My mother's name when she died was Adina Carrington, and my grandmother's name was Eliza Anderson. My mother's maiden name was Forest but my grandmother married again some years later after her first marriage. Carrington is the name of my mother's second husband.[8] My grandmother had a son in addition to my mother. His name was Elisha and he was four or five years younger than my mother. He was alive when we left Panama, but he died very young. He was as tall as my mother was short. He was very gentle, very sweet and quiet. I remember he was very loving to me because I was a quiet child. I was not lively. He'd let me sit on his lap and he would talk to me. I had a picture of him, but I am such a gypsy in wandering around that I lost it somewhere.

As a small, young girl, my grandmother was a household servant and a companion to the daughter of one of the wealthy Panamanian families, that

7. In an unrecorded interview, Springer stated that her father, after viewing her, threatened to harm her mother, whom he blamed for her condition.

8. In the early 1960s Adina Stewart married Barbadian-born Dalrymple Carrington. Born in Jamaica on February 28, 1870, Eliza Anderson went to Panama as a young girl and considered herself to be Spanish culturally. She was the youngest of several children born by Edward and Sarah Austin. Eliza lived to be 104 and her mother reportedly lived to be 125. Program, Recognition luncheon for Mrs. Eliza Anderson on her 100th birthday, March 1, 1970 (MSK PP).

group many of us called the robber barons (*laughs*), one of those ruling families.[9] Throughout her life as a young woman, she traded on this. She was the child of the house, so she had some clout. When you talk about Panamanian justice, you see, you knew somebody with clout. Just like in the United States, if you know someone, it moves the agenda for you. My grandmother was a very tiny lady. Extremely independent. Abrasive. Litigious. You could not talk sharply to her, and she never *forgot* anything you said to her. Always she would go to court for anything if you troubled her, and she troubled very easily. And God forbid if you were a foreigner, if you were a West Indian and not a Spaniard and you bothered my grandmother or you had some problem with her and you took her to court. The judge would let you know you were bothering the person associated with this famous family, and your justice was sometimes limited. (*Laughter.*) So my grandmother was a lady very feared because she would take you on. Everybody knew her. My mother told me these stories. All of this took place in my grandmother's young life.

My grandfather died very early when my mother was a child. But before that time my grandmother with her tiny, aggressive self was embarrassed by my grandfather because he was too pious and he let people do things to him. If a man spoke harshly to him or hit him, he would pray for him. (*Laughs.*) My grandmother didn't understand his behavior. It infuriated her terribly, and I think this is the basis for the weakening of their marriage.

On one occasion he had a difference of opinion with a man and the man knocked him down. He then got up and prayed for the man and said that he was a Christian and he would not use his hands. So the man knocked him down again. (*Laughter.*) Well, after they came and told my grandmother, she hitched up her skirt and went out and charged into this man. And when she got finished with that, she charged into my grandfather. Grandmother was so humiliated by this that she wouldn't have him in the house. My mother said my grandmother was so outraged with her husband that she called him every kind of coward that you could think of in Spanish. And my mother ran underneath the bed. They had high post beds. That marriage in due course got dissolved. No, she couldn't stand weak people. And she thought my mother was going to be like her father.

Doña Luisa was something special. In the Spanish community, they called her Doña Luisa. In the West Indian community, Red Liza. (*Laughter.*) To be

9. Panamanians largely referred to the leading families as *rabiblancos*, or whitetails. See Walter LaFeber, *The Panama Canal: The Crisis in Historical Perspective*, 2nd ed. (New York: Oxford University Press, 1989), 50.

derogatory, they called her Red Liza. She had big brown freckles and kind of copper-colored red skin from the sun.

As I said, my grandmother was always an independent woman and was an aggressive little businesswoman. She fed a portion of the men who worked building the Panama Canal when my mother was a child. Every day my grandmother prepared the midday meal for them. This business was a kind of restaurant, and she had women working for her. They grated the coconut and seasoned and prepared the food. They used these pans that are in three and four tiers. On the bottom would be the hot soup. Even today out of my family's tradition, I do not feel that I have been properly fed until I have had some hot soup with what I'm eating. The hot soup kept the rest of the food hot. On top of that would be the meat, and then there was rice and what they called the breadkind, plantains or cooked greens. And on the very top there would be a sweet, cassava pudding, pone. These young women would deliver these three or four layers of food to the men whose names were marked on the pans. They would get on a certain train and go down on the lines to take the luncheon. I guess there must have been many other folks doing this. But my grandmother had a flourishing business of feeding the men on the lines during the building of the canal.

After that, my grandmother was a farmer and she sold food as a market woman. That's what she did until she was quite old. With her second husband she had a farm outside Panama City. I remember it was way on top of a hill. It was very high because she had to stop the car kind of on the side of the road. She was nimble. She just went like this up the hill [*indicates rapid motion with her hands*]. And I was breathing hard, walking up to this place. This was the first time I ever saw such a variety of fruit growing. That was quite an experience. She would walk with her machete and show me ginger, turmeric, varieties of mangoes as I have never seen before or since, many kinds of bananas. I had seen small bananas like those before, but in East Africa. They did not turn yellow. They were ripe. Then I saw the red bananas. I saw avocados. This stuff would just rot on the ground because she was not able to take care of it. She could not farm it anymore. She was eighty years old and needed help. Her husband had died two or three years before. This was peasant farming, so who was going to work for her? She was up there alone.

This was all in the process of me trying to persuade that old doll to come to the United States for twenty, twenty-five years. I remember my grandmother having such strong views of the United States. I think she thought that everybody lived in wooden boxes, and you didn't have a lot of earth around you. She was concerned about this since she was a farmer. She thought you lived in a shut up place, so she resisted coming to the United States for many, many years for that reason.

I had just turned seven when we came to the United States in 1917. The story is told that my grandmother tried very hard to get my parents to leave me in Panama until they found their way. But my *wonderful* young mother with not a clue as to what life would entail here told my grandmother that if she had to suck salt in the United States, I would be right beside her. She wasn't trained for anything in the United States. She had never worked anywhere. When she first came here, she worked briefly as a domestic. But she told her mother she would give me a little of the salt, and we would drink saltwater together. She would *never* leave me with anyone. I have always appreciated that. The indignities that were foisted upon a child left with relatives in that country I know about, because many of the women that my mother knew and who came here after her had stories. They left their children behind at first and brought them when they were ten, twelve, thirteen years old. So I saw some of what could happen firsthand. But that was my grandmother, and they said she loved me very much.

We wanted my grandmother to come here because as she got older and her husband had died, she had cataracts and wasn't seeing very well. The local minister whose church she attended took on the responsibility of writing to us about her. Since the mail system except in the United States and maybe a few places in Europe was horrible, we sent money to him for her because he was able to get mail by way of the Canal Zone. The postal service was better there where he had a post box. We took care of my grandmother in this way. My cousin Clarence Scott, whom we call Scottie, tried to keep track of the money we sent to the minister. He tried to make sure that things were looked after for my grandmother. Before he came to the United States to live, he would write to us and tell us what he thought was going on with her care.

We were instrumental in helping Scottie to come here. He remained the same concerned, gentle person close to us. And if my grandmother said he's my relative, then he's my relative. She never tried to explain how he is a relative, but she was very good friends with his mother. He's over six feet, but as a young man he had a much bigger body. He's a sick old man now. He's thin framed now and as gentle, always laughing. I have never in forty-five years heard him raise his voice or be ugly with anyone.[10]

My mother would go back to Panama periodically and, of course, try to talk my grandmother into coming here. She told my mother in no uncertain

10. Clarence Eleazor Scott (1908–1993), who came to the United States in 1948, died two years after this interview.

terms why she wouldn't come here. So my mother went down again and said, "You know, you're alone. We'll get a place for you in town." In due course, a distant cousin wanted money and my mother bought his property, a beautiful piece of land, loaded with water. It was less than an acre. Then she just sent me a telegram saying that she had bought it and what money she needed. (*Laughter.*) It wasn't a great deal, but by my standards in those days it was a lot of money. I then went to Panama and talked with my godfather, who was a builder, about building a house for my grandmother. I came back and borrowed money to build this house and later more money to improve the land, because my grandmother said there were no trees. There was just grass. So Scottie, who was then a very young man, got all of his young friends to help with the land. They thought this was very wonderful, fertile land. They planted the fruit trees that my grandmother wanted planted now that we'd brought her from her farm down into this city. We fenced it in. It was a very nice area, this place called Pedregal.[11]

After my godfather built the house, my grandmother wouldn't live in it because she said that my godfather used my money badly, that he bought old lumber and the rooms were too small. A little woman all by herself. She said she didn't like the house he built, and she would never live in it. (*Laughs.*) That was my grandmother. Well, anyway, the wood ants began to eat the house, because no one was living there and taking care of it. So we rented another place in town close to the house of some of my mother's friends. That was a good arrangement. But eventually we got her here because these same friends were coming to the United States. Her eyes were getting bad and people were robbing her blind. So at ninety-four she came here and lived here for ten years. She died at 104 in 1974.

How did you know you needed an act of Congress to bring your grandmother to the United States?

Oh, I think my son, Eric, checked out the legalities of it when we began to do all of the necessary papers to bring her here. He then got the services of our congressman. The purpose of that act of Congress was to indicate that this ninety-four-year-old woman was not coming to the United States to be a public charge, that I had a home, which was adequate. My son is a lawyer and he had an adequate living and was supportive of bringing my grandmother here. She was the only close relative we had remaining in Panama.

11. Lying just outside of Panama City, Pedregal had the character of a rural town. With Panama City's expansion, Pedregal has now become part of it. Correspondence from Eduardo Watson R., Panama Info-Doc Services S.A., Panama City, Republic of Panama, December 10, 1999.

Panamanian Immigrant in Harlem

When she came to the United States, she was always busy teaching my mother how to grow up. I'm a woman, but my mother was still her child and she was critical of her. And when she was not critical, she would sit in the kitchen and say, "You know, I never thought that you would do so-and-so so nice. I thought that you would grow up a careless young woman." She said this because my mother had become a fanatic housekeeper, and my grandmother had not thought much of my mother's ability, I guess, at those sorts of things when she was a little girl.

My grandmother spoke Spanish when she was angry, irritated, or when she prayed, because I don't think she thought English-speaking Gods understood her as well. (*Laughter.*) I would hear her speaking and muttering in Spanish. But when she was annoyed about something, she would really let you know. When she was angry with my mother, she would tell her, "When I was Doña Luisa, you could not treat me like this!" Or she would say things like if she wasn't in the United States or if she was in Panama, my mother would not treat her the way she did. She said that my mother was doing or saying something to her because she was not the person she used to be, because she was now old.

What was my mother doing to her? She would say, "Mama, in the United States you eat this kind of breakfast." My mother gave her cornflakes. Well, my grandmother didn't understand these things. In Panama, she drank her early morning tea at four and five o'clock in the morning, and by eight or nine o'clock she had worked for many hours on her farm and would then sit down to a sturdy meal. She had breakfast, which consisted of meat and breadkind —by breadkind, I mean some kind of starch, a root vegetable—freshly cooked bread and tea. She might have codfish or fresh fish and plantains and dumplings, dates and cocoa. She would have at eight o'clock or nine o'clock in the morning what would be for us lunch. When she came here, she was up at 5:30. We didn't get up at 5:30. So the cultural differences, the way we cooked and ate in the United States, took some adjustment. My mother was an excellent cook, and she seasoned and cooked in the way they did in Panama, but we had absorbed a whole lot of new ways in the United States. So when she gave my grandmother cornflakes and bananas, she tasted it and promptly spit it out. (*Laughs.*) "What this?" No, she was something to deal with.

Did she ever get used to that?

My mother didn't give her cornflakes anymore. No, my mother made the changes. It wasn't difficult. Just don't give her what would be a standard American meal at nine o'clock in the morning. Give her a heavy meal, a substantial meal.

What was your grandmother's religion?

She was Presbyterian, Episcopalian, that kind of mixture. She joined the Presbyterian church just around the corner. Loved the minister, liked his wife and was very happy.[12] She wasn't a deep churchgoer, so let me disabuse your mind. She wasn't devout. But that church was *good* for her. She was happy. The minister came to see her every week, and he didn't talk to her about religion. He sat there and talked to her about the world and about how she was doing and what she liked and what she didn't like.

Tell me about your father.

My father came from the West Indies by way of England to work on the Panama Canal, as many West Indians did. In due course, he married my mother, unfortunately. (*Laughs.*) He had some semiskilled, clerical job, because he wore a clean shirt and cuffs. He read and wrote fluently and knew mathematics inside out. But, of course, he didn't get paid what he should have gotten because there was a gold and silver rule. He was paid the black wage even though he was doing work that a lot of the *white* workers were doing.[13]

When I came here I was pretty good with mathematics. When I was five in Panama, my father, a West Indian, believed a child should begin to learn. I had to learn the multiplication tables, the division tables, and subtraction. I would have to stand against a wall and recite them. Whenever I missed—and between five and seven you miss a lot of things, and you forget—the teacher who was my father's friend would crack my fingers with a twig. Now imagine a five, six, or seven year old reciting "twelve times one is twelve, twelve twos are twenty-four, twelve threes are thirty-six." You were supposed to know your tables from one to twelve.

In the house my father would not allow my mother to utter a word in Spanish. It was a very harsh, very severe situation. That marriage ended shortly after we came here. I put these and other experiences in the back of my mind and don't talk about it because what I remember was unpleasant and cruel in a child's mind. In an adult's mind it was cruel. He was mean to my mother also.

I had one sister whose name was Hélène. She died when she was three years, nine months, fifteen days. I was five. They said she didn't live because

12. The church's name was Westminster-Bethany United Presbyterian Church, located on Howard Avenue and McDonough Street in Brooklyn. The pastor was Reverend Claude C. Kilgore when she joined the church. Later, Reverend C. Herbert Oliver became pastor.

13. Virtually all blacks performed the heavy, dirty, dangerous unskilled labor and were paid according to the lower Panamanian silver standard, while U.S. whites were favored for the highly skilled crafts and mechanical work and received wages based on the higher U.S. gold standard.

Panamanian Immigrant in Harlem

she was so bright. She was, they said, born old. She did not like children, and she didn't like me especially. She always was with adults. She was very charming, and she lisped. But her conversation was an adult conversation. She was a *very* bright child, and she died of spinal meningitis. We came to the United States about a year and a half later.

When I go to New York, I have to go to Ellis Island and visit it as a museum, because this was my family's port of entry to the United States. I even remember the name of the boat we came here on, S.S. *Alianza*. My mother never let me forget it. (*Laughter.*) You know, people came here in all kinds of ways—with little bags on their shoulder, in steerage. I think it was very important to my mother that we came here on full passage. So she never let me forget that we came on the S.S. *Alianza* and that we weren't in steerage.

The one thing I remember about the trip is that the boat stopped in Port-au-Prince[14] after we left Panama. It is a play on the mind because I thought we went to the post office in Port-au-Prince, but I didn't know anything about post offices. Strange things stick in a child's mind. It was a little building with a pointed top. Now there may not be any reality to this, but this is what I remember. I remember the little boys would *dive* when people would throw money in the water, and then they would come up with the money in their teeth, which they could keep. I understand that it's still being done. I remember this because, you know, you're awed. I'd stand by the rail looking at them.

I remember Ellis Island because this was a sea of people. I'd never seen that many people in my life! They were all colors, all sizes. They were all speaking something different, many of them, because they were coming from all over the world. For many people, whoever was supposed to meet them was not there yet. There were Spaniards who were having trouble communicating, so my mother acted as interpreter since she was bilingual.

I remember that the cousins—my mother said that these were our cousins on my father's side because I didn't know them—were there early.[15] When we got there, they were there! This was a contrast against the people who were crying because there was no one to meet them. We went (*claps hands to indicate "quickly"*). Our papers were in order. We had funds—modest. We had somewhere to live and people with whom we were going to live. Evidently our physical examinations showed that we were healthy. So all of this had fallen into place. We had no problems.

14. According to the ship's manifest, the S.S. *Alianza* departed from Cristobol, Panama, on July 26, 1917, stopped in St. Marc, Haiti, on July 30, and arrived at Ellis Island on August 4.
15. The ship's manifest lists one cousin as James Reece of 135 West 143 Street.

Panamanian Immigrant in Harlem

I remember the physical examination and the people who were crying. I didn't know why they were crying then, but years later I learned that people were sent back, or either were stopped from coming in because they were sick. There was a very high incidence of tuberculosis. I learned these things twenty-five, thirty years later when I read about Ellis Island. Everybody I knew, that I worked with, was a foreigner, or their families had all come from someplace else—from Italy or from Poland or from Germany. I lived among my own Caribbean people and Central American people. So as a colored American I lived in a very different world.

What were the working conditions for your mother as a domestic?

In those days women worked as domestics for $2.10 a day—ten cents carfare and two dollars. People would accumulate all their dirty clothes for a month and then pay you $2.10 to wash and clean and do all of this work. When you washed clothes, you then boiled them in a big boiler, and you would have to hang them up on the roof. In February the sheets would freeze before you were able to get the clothespins in them. The person you worked for was only a little bit better off than you, but they could afford to pay you. I think my mother worked as a day worker maybe for a month. Then she said, "Never! Never!" When she talked, she was very dramatic. I think what finally broke her back was this incident. After working for eight hours washing clothes— and I think this lady gave my mother a hard-boiled egg and a stale roll for lunch—my mother did not get paid at the end of the day. This lady told my mother that her husband had not come home and she could not pay her. My mother said, "No?" Then she went over to the lady's china closet and held it and began to shake it. The lady went into her bedroom and found $2.10 and got rid of my mother.

The humor and nerve of my mother was something else. An American friend of ours who was a great chef said to my mother, "Diana [pronounced Deeana],[16] with your seasoning and cooking ability, we could make you a chef in a small place." He got her some celluloid cuffs and a little hat with a poof, and she went to employment agencies. When she felt she had improved enough, she applied for a job as a chef, or maybe they called it a cook, in a very fancy little French restaurant. The cooks were all women, but they were all rather substantial women. My mother was short and small, thin. They looked at her and said she must be something very special if she came from the other side. By "other side" they meant that she was from the Caribbean,

16. It seems that Adina's name went through some changes in the United States.

was a foreigner. When the waitresses came in and started giving their orders, my mother was flabbergasted. The first two things she was told to make were "oysters à la Somerset" and "eggs à la goldenrod." She said (*laughter*), "What do these Americans eat?" Well, to make a long story short, she started spinning around, and the experienced cooks in this little French restaurant saw that she was terrified with this, and they said some very harsh things to her. Since the waitresses weren't getting their orders out, the owner said to my mother that she could stay and be a dishwasher. That was the end of my mother being a chef there. It's probably a family trait that we do these strange things.

In due course, my mother decided to go to school. She loved the work of a beautician and went to school to become a beautician. After becoming a hairdresser, my mother never worked in anyone else's place a day! What was so heroic about my mother that I did not appreciate until very late was her decision to go to school, and only having a limited English education she had to take the state board exam in New York with all of these medical terms. When she graduated weeks or months later, she saved her little money and opened her own business and worked there until the day many years later when my son and I forced her to sell the shop.

We made her give it up because the neighborhood became dangerous. The neighborhood was becoming part of a center for all kinds of illicit things. As against today it was infantile, penny ante stuff. We had moved to Brooklyn [730-A Macon Street] by then, and my mother's shop was in what they called Spanish Harlem. She was Spanish-speaking and everybody loved her. But the young dope and prostitution lords wanted to use her basement, which she refused. The beauty parlor was street level, a big basement apartment was downstairs. They would call her *la señora en frente*, you know, the lady in front. They said they would pay her well. As a show of their good faith to her, they started out by flooding my mother with business. All the young girls who were their workers would come there and have their hair styled. She was so busy, and she had two or three other operators working with her.

When she refused to cooperate, life became difficult. All of the business they sent her was cut off. They'd leave dead rats, dead cats in front of the door. When the FBI came, they found dope stuck in the crevice between the window and the door of the building. They came in and asked my mother about it, and she said she didn't know anything about it and didn't know anybody. Maybe the FBI was rounding them up, so they stuck this dope in there. The dope peddlers knew that my mother was never going to say anything about them, but they simply wanted her out. They wanted that place. They shot out the plate glass more than once, and even in those days the insurance was high.

When the worst of this was happening, I was out of the country. By that time my son, Eric, was living in Pittsburgh. It was in the fifties. But a good friend of mine—he was a black American Southerner named Donevant—he was a real estate person handling her affairs. He kind of kept track of her. Since this was beginning to get dangerous, we made her give it up. That was sad. If I had been more intelligent, I wouldn't have done that then. The ambition of her life we destroyed. But they would have hurt her. In any case, this is one of the things I do in a small way regret. Maybe we saved her life, but we destroyed something else.

Fortunately, I was busy enough in my life that she could share in a number of things. She was able to go to Africa. We stopped in Europe on our way to and from Africa. We stopped in Paris; there were some people we wanted to see there. She was very involved in what I was doing. Whether I was home or no, my home was an open house and Africans stayed there. My mother was very active in the block association to keep our block nice and participated when we had block parties. She would cook. A very talented, vivacious lady. If she had had an American education and had been more knowledgeable about this society, she would have been just tremendous. Bright! Bright! Bright!

Then my mother, this enterprising lady, had her own "overground." She would go to Panama, and she would tell people, "Oh, come to the United States. My daughter, you know, is a union official. She'll get you a job." And people would arrive at four o'clock in the morning, straight from Panama. I knew nothing about it. The bell would ring and my mother would be coming downstairs—we had a large old brownstone in Brooklyn—and she would say, "Well, May, I just said in passing when I was in Panama . . ."

Did she give you any house rules when you were a child concerning having company while she was working?

No, I was very good about that. She never had to say to me you cannot have somebody in your house. But back then, children and their parents had a different relationship. I assumed that if I had done something that my mother didn't want me to do, I would get in a lot of trouble. I tried to get a job, which she didn't know about. But what could really get you in trouble was bad behavior. Unh, unh. No. No. No. No. No. My mother was small but fierce! You just did not know that children talked back to their parents and children disobeyed. The kind of permissiveness that we have today was just not tolerated in my mother's household or with any of the children that we knew. I was a door-key child. I had a small key around my neck. By eleven, twelve years old, I was an old person. And everybody sort of looked out for one another's children. If my mother's neighbor saw me doing something, she would come to visit her and would tell her about me. They didn't have telephones.

I had three vices. One, I used to hop ice wagons. When the ice wagon would start off with the horse, you would jump on the back step. Of course, the driver would chase you off. But it was great pleasure jumping on the ice wagon as it began to roll down the street. Now, that was not proper activity for a girl. The little boys hopped ice wagons. So anyone who saw me hop an ice wagon would tell my mother.

In those days, the icemen brought the ice up. We always lived on the top floor because the rent was cheapest there. Today the rent is more expensive because you have a view from the top floor. So we got ice on Saturdays, I think, a seventy-five-cent piece of ice and a thirty-five-cent piece during the week. You would carefully wrap it up in newspapers, so it would last a couple of days. And you would always have a window box outside the kitchen window to put certain foods that wouldn't fit in the icebox. That was your other refrigerator in the winter. My job was to empty the pan underneath the icebox, because the water would run over. I would forget very often. Ooh, my dear! My mother would have a fit.

The other vice I had was shooting emmies, playing marbles with the boys. A few girls played, too, but it was frowned upon. Well, when they saw me doing that, they'd tell my mother, come over and have a cup of tea with her that evening. So whenever my mother would say to me when I was going to bed, "Miss Maida," I would know I was in trouble. Somebody had reported something I had done.

My third vice was belly whopping. When there was snow, you'd throw yourself on the sleigh and slide down the hill. In Manhattan there was St. Nicholas Park where children used to go sleigh riding. My mother told me the one thing that no girl should do was go belly whopping. After all, you were going to grow up and be a young lady and you might hurt yourself. But I loved to go belly whopping. I didn't think I was a tomboy because I'm not that athletic. But I enjoyed it. My mother was disgraced. She was outraged. So these were my vices. These things kept my mother in a dither. I was always doing one or the other. Our next-door neighbor, Mrs. Murray—our buildings were numbered 135 and 137 on West 142nd Street—would not tell on me, but she would talk to me because she thought my behavior on ice wagons and shooting emmies was not really good.

Mrs. Murray always included me in whatever she was doing with her children. I was friends with her daughter, Dora. At age seven, we were in the

Catholic school, St. Marks, together. When I was maybe ten years old, I saw a pattern of a dress with a little waistline. And my mother said she would buy the material. She was so pleased that I wanted to do something besides hop ice wagons. (*Laughs.*) A friend of hers who was a very fine dressmaker cut out the pattern for me, and I made a dress for Dora and me with little tam-o'-shanters to go with it.

Mrs. Murray started helping my mother find her way in, as my mother called it, "the United States of America." She was introducing this Panamanian mother to the American social mores. Mrs. Murray loved young people. All of her weekends were devoted to her children. She took me under her wing and introduced me to the American system. She took me for my first library card in the 135th Street library. She took me on my first kind of family picnic, my first museum, things like that. She was a beautiful Creole lady, butter-colored and graceful manners. They were from New Orleans.

Mrs. Murray's mother kept the house and her two grandchildren. I think I almost lost my family relationship with them when we were learning how to make taffy. When her grandmother was out of the house, Dora and I pulled this taffy and stuck it all over the kitchen and couldn't get it cleaned up in time. And we spilled hot water all over the floor. Her grandmother said that it was my fault, as she called me, "that ole big-legged gal next doe [door]" (*laughs*), because I was short and small but had very fat legs. But Mrs. Murray forgave me. She knew that children do these things. Mrs. Murray and her family remained close and were a part of my life until she died. Both of her children died as young adults.

Both Mr. and Mrs. Murray worked. For a *colored woman*, Mrs. Murray had a very fancy job. She worked for a very prestigious pharmaceutical firm, Ben Diner and Schlesinger. At that time, it was very unusual that a person of color was working in any capacity with any firm. Her husband was a very proud Pullman porter, because those were good jobs in those days. You never *saw* a great deal of him because he was on the road all the time. But he was meticulous. He was always so spotless in his uniform and his shoes. They lived well and had a very nice home.

When I was given the Rosina Tucker Award of the Brotherhood of Sleeping Car Porters in June last year [1989], I talked about how Dora and I as children used to fold and stuff leaflets for Mr. Murray that told of the problems of the porters and their demands. I didn't know what I was stuffing or what Mrs. Murray was doing then when she was inviting these ladies, porters' wives, to her house. This was before the porters became a really potent organization. These men were trying to organize and they would carry their leaflets on their run. As they stopped off different places, the men who were working with them would get the material and circulate it. I learned that this was a porters' organization years later. Pops Murray was wonderful. He would laugh and tell me about those times, when many years later my husband Owen, Eric, and I lived in the apartment on the top floor of the brownstone that the Murrays had bought at 218 Edgecombe Avenue after moving from 142nd Street.

Dora and I started school together at St. Marks. This was a mixed school. We were the only two colored children in that class, 2-A. We sat together in double seats. The teachers were all maiden ladies or nuns. In those days a woman could not be married and teach school. You had very rigorous training in the classroom. You had to do your homework.

Was this integrated school, St. Marks, in your neighborhood or near?

It was in the neighborhood! You know, you didn't talk about "integrated" schools in those days. In my block on 142nd Street, the owners of the grocery store and the drugstore and the butcher were white and all lived in the neighborhood, lived upstairs, above the stores. So I didn't know anything about the word "integration." That came later. (*Laughter.*) With the first apartment my parents had—their marriage ended very shortly after we came here—the superintendent had an apartment in the cellar with his family. In those days, we called them janitors. He was white. His children and I went to the same school. They had their other things they went to that we didn't go to. Then as Harlem began with the waves of people coming from the South and from the islands, the white community began moving out and your community began to be more colored.

When I went to the public school, P.S. 90, the teachers were tough also and they taught you, because the classes were mixed. But teachers in the public schools told parents, all the black parents I'm sure, that your child shouldn't take this course or that course because they wouldn't get a job, they wouldn't be able to find any work. They would say the black child should take some industrial course like basic typing or the boys should go to school and learn a trade. This was flagrant.[17]

When I was in sixth or seventh grade, my mother didn't know the Ameri-

17. White educational administrators' discouragement of black children from pursuing higher aspirations was a systemic problem nationally. Osofsky, *Harlem*, wrote that school administrators said that they hesitated to encourage blacks because they feared that "it would only lead to frustrations after graduation." Rarely were black teachers allowed to teach in mixed schools. Springer commented that she did not see a black teacher the first four years after coming to the United States (200).

can system, but she resented the fact that a counselor or the teacher would tell me that there was no way I could do whatever it was I wanted to do at the time. You see, we had to write down what we wanted to do. They would talk to you in the class about this. I guess this was the counseling that she was doing with the black kids, to discourage them from wanting certain goals. She wrote to my mother about this. So my mother went to school and chewed that lady up and down, never using a vulgar word. No, not being abusive. No. That's what people very often do when they're angry, curse and be very vulgar. Not my mother. She said, "Miss Teacher, how do you know? How do you know?" Because I had all good marks.

Were you aware in your neighborhood of aggression toward black people? Were you aware that there were certain boundaries you shouldn't cross?

Aware of boundaries, but in the language of integration, segregation—no. We were different. We did different things. We didn't go to the same social things as whites. By the same token, not only did we not socialize with whites, but the American colored community was a separate entity from foreign-born blacks. In my mother's life, our enclave was generally the people who were culturally like us—blacks from the Caribbean and Central America. Colored Americans dealt with people culturally like them. But because of our similarity of circumstance, we did some things together.

For example, the Negro church was the cultural unit for all blacks, the social center, because this was the place where you had theater and concerts. This is where the artists and poets performed. This was your religious community and your social community. So in this all the colored community shared. This was a part of the social outlets and the opportunities for black people to show their talents. We had entertainment in the church basement, as well as readings and entertainment in your home. There was certainly much more of that kind of entertainment available to us than there is today where everything costs a lot of money.

I ran across some information that said you had a piano at home when you were young.

Yes, of course! Well, in every household your child learned some musical instrument. My mother got a piano. She bought it on time. (*Laughs.*) She paid weekly money for it, because her child had to learn music. Some children played the violin. Girls didn't play trombones and things like that in those days. So we had a piano, and I went (imitating a simple scale) dee dee dee dee dee dee. (*Laughs.*) When adults came to my home, they played this piano. People entertained at home, and so you would have Saturdays and Sundays for this.

Panamanian Immigrant in Harlem

In one of your letters, I read that among the people you saw in church were Florence Mills, Ethel Waters, and Bert Williams.[18]

My husband Owen was a collector of black art entertainment. He was a great collector of records, and he had all the records of Bert Williams. He did wonderful mimics of Bert Williams. You would not generally think so because he was a quiet, serious person. But he was a great mimic. Eric still has some of the old OKeh records.[19] Florence Mills played in local theaters. I think she was one of the first [black] people in a Broadway show, early on. So she did not do as much in my youth. She was beyond that. She was a really big personality in the theater. But almost every great artist gave of himself or herself in the black church. It was a part of the social responsibility. It was part of the strength of the church. There was a social environment that was much more community oriented, and the Negro church played a multiple role.

A friend was talking to me a few days ago. She said, "You know, on Sunday morning we went to Sunday school. Then, I went to church with my parents. Then we had dinner in the church. Then in the afternoon at four or five o'clock, we went to BYPU [Baptist Young People's Union]. Then you had evening service. And then if there were special occasions like readings or a cultural program, we went to that." It was a kind of welcome. Your life was centered around the church. The events of the day people discussed in groups. As they still do, people visited the sick. But visiting was certainly, from a child's point of view, almost like a family relationship. My mother would make her specialties, something cooked or a basket of fruit, and I always went with her. When somebody moved in the neighborhood, you went to invite them to the church and found out what was their denomination. We were not Baptists, but I would go with all my little friends who were Baptists. Church for my mother was high church, because all the people from the islands (*laugh-*

18. Internationally acclaimed actress Florence Mills (1895–1927) used her status to comment on racial injustices. She first appeared in the musical *Shuffle Along*, which was written, directed, and performed entirely by blacks. Her funeral was the largest in the history of Harlem at that time. See Park Net, National Park Service, "Florence Mills House, a National Historic Landmark, Places Where Women Made History," A National Register of Historic Places Travel Itinerary, www.cr.nps.gov/nr/travel/pwwmh/ny24.htm (accessed March 18, 2003). Ethel Waters (1896–1977) was a singer and actress. Appearing on Broadway and the movies, she was nominated for an Oscar in 1949 for her role in *Pinky*. Antiguan-born Egbert Austin Williams (1874–1922) was internationally renowned as a singer, comedian, and an actor in the minstrel tradition. He appeared on Broadway in the *Ziegfeld Follies*.

19. The OKeh record label started the black music recording industry with the recording of Mamie Smith's "Crazy Blues" in 1920. See David Edwards and Mike Callahan, "OKeh Album Discography," www.iconnect.net/home/bsnpubs/okeh.html (accessed March 18, 2003).

ing) were all Anglicans. I laugh because there are so many recollections later of people making fun of these people and their high church.

Then, in addition of course in my family, my mother was a member of the Garvey movement. This was a place of great innovation, because you had Marcus Garvey talking about "Don't buy where you can't work" and a back-to-Africa movement. You listened to great oratory. At nine years old, I was listening to great stuff. The woman that made a great impression on me—because I had never heard a woman speaker before—was Henrietta Vinton Davis. She was a very highly trained American woman and was one of the leaders in the Garvey movement and one of the great advisers. Perhaps if Garvey had listened to her, he would not have done some of the extreme things, which permitted the American government to charge him with all sorts of things and chase him out of the country. Only recently when I looked through the *Sage* compilation of women, did I realize for the first time that Henrietta Vinton Davis was an American woman. I had thought she was part of the West Indian entourage. At nine when I saw all of these men posturing and talking and reshaping the world, this woman could just hold you. I would sit there in attention and with awe. She commanded an audience. As an adult I have read of her fine dramatic training. This one woman and Garvey's wife [Amy Jacques] were so compelling.

So Harlem was the center of the cultural ferment. Everybody was coming from everywhere to be a part of Harlem. And then, of course, later came what is called the Harlem Renaissance. I lived in a community where all of that developed.

UNIA Hall was five blocks from where we lived. We were there Sunday morning and Sunday afternoon, or maybe you went to church Sunday morning and went there in the afternoon. There were always hot political issues, and my mother was always there, and I was with her. There were no babysitters. We didn't know that word. Only very wealthy people have people to take care of their children. Your children were taken care of by a relative, or everywhere you went, your child went with you. We had no relatives. So life was very, very different. You were very closely tied to your family. My mother was one of the Black Cross Nurses. I remember her marching in a Garvey parade as one of the Black Cross Nurses with her white uniform, a nurse cap, and a red, black, and green cape. She was not a nurse, of course, but she knew the smelling salts and other emergency remedies. There was Garvey with his hat with plumes and all the pomp and circumstance. And I'm marching right along with my mother.

Marcus Garvey was attempting to develop what you call today real estate ventures. So Negroes began to buy property and fix them up. My mother was a member of the Terry Holding Association, probably a three-dollar shareholder, a minimal shareholder.[20] We never had any money to really invest. Some people made great investments and did very well in that limited period.

Don't forget, there were such restrictions as to what the Negro could do. If you walked to the movies at Loew's on 125th Street, you had to sit upstairs. This was in our community! My mother was fierce about those things and did not care to sit, as she called it, in the poop deck. I guess on some occasion I must have gone there with her to see something. But she would not permit me to go. I went to the movies in my neighborhood on the corner, and they didn't have an upstairs balcony. There were stores that you were not welcomed in. You could not go into and sit down and eat in Childs Restaurant in the middle of 125th Street. In the stores in my *own* community on 125th Street, you never saw a nonwhite person working there. This was seventeen blocks away from my home and was the shopping center. There was a big department store that did not hire Negroes. "Don't buy where you can't work" was the Garvey theme picked up later on by Adam Clayton Powell Jr. In my own small way, I picketed up and down those streets against Blumsteins and other such stores. I was a little older then, and this was with the Fellowship of Reconciliation.[21] This was around 1934. At that time I was an activist in the American labor movement and was busy with everything that was going on with protest. So that tells you about this black and white community. And after three o'clock, we children didn't cross certain boundaries, or you would fight for your life. Because it still was an Irish, an Italian, a Jewish mixture you had in this community.

Oh, there were many things that were wrong. I first heard of Frank Crosswaith and A. Philip Randolph as soapbox speakers. Later they became my friends, and Randolph, my mentor. You had limited access to the press. So the street corner was the people's place. Anything you had to say, you got up on a soapbox and put up the American flag and articulated that. These men

20. The Terry Holding Company was established by Watt Terry. A Virginian by birth, he moved north in 1901. Starting with fifteen cents, he made a large fortune in land speculation in Massachusetts before settling in Harlem in 1917. He was reportedly one of the wealthiest blacks, if not the wealthiest, in the United States. See Osofsky, *Harlem*, 119.

21. The Fellowship of Reconciliation began in England in 1914 as a movement against the horrors of World War I. In 1919 it was founded as an interfaith international organization committed to fighting injustices through nonviolent means. See Fellowship of Reconciliation, "History and Supporters," www.forusa.org/about/history.html (accessed March 18, 2003).

were *passionately* discussing the state of the American Negro. Don't forget, you came out of World War I, the war that you had fought for other people, to improve their lives, and you find that you came back and they were ready to lynch you! Lynchings were going on, and you could see the pictures of people being tarred and feathered in the Negro press. You heard the stories of repression and the jobs you could not have! Don't forget that A. Philip Randolph during World War I was called the most dangerous Negro in the United States.

I heard these people on the street corner, because my mother was a street corner person. She was listening to everything. My mother always knew who was speaking where, because some of our friends, some of the Caribbean people, were among the noisemakers on the corner. Whatever terrible work you did during the weekdays and on Saturday, hitting rocks or doing whatever menial job, on Sunday you were a man or a woman. Many meetings, just Sunday afternoon gatherings, were held at my house. My mother was an extraordinary cook. She would cook fricasseed chicken and fried plantain and rice and peas and coconut bread or coconut cake in the summer when you could get all these things.

We shopped "under the bridge," as they called it where you got all the Caribbean foods, spices, and seasonings. "Under the bridge" was downtown on the East Side and it was in Harlem underneath the New York Central Railway. You were able to buy things cheaper in the summer. It was an open-air market that catered to this diverse community of foreigners. They've closed that now and you have an indoor market.

My grandmother would send some things to us from Panama from her farm. During these gatherings men played music. People recited. People talked politically, *passionately* about discrimination. I don't even think it was called that word, but they talked about just the oppression people faced.

Were you aware as a child of any discussion of the conflicts between Randolph and Garvey?

By the time I was really aware of that, I was older and maybe away from home and had read some of this. But as a child at home, no. No. When we came here in 1917, Randolph was talking antiwar. J. Mitchell Palmer was the attorney general. He considered Randolph one of the most dangerous men in the United States, and so of course you read that. You know that in America that there was a division, a feeling of black Americans that *maybe* this is a chance; we will serve the country. Maybe we will get respect for our citizenship. And Randolph was saying this is a war that you have no business being in. That kind of talk I heard because the adults were talking, all of these

Caribbean people were talking about the situation here and having opinions on it. They weren't talking to me. (*Laughter.*) They had conflicting feelings as to what was happening in America.

Did you ever get a sense that people were denouncing Randolph?

Never! Never! They thought Randolph was a great man, that he was speaking to the hurt of black Americans.

What do you now think about some of the ads selling hair straighteners and skin lighteners that were in the organ of the UNIA, the *Negro World,* and other black papers?

All right, this was dollars, evidently. They were selling newspapers. And you know enough about what we do today, I mean our whole society, what kind of contradictions we have. You know that in this society *still* the question of color is very alive and well. You look at all the creams that can make you fairer and all of the things that you do to your hair. Yes, it's a part of a contradiction. We still are full of contradictions. (*Laughter.*) It's better now, though. I think we are respecting ourselves more. But skin lighteners were very prominent. Part of the income from all the Negro newspapers was from these ads about bleach creams. You cannot live in a culture, in which you are 10 percent or less of the population at that time, that denigrates you because of color and not be affected negatively. Within the black community there was this demarcation—the lighter you were, the more opportunity, the better job you could get. This was true until a few years ago, quite.

Did you have an understanding that these skin lighteners could be dangerous?

No! I think I knew when I was a teenager someone who suffered from this. You knew someone who got sick and broke out in all kinds of bumps because they poisoned themselves with these skin bleachers. But you were not talking in terms of health, and you did not know the scientific reasoning. This is your generation. And since nothing like that could be used in my house, there was never a problem. My mother would kill me. (*Laughs.*)

Her threat always was with anything I did to displease her that she would kill me. And when she was annoyed with me even when I was an adult, she would say, "You know if I had had you in the hospital, I would disown you." She would say this to me because I would wear subdued clothes and not bright colors. She said I did not have a little dash of paprika. My tastes were so limited. She said it when I sent my six-year-old son to his first camp, and my husband agreed with her. How could I be so cruel as to send my only child with all of those strangers? She thought that was the worse thing I had ever done. But Eric as an old man has happy recollections of camp.

I wanted to take him out of that cocoon and put him in an atmosphere where he would be with other children, where he was not special. I thought this camp would make him a more social person and not pampered so by this family of his. Six of his seven first cousins were older than Eric, and one of his cousins was the senior counselor of the camp. Eric was my mother-in-law's very special child, I think for the reason that his father was a very fragile child and they did not expect him to live. So she was so grateful that Owen grew to be a man, married, and had a child. While she loved her daughter, Owen was very, very special and tender to her. This family even today is like this, very close. I come from a small and narrow family and for all intents and purposes am an only child.

What made Eric's camp experience look worse in my mother's view was that he got off the bus looking very grimy and happy, with scratch marks on his legs. If he had gotten all of that at home, this would just be boys' play. But the fact that he went to camp against her and my husband's wishes, she said, "You see. Look at this boy! Look!" My mother was fierce about her grandson. What I learned was that no one had ever had a grandchild other than my mother. No, she was a very special lady.

In an autobiographical sketch I found in your papers, you wrote that young Africans, mostly from Nigeria, stayed at your house during the summer in the early twenties.

Well, as I have told you, my mother from the time we came here was involved in the Back to Africa movement. The Nigerians we met were going to Southern colleges and working in New York in the summer, and we were part of a network. My mother had a room to rent and someone would be recommended. In this way over four or five years, this helped to pay the rent. I remember only one particular student. His name was Said Ibrahim. He was a very introspective man. He was more serious than the other people who had stayed with us. I remember him because he thought that my mother should not let me go out to play, that I should be studying something that I had no knowledge at all about, some higher mathematics. I was a reader so that was not a problem. But he thought my mother allowed me to be too frivolous. He would talk to my mother in the evenings about my frivolity. Instead of jumping rope and hopping ice wagons, I should be studying. So I would never forget him, because if I had known the phrase then, I would have said, "Later for you." My mother took him seriously and thought he had a good point. She worked during the day and couldn't control what I was doing. I would quickly do whatever it was I was supposed to do in the house and then go play.

The other reason I remember Mr. Ibrahim so well was that he told my mother the reason I should study math was that I should be the first black aviatrix. He and my mother knew Herbert Julian, a man from the Caribbean who was called the Black Eagle. Once he was flying to Africa in an airplane and I think he flew over a river and dropped in it. (*Laughs*.)[22] Later he was heading the Ethiopian Air Force and buying their planes. He was always an entrepreneur. He was the best PR person, a great name. And he was a very, very dashing man. Many, many years later, when we were on the same plane, I spoke to him and he remembered my mother. I think he may have told my mother also that I should be an aviatrix. So you know I didn't like this man, Said Ibrahim, *at all!* He wanted me to be sitting in the house studying math all summer when my friends were having so much fun. This man was a scholar. I didn't know anything about scholars. I just thought he was a nuisance. (*Laughs*.)

What were your early experiences with intraracial hostilities?

There was hostility against people from the Caribbean, West Indians, Central Americans. They said we were clannish, we talked funny, we cooked with strange-smelling herbs. You know, you pick on all kinds of trivial things to disassociate yourself. The American Negroes are being stressed and pained and humiliated and discriminated against, and I think this was a natural lashing out at someone who was different. Because you are so pained, you are looking for a scapegoat. Of course, when you are old, you can rationalize what happened. But the bottom line was that employers dumped on both of us.

And I do say that in that period, many of the people from the Caribbean arrived here very politicized. When we came here, my family got immediately involved in the Garvey movement where there was *hot* debate and discussions by West Indians about the conditions here. There were no laws against discrimination. You called the people what you wanted, you chased them off the job, you paid them as little as you wanted. There was no FEPC [Fair Employment Practices Committee], no Social Security for blacks or whites, no unemployment compensation, no Wagner Act.[23] For the poor whites—

22. Herbert Fauntleroy Julian, who was born in Port of Spain, Trinidad, became an officer of the UNIA, which had as one of its auxiliaries the Black Eagle Flying Corps. In 1924, after collecting funds through newspaper advertising, Julian announced he would fly to Africa. Although he did not have sufficient funding to keep to his July 4 departure date, he proceeded anyway because there were strong indications that postal department agents would prosecute him for mail fraud. A crowd of thirty thousand met him at the 139th Street pier where he took off in a Boeing hydroplane he had never flown, named *Ethiopia I*. After the right pontoon ripped away, Julian was forced to nosedive into Flushing Bay, miraculously surviving with only a broken leg. See David Levering Lewis, *When Harlem Was in Vogue* (New York: Knopf, 1984), 111–12.

23. In 1941 Franklin Roosevelt established the FEPC as a wartime measure against discrimination by the government and defense industries after Randolph threatened a march on Washington. The 1935 National Labor Relations Act (Wagner Act) barred certain antiunion practices and established the right of workers to form unions of their choice.

Panamanian Immigrant in Harlem

and the majority of whites were poor—there was a song, "Over the Hill to the Poor House."[24] The employer would retire the mules that worked in the mines, but the worker, black or white, was on the dump heap after he finished with them. So we mutually were abused. There was no government intervention to alleviate the conditions of the nonworking poor. *All* of this legislation came many, many years later with the advent of Franklin Roosevelt.

So if as an old, old woman I still reflect on the positive aspects of the American labor movement, it is because it made not the leader of the union but that amorphous mass of workers down there, a people who could live with dignity. The union structured health centers, their own vacation centers, set up colleges to train their people. So I have an unending love affair with the American labor movement. I make no apologies for whatever has been found to be wrong with the American labor movement, but so much has been right that I will always be an advocate. The strongest working-class Republicans can afford to be so because the American labor movement did the kinds of things which *made them whole*. This or any other society will never be a classless society, and that is true whether it is the Soviet Union or the United States. But to the degree that a government can be challenged and workers can have the right to help to determine their hours of work, conditions of employment, redress of their grievances, it's the labor movement that made this contribution on behalf of the working class. I remain a member of that class without apology.

When did you first start to work?

Between ages eleven and thirteen. Since I was tall for my age at that time, although I've never grown an inch since I was eleven, people thought I was older. My mother, who was short, despaired, because she felt she was going to have a giant. I had big feet, big hands, and was five feet four inches. My friends—I had become Americanized by then—went to work in the summer. Children went to work at age fourteen because most families had six, eight, ten, twelve children. The oldest child and particularly the girls got out and worked. Everybody tried to get a job, to help yourself, help your family.

An older friend was working in a factory and said to me that she could get me a job there as something called a pinker. A pinking machine had a small wheel that you used to cut these jagged edges that you see on the seams of garments. In those days, they did them by hand. You would put the edges of the garment on this machine and you rolled this little wheel around very quickly to make the jagged edges. Then it went to the operators. I had never

24. "Over the Hill to the Poor House" was originally a poem written by Will Carleton in 1897.

Panamanian Immigrant in Harlem

seen a pinking machine, this little wheel. My friend described it to me. She had used pieces of paper for the garment to show me how you worked the machine.

So when I went to the factory and was asked did I know how to pink, I said yes. They showed me the machine and gave me a bundle of work. I sat down and I began turning the wheel. With the first bundle that they gave me, I cut the center fold of the skirt instead of the side seams that were to be stitched. So I made an opening that the designers had not planned. Fortunately, the employer came over — it was a husband and wife team — and he looked at this bundle. Since it was new work, he wanted to see what I was doing, if the cutting was straight. I was evidently quick. When he saw I had cut the center fold open, this man screamed. He said he'd throw me out the window. His wife, who must have been a compassionate, loving woman, came over and said after all the commotion as he was chasing me out, "This girl has nerve. Let's give her a chance."

I worked there the whole summer, and I caught on. I was quick. I did a lot of other things. The wife encouraged me not to go back to school, that I could stay there and work and move up in the factory. But I didn't. The garments were for a very fancy house, a place called the Tailored Woman, which had expensive, fine-tailored garments. This was one of the most daring experiences for a young girl who had never seen this little machine grinding out jagged edges. That's one experience I'll never forget. That man's rage! Well, he was justified. (*Laughter.*) There may have been two pinking machines. And they were busy and had a lot of work when they took on this absurd young girl.

In that shop, there may have been five black people. It wasn't a large shop, there were about thirty, thirty-five people. The rest were Italians, Jews, a few others. There may have been a Spanish person. In the industry at that time, none of the power machine operators were black. None! Most of the owners of the shops were Jewish and Italians.

How did you get to work?

Oh, listen. The subway fare was ten cents round-trip. I guess I either took the bus or the subway. Ten cents transportation, fifteen cents for lunch. Ten cents for a sandwich, five cents for a soda. Or either I took my lunch from home after my mother found out that I was employed. At first, she was very much opposed to my working. But our financial circumstances made her concede that if I was helping myself, I was helping her. I could save the money I earned in order to go back to school. Some of my other friends were working doing different things. These friends were not from my neighborhood. It just

Panamanian Immigrant in Harlem

46

so happened that most of the children in those days and the people who were our family friends were all in better circumstances than we were. My little friend, Dora Murray, never worked.

By age thirteen, I had had a couple of jobs. My friend was working in this airbrush factory, and so I went down and got a job there. Women were wearing what looked liked hand-painted garments which were fashionable at the time. The designs were done with an airbrush, a stencil. You laid out the stencil pattern and with an airbrush you made the design. The colors were marked one, two, three, four, five. It was piecework. I was very good at it; I was very fast. I was precise, so there was no damage because I did not spill over the pattern. The end of the week I had earned about seventeen dollars. This man said that I made mistakes on the work and he would not pay me. So I cried and went home that Friday night.

My mother didn't know I had this job until about midweek. She went to work a half hour before I left the house, and I got home before she did. I'd push my work under the bed, start burning up the dinner. (*Laughter.*) She's coming home from work, and she's tired and she's not really noticing. But by the third day she knew something. People worked on Saturdays in those days, but my mother took the day off and went to the factory. I had all the slips of the work I'd done. I wouldn't give them to him after he wouldn't pay me. My mother was small, but as she said, "*pura Latina.*" She was a pure Latin. She told him off. She did not use vulgarity, but she used her eyes and a way of stamping her feet. And when she would really take off, then she would tell him in Spanish what she wanted him to know. What she finally told him — this little short, small, thin woman — was that she would eat him without salt and leave him with his head hanging out. He paid me. Never wanted to see me or my mother again. And that was the end of that job. I don't think I worked anymore that summer. I think my mother promised to eat me without salt. (*Laughs.*) I caused my mother so much trouble trying to be helpful.

From that job, she let me spend most of the money. I've always had a rocking chair. As you see, even at this old age I have an antique rocking chair in my bedroom. I wanted to buy a chintz print to make a seat for the rocking chair and a bedspread to match. She permitted me to use that money. She said she thought I had earned that. I guess the print was maybe ten cents, twenty cents a yard. I must have used three or four dollars to make this outfit for my bedroom. These experiences are kind of landmarks in your life when you are beginning to be an adult.

There was one instance that was the most searing experience. My friends were applying for a job at the telephone company. You took an oral test and a written test. What I was told then was that my enunciation was good and that my written test was very good. But the woman in charge *said* to me, "What white mother would want you to sit next to their child?" I had said I was fourteen, but I was eleven years old, and I was devastated. (*Chuckles.*) All the operators sat together on the switchboard lines, and it was for that reason I was not considered. That's hard to accept today when you look at the telephone company and the diversity of the people who work there. But racism was *blatant*. There were no laws. There was nothing an employer could not say or virtually do to a person of color.[25] It was a very different world. Racism is still here. It takes subtle forms. And if there are overt forms, there are ways that you can begin to challenge it. That experience was all very strange and very difficult. As old as I am, that experience, *despite* a long life of a lot of other very good experiences, remains stark with me. *This* was the first time I had this very *open* hostility.

When I was older, I worked with Madame Malone. I had worked at Poro College because my mother had forced me for two or three summers to take hairdressing. That is where I met Madame Malone. She had Poro schools in many parts of the country. She was a very religious woman. At midday every day in the school, you stopped for midday prayer.

You see, my mother had a great passion. She wanted to become a beautician and thought that I would become a beautician, too. And because I would have been trained in the American schools, I would go further and learn all the new innovations to develop a large business. This was in the back of her mind all these years, and her ambition. Before my mother went to beauty school, she made me on my summer vacations go to beauty school, go to take hairdressing, which I hated! I went to Poro school on Seventh Avenue in Harlem and took the course and passed it. I never worked as a hairdresser one hour in my life! I despised it! I hated it! I didn't want to wash anybody's hair. My mother loved it—manicures and all of that.

Because New York was her second headquarters, Madame Malone was here a lot.[26] She took a fancy to me and gave me a job as a receptionist at the college. That summer, I was one of the students. She would call me into her office and apartment back there and talk to me. She thought I had a future,

25. The New England Telephone Company barred the employment of blacks and Jews as operators until the 1940s. No blacks were hired in any capacity above that of janitor in the entire Bell system into the 1930s. Stephen H. Norwood, *Labor's Flaming Youth: Telephone Operators and Worker Militancy, 1878–1923* (Urbana: University of Illinois Press, 1990), 42–43.

26. The first Poro College founded in 1917 in St. Louis served as the base of Malone's operations.

that I had a presence, and that I was well spoken. So she wanted to teach me to travel on behalf of the school. They wanted to train me to be a teacher. By then, I guess, somebody must have told her I would never be a good hairdresser. (*Laughs.*) But anyway, that was her hope. This is how I got close to Madame Malone.

You called her Madame Malone?

Oh, yes. Oh, yes. You were very proper. I tell you, we prayed every day. (*Laughs.*) Every day.

My first impression? Awe. She was a soft-spoken woman, but very correct and very, very traditional. Just extremely correct. I thought too correct for my taste. (*Laughs.*) This is how she impressed me. When she spoke, you listened. She would dress as befitted a lady of her station, the head of an organization. She always had on hats and gloves and muted shades when she walked out. She wore *no* flamboyant colors and wore very nice things. You could look at her clothes and see that it was, as we say, "high-class stuff." (*Laughs.*) I remember her having a faint smell of lavender.

By the time you first worked summers at Poro College, you had spent a number of school years enrolled in an industrial school.

I spent three years at Bordentown Industrial School in New Jersey. The first time I went to Bordentown, they rejected me; they sent me home. All of the girls who went to Bordentown had to be young ladies. But I was not a young lady the first time, although I was tall for age eleven. I was the correct grade, and they accepted me, but when the matron, Mrs. Davis, asked me what you ask young ladies, I didn't know what she was talking about.[27] So she just said to my mother, "How old is this little girl?" My mother hung her head and said I was eleven.

I returned and was accepted when I was thirteen. This school especially sought children who came from one-parent homes. I did not know the kind of school it was until many years later when I saw a story about it in the *New York Times*.[28] This article mentioned that I was one of the graduates. Bordentown was a church-oriented boarding school as most of those institutions were. You lived in a dormitory. My first year I think we were three in a room. After that, we were two in a room. I would visit my mother at Christmas and Easter. People didn't have that kind of money to go home often. But my mother would come and visit me.

27. Minnie Davis, matron of the girls' dormitory for twenty-one years, resigned in 1941. She had asked young Maida a question concerning menstruation.
28. "School in Jersey Aids Negro Youths," *New York Times*, November 21, 1948.

Panamanian Immigrant in Harlem

49

A student that stands out in my mind was this beautiful young Indian boy, Charles Irquoit. He was mixed Indian and Negro. He had a great, long hooked nose and walked as though he was barefooted or had moccasins on. He had a thrilling voice. I don't know why I remember him except he was so beautiful and so kind. He was a tall young man. He moved quietly. He talked quietly.

Since it was an industrial and agricultural school, you spent part of so many days a week sewing and cooking and doing those sorts of courses. You raised most of the food. But you also had academic courses. Because most of the men and women were first-class brains, were scholars, they gave you so much. I think I still read a lot today because of my history professor and a woman named Frances Grant.[29] She taught English literature. Every year she would travel to some part of the world. One year it would be Europe, and then it would be in Latin America. She would come back and draw word pictures for you. My interest in reading and my curiosity—I'm not educated, but I'm fairly well read—came out of this background.

My history professor's name was Mr. Williams.[30] He graduated from Harvard. It was said his father had been a janitor there. That's how he went to Harvard. His talk fascinated me. I never learned anything in public school very much about ex post facto law and the slavery codes and what happened after the Revolution. He made history poetry. He was a giant of a man. He must have been six three or four with great big lips and coal black in color and great big feet. When he walked across the room and talked about the history of the United States and the politics of black men and women like Sojourner Truth, I sat in awe with my mouth open. It was music. It was music.

So at Bordentown the history of the American Negro became alive! The music of America, which I had been introduced to in the Negro church, was kept alive. Big names, people like Paul Robeson and Dr. Du Bois walked across your stage, ate in the dining room. You served them! If I was lucky and it was my week to work in the teachers' dining room, I saw all kinds of people. They made a circuit of the black schools. *These* were the people I saw. They would

29. For more information on Frances O. Grant, see Maurine Rothschild, "Frances O. Grant, Interview," in *The Black Women Oral History Project*, vol. 4, ed. Ruth Edmonds Hill (New Providence, NJ: K. G. Saur Verlag, 1991), 361–421.

30. In 1918, Thomas Calvin Williams began teaching history and civics at Bordentown and served as the school's assistant principal. He retired in 1946. Alumni remember his commanding presence and proud demeanor and recall that their secret nickname for him was Blue Steel because of his dark color and strong presence. For information and literature about Bordentown, I am indebted to Richard Gross, alumni Arthur T. Harris and Nat Hampton, and former Bordentown teacher Helen M. Roberts. See the school newspaper, *The Ironsides Echo*, June 1955.

Panamanian Immigrant in Harlem

come on some special occasion and speak to a class and always address the entire school in the assembly. The best voices like Roland Hayes came.[31] Roland Hayes was this great star that could not really be recognized in the United States but could sing *lieder* in Germany. (*Laughs.*) A great voice. You name it, I've seen them on the stage in this little industrial school. Although this was an industrial school, not for the supposed intellectual, the quality of the teachers as I continue to reflect on this was just amazing. Somebody ought to write about the contribution of these people to the black schools.

Most of those brilliant men and women, that one percent graduating from excellent institutions of higher learning, found there were very few places they could be employed. William Hastie had just graduated from Amherst before he came to Bordentown as a science teacher.[32] That's how I met Judge Hastie. When he was, many years later, a very famous person, I was thrilled that he even remembered me. Possibly he did because we had a lot of mutual friends. One of them was Lester Granger, whose wife was the registrar at Bordentown.[33] Lester was the commandant there. Lester Granger took me under his wings after Bordentown with the various things I was doing. He became the executive secretary of the Urban League. I was a member of the Urban League.

At one time when Lester was the executive secretary, he tried to get a scholarship for me at NYU. He thought I was very bright and thought, in terms of my work in the labor movement, there were all these special courses that you could take with a scholarship. Since I was a married woman with a child and working, he thought I might get this grant. But I did not get it. That was one of the horror days for me. When I walked up to the building for the interview, my petticoat fell off in the street. A lot of young college people were sitting on the steps until their next class and they laughed. I stepped out of it and put it

31. Roland Hayes (1887–1977) was the most acclaimed black tenor of the first half of the twentieth century. He sang opera, black spirituals, and African folk music. Library of Congress, "Tenor Roland Hayes," Imagination, American Treasurers of the Library of Congress, www.loc.gov/exhibits/treasures/trio32.html (accessed March 18, 2003).

32. William Henry Hastie (1904–1976) was a lawyer, educator, and government official. He graduated as valedictorian of the prestigious Dunbar High School in 1919 and of Amherst College in 1925. Hastie taught for two years at Bordentown to finance further education. In 1930 he graduated fourteenth in his Harvard Law School class of 690. He served as the first black governor of the Virgin Islands from 1946 to 1949. In 1949 he became the first black judge on the United States Court of Appeals. See Beck Cultural Exchange Center, Inc., "William Henry Hastie," www.korrnet.org/beckcec/hastie2.htm (accessed March 18, 2003).

33. Granger met his future wife at the school and married her after one year. Harriet "Lefty" Lane Granger held the position of bookkeeper from 1916 to 1951. Lester Granger, interview by William Ingersoll, 54–81, Oral History Project, Butler Library, Columbia University, New York, NY; *The Ironsides Echo*, June 1955.

Panamanian Immigrant in Harlem

in my purse. But I was so shaken by this that I arrived in the professor's office a basket case. I called Lester after the interview and just told him I mumbled like an idiot. When I told him my petticoat fell off, he couldn't stop laughing.

How did you get to know your first husband?

Owen Springer and I lived in the same neighborhood; we were neighborhood children. I think I'm five years younger than he. So he was one of the big boys in our block. Everyone knew everybody in our neighborhoods, and parents looked out for other people's children. All of our families shopped in the same neighborhood stores and talked to one another because we all came from somewhere else. Owen's family was Barbadian and mine were Panamanian. He had, I think, four aunts and an uncle living in the same block. Owen was one of the big boys that sort of looked out for the younger kids in the block, and I was one of those in a whole group.

The people in our block were very close. I remember in those days, the politicos having block parties. The Democrats controlled the area. They used to cordon off the block so that at one end of the block they had lemonade and cookies and cake for the children and fruit and nuts and hot dogs. And at the other end of the block they had beer and other things for the adults. They were buying your vote. In those days, there was a joke about them registering tombstones. That was the democratic process at its best. (*Laughs.*) I didn't understand all of that, of course, but I understood that this meant that they were cheating in some way. None of the organizations were clean, but Tammany Hall was a cesspool. J. Raymond Jones was considered the black political genius. They called him the Fox. He was very strategic in black political affairs; he delivered the black vote. He was a dispenser of goodies, got all of the political crumbs. (*Laughs.*)[34] I think Mayor David Dinkins is married to a relative of his.

Owen worked in an ice cream parlor owned by a German. As I said, in the community in those days most of the store owners either lived above their stores or close by. The ice cream parlor was on the corner of our block. We went—Dora Murray and maybe another friend—down to the parlor, sat on the stool, and had ice cream. I would eat pineapple temptations. Owen would buy ice cream for the three of us. I'm sure he didn't go home with much

34. J. Raymond Jones was from St. Thomas, the Virgin Islands. He gained his name "the Fox" through the legendary reputation he had fighting corruption and election fraud. In the 1960s he became the first black leader of Tammany Hall. Charles V. Hamilton, *Adam Clayton Powell, Jr.: The Political Biography of an American Dilemma* (New York: Macmillan Publishing Co., Inc., 1992), 113–14.

money. If they paid him five dollars a week, I guess we ate two dollars a week. (*Laughs.*)

I couldn't go in by myself. The neighbors would tell my mother. Children were not as independent and abrasive then. They did not talk back to their parents the way children do today. It was a very different psychology of child and parent. Your parents worked, your parents were right, and that was that. So we'd always be a group. You didn't go off somewhere. I guess some individual children did, but it wasn't done in my house or no one else's house that I knew, friends of mine. We did not disobey our parents. We found substituted ways of getting around them. But I wouldn't go off somewhere. No. No.

We didn't have television and all of the things that children have today. Let's see, what did we have? Victrola with a big horn. We didn't have a radio. We didn't have a telephone. We had a movie house on the corner. Everything was right in the neighborhood. If Owen wanted to take me to the movies, he would take me and two of my friends. If I was sitting alone in the movies at ten years old with a boy, my mother would be at the movie because one of the neighbors would have told her that I had gone into the movie with that Springer boy. (*Laughs.*)

Oh, I know the worst thing that happened to me. I think I was eleven. I had measles and Owen came to my house to ask my mother how I was doing. He heard I was sick. I think she was polite to him. After she told him I had measles and closed the door, she came in to me and said, "Who is that long man at my door asking about you?" I guess my fever went up ten points. So I told her his name, and I told her she knew his mother. Then Owen and I lost track of one another. There was nothing more involved than that until way up in my high school days. When I became a teenager and a boy could talk to a girl, I knew he was interested in me.

By the time I was nine or eleven—I knew this later—Owen had intentions on me. He would always ask my little friends if I wasn't in the block or if my mother had gone somewhere, if I was with my mother or where was I. His mother told me after we were married that he had told her that when Maida Stewart grew up, that little girl up the street—he pointed me out to her—he was going to marry or court her. So that's that. Everybody knew everybody's family and their family history.

Were you working for Madame Malone when you started talking to each other?

Oh sure, sure, sure. By that time, yes. Not seriously, I don't think. Maybe seriously. Honestly, I don't remember that detail anymore, because I don't think I was serious about anybody. When I determined that I wanted to grow up very quick, I wanted to get married and go to school. By that time, I was rebelling

Panamanian Immigrant in Harlem

against my mother in a very modest way after I graduated from Bordentown — not rebellion in talking back to her and rebellion in staying out late and doing independent things. Noooo!

My mother was interested in me going down the aisle in a veil. No, I didn't want that. I was terrified. In the second place, we didn't have the money. Neither of our families had the money. I begged her. My mother would have borrowed, and we would have been in debt for the next five years knowing her, because she would have pulled out every stopper. "My only child." I was always the one thinking about money and how you pay for things. My mother was the expansive person, that you *did*. She said I would put shame in her face, because there would be a feeling that there was something wrong with me, that there was some reason (*laughs*) I was getting married, that I was pregnant, which she knew I wasn't. She said she had to invite her friends. So my compromise was that I would agree to a wedding reception, but that I did not want to be married in a big ceremony with the veils and the marching down the aisle. Owen came from an *enormous* family. So between my mother and mother-in-law, everything at that wedding reception was prepared by them. There was *nothing* except maybe toothpicks that they didn't make. Even some of the drinks they made. It was a typical Caribbean wedding reception with mauby and ginger beer and rum. The mauby and the ginger beer were made by my mother and my mother-in-law. No. I won that battle. As I say, we would have been paying for it for five years.

Well, my wedding reception was held at Madame Walker's salon, which was rented for social occasions. Madame Walker was a millionaire and as a commercial venture had this public place which was considered a very nice quality place opened for the black community to do the social things—I think we were the colored community.

What were your intentions about school?

I don't remember what I wanted to be at the time. I knew the one thing I was not going to be was a *hairdresser*, because I've already graduated from hairdressing school. I had an agenda. I was going to get married and go to school. I'd be an adult in my own house and, you know, grown up! But less than two years later, Eric had some opinions about that. Eric was born. (*Laughs.*) So intermittently, all my life, I went back and forth with some schooling.

When I became pregnant, I read all of these books about prenatal care. And the more I read, the more ignorant I became. I kept running to the hospital, because I kept getting these false alarms and was terrified. We kept a bag packed and Dora Murray, who was then a government worker, would take time off to run to the hospital with me. They got so sick of the two of us.

Panamanian Immigrant in Harlem

(*Laughs.*) My husband had paid whatever the amount of money was for the hospital *months* before. Then when the time really came, I was so petrified that I wouldn't move. I just kneeled on the floor until my husband came home. Somebody called my husband from his job because I wouldn't. When Eric was born, Mrs. Murray and Dora outfitted his room. They bought his crib, bassinet, baby's tub with a dressing table that he pulled on. Very fancy. Until Mrs. Murray's death, she was my second mother.

When I first married, I lived in the building my mother-in-law lived in. For the first moment I lived in their apartment, five rooms. My mother-in-law and her second husband just wanted a bedroom and her kitchen to cook on the weekends. And then I got a small apartment on the top floor, a four-room apartment, as soon as one was vacant. This building must have had six floors. So we had a whole big family living in that building. My sister-in-law was downstairs; the deacon's sister was across the hall on the floor the deacon lived on. The deacon was my mother-in-law. And then across the street and at the top of the block, oh my, there were others. One hundred West 142nd Street was my first married address.

How did she get the name "the deacon"?

I gave her the name "the deacon." The deacon was always preaching to me, and then she was a deacon's wife, her second husband. Well, I just thought it was a fun name. She was so good to me. I loved her. And so everybody then called her the deacon. She was trying to teach me how to be a sensible adult. That's all I can tell you, because I was not a sensible adult. To this very day the relationship with all the Quintines[35] has been very good. If I had anything to learn from the family, I certainly learned what family relationship meant. From A to Z, they were all wonderful to me. The deacon was something else. She just didn't live long enough. She had a stroke. Eric was five or more when she died, because he called her "the deacon" too. She was funny; she didn't have a voice, but she would love to sing to Eric when he was a baby. Put him on the end of her knee and sing to him, and we would fall out. Oh dear, she was good to me, very good to me.

You told me that Owen was a coach for a warm-up team.

Owen was always interested in basketball. His team, the Metro Diamonds, was the warm-up team for basketball players who were the forerunner of the great stars who did the fancy stuff holding the ball. They weren't the Harlem

35. Quintine was the maiden name of Owen's mother, Beatrice. His father's name was Joseph Springer. At the age of eighteen or nineteen when Beatrice married, her marriage certificate listed her as a seamstress and a spinster. The name of Maida Springer's sister-in-law was Eugenia (Gene) Payne.

Globetrotters but I do not remember the name of the team. [The New York Renaissance Five, popularly known as the Rens].[36] They played at the Renaissance Casino Ballroom. Owen's team did the opening game thing and their guys were good, but they were not the big stars. On Sunday mornings when Eric was a baby, Owen pushed him in a baby buggy to the basketball practice. He was one of the early men, I thought, to push a baby buggy, because men didn't used to push baby buggies. And I was so pleased. If they were practicing in a court somewhere, he would just take the baby and all the guys, you know, whoever wasn't up, they were looking after Eric, rocking the carriage or doing whatever. Every Sunday morning in the spring and summer, he was gone with Eric.

Once Eric was ill. He was a baby, maybe a year old. He had some childhood thing. When I went into the Renaissance to get Owen, I left Eric in the cab. The man could have just driven off with my child. But it wasn't like it is today. I was crying and going on. The cab wasn't going fast enough. We only lived four blocks. . . . I lived on 142nd Street and we were going down to 138th and Seventh Avenue. The cab driver was commiserating with me. At the Renaissance they told me that the game was on and Owen was on the floor. So I made a big fuss and screamed and carried on about my baby. I wanted Owen to come with me, to get off the floor and stop doing whatever. This is my child, sick! So there was no being rational. I said, I'll pay any ticket price you want. Then somebody came by and said, you know, that's Owen's wife. So they let me in. I went up on the floor and screamed there. (*Laughs.*) Oh, I am sure I behaved terribly. You know he went with me to the hospital. I told you that he was wise beyond his years. And he just sort of said, May, May, May. . . . He just calmed me down and made whatever arrangements he had to make and got off the floor. If he was coming, then it was all right. But I had no reason, no reason; basketball my foot.

You talked to me about how very neat Owen was.

Oh my goodness, don't remind me (*laughter*) how neat he was. This was my exposure, my first experience. He took off his socks and *folded them* to put them in the hamper. He folded his pajamas *neatly* and put them in the hamper. When he sliced meat, it was like the chef's slice that you could run a skewer through. He was very neat, very meticulous. I felt crazy. I had never seen anyone do anything like this.

36. The Rens were a professional basketball team founded by Bob Douglass in 1922. Composed of the most talented group of players for its time, they disbanded in 1948–1949. See Harvey Frommer, "Remembering the New York Renaissance Five," Travel Watch, www.travel-watch.com/renfive.htm (accessed March 18, 2003).

Panamanian Immigrant in Harlem

Did he ever say anything to you about your habits?

No. I wasn't untidy. But by example I think he tried to show me. Eric to this day . . . you see those coins lined up over there? Owen always knew exactly how much change he had in his pocket. He was very neat about that. He would always roll up the pennies, the nickels, and the dimes. To this day, my son, who is an old man now, does the same thing. You see that over there? I had that box full of loose change and Eric brought the papers back—Look! See them there—to roll them up. Honestly!

(*Laughter.*) He has picked up some of his father's habits?

Many, many. Most all of the good ones. Yes, most all of the good ones.

Do you consider your son to be like you?

Like me only in the sense that he believes in the community beyond himself, and he thinks he has a social responsibility. In that sense, he is like me.

Did you and Owen have the same goals or outlook on raising Eric?

All of his early life, as a baby and as a young boy, yes. Where we had problems was his junior high and high school years. Owen felt that, given this racist society, I was attempting to set standards for Eric that would help to mislead him to have higher expectations. Owen thought that Eric should get everything he could in terms of learning; it wasn't a question that he thought his son should be limited. But he thought I had a very different view. Well, I worked in an atmosphere, in the trade union movement, where I was always seeking ways that would lead to greater opportunities, programs that children were involved in. This is where we differed. Owen felt that I would give Eric the kind of false expectations that would hurt him. I couldn't see that. We were ideologically different.

What kind of work did Owen do?

He worked for a firm called Claudius Ash and Son. It was an English firm that made dental instruments, and Owen learned from the ground up. He was very skillful, and he was mechanically a genius. I think he started there as a late teenager and learned the skills of repairing and adjusting these instruments. These dental instruments were among the finest instruments made. The Germans and the British were making the fine steel dental instruments. So *Mr. Springer* answered all of the questions pertaining to assembling, repairing, and adjusting these instruments.[37] Since they would come packed from Britain, they would always need adjustments, and dentists would have questions about them. They would call from all over the country. When these

37. Maida Springer emphasizes the name "Mr. Springer" in this way because it was not customary for whites to knowingly accord the title of "Mr." or "Mrs." to blacks. Whites who called the firm and spoke to her husband assumed he also was white.

Panamanian Immigrant in Harlem

dentists traveled to New York—those who were from out of town—and would go over to this firm in New Jersey, they were always surprised to see that *Mr. Springer* had a brown face. (*Laughs.*) He was very, very, very bright. When I would say, "But Owen you don't know how to do that," he would always say, "Well, May, but who taught the first man?" He was very talented. He could make anything. My son has some of his manual talents. For exercise my son builds mobiles, and he can build furniture—precision things. As well he's a fine lawyer, they tell me.[38]

Would Owen travel to New Jersey to work?

Yes. We lived in New Jersey for a short time. Originally the firm was in New York, and then they moved and they had a big plant in New Jersey as their business expanded. We lived in East Orange and the plant was a little bus ride away. Then, of course, when World War II came, the firm closed down because they could not get supplies and the Depression had hurt them. The stock market crash in 1929 affected everything. We suffered as a result of that because Owen had a cut in pay. And the business continued to go down. By 1939, you saw this very fine firm was going, going, going, and the war clouds were overhead.

How long did you live in New Jersey?

A very short time. (*Laughs.*) Owen was there a longer time, but I moved back to New York. I was not mature enough for New Jersey life. I was an urban child. In New York City when you rented an apartment, it had an icebox, a stove. When we went to look at this two-family house in New Jersey, it had a coal stove furnace in the basement for heat, a gas stove and a refrigerator, but the gas stove and refrigerator were only there temporarily. You bought those things yourself in New Jersey, but nobody bothered to tell us. The renting agent didn't tell us that. So on a freezing November day, we moved into this house with this beautiful, big coal stove—I had never been near a coal stove in my life—and the vast kitchen with no icebox and no cooking stove. Those were disastrous times. Everything that one could do wrong, I did wrong, like flood the boiler. In the morning, Owen would do whatever you did to the furnace and then go to work. Then I would have to call him, because by midday I had done something horrendous. It was awful. He would come and find smoke that first week or so until we got a gas stove in the kitchen. I would do something wrong which would cause this coal stove to be smoking. And then

38. In 1971 in Pittsburgh, Pennsylvania, Eric Winston Springer and John Horty founded Horty, Springer & Mattern, P.C. With a national reach, the law firm was the first of its kind to devote its practice exclusively to the health care field. See Horty Springer, "Legal Services, Attorney Bios, Eric W. Springer," http://www.hortyspringer.com/LS/bios/bio.springer.htm (accessed March 18, 2003).

this little two or three year old and I would stand out in the yard, both of us crying. (*Laughs.*) No, Owen endured a lot.

What did he do after the plant closed?

Oh, he went into the wartime industries in the shipyards of Baltimore. He was working away from home, and it was a hard living because the people who were renting rooms to these men doubled them up. They would rent the same room to two people, one who was working night and the other one was working day, because the shipyards ran twenty-four hours. I did not know really the hardships until many years later because he did not tell me. He would, of course, come home for the weekends or whatever his days off were. But he never complained and told me how difficult it was then.

What were your impressions of the Depression during the really bad part of it?

You saw the things that were happening, not daily, but minute by minute. You saw all the people you knew whose plants had shut down, who were out of jobs, *able-bodied* people. You saw the Hoovervilles, the shacks that the people were living in around the railroad yards. You saw people you knew selling apples on the street. Almost every family you knew was touched by the Depression. No, we saw it firsthand. The limited jobs that American Negroes had became even more limited, because with the pressure and the needs caused by the Depression, competition for jobs—jobs that normally white Americans would not take—increased. White Americans were then fighting for those jobs. Oh, you saw it in abundance, in abundance—the people who were homeless, the people whose children had to go to work, find some kind of job and not continue to go to school.

While our very modest living was lessened, and by the thirties I knew I had to go to work, we never suffered any of the real deprivations like not being able to pay your rent, not having food in the house. Our life was simply more stringent and more difficult, but we never had any of the deprivations that some of the people with a lot of children, people with older parents had. By that time my mother was considered such a fine cook that she was a chef in a very nice small restaurant. And then she was going to school to become a hairdresser after which she opened her own shop.

I had not worked since marrying. I had worked for Poro College for a few months just before I got married. So I went to work in the garment industry when my husband got a large wage cut. Well, for ten dollars or fifteen dollars you fed your family for the week. So I had to find work. I was surrounded by all of my husband's family, so child care was not a problem. My mother, my mother-in-law, my sister-in-law with seven children helped care for my three-year-old son.

Panamanian Immigrant in Harlem

2

In the Cauldron of Local 22 Politics

In May 1933 Maida Springer joined Local 22, the dressmakers' local, of the International Ladies' Garment Workers' Union. The strongest influences on her early union outlook were Socialists like A. Philip Randolph and Frank Crosswaith and former Communists like Charles "Sasha" Zimmerman, manager of Local 22. In this chapter, Springer demonstrates how the close relationship among these leaders enabled her to combine civil rights and labor activism. Springer explains how these relationships contributed to her overall positive assessment of unionism and played a role in how she assessed Communist activists in the union.

In recounting the excitement with which she approached labor activism, Springer also relates the consequences it had for her personal life. Unable to reconcile their divergent views of family life, she and Owen divorced in 1955. Owen Springer did not trust the labor movement to work in the best interest of blacks and viewed her activism as a hindrance to attaining the kind of life he envisioned for his family. Yet for Springer the positive benefits of union membership could not be denied. By 1935 the union had a thirty-five-hour work week and wages were steadily rising. In 1937 union members had the first employer-financed fund for workers' vacations. In 1938 they gained a health and welfare fund. And in 1950 severance pay was made a benefit.[1]

In support of Owen's perceptions of the labor movement, Springer outlines the nature of race and gender discrimination within the ILGWU and the garment industry. Still, the ILGWU was noted as one of the most progressive unions of its day. The American Federation of Labor (AFL), the umbrella organization of the labor unions, had a starkly different reputation. Black leaders were often met with silence or rebuke from the AFL in their efforts to get the federation to deal effec-

1. Jerry Schwartz, "Labor Leader David Dubinsky Dies at 90," Associated Press, September 17, 1982.

tively with the racial exclusion practiced by its affiliates and to commit resources for funding African American organizers.[2]

In contrast, by 1928 Communist Party (CP) policy was aimed at the recruitment of African Americans, including labor activists like Springer. Communists had a strong presence in her Harlem community and were engaged in ongoing campaigns against racial discrimination in employment, police brutality, and lynching. Springer recounts her experiences and strong ideological disagreements with Communists. Within her social circle was a strong belief that the CP had an opportunistic concern for blacks. During this period the CP was vying with the NAACP for control of the Scottsboro legal defense, a case that would gain international notoriety for the persecution of nine black youths falsely accused in 1931 of raping two white females in Alabama. Fearful of the possibility of sullying its reputation by defending potential rapists, the NAACP had delayed in sending representatives to investigate. The organization's hesitation allowed the CP to gain a foothold in the case. The NAACP and CP continued to lobby the defendants and their families on the issue of which organization could best represent their legal defense. By 1935, however, the NAACP joined efforts with the party's legal arm, the International Labor Defense (ILD), and other groups to form the Scottsboro Defense Committee. Although the defense was able to keep the nine youths from execution, the defendants were still convicted and spent long years in prison where they were brutalized by prison authorities.[3]

In relation to her activism, Springer discusses her perceptions of and experiences with a specific group of former Communists known as Lovestoneites who were expelled from the party in 1929. These included Edward Welsh, Zimmerman, and the group's leader and former head of the American Communist Party, Jay Lovestone. Born in Manhattan in 1902 of an African American father and white mother, labor leader Edward Welsh was among the few black Lovestoneites that Springer knew. In the 1930s he worked as a volunteer organizer for Local 22 and taught classes at the Harlem Labor Center. He organized for a number of different unions in the United States, in the Panama Canal Zone in 1950, and in East Africa,

2. Since 1917, the AFL had endorsed resolutions calling for black organizers with the proviso of funding availability. Year after year, however, the AFL claimed a lack of funds, even when the Urban League offered to raise half the needed amount. See Reginald A. Johnson, "The Urban League and the A. F. of L.: A Statement on Racial Discrimination," *Opportunity: Journal of Negro Life* 13 (August 1935): 247, posted on the New Deal Network, http://www.newdeal.feri.org/opp/opp35247.htm (accessed April 14, 2003).

3. Four of the defendants were allowed to walk out of prison in 1937, two were released in 1944, two were paroled in the mid-1940s, and the last one escaped prison in 1948. In 1976 Alabama Governor George Wallace pardoned the sole surviving defendant, Clarence Norris, for a parole violation of leaving the state after his release, and he was declared "not guilty."

In the Cauldron of Local 22 Politics

where AFL-CIO President George Meany assigned him to the International Confederation of Free Trade Unions (ICFTU) in 1961.

Springer recalls that one of the salient stories about Welsh concerned his rebuff of Soviet leader Joseph Stalin during factional disputes. The incident happened while he, along with Lovestone, Zimmerman, and others were in Moscow in 1929 to appeal the policy decision of the Executive Committee of the Communist International (Comintern) to turn over the American party leadership to William Foster. Zimmerman reported that Stalin singled out Welsh in the Lovestoneite group to shake his hand because he was black. Welsh turned away from Stalin and toward his colleagues and reportedly asked in language laced with cursing, what did Stalin want from him? Harry Haywood, the only black in the Foster faction and a strong supporter of Stalin, recorded this incident in his autobiography. Welsh's behavior and support of Lovestone appalled him.[4]

The only convergence of opinion between Springer and Haywood on Welsh was that he was handsome. Springer calls him a "bronze Adonis" and remarks on his remarkable teaching abilities. She would later be drawn closer to him and his wife, Miriam Spicehandler, through her friendship with Miriam's sister, Evelyn Scheyer. She would continue to have contact with Welsh during her period of African activism when he was in East Africa. In 1964 he returned to the United States and worked for the New York City Central Labor Council.[5]

Charles "Sasha" Zimmerman (1897–1983) emigrated from the Ukraine at age sixteen and began work in the New York garment industry. His commitment to social change led him to join the Amalgamated Clothing Workers of America (ACWA) as a charter member, the ILGWU in 1916, the Socialist Party in 1917, the Industrial Workers of the World in 1918, and the Communist Party in 1919. He retired from the ILGWU in 1972. As Springer notes, ILGWU president David Dubinsky continuously referred to Zimmerman's time in the CP as his "years of sin." This treatment clearly drew the ire of Zimmerman who did not become the unrelenting "cold warrior" that Jay Lovestone would.[6]

An immigrant from Lithuania, Lovestone (1897–1990), née Jacob Liebstein, was

4. Charles Zimmerman, interview by Henoch Mendelsund, 521, 1976, General Collection no. 5780 (ILGWU Archives); Harry Haywood, *Black Bolshevik: Autobiography of an Afro-American Communist* (Chicago: Liberator Press, 1978), 294, 304.

5. Bio Sketch, 1974 program for the Third Annual Award Dinner Dance of the Black Trade Unionists Leadership Committee of the New York City Central Labor Council, Welsh Papers.

6. Philip S. Foner and Ronald L. Lewis, eds., *The Black Worker from the Founding of the CIO to the AFL-CIO Merger, 1936–1955*, vol. 7, *The Black Worker: A Documentary History from Colonial Times to the Present* (Philadelphia: Temple University Press, 1983), 643; Zimmerman, interview by Mendelsund, 1076–77.

one of the founders of the U.S. Communist Party. A loser in the factional fighting that secured Stalin's ascendancy, he was demoted as general secretary and subsequently expelled, but he tried for years to reenter and reform the CP. By 1941, however, he had become a rabid anti-Communist, working first with Dubinsky as director of the ILGWU International Affairs Department in 1943 and by 1944 with Meany as head of the Free Trade Union Committee. From 1963 to 1974 he served as director of the AFL-CIO Department of International Affairs. Always a controversial, clandestine figure, Lovestone secretly built a working relationship with CIA counterintelligence chief James Jesus Angleton. Angleton is noted for his paranoia about Communist infiltration, which resulted in actions that helped to undermine CIA operations and hurt morale.

Springer reflects on the differences that developed between Lovestone and United Auto Workers (UAW) leader Walter Philip Reuther (1907–1970). Reuther helped to organize the UAW, becoming vice president of the union in 1942 and president in 1946. In 1952 he became president of the CIO and helped to bring about the merger of the AFL-CIO in 1955. Reuther and other CIO leaders strongly disagreed with the AFL's international anti-Communism. Following the merger, CIO leaders' efforts to dilute the power of Lovestone, who was the major adviser to Meany on foreign affairs, were ultimately unsuccessful. Continuous disputes with Meany on both domestic and international issues eventually led Reuther to remove the UAW from the AFL-CIO in 1969.

Springer reports on David Dubinsky's close relationship with both Lovestone and Reuther. Dubinsky (1892–1982) was born in Brest-Litovsk, Poland, which was controlled by czarist Russia. For his role in a bakery strike, he was sentenced to Siberia but escaped to the United States, arriving in 1911. He became head of ILGWU Local 10, the cloak cutters' union. In 1929, he became ILGWU general secretary-treasurer and in 1932 president until his retirement in 1966.

Springer recalls that Dubinsky, along with Randolph and Lovestone, supported her later move into international affairs. As a staff member with the AFL-CIO Department of International Affairs, she would have significant contact with Meany. William George Meany (1894–1980) was born in Harlem into a large Irish Catholic family. He followed his father into the plumbing trade and became business agent for his plumbers' local in 1922. In 1934 he became president of the New York Federation of Labor and as a lobbyist worked with Governor Herbert Lehman for passage of labor legislation. In 1939 he became secretary-treasurer of the AFL and in 1952 its president. In 1964 he was among those who gave crucial support for the inclusion of Title VII in the Civil Rights Act, a provision outlawing discrimination in employment. Springer speaks of conflicts between Meany and civil rights leaders over the pace of civil rights reform within the labor federation.

Springer's domestic labor activism led her into the circle of women reformers and union activists connected with the Women's Trade Union League (WTUL). The WTUL was composed of working women and middle- and upper-class reformers. Many of the WTUL leaders, including Frances Perkins (1882–1965), secretary of labor under Franklin Roosevelt, and WTUL president Rose Schneiderman (1882–1972), were galvanized to labor activism by the tragic events of the 1911 Triangle Shirtwaist Factory fire. These women and others in the WTUL served as role models for Springer. In various portions of these interviews, she speaks of their towering influence on her activism and the connections they had with one another.

Hilda Worthington Smith (c. 1889–1984), WTUL activist, turned her family's estate into a workers' school called Hudson Shore Labor School. Springer attended Hudson Shore and later as a union educational director took delegations of workers to the school. Hudson Shore represented a continuation of the work Smith had started as director of the Bryn Mawr Summer School for Women Workers (1921–1934), a school she had cofounded with Bryn Mawr College president Martha Carey Thomas. The curricula for Bryn Mawr and Hudson Shore represented a collaborative effort involving the Women's Trade Union League, trade unions, and students. By 1927 Smith served as director of the Affiliated Schools for Workers, a consortium of labor schools. A close friend of Eleanor Roosevelt, Smith participated in organizing federal workers' programs during the Depression. From 1965 to 1972 she was a program analyst in the Office of Equal Opportunity.[7]

Another activist, Caroline Ware (c. 1900–1990), became a supporter of Springer's projects, helping to underwrite her pamphlet, "Pioneers of Negro Leadership," in the late 1960s, which featured labor pioneers in Chicago. Ware and her husband, noted New Deal economist Gardiner C. Means (1896–1988), had a farm on many acres of land in Vienna, Virginia, which served as a respite for visitors like Springer seeking escape from the meanness of 1940s Washington, D.C., segregation. Ware was a writer on cultural history and a Howard University professor.

Springer first met Ware through Esther Peterson (1906–1997), who also served as her role model in the WTUL. Esther's husband, Oliver, who was once the librarian at the Bryn Mawr Summer School for Women Workers, was the first to acquaint her with the labor movement. He took her to hear Sidney Hillman, president of the Amalgamated Clothing Workers of America (ACWA) and to view the horrible conditions of slums and factories. After meeting Smith, Esther became a gym teacher at the Bryn Mawr school. She went on to work as a union organizer

7. "Hilda W. Smith, 95, Educator," *New York Times*, March 14, 1984; Suzanne Bauman and Rita Heller, *The Women of Summer: An Unknown Chapter of American Social History* (Filmmakers Library, 1985), film.

and educator for the ILGWU, ACWA, and the American Federation of Teachers. Peterson also served as a legislative representative for the ACWA and the AFL-CIO before Congress, as a lobbyist for such causes as child care in federal agencies and departments and equal pay for women, and as a consumer advocate, pressing for laws to uphold truth in advertising and nutritional labeling. She held appointments under Presidents Roosevelt, Kennedy, and Carter.[8]

Other role models for Springer, Fannia Cohn (c. 1885–1962) and Pauline Newman (c. 1888–1986), were known also for their legendary work in the ILGWU. A pioneer in workers' education and holding the distinction in 1916 of becoming the first female vice president of a major union, Cohn extended her expertise beyond the ILGWU to help sustain other union and independent workers' schools. However, Cohn had a long, contentious relationship with the male leadership of the ILGWU, and in August 1962 they sought to force her out by giving her an unsolicited retirement party. She refused to give up her life's work, but died four months later.[9] Pauline M. Newman (c.1888–1986) served as educational director of the ILGWU Health Center and the union's first female organizer. Born in Lithuania, she became a child laborer in the United States and worked in the Triangle Shirtwaist Factory where later many of her friends were among the 146 who perished in the fire. During the 1930s she served on various federal labor advisory boards.[10]

∽⚬∾

The first time I guess I ever saw Randolph in a meeting was when I was twenty-two and married. I knew him by name earlier and had seen him on street corners, because Philip Randolph, Walter White, and Marcus Garvey were well known.[11] You knew the people who were writing and doing things for blacks. You knew some of the things Randolph wrote in the *Messenger*, and you heard his name during World War I as part of the group of blacks

8. Esther Peterson, interview by Martha Ross, 1978, transcript, 1–6, 16, "The Twentieth-Century Trade Union Woman: Vehicle for Social Change," Oral History Project Program on Women and Work. (Ann Arbor: University of Michigan, Bentley Historical Library); J. Y. Smith, "Consumers' Advocate Esther Peterson Dies," *Washington Post*, December 21, 1997.

9. Annelise Orlech, *Common Sense and a Little Fire: Women and Working-Class Politics in the United States, 1900–1965* (Chapel Hill: University of North Carolina Press, 1995), 169–203.

10. "Pauline Newman, an Early Organizer of Clothing Workers," *New York Times*, April 10, 1986.

11. Walter White (1893–1955) served as NAACP executive secretary from 1931 until his death. Within the organization he often clashed with W. E. B. Du Bois. White, who had blond hair and blue eyes, passed for white as an investigator of lynchings in the South.

In the Cauldron of Local 22 Politics

and West Indians who were articulating about everything. So outside, I had heard him. He would just talk in general about the issues in our community because these were soapbox meetings on the street corner. This meeting I went to at age twenty-two was, I think, a union organization-oriented meeting and was inside. At this meeting, Randolph was talking about interracial justice. His position was that the employer was prepared to discriminate against anyone as long as he could get you cheaper, pay you nothing, give you no conditions, and use the black man and woman as scabs and strikebreakers. For me this was a very different approach to understanding the problem of exclusion and discrimination. His was a larger perspective.

I spoke about this meeting at the commemoration for the A. Philip Randolph stamp [issued February 3, 1989] as one of the five people asked to speak on that occasion. In that audience were at least two people who knew Randolph at that time and remembered this part of his history. They were among the Socialists and they are still Socialists. It was marvelous for them to hear what I had to say about those days. These were people I knew and had worked with on committees. I told them that I had wanted to hear what this black Socialist had to say. I had never seen a black Socialist. (*Laughs.*) I thought all Socialists were white. So I went to *hear* him because now I was an adult, I was married, I had a child, and these were troubled times. This was during the Depression before I had gone to work and become a union member. I shortly would. And the union I became a member of worked closely with Randolph. But then he was talking about the rights of workers and the dilemma of black workers and white workers who could be easily misused and abused, doubly so for the black worker. He said there must be an understanding by the white worker that he could be undermined by excluding the black worker, and that there must be a joining.

So I told those at the stamp commemoration that Randolph really turned my head around at that meeting when he was discussing his Socialism. He excited my interest and challenged my mind to think about something besides the prejudice against the black community. I owe him a debt of gratitude for this. I got a Ph.D. education in survival from Randolph and an awareness of a struggle and of black and white relationships. He was never angry. He was never bitter. But he *never* deflected one iota from what he believed. Oh, what a man.

When I was twenty-two, I never believed that I would be able to sit with Randolph, talk with him, travel with him. If anyone had told me that later in my life A. Philip Randolph would be a family friend, would be my mentor, that I would be marching with my five- or six-year-old child with the Brotherhood of Sleeping Car Porters when they won their contract, that I would be marching as a *delegate* from the dressmakers' union of the ILGWU, I would have thought it inconceivable. I would have thought it inconceivable that I would become part of that inner circle of the Randolph family, that Randolph would be calling my union to say (imitating the speech of Randolph), "Now, Sasha [Charles Zimmerman], now Dave [David Dubinsky], we would like to borrow 'Maydia'" to do whatever it was they were doing. I really began to know Randolph by 1936, right before the time I was a delegate for the Brotherhood march. And by the time the March on Washington was planned in 1941, I was on a first-name basis; I could call him "Chief."

His wife was Lucille Randolph, the very elegant and beautiful society grand dame whom many people misrepresented and misunderstood as flossy-headed. She was a highly educated woman. She went to Howard and became a teacher.[12] Then she came to New York and became a fine beautician and worked with Madame C. J. Walker. They were colleagues. She was a representative of the Walker style of hair care. I guess after Madame Walker died, Lucille had a very fine beauty business with a very fastidious clientele, largely white. Then she and Mr. Randolph met one another, and they married.

Lucille Randolph was a Socialist. She had a deep, incisive mind and was single-minded about Buddy, her husband. They called one another Buddy. And really she was the backbone, the financial doer in the Randolph relationship for many years. It was her money and her business that made it possible for Randolph to carry on the work for the Brotherhood with no money, no pay. She virtually lost her business because of opposition to Randolph's activities, because this was something wealthy people didn't want to know about.

Lucille Randolph would test those who were getting close to Randolph to see how serious they were about the labor movement, how serious they were about the Brotherhood. And for whatever reasons, I evidently passed the test. I did not know, of course, I was being tested, but she had her own litmus test as to whether you were a part of the movement or no. I became very fond of her and she of me. Everything the Randolphs did had a purpose in terms of an agenda for the race. I spoke about her at the commemoration of the stamp for Randolph, because most of those young people didn't know Lucille Randolph. When she became so ill, Randolph would sit and tell her the day's things and read to her every night. If you have not read Jervis Anderson's book,[13] please

12. The former Lucille Greene was once a Virginia schoolteacher.
13. Jervis Anderson, *A. Philip Randolph: A Biographical Portrait* (Berkeley and Los Angeles: University of California Press, 1972).

do, because what he's saying about the relationship of Lucille and Philip Randolph is true. I respected Lucille Randolph very much. She was so elegant. Labor people tended to wear baggy skirts and flat shoes and flat hats, berets and tam-o'-shanters, including myself. She always made me feel self-conscious. (*Laughs.*)

How did you decide on the garment industry for work?

I had some sense of the factory. I had gone to an industrial school in Bordentown where dressmaking was part of what I had studied. So I went to work in a dress factory. This was my first time back after my great experience as a pinker when I was a young girl. I guess I must have begun working at the end of 1932. Again some of my older friends were working in factories. The factories had signs out, looking for workers, and I shopped around. I was *outraged* at one factory I worked in because we had to repair garments or do work over and not be paid for it. And if you didn't like it, you could go. Everything was nonunion in 1932. Well, certainly there may have been some union shops, but the unions were too weak. The garment workers' union certainly was too weak then for management to pay any attention to them.

I went to work in one factory and then another. This was piecework. You were earning nothing and you were working. Car fare was still five cents, and I took my lunch. I had worked in one shop that closed down with our wages. We had not gotten paid for two weeks because the contractor was not paid by the manufacturer. On Monday when we went back, the loft was empty. The contractor had moved out that Saturday afternoon and Sunday. (*Laughter.*) The industry was so unregulated and wild.

The general strike was 1933, August. Let's see, I was twenty-three. I think I became a member of the union in May. It was after I joined that the Roosevelt administration made the changes in legislation. We later said that the NRA [National Recovery Administration] was the Magna Carta for labor.[14] That workers should and could have representation really was a whole change in the climate of America.

Tangentially, I helped organize the workers who came in after the 1933 general strike, when we would not accept the NRA's minimum wage codes. They were grabbing a lot of people to help with organizing, because you're trying to keep order and you're trying to get things done. The union was pretty

14. Two government agencies, the NRA and the Public Works Administration, came out of the 1933 National Industrial Recovery Act (NIRA). Section 7a of the NIRA gave workers the right to organize unions of their choice. After the Supreme Court declared the NIRA unconstitutional, Congress passed the National Labor Relations Act (Wagner Act) in 1935 to again secure the right of workers to form unions.

much overwhelmed by the people who flocked in to become members. I became a member of the strike committee. The general strike was very short. I then worked with them in whatever I was assigned. This wasn't organizing. This was keeping order. This was signing people up who were just coming in, in droves. Then after that I remained a part of the *active*, they called it, of the union. They began force-feeding groups of us who continued to be active, so that you were sent to different classes in order to develop some sense of history. I was excited and wanted to know more because I felt so limited. I *drank in* everything and people began to point me out and a lot of other people, black and white. Most of these folk who were grabbed dropped off.

One of the miracles after the general strike and when the unions were recognized and got agreements was the institution of what we called the "registration of contractors" in 1935. There was now a responsibility by the primary employer for the wages—not the little man who worked for him, the contractor, but the primary employer, the manufacturer whose label was in the garments. Really, it was a revolution. You had a structure set up in this volatile, piece-rate industry where each worker working for the same manufacturer and making the same type of garment was paid the same price for it. This is out of the heads of these labor leaders!

When the registration of contractors came into effect, we began to do what is called "settlement" on the jobber's premises, or the manufacturer's. All workers employed in the contracting shops of this particular manufacturer were represented by someone. Every contracting shop designated a committee to settle prices with the manufacturer. This was volunteer work. So six or ten of us, representing the workers in the different shops, and these contractors for the same manufacturer, would meet with the management's representative and a union representative to agree on the prices of the garment. We met in those days on Saturdays to settle prices. So all of the six, eight, ten shops working for the manufacturer had a printed document which said you are paid so much for this seam, this snap, and the rest of it.

Working on price settlements was my introduction to activities in the union. The union was crying for people to volunteer and work and go to meetings, learn parliamentary procedure, learn the agreement. What were our responsibilities? What was the employer's responsibility? This was a great education. I was on the price committee and was doing various things, getting into the work of the union community.

Later on as a very young officer of the union when I was education director of Local 132, I was on the War Production Board and was accepted as a constructive participant in the war effort. The unions agreed that they would not make demands during the war despite the fact that munitions manufacturers and these other folk had cost-plus programs that netted them millions of dollars. But this was our sense of patriotism.

Now, where do you want to go from here? You know, you have me on a subject that still excites me, because I was there in that beginning. Young people today take for granted pensions, hospitalizations, birthdays off, and a lot of other things that were fought for. They think that these benefits came down from heaven and somebody gave it to them. But *this*, people challenged and fought and in some instances died for on behalf of the workers. Today, there are hundreds and thousands of children that have been able to go to school because their parents earn a decent wage and because there was not a minimum wage for the black worker and another kind of wage for the white worker. We had to fight that within the union, too, because there were parts of the country where workers couldn't even sit in the same room together. Black workers had auxiliary contracts. The union had to fight that within its own reserves. So I'm not trying to give us marks of angels. I'm saying to you that without the labor movement the American worker would have been still in the Dark Ages. I hope that we will see ourselves again and that there will be a turnaround. We are so sophisticated now that we do not remember from whence we came, that is working people. And when I talk about working people, I'm talking about nurses and doctors and teachers. They are workers, too.

Why didn't I drop out of active union membership as others did? In the first place, I wanted to know more. I was a married woman with a child, and I was not going to go to school. I was interested in the philosophies of these men and women. I was having doors open to me, to a world I would not otherwise have been privy to. So for me it was a learning experience. Also, I was getting improved wages as a result of my participation. It was a whole new world. It was a whole education. And it was so fast. It was so rapid. It was hard to keep up.

The collection of young people who were a part of the intellectual ferment called themselves the *actíve*. Out of that group, most of us remained involved in the union activities—became officers, became educators and educational directors, research persons and editors. Most of them, see, were young men and women who were graduates of NYU, of Brooklyn College, of Hunter. So you had a great intellectual cadre of young people, all of whom remained and whose families were foreigners and some of whose parents were workers in the needle trades. There was a shared social philosophy about the labor movement and a commitment. This meant that some of them continued going to school but came back and worked as representatives and officers of the union.

Leon Stein and Miriam Stein, his wife, and I became firm family friends. Leon Stein became the editor of *Justice*, the ILG's newspaper, and wrote many books. He retired as the editor of *Justice*, and he lectures now and did a pictorial history of the garment workers with someone else. Miriam Stein would review all of the books, labor and otherwise, for *Justice*. Their son was interested in international affairs, so Leon Stein brought him to me when he was going to go to work in the Congo. I had just come back from the Congo. Whether I was in Washington or whether I was somewhere else, we remained friends down the years. *They* were among that young group of intellectuals that we knew. I wasn't a part of the intellectual group. But by osmosis I absorbed some of what was going on. This involvement in the union was my university and has taken me to all kinds of universities and provided me with many experiences.

There were a variety of things you did for the union, but none of these were things that anybody got paid for. As an active member you took on this responsibility and volunteered. I did not settle prices for operators until I was a business agent.[15] I controlled about sixty shops represented by many manufacturers or jobbers. Settling prices for operators was part of the work I was then paid to do. I was the union's representative, and there was management's representative and then the various committees. Once we made the agreement, I would sign it for these shops.

Did you know of any other black women who were as interested as you were in the union?

Oh, yes! Oh, yes, yes. Later on there were young women, some of whom went to the Harvard Labor Management School. There were those who were Spanish-speaking like Marie Calera and others who did a lot of work to help to create the Cornell Labor College through which thousands of workers go. Now the AFL-CIO has one of the most sophisticated labor centers in the country which *all* of the unions draw on.[16] So we're walking a very different mile these days.

Mabel Durham-Fuller was a part of the education department of Local 62 [the Undergarment Workers' Union].[17] We were great friends. She had a sense of humor, a marvelous wit, and was very bright and hard-working. I admired her greatly. Local 62 was very active. I met her through various educational

15. Springer was the second black business agent for Local 22 and the first to control a district. Edith Ransom, the first black business agent (1937–1939) and the first black on the staff of Local 22, had settled prices for finishers but did not control a district.

16. The George Meany Center for Labor Studies located outside Washington, DC, in Silver Spring, Maryland.

17. Local 62 is now Local 62-32 of the Union of Needletrades, Industrial and Textile Employees (UNITE).

In the Cauldron of Local 22 Politics

classes. The oldest woman who was part of the day-to-day union business but was never a part of the social ferment was Edith Ransom. She settled prices for finishers. I think she was on staff right after 1933, and was perhaps the first black person on staff in Local 22.

There is an amusing story from that early period. The union developed this wonderful play, *Pins and Needles*,[18] which ran on Broadway and went all over the country. Since I was one of the activists on this committee and that committee and every committee—a face that was familiar to them—they tried very hard to put me in the cast of *Pins and Needles*. My reaction to this was I could not dance, I could not sing, and I wasn't pretty, and what did they want from me? So I was never persuaded to join the talent group that went into *Pins and Needles*. I knew then I could not join, you know, I still had a small child; and after the play became so successful, they were traveling around the country for weeks and weeks at a time. But mainly I had no talent for this! So eager was the union to involve what they thought was their potential and to have a very democratic show including Negroes and Hispanics. And I think in the back of their minds the assumption was that all Negroes dance and all Negroes sing, but I couldn't do either. My husband had told me early on that I had a good voice for cooling soup, because I would sing to this little boy when he was a baby. (*Laughter*.) So my opportunity to be in the theater was lost. That was one thing I was intelligent about.

Who were some of the other people who involved you in union work?

In my own case, the person most closely related to me was the then manager of Local 22, the dressmakers' union, Charles Zimmerman. Before I got to his attention, there was the business agent, the man who was responsible for servicing this shop I was working in. His name—I don't even know his English name—was Smoliah Margolin. He dealt with our shops daily. This was in my very early period right after the general strike. Margolin was the one who said to me when I was a hand worker, "Maida, you put so many stitches to a 'hinch' [inch]." If ever there was a teacher, he was it. Smoliah Margolin was that union representative in Local 22 who helped to settle prices. When I was on the price committee, he took me down the path of dealing with management, so that I didn't get angry and incoherent but informed and challenging. There's a world of difference!

Smoliah Margolin is a Jewish name. He was from Eastern Europe and he was one of the early workers in the sweatshop industry in the United States.

18. Local 22 members accounted for 90 percent of the dramatic group of the 1938 production *Pins and Needles*. The play had a successful run from 1937 to 1941, which included a stint on Broadway and a White House performance. Zimmerman, interview by Mendelsund, 642.

He said to me, "Maida, the only thing the employer didn't ask us to do was to bring money from home to pay him," because Margolin walked with his machine on his back! He was one of those who represented that history. In the East Side ghettos you worked all day, and afterwards everybody in your family worked at home. The little child cut threads and the others did other things. Everybody in the family *worked* at home, because there was an understanding in the industry, if you don't work Saturday or Sunday, don't come in Monday. So this was a sweated and exploited industry. And Margolin was the person who kept challenging me to learn more and to do more. He encouraged me to register for the parliamentary procedure classes and to register for the classes where you learn about the union contract. So one had to make some hard decisions.

While my husband had to accept my working, he did not have to accept all of this other business I was doing, and he took a dim view of this. (*Laughter.*) I don't think he was *ever* enthusiastic about it, but whenever there was a crunch, he would always come down and support. No, he *never* liked my union activity. Never. (*Chuckles.*) In due course, he became a member of the Transit Authority, but he was never an active unionist.

Years later he went to work for the Transit Authority after he left the wartime industries in which everybody made a lot of money. He had made a very good living, but it was a very *hard* living. He took the exam for the Transit Authority after the war and after the fight had been made for Negroes to work in the subway change booths and as motor men. He passed the exams and was a part of that first wave of blacks hired. At that time blacks working in these positions were, you know, still quite new and unusual. This was a whole, wonderful political time, I think, which softened his attitude about union activities. But my *strong* involvement I don't think ever made him happy.

His hobby was painting and drawing, so he then involved himself more in his artwork and had many, many one-man shows. As a matter of fact, when he died [in 1974], a whole artist group that he had belonged to came to his funeral in honor of the work that he had done. Some of his paintings and drawings were used by the Transit Authority. Eric had a cellar full of his father's work. Look! (*Pointing to a painting of fruit on her dining room wall.*) There is a still life. That's excellent, isn't it? The one in the kitchen is also one of his still lifes. Owen would quietly just go off and sit in the backyard and paint. He did a lot of portraits. He would always paint me with an African headdress and stuff. I am sorry, but I used to have some early African portraits that he did. They got lost in the shuffle somewhere.

Owen had an interest in what was happening on the African continent.

Read a great deal. Oh Lord, he read! And then, let's see, early on, after 1945, people began coming to our house in Brooklyn from Africa and he would be quietly listening. He had a concern about Africa, but I think he tried not to show it too much because he felt I would go off the deep end. (*Laughter.*) He didn't trust me. No, he was a man of very many talents, very bright. He did not have degrees but, oh Lord, he was so smart. Read blueprints for pleasure, could build anything.

Did you ever resolve your differences about unionism?

Oh! Never! No, it got worse because after the general strike and my involvement in the union increased, it was very troublesome for him. When I became a union member, he did not think that was going to do me any good or our family. And our family was three, just Eric and he and myself. This was a disciplined, decent, proud man. He was a good family man.

Did the two of you share friends?

Well, we shared those early friends who grew up around with us. And when Owen was involved with basketball, we had those mutual friends. When I became an active union member, that dissipated. Our friendships began to change because I was so busy learning about the labor movement.

He was never enthusiastic about my involvement, but I was on fire with it. I had seen myself move, and my wages went up two or three times after the union contract, after 1933. Here I was going away to summer school events. Here I was going to all kinds of lectures with the Rand School for Social Science, later the New School. And the Hudson Shore Labor School was my Bryn Mawr. So instead of going home at five o'clock, I was involved with the union. It was between my mother and my mother-in-law and my sister-in-law that I was able to go to a union meeting and then come home.

By 1936 I was a young active trade unionist taking training courses for workers at the Harlem Labor Center, and there was a lot of interchange with the Labor Center and the Brotherhood offices. Classes at the Harlem Labor Center were structured, so you didn't have to stay downtown or go back downtown for everything. I lived in Harlem. I took classes in parliamentary procedure, union contracts, the history of the labor movement there. The Labor Center was in the 300 block of 125th Street.[19] It was just down the street from Brother Randolph's office, the headquarters of the Brotherhood of Sleeping Car Porters, which was at 217 West 125th Street. Too bad that building got torn down because it should have been a landmark. So much history in that building.

19. The address was 312 West 125th Street.

In the Cauldron of Local 22 Politics

Trade unionists were delegated from all over the labor movement to attend meetings at the Harlem Labor Center. Black and white workers were made delegates to go to there. We were talking about egalitarianism and fraternity, and there were classes on social issues. You had a lot of very dedicated trade unionists, but these people didn't live in the black community. Since they lived in Queens and in Jersey, on the night they would go to the Harlem Labor Center we'd all go to supper together and afterwards we'd all go up to Harlem to the Center.

Among other things, they were trying to make sure they kept the Center integrated, which wasn't easy. After the first excitement of winning the union contract, a lot of people fall off. The interest wanes. It's inconvenient to come to Harlem if you live downtown or in Queens or New Jersey. I'm sure people felt, I can do this downtown. Why should I go to Harlem? When I left the Center, I could take the bus home. I was fifteen minutes away. Or somebody would drive me who had a car. Few people had cars. We went everywhere by bus or trolley or subway. It wasn't like today when all sixteen year olds seem to have cars. (*Laughs*.)

Frank Crosswaith was director of the Harlem Labor Center. He chaired the Negro Labor Committee and carried on the activities for all of the various unions that sent their delegates up there for classes. They had some wonderful training classes about another world, another way, workers, classes that kind of opened your eyes as you listened. This was a very liberal education. And I guess I was very fortunate for the reason that I was able to be active; even though my husband took a dim view of my activism.

Crosswaith was also on the staff as a general organizer for the International Ladies' Garment Workers' Union. Formerly, he had worked with Randolph in the Brotherhood as an organizer. He had worked with coal miners. I think he was the first person I heard speak on the conditions of the coal miners, and he was eloquent. He said that the bosses took better care of the animals than human beings. The animals were worth something to them. The worker was expendable. I had a liberal education from good people, good people, very talented people. In due course, he had a position with the city under Mayor Fiorello La Guardia.[20]

These two men, Randolph and Crosswaith, were called the silver-tongued

---

20. Upon Randolph's recommendation, La Guardia appointed Crosswaith Commissioner of Housing in 1942. Fiorello Henry La Guardia (1882–1947), mayor of New York from 1934 to 1945, was noted for his reforms on behalf of labor and the poor, his fight against corruption, and his efforts to modernize New York. See A. Philip Randolph and Richard Parrish, May 1, 1975, transcript, Interviews file, box 1, APR Papers.

In the Cauldron of Local 22 Politics

orators. They were very devoted, aggressive, active Socialists. They were the street corner orators inveighing against the social ills of our time. These two men were always advocates of social reform and all the progressive things that the Socialist Party stood for, and they were among those who were a part of the welcoming delegation when Eugene Debs was released from prison.[21]

The world was small. There weren't too many black people, colored, Negro . . . (*Laughs.*) You see, all of these terms are semantics. If you don't respect me, if I do not have an opportunity to do what others do, then all these different names do not open a door for me! Unless I'm prepared to challenge you and to develop what I need in my head to fight you, the name you call me does not matter—whether I am an uppercase Negro or a lowercase negro, colored or black. Now, I am an Afro-American, I think.

(Laughing.) African American now.

You're young, so you know. I'm old. Since I have very little respect for the semantics of race, I don't keep them in my head. You realize that our various titles I find a source of irritation.[22]

What classes or teachers stick out in your mind from the Harlem Labor Center?

I think learning the basics of parliamentary procedure. It was taught by a young university professor, Julius Manson, who was also a part of the social and political philosophy of the labor movement, and I think in the early day probably gave his time for free to the union.[23]

Then there was Eddie Welsh. One of the things that is written about him a great deal is that he is alleged to have told Stalin to go to hell. (*Laughs.*) If you've read anything about Eddie Welsh, you know this. In later years we were personal friends. Here was this bronze god. He taught at the Harlem Labor Center, which offered history, philosophy, and that wonderful word, dialectical materialism, an understanding about Communist theory. He taught some

21. Eugene Victor Debs (1855–1926) and Randolph were arrested within a few days of each other in 1918 in Ohio by the same Department of Justice agent. While Randolph spent a few days in jail, Debs received a ten-year sentence under the Espionage Act for a speech he gave opposing World War I. The year after Debs had gained a million votes in the 1920 presidential election, President Warren G. Harding commuted his sentence to time served. Debs was a five-time Socialist candidate for president. See Eugene V. Debs Foundation, "Personal History, Eugene V. Debs," http://www.eugenevdebs.com/pages/history.html (accessed April 14, 2003); biographical material, box 1, folder 2, APR Papers.

22. This part of the interview occurred September 14, 1990. Springer's comments are in the context of the debate spawned by Jesse Jackson concerning racial nomenclature. See *Ebony* 44 (July 1989): 76–79.

23. Julius J. Manson (d. 1998) served as a labor negotiator for the New York State Board of Mediation, as chapter president of the New York City Humanist Society, as the American Humanist Association's NGO representative to the United Nations, and was a professor emeritus at Baruch College. See "Manson, Julius J., Ph.D.," *New York Times*, November 12, 1998.

of those classes that provided an understanding of the worker's cause and the worker's right to be a part of the structure of society with dignity. By intellect and by concept, he was, in my view, a first-class brain. He was a terrific teacher, an excellent teacher. He could make a dull subject alive, and that's the mark of a good teacher. He can take a dry history of the labor movement and pace up and down and talk to you about it and make it alive! Eddie Welsh was a Lovestoneite. I didn't know this when I was sitting there in awe as he was moving back and forth across the room with his six-foot-four self, this bronze Adonis.

Then there was Fannia Cohn. She was not a teacher, but she was in the education department of the ILG. Fannia had been the first woman to become a vice president in the ILG, and she was critical of her male colleagues. I think she made life so uncomfortable for them (*chuckles*), that in due course she was not a vice president anymore. She irritated people because she was getting old, and I think many people thought she was out of step with the times. She was being isolated, and the young intellectuals were the movers and the shakers. She was an old intellectual who talked still with a heavy accent, and many people thought she was a nuisance. I guess this was in the forties.

But Fannia was a woman who believed in books and believed in the power of thought. She was a force for many years in the whole educational structure of the ILG. Whenever you saw her, she'd hold your sleeve to talk with you about books. Many people looked at her as a bother sometimes, but she was a treasure for me. Fannia was a resource. If I wanted to talk about camp, at the tip of her fingers she would say she thought Eric ought to go here or I ought to apply for this. Eric elected not to go to any of those camps, though. When I was distraught about what was beginning to happen on the streets of New York—it was nothing compared to what happens today—and I was in the national office, I went to Fannia. When I told her that I had to get my son out of New York, she ran down on the tip of her fingers a list of schools. And Eric went to one of those schools; he went to Oakwood, a Quaker school in Poughkeepsie. It was a good experience for him. So she was my kind of quiet resource.

The woman who was a part of that whole labor education history, Hilda Worthington Smith, turned her home on the Hudson into a labor school after her parents died. She gave her home, Hudson Shore, possibly in the forties, because I went to Hudson Shore in either the late thirties or early forties. I began giving weekend seminars in the forties as educational director of Local 132.

A young woman of her class did not go to work anywhere. They did community service and worked in the settlement houses, in the working-class communities. It is in this context that she became involved with workers. She was part of that tradition of the educated upper class like Mrs. Roosevelt who were concerned with the ills of poor families, the problems—it had nothing to do with blacks—of women having babies every nine months, the poor living conditions in these tenements, the men who were losing their jobs all the time. It was a terrible time. You've read enough about the history of the American working class to know how terrible it was for American workers in this country. These women saw these conditions, particularly on the Lower East Side.

Hilda Smith was an educator and wrote a book about women workers and her own involvement with labor as a woman to the manor born called *Opening Vistas to Workers' Education*. They called her Plain Jane.[24] Hilda Smith was very, very active. Before opening Hudson Shore Labor School, she worked at Bryn Mawr as one of the people doing programs for the Women of Summer [Bryn Mawr Summer School for Women Workers] because she was always interested in the working class. I think I had met her in New York before Hudson Shore was opened. When I began going to institutes at Hudson Shore, I met her really in a very personal way. The women who were close to her in the labor movement and with whom I had a lot of association sort of drew me into her circle.

Dr. Caroline Ware was a friend of hers, which helped to cement my relationship further, because Dr. Ware took me under her wing. We became friends in 1945 and remain friends to this day. Dr. Ware is now ninety and is in a retirement village.[25] She gave seventy-five acres of her farm for public property, so that they would not cut it up into little divisions. A magnificent park in Virginia.

As a result of this relationship among Hilda Smith, Mrs. Roosevelt, and Pauline Newman (who was from the labor movement), when the Roosevelts went into the presidency and began to do all these challenging things, women like Hilda Smith were drawn in to develop programs and projects. They were educators. It is in this context that I knew them. During the wartime, Hilda

24. Smith was given the name "Jane" by her Bryn Mawr College roommate in 1906. Unlike the other women who wore their hair pinned up in what were seen as sophisticated styles, Hilda wore a pigtail down her back in the fashion her mother deemed appropriate. See Hilda Worthington Smith, *Opening Vistas in Workers' Education: An Autobiography of Hilda Worthington Smith* (Washington, DC: Privately printed, 1978), i.

25. This section of interview was conducted on March 23, 1990. Ware died the following month on the fifth.

Smith helped to develop the women's corp. The CCC camp was for young men, and they called what she was doing the She-She-She camp [Camps and Schools for Unemployed Women]. (*Laughter.*) [26] The idea then was that you should have a CCC component for the young, working woman who was unemployed. She-She-She Camp was not its name, but the men mimicked it and called it that, because women were not really accepted. They were not people. (*Chuckles.*)

Would you meet union personnel coming around to your shops trying to get people to join up before the 1933 general strike?

I saw no one in 1932 when I started working. I never worked any place long enough. (*Laughter.*) But the union was flat on its face. From season to season, they would have a union and then they wouldn't have a union. The employers would barter with one another, and they would break the union. What the employers would try to do subsequently in those days was to take in women to work in the skills that only men had been working, so that they could break the back of the men. The rebirth of the ILG was in 1933. We blacks were not a part of the top skills of the industry; therefore, we were not represented proportionately as a part of the masses. But in those days whatever we did, we shared in the activity and the work. I would be misrepresenting the facts if I said to you that I believed that everyone in the International Ladies' Garment Workers' was pure at heart. No.

Many leaders of the garment workers at that time were former members of the Communist Party. They were Lovestoneites, Trotskyites, anarchists, Social Democrats. Local 22 had a very strong Communist group. Charles S. Zimmerman, the manager of Local 22 in those days and later a vice president of the ILG, had formerly been an ardent Communist. President Dubinsky never let him forget in *any* public place that he was a former Communist. (*Laughter.*) Zimmerman was a Lovestoneite, and the Lovestoneites broke away from the rigidity of the Communist Party that was authoritarian, you know, following decisions from the top and no discussion. Lovestoneites believed in the principles of a more egalitarian society but felt that the worker could not be dogmatic and believe and function on that basis.

26. Smith organized the Camps and Schools for Unemployed Women which the press coined "She-She-She." The camps offered training in home economics and health education and provided recreation and some workers' education classes. Smith noted that the camp experience gave some women the first opportunity to engage in sports activities. Future vice president Hubert Humphrey was in another of her programs for unemployed teachers. Smith, *Opening Vistas*, iii; "Hilda W. Smith, 95, Educator," *New York Times*, March 14, 1984.

In the Cauldron of Local 22 Politics

The Lovestoneites were a very small group, but their influence ranged very wide. The leader was Jay Lovestone who just died at ninety-one.[27] Jay was never a garment worker, was never a worker. He was an intellectual, a tactician, a theoretician, an adviser in the American labor movement, as were many other intellectuals. This man became a personal friend.

One of the *reasons* I felt so strongly about Jay Lovestone until his death was the fact that he was very honest. He had been told somewhere that my mother had been a member of the Garvey movement. He had met my mother, and he had known Marcus Garvey. So he would talk to her about Garvey. We used to have dinner with him. He told me why he was for the Garvey movement, why he was against it, and he talked about his change in feeling. Told me about a lot of the other people he knew in the international movement. Ho Chi Minh. I got a Ph.D. education through my association, just listening and asking questions. He never asked me to be a virulent anti-Communist or to politicize anti-Communism in Africa, so I can never say that. But he had a pulse on everywhere in Europe. Then it extended. He was a harsh anticolonialist. Therefore, he was a supporter of the African independence movement.

If you said you were going to do something, he expected you to do it. I remember once I came back from somewhere and I owed him an article. I had said I would do an article for the *Free Trade Union News*, but I had some ailment and didn't do it on time. Oh, he wrote a note to tell me that I'd made a commitment. I made sure I got that article out there straightaway.

Jay Lovestone was considered the hard-liner on anti-Communism. He had very deep anti-Communist beliefs coming out of the fact that he was formerly the head of the Communist Party in the United States. Broke with them because he felt that they could not demand blind faith from the American worker, because over there in the Soviet Union they did not know the circumstances here. He was a first-class brain. And I considered myself very fortunate that he considered me sufficiently intelligent to pay attention to me, because he had little patience with people whom he felt had no substance. It was in this context of him working for the ILG that I met him. By the time Lovestone came on to the International Affairs Department of the AFL-CIO, my relationship to him had been established. And I do believe that he was among *those* persons—Randolph and himself and Dubinsky—who agreed with the AFL-CIO leadership that I should come to Washington in 1960.

As a business agent of the International Ladies' Garment Workers' Union,

27. Lovestone had just died within the past two weeks of this interview of March 23, 1990.

I was not a high policymaking officer, but I was good in my field of representing the workers and taking care of the business of the union. And ours was an internationally minded union. I come out of a union with all these people, the nationalities, passionately concerned about social justice. They supported all of the policies against Hitler and Mussolini. They spoke about Haile Selassie. I raised money for the civil war in Spain. *We were* a part of that international world, and in New York City you are a window on the world.

After World War II when we knew the changes that were taking place, I came back from Europe in 1945 and said you have to watch what is going to happen. You cannot send men to fight for freedom, which they cannot have in their own countries. I had met Jomo Kenyatta. I had met Ras Makonnen. I had met Peter Abrahams, a South African who was a writer.[28] I had listened to the people from the Caribbean. In London all of these people from the dark countries were fighting the war for freedom and independence. And I had a firsthand, face-to-face set of discussions and heard the feelings of these men. Una Marson, who worked for the BBC, involved me in making broadcasts to the Caribbean, way down six feet below the earth during wartime in England. Jay Lovestone listened to me and did not think I was crazy. He said, "There are going to be a lot of changes. And we will be encouraging trade union leaders."

When a number of trade unionists were coming to this country in the early days, I went to him and said, "I would like to have a luncheon for Tom Mboya to meet the educational directors of our various unions so that he can share a point of view with them. They can learn from him. He can learn from them." Without batting an eyelash, he worked it out. So he was supportive in those things, and so he had my undying respect and admiration because he didn't have a double standard. That was my relationship to Jay Lovestone.

And I'm sure you've heard of criticisms of Jay Lovestone.

All over the world. (*Laughter.*) That's normal. Yes, he was considered a "cold warrior." And within the American labor movement, he was certainly roundly criticized. If he were alive now since the dissolution of a lot of things in the Soviet bloc, he would sort of sit back and smile. He wouldn't even have to say I told you so. The villainy of some of those and the brutality of Stalin would speak to that directly. So I cannot and will not try to defend the fine-tuned mind, the absolute political animal that Jay Lovestone was, because he lived for all of the international work that he was doing. What I know is

28. Peter Henry Abrahams was born in Vrededorp, South Africa, in 1919. At the age of twenty he left and eventually settled in Jamaica.

In the Cauldron of Local 22 Politics

that for me in my relationship to him, he never had a double standard. And for me, he never asked me once to be a cold warrior.

I was never a member of the Lovestoneites, but people said everybody I knew was a Lovestoneite. Very often people would tease and say if you want to find the Lovestoneites, go to Springer's office. (*Laughs.*) This was not by design or choice. I had friends who were Lovestoneites before I ever met Lovestone. I guess I really started to know Jay in the late forties.

The first time I met a couple of Lovestoneites was in a Harlem community group that held discussions regarding workers. I did not know at first what some of these people were politically. I learned that later. But I was attracted to them, and they were interested in me. The first one who talked to me about Lovestoneites was Cornelius Graham, a black Lovestoneite, because the name Jay Lovestone went across the top of my head. I didn't know of him. Cornelius was a printer. That was very unusual for those days. One of the Lovestoneites owned a printing shop in which he worked. Among the things that they did, they attended Harlem meetings. I went to all meetings. And I saw the people who were—and this is a meeting in the black community— were trying to build a political nucleus. I think I got up and asked some innocuous question. But that was enough to start a chain, and I became friends with Cornelius, and this one and that one. You know, he is a union guy! Cornelius Graham sat down and talked to me as a Lovestoneite about international politics, when he was trying to proselytize me. (*Laughs.*) He talked to me about something of this narrow group and a little bit of the history. Jay never told me anything about the history of the Lovestoneites. It wasn't Lovestone, it wasn't Zimmerman trying to proselytize me, it was this man.

There was another black man whose name I forget, who was a Lovestoneite. As a matter of fact, Eric's first really paid summer employment was with this man who had an office downtown. He repaired typewriters. Again, the building that he rented was owned by a Socialist and a Lovestoneite. That history I learned later. All of this came out of this friendship with Cornelius Graham, who then introduced me to this political colleague who was a Lovestoneite.

Did you know Arthur Boyer, who became a business agent for Local 155 [the Knitgoods Workers' Union]?

Arthur was a strange kettle of fish—very bright, very handsome, was a Lovestoneite. "Strange" is the wrong word. I should say his wife was strange, not Arthur. (*Laughs.*) He had a very devoted, brilliant wife who was white. When Arthur died, she was widowed early. But she fought *tooth and nail* everything and everybody, so that Arthur had a place in the sun. She was ferocious about him. This was her husband, and Arthur was who he was, and you damn well better recognize it. She was a Lovestoneite, too. Arthur in my view did not come out of the same intellectual base. He moved into it. She was a part of that base earlier. I think that was the difference I saw. And this attitude of hers had something to do with race. My guess is that she would feel that he was not getting the recognition he was due.

When did you get to know Minnie Lurye Matheson?

In 1933. She was one of the big wheels in the general strike. She didn't pay any attention to me. She noticed me later, because she was very close to Sasha, as Jennie [Silverman] was, even though later on she hated him.[29] I never understood why. They did not have an intimate relationship. There may have been some political or cultural differences. But the Lovestoneites were a very, very close, small but effective political unit. They talked about people whom they thought had potential. None of this I knew at the time. Minnie then moved on to Pennsylvania. She worked for the ILG in Pennsylvania because they were having to stretch the resources of their intellect and organization skills. So Minnie was moving. The ILG sent Minnie to Detroit to help Walter Reuther.

Did Minnie Lurye Matheson maintain a relationship with Jay Lovestone since she had once been his secretary?

I don't know. Minnie did not talk to me that much. She talked about union business. About Jay there are very few things that people know.

People didn't talk about him too much? (Laughs.)

They talked about him all the time. (Laughs.) Some of it was a figment of their imagination. There was so much mystery around him, always, and he played it so close to the vest. If you don't know a person, and there is an aura of secrecy about the person . . . Everybody in the world he knew, in terms of political movement, but you did not know whom he knew. And you did not know how close the relationship was. So that there were always stories. I wasn't someone that was a part of his inner circle.

Did you ever get a sense while you were doing international work that there was CIA involvement in what you were doing or what others were doing?

You can't walk in that world from the later 1940s on and not be aware of an aura of the complexities of the time. I would be misleading you if I told you I was never aware of alleged CIA activities. We worked in that sort of a cauldron, the politics of those times. If you were not part of the anti-Meany

29. Silverman joined the Young Communist League and was a supporter along with Zimmerman of Lovestone's leadership. See chapter 3 for more discussions of Silverman and Matheson.

In the Cauldron of Local 22 Politics

and Lovestone group, no matter what you did you were wrong. I was surprised to find that a writer recently called me a Lovestone operative and said a lot of things about me that are not true. He was taking literary license.[30] But in those days the challenge went beyond Lovestone. He was in the shadows. The hard-line politics of the AFL-CIO itself brought forth challenges. Early on in Africa it didn't affect me or any work that I was doing for the reason that I tried to do what many Africans in a few countries wanted and appealed for, like educational opportunities in the United States and very special projects at home.

Did you ever have a speaking relationship with Walter Reuther?

You know, I was a peon down there. Walter Reuther was the head of the CIO. Yes, he knew me. Well, he had to know me because I would have come to his notice because of the 1945 England tour. One of his officers was a part of that tour. And, of course, he knew me even a little more so because I was someone that the ILG thought well of. I remember that long, vicious strike of the UAW, and the ILG was just supportive. There was money and support because DD [David Dubinsky] admired and liked Walter Reuther *very much*. This is true! Walter was his fair-haired boy. Reuther was on the platform of this meeting; it was a membership meeting, pulling for support of the UAW. And when I came in to the meeting, somebody pulled me on the platform to make some kind of remarks. This was not a part of what the agenda was. It was just an added something of support, I think. Yeah.

How do you think Dubinsky regarded the friction between Lovestone and Walter Reuther since he was supportive of both of these men?

My guess is—I haven't a factual clue—that he would have voiced opinions to Jay about Walter. Similarly, he would have voiced opinions to each. He would have attempted to point out something positive. He cared for Walter Reuther, this young man, and he respected Jay Lovestone.

What do you know about the internal fighting that was a part of the 1926–1927 cloakmakers' strike of the ILGWU?

It was an ideological fight. That fight was going on in the twenties when I was in school. I didn't know anything about that fight. But I was enmeshed in it because it was so bitter. When I became an active member of the union and the Communists were still trying to take over the garment workers, you were constantly being proselytized. They sang a doggerel, "Dubinsky's union

30. Ted Morgan in his biography of Lovestone dubs Springer "Lovestone's Africa agent." See Morgan, *A Covert Life: Jay Lovestone, Communist, Anti-Communist, and Spymaster* (New York: Random House, 1999), 304.

is no good union, is a union by the bosses."[31] So there was a political agenda. The union consolidated around 1933 after the general strike. We had our battles with the Communist Party for years after that, but they were never able to control Local 22 or the International [ILGWU]. The real break came for those people who were still intransigent about the Communist Party with the Stalin-Hitler pact [the 1939 Nazi-Soviet Non-Aggression Pact].

Early on in the *serious* days of proselytizing in the late thirties, committees from the Communist Party would come to my house on Sunday morning, you know, to talk and to raise questions as to why, why I a black person . . . they lynch black people in the United States. They would talk of all of the things that were wrong in this society and wrong with the union. These were people that were willing to share with you, to be with you, but don't live next to me. (*Laughter.*)

Really, you felt that?

No, I knew it later. You know, there are subtle ways that you learn things. You could come to my house. You could come to my community to be with me. You would share things in *my* community. All right. I could not come into your community in the same way because you may live in the house where the elevator man says, "You have to go to the back to the servants' entrance." These things have happened. I am not saying that the Communist member was responsible for that. But they would support you in your community, while they lived in a society that they hadn't changed yet. They would use the excuse that when the revolution comes that would all be changed. (*Laughter.*) I'm being facetious on this, but no, you saw the very sharp (*claps hands twice*) differences. There were some who shared your living and your problems with you, but that was a minority.

So I was considered by them hopeless and beyond repair. Here I am an active member of the union. If I had come along and said that the union is really no good and nothing they say or do is right, it would have been a great feather in their cap if they could have captured me.

I was untrusting of their motives. But they were saying *all* of the right

31. There are a number of variants to this song, which arose in the late 1920s and is attributed to the rival Communist Needle Trades Workers' Industrial Union. One version goes, "The Cloakmakers Union is a no good union, it's a company union by the bosses. The old cloakmakers and the socialist fakers, by the workers are making double crosses. The Dubinskys, Hillquits and the Thomases by the workers are making false promises. They preach socialism but they practice fascism to save capitalism by the bosses." In Stanley Aronowitz, *False Promises: The Shaping of American Working Class Consciousness* (New York: McGraw-Hill, 1973), epigram.

things. Very engaging. *All* of the right things. You cannot live in this society at that period and not at least listen. The structure of this society was *so* prejudiced. You couldn't have a job. You couldn't ride. You couldn't be employed as a bus driver. You could not be employed as a subway motorman. These things were effective. You could not sit in the theater wherever you wanted. There were hotels and other places that you could not and didn't dare go. The Communist Party spoke of these things. The Communists reasoned that with all of these ills in this society, you had to change the structure, and that structure change then had to be drastic.

You didn't know anything about the social order in the Soviet Union except what the Communist Party told you. You'd never been there. And they would tell you anything—that after the revolution all of the bad people in the Soviet Union were no more. Everything was wonderful. There wasn't a gulag. There was nothing like that. It was a paradise. It was a pure egalitarian government. Everyone was the same. (*Chuckles.*)

I knew sufficiently enough about history to know that was not so. In the most perfect societies, we are not egalitarian, whether it is the church or anything else. The minister and the pope and the priest have a different standard of living, which immediately removes them. They are not a part of the mass. It was too good and too sweet what they were saying. And I knew enough about some of the fakery of some of the local Communist Party members, so I didn't need to fight them on that score. They were not going to *use* me, but they had *all* of the angles for capturing the hearts of a disturbed and a distressed and a downtrodden people. God knows there were enough ills in the United States for the Communist Party to be a source of great comfort to you.

Would Communist Party members just drop in on your house, or would they say, "Hey, we're going to come over."

No, no, no tell you . . . no, no, no, no, no, no. Groups would come, you know, they knew where you lived. I was an active person in the union. They tried to proselytize me. By this time I am committed to Local 22 of the International Ladies' Garment Workers' Union, and I don't see the union the way the Communists do. I think that the union is moving along the ways to help the worker. The Communists in my view were concerned with an international political agenda, which I did not want to be a part of.

After we talked about fundamental things that I thought the union was doing and that I was a party to and that I was given an opportunity to serve, they would keep talking. And then I would get nasty. I would ask them, "How many colored people live in the building you live in?" Because it was time for me to do something with my child. It was time for me to cook my dinner.

(*Laughs.*) You know, it's Sunday! Maybe I've just washed the clothes. And then I would make it awkward sometimes by saying, "Don't you have anything to do in your house?" I'm looking at my watch. I have to clean my house. I've got to go to work tomorrow morning. I have this child's clothes to iron. Saturday, I went shopping or I worked half a day or I was at a union meeting. I washed Saturday night. So they were a nuisance.

But they would come again?

Oh, of course! Oh, you don't give up. Before I became a staff member, they had stopped, because they had given up on me. I was still working in the shop when they were busy with me. They would offer me trips, a free week-end. They had camps where you vacation and had great meetings and theoretical dialogue and practical discussions on how you were going to change the union, and you sang and you danced. We [the ILGWU] had Unity House, and the Communists had a variety of places that they had bought. But I didn't have time, really. And when I took the time I was going with my union people. No, it was a tough life. In those early days, you had meetings or classes three nights a week. I don't know what I would have done without my mother.

They would come to you because of your involvement with union work?

Of course! I was a union member. They were active in the union. The union was their base to take over the country. The Communists were workers in the factories. As a worker in the shop, they were a part of whatever had to do with the workers' rights in the shop. In later years many of the chairmen of my shop were Communists. If the workers in the shop voted for a party member for chairman or to be on a committee to divide the work or to settle prices, that was that.

The Communists always sought the leadership positions. Most people are not willing to give up a lot of time, but if you are a party member or if you are in any organization, you are going to work toward getting the best results that you can. They were doing that for the Communist Party. They wanted to eat the business agents without salt, and I was one of the business agents. They would say that the union was no good and that you weren't doing your job. I had double jeopardy, because how *dare* the garment workers elect a black woman to be an officer of the union. Now, this should be reserved only for a member of the Communist Party when they took over the union, maybe. (*Laughs.*) So I had a great deal of fun with that.

If the shop elected a member of the Communist Party—I'm there as the business agent running the meeting—that person was elected. I had no problems with that. But I made sure I did double duty in that shop to service complaints, to be sure that the adjudication of the work was efficient, that that party member did not use the position to give only his favorites work. The sizes and colors of the material in a bundle determine how well you can organize your work and how fast you can work. The person who does the division of work is in a very strategic post in a shop. The people who do this job do not get paid. They may get paid for time lost, but you've lost your momentum. So if you organize this task properly, in the morning you go in early and make sure everyone has work in their basket, and you checked at night before you go home. You have a committee and you work with the employer on the priority work. It is a very strategic post. So if someone wants to make you look bad and has control of the shop and *you* lose control of it as the business agent, you're in trouble.

For example, ours was a piece-rate system in the garment industry. If the shop chairman was Communist or if some of the members of the price committee were Communists and they went with the other various shops working for the same manufacturer to settle prices at a central location, as a business agent you could lose control of the shop if you did not get the prices you wanted. You may come out of there not getting the price you wanted. You may have made a compromise. If the chairman or the price committee didn't like the price, they would condemn it and make a ruckus in the shop and everyone would get unhappy. That can destroy a shop. Look! In your classroom, you could have one person who could disrupt your classroom whether the issue was germane to whatever you were discussing or no. You could have someone go off on a tangent, and they'd be talking about something completely different from what your assignment was. (*Chuckles.*)

So the Communists continued to do what they thought they needed to do to disrupt the shop, to control the shop, to do their political work. But we were strong enough, the rest of the workers in the shop, to overcome that. Many of these young Communists in the shop would do their job. The chairman would divide the work. He would call the shop meetings, and I would preside at the shop meetings. At shop meetings they would get up on the platform and say whatever they wanted to say. He would or she would do their best to have people attend their cell meetings, run for political office. Now, as activists in the union, every right the union member had.

So did they tell you what would happen once they had control of the union?

No, no, no. You are not talking about controlling just the union. You are talking about changing a political system in the United States. Bugger the union! (*Laughs.*) The union would be able as a motive force to change the ills of the social system in the United States: the jobs that you can't get, the houses you can't live in, the trains that you have to sit in the back of the car or behind the soot coming from the engines. I mean, these were the things that they were addressing. Here is the basis of the Communist thrust, which is very engaging. The masses of people are workers. The conditions under which employees worked were bad. If workers control the means of production, there would be no multimillionaires, and the society would be more egalitarian. OK. This is a good argument. You know the one that goes "Workers of the world unite. You have nothing to lose but your chains." All right.

So that is the approach, and it was a moving one. It just happened that I didn't believe them. (*Laughter.*) Number one. I did not believe that a workers' group such as the Communist Party was going to win control of this great diverse country, the United States. I did not think that they were going to move into the South and change the conditions there. I was suspicious of a white worker telling me how he or she *loved* me and was working on my behalf. Fortunately, that was played down, so that you were talking on a mass basis.

And don't forget I had my people in the ILG and the intellectual crowd that I dealt with as sharply opposed to the Communist Party ideology and constantly warning against the authoritarianism and what really had happened inside Russia when the Communists won in 1917, this history, this politics. Just as the Communists were busy proselytizing me, the group that I dealt with in the international field—these were the men and women from Eastern Europe and from Asia and from Spain—had a very different concept of the world—certainly a social democracy which gave better opportunities to the working men and women, a more egalitarian society, one in which people voted for something, people had a voice in something, and which as much murder was not committed. You know, mine is the only right way. You had, similarly, religious walls. Mine is the only right religion and everyone else is wrong. So I guess I just don't believe in authoritarianism.

On that question I was never *tempted*. Maybe, early on, it was because of the kinds of friends I had. In those days I read widely. I read, read, read. And I was here long enough to know that while this is the most wonderful place on earth, it leaves a great deal to be desired if you wear brown skin. But I didn't think that my Soviet colleagues would be any different. So I never bought that line. I believed that there was an opportunity in which men and women of color could participate without being patronized as much as I thought the Communist Party was patronizing me. I think the thing that offended me was that I always felt that I was being patronized. I think they loved me too much. (*Laughter.*) And I'm always suspicious of that.

Did you ever meet any Communists who may have not have been such ideologues?

In the Cauldron of Local 22 Politics

OK. Sure. Go to lunch with them. Talk to them. Fight over a drink or cof-fee. People I liked very much. But they were not going to proselytize me. They were not going to be successful at it. Sure. Of course. Some of my shop chair-men were people I liked very much, but you made sure that *you* did *your work*, so that they did not destroy the workplace. And that sometimes took a little doing. Everything that the leadership of the union said from Dubinsky on down, they would attack it. They would come in every morning with some-thing else from the *Daily Worker*.[32] They would take all of the issues, what-ever the top leadership of the ILG said, and attack it. You would constantly have disorder; they worked at disorder. Oh, yeah. There were a lot of Com-munist persons I liked. I'd fight with them.

You told me once that you and your husband Owen had political differences.

Yes. Well, Owen was five years my senior and very mature for his age. And, of course as a citizen, he took a dim view of anyone who was a member of the Democratic Party in those days. We saw all of the limitations. The city politics, the machine politics was terrible if you paid attention to it. He knew the history of American politics in the big cities and in the South, the history of segregation and discrimination whether you were South or not. Maybe in one area it was a little more polite, but there were great, great limitations on where you could be employed, how you were treated. Owen felt very strongly about the Democratic Party's history with that. He was very anti-Democratic Party. And so he was a very staunch Republican. While I lived in New York I did not belong to the Democratic Party, either. But I supported third-party groups. So Owen and I had differences.

In those days his feelings were so strong. However, in the 1932 elections when Herbert Hoover promised the country that they would have a chicken in every pot, that sickened him. We were seeing the Hoovervilles. It was the Great Depression. We had come through '29. People did not have jobs or houses and Hoover was talking about a chicken. Owen voted for Roosevelt in that next election [1932].[33]

Did he ever have any conversations with you about the Communist Party mem-bers who would come by your house?

32. A newspaper founded by the U.S. Communist Party in 1924. At its height it had a cir-culation of thirty-five thousand papers. Publications ceased in 1957 during the political re-pression of the McCarthy period. See Spartacus, "Daily Worker," http://www.spartacus.schoolnet.co.uk/USAworkerD.htm (accessed April 14, 2003).

33. In Franklin Roosevelt's second bid for the presidency in 1936, Northern blacks switched en masse from the Republican to the Democratic Party. After blacks in the South gained the right to vote, the formerly all-white Democratic leadership of the South began to switch to the Republican Party with former presidential candidate and segregationist proponent Senator Strom Thurmond of South Carolina leading the way in 1964.

Well, he took an extremely dim view of them. I think part of that stemmed from the fact that he believed that they were false friends, that they were users. I think the Scottsboro case certainly had an effect on his views. He strongly believed in the NAACP. His views were colored largely by his belief that the Communists were insincere and blacks were only a pawn. When they came, he was polite. He never insulted them, but he would leave the house. He would never do anything to offend me, to humiliate me. He would speak to me about his political views because he felt that I had a very immature head and I didn't know what I was talking about or what I was doing. (*Laughs.*) He also had originally some strong views about the labor movement. The history in those days of blacks in labor unions was not good. You had very exclusionary policies in many unions. Ah, yes.

What were the lowest paid jobs in the industry?

I would say that the lowest paid job would start with the pinker. A cleaner. A cleaner is the person who cuts the threads. An examiner. These were weekly salaried jobs. Before the garment goes out it has to be examined to see whether it's stitched right. If there are any mistakes, you take it back to be repaired. After the garment is made, there's a head examiner who then goes over that also to see what is to be done on the garment, to check it and return it to the operator if there are any errors. The garment cannot go out until the head examiner says so.

Then you have the operators. Now this is the mass of the workers, the operators. Depending on the price of the garment they made, they can be highly paid. They used to be highly paid. The industry is in very bad shape today. But the operators could make a good living. If you worked on cheap garments, you had to make more garments. You rushed more. But on the middle- and the high-priced garments, of course, you could take more time. The work you do is detailed and fine, and you're paid well. The pressers, like the operators, were piece workers, and they could make a very good living.

The cutters were very skilled. They were considered the aristocrats of the trade because they didn't soil their hands and they didn't (*Springer breathes heavily and quickly for emphasis*) have to rush to sew garments that way. They were week workers. They didn't work by the piece. Today I'm told there are all kinds of arrangements where cutters have a different system where they do things by the piece. Then of course you have the sample makers. They are week workers also. They are salaried people who make the sample first. The garment goes out to see if the style is right. Then that sample is sent to the shops to be copied and made.

So you start from the bottom with this group of floor workers: pinker, cleaner, examiner. A finisher is the hand worker who sews the buttons, makes the hems, does all of the trimming. They would be considered among the category of low-paid workers, too. But this, too, depends on the shop, of course, and the garments you are making. Today so many things have changed. You have all kinds of positions now like buttonhole makers. People who used to sew buttons by hand don't do that anymore. A machine now does that. Hems on garments today are generally all done, except for very high-price stuff, on a fast machine called a felling machine.

Most black men worked delivering the finished garments. They had these covered garment trucks you've seen in films if you have not been in New York and seen them. In the industry you're only a couple of blocks from the manufacturer. In those little contracting shops you made the garments, and then they ran them on over to the jobbers' and manufacturers' premises to deliver them. Black men also worked on the tables semihelping the cutters assemble garments, running various kinds of errands, keeping the shops clean. Some of them did many things, because they learned on the job. They could fix the machines, and the straps were always breaking on the machines. They worked on the table, sorting out work. And this was a skill, but it was considered low category, an unskilled job.

Now this situation I'm talking about was when I went into the industry. And because of the lack of skilled black men, that is why I remark about this black cutter I knew. No, he was a *Negro* cutter I knew at that time. I worked in the same nonunion shop with him before it became unionized after the general strike. This young man was a fine cutter. He was from Barbados, and his name was Carl Clark. We remained friends until I think I left and was working in Washington and overseas. He was mathematically very good. And that you need if you're going to be a cutter, because you've got piles of cloth that you can destroy if you don't lay them up right and if you don't know how to read the pattern. He was very low key; he was never a noisy activist like me. He was a very gentle human being. He, I guess, was a little older and had been around working in the industry always in nonunion shops. In due course after the general strike he became a union member and he worked around. When I became a business agent of the union, he worked in two or three of my shops. Yes, he was a very, very, very nice human being. I remember a friend of his who was very, very talented. We helped to put him as a tailor in what they call the Gold Coast—Bergdorf Goodmans, Saks Fifth Avenue. Carl Clark was a very decent person and very skilled and really in the early years never got his due.

The situation back then is not true today. Black men today are cutters, they are operators. I think black men will never be any mass group of operators as white men, certainly the Eastern European Jews and the Italians and the other men who were machine operators and the tailors. But they are sprinkled in the industry from designers, owners of factories. Minimum. But they're doing all of the various jobs. When I went into the industry, their role was very minimal. You had a lot of black men as pressers. And as that developed, they earned a good living as pressers. So that was black men.

Black women were pinkers, examiners, cleaners, finishers, and some operators. And of course today they are the majority. Black women are working in the factories in all kinds of categories. But as I said, the industry is shot to hell. (*Springer slaps hand over her mouth in an attempt to take back the last sentence.*) But they are in *all* phases. In my time women were moving into the very skilled operations. Before World War II there were not that many black women in the needle trades. The unskilled women were still focused in household work and in some other industries. After 1933 many moved into the needle trades, and the real open door came after the beginning of World War II, when there was a great influx of Hispanic and black workers.

Would you say that most of the skilled blacks in the industry were West Indian?

No. It happens that some of these people I speak of were friends. Many West Indians came into the United States with skills because they did not have in their countries the prejudices of exclusion, denial of opportunity, to the same extent as was the case in the American South. There they were all black in their countries. So they were the seamstresses, the carpenters, the local doctors and lawyers. Many of them in the high professions were trained in England. They learned skills in their countries, but they didn't have the American factory system.

When one of the women that my mother helped to bring here in her underground (*laughs*) went to work in a factory, the employer called her a shoemaker, told her she didn't know how to sew. She came home devastated! She said, "Me! I turned out all of the bridesmaids' outfits, made suits for men." But she didn't know the factory system. She cut her material herself and made a garment at a time. Here they gave her a bundle of work of pieces and she took forever to put them together. (*Chuckles.*) But within a couple of weeks, she had gotten the hang of the system.

But many West Indians did not come here with a skill. They came to the United States for an opportunity. Many came as farm workers following the crops.

When I came into the industry in 1932, I came in as a finisher, a hand worker, sitting at the table doing the hems and the buttons and the trimming and the necks. In that first shop after the general strike I think there were maybe eight people doing finishing work, two of us blacks and six whites—Italian and Jewish and whatever. The world. Because, you know, Local 22 used to boast that it had thirty-two nationalities in its membership. I don't think anyone ever counted, but the workers were every nationality and Jewish, and the owners were Jewish.

When I became a business agent, I do not think that I ever had a shop that had more than 10 percent of the workers who were blacks. Never. I think we blacks represented maybe 10 percent of the country. In addition, the section of the shops I represented as a business agent was the middle range area, making a good garment with good fabric. The garments were mass produced, but there was a good range of garments.

The cheap garment you ran off in section work by the yard. The top-range garments sold wholesale for hundreds and hundreds of dollars. The cheaper the grade of the shop, the more black women you had working in those shops. That changed during my years as an officer of the union. More skilled women came in who were good operators or grew up in the trade and took advantage of moving from one craft to another.

I was a finisher and then I became an operator. I wasn't very good because a great deal of the time I was out of the shop representing the union. I wasn't a rapid operator earning two hundred dollars a week. I was so busy in those days with the union that I didn't have much time to work. And this union activity is as a volunteer.

Here's a story about a shop I was working in in 1942. During World War II —I think this was just before I became education director of Local 132, the Plastic Button and Novelty Workers' Union—there was a dinner at the Waldorf-Astoria. This was really a big wartime effort. Madame Litvinov and Madame Chiang Kai-shek and Mrs. Roosevelt were the principals at this luncheon. I don't remember whether it was a bond rally or what, but the union was very, very, very involved in World War II effort. The union had tickets for this event.

So they called my shop and said, "Maida, Sasha wants you to be part of the delegation going to the Waldorf-Astoria for this wartime luncheon." I said, "Yes! How can I go?" I had good shoes on. But, I said, I have just a skirt and a blouse on. The owner of the shop was standing beside me, hearing me. He said, "Oh Maida, don't worry about that. We'll dress you. You will go!" It was the kind of shop that had some social conscience, and they liked me. They felt very pleased that a member of their shop was very active in the union. They pulled the garment off the dress form. Had it pressed. I think I wore size ten. The chief examiner loaned me her coat. Somebody else loaned me a nice purse. Everyone in the shop was putting out their best things for me. I went to the Waldorf-Astoria and met the delegation representing the dressmakers' union, looking like a first-class *elegant* dressmaker.

That evening we had an executive board meeting of Local 22. I was a member of the executive board as a chairman of a committee. I had my good shoes on, but I had my sport coat on and a tam-o'-shanter—I still wear them today—and my skirt and blouse. Well! The delegation that was at the luncheon laughed, and they said, "Cinderella has gone back into ashes."

3

Educational Outings, Strikes, and Struggles for Equality

In Springer's narration of her activism during World War II, she speaks of the racism in the union and society at large, her relationship with various labor and civil rights activists, and her rise in the union hierarchy. Local 22 manager Charles Zimmerman played a major role in grooming her for leadership positions. During the war years he placed her as educational director of the ILGWU's Local 132, the Plastic Button and Novelty Workers' Union. The products made by Local 132 workers included apparel and millinery parts and ornaments, jewelry, cigarette and makeup cases, big frames, radio cabinets, umbrella handles, and industrial cleaning rags. Through her stories Springer demonstrates how she became adept at confronting the racism of this diverse group of workers and their families as she served in this position.

Within the social context of the ILGWU's support for anti-Fascist struggles against the governments of Benito Mussolini, Francisco Franco, and Adolph Hitler and support for Jewish refugees, Springer tells of her participation in a strike against an industrial cleaning rags plant that hired followers of the Father Divine Peace Mission movement as replacement workers. Father Divine was a powerful black cult leader and businessman who built a mass movement of thousands during the Depression. The great majority of his followers became known as "Angels." Angels gave all their property and donated their wages and labor to Father Divine in exchange for his ministry and food and shelter in "peace missions," which were also called "heavens." Those classed as "Children" were fellow travelers who were not willing to part with all their property but followed his teachings and lived in the peace missions. As part of their total submission to Divine as God, followers renounced all familial relations and gave up sexual activity. Springer recalls the humorous twists of incidents as she served as the contact person for negotiations with the Father Divine movement.

Although Springer did not share the movement's religious and labor views, she speaks of the movement's misrepresentation and sensationalism in the press. During this period Father Divine's most celebrated purchase, a five-hundred-acre estate located near Hudson Shore Labor School and across the Hudson River from the Hyde Park mansion of President Franklin Roosevelt, served as fodder for the newspapers. During educational weekends for Local 132 members at Hudson Shore, Springer provided workers with opportunities to view for themselves the operations of the Divine movement. The Divine movement was able to circumvent racially restrictive neighborhood covenants by sending in white followers to purchase exclusive properties. In this case, however, the previous owner, Howland Spencer, knowingly sold his estate to Divine to embarrass the president and foment greater dissention between him and Southern segregationist congressmen. The Roosevelts responded by making light of the situation. Eleanor Roosevelt later wrote in her article "Some of My Best Friends Are Negro" that while some of her neighbors were alarmed that Divine had moved there, they were never alarmed about the presence of African American dinner guests at Hyde Park.[1]

Pauli Murray (1910–1985) was among Eleanor Roosevelt's and Springer's best friends. Springer recalls that Murray and her sister and nephew would spend an occasional weekend at Hyde Park. Murray was a poet and writer, a civil rights activist (participating in lunch counter sit-ins in the 1940s), a lawyer (graduating from Howard University first in her class and the only woman), a founding member of the National Organization for Women, and the first black woman ordained as an Episcopal priest. Through Springer's friendship with Murray, she also had an occasion in 1957 to socialize with Eleanor Roosevelt. Roosevelt by this time knew of Springer through the Women's Trade Union League (WTUL) and Randolph's labor and civil rights causes and her membership in a 1945 four-woman labor delegation trip to England. When Springer accompanied Murray to Eleanor's Manhattan apartment for tea and conversation, she witnessed how the former first lady used what Springer called her "quiet connections" to further the cause of social justice.[2]

Among the cases Eleanor Roosevelt looked to her husband for redress during the World War II period was that of black sharecropper Odell Waller, who claimed self-defense in the murder of the white farmer who took his entire crop. Denied his right to a jury of his peers because of the poll tax, Waller was tried and sentenced

1. Robert Weisbrot, *Father Divine and the Struggle for Racial Equality* (Urbana: University of Illinois Press, 1983), 73–74, 110–11; Eleanor Roosevelt, "Some of My Best Friends Are Negro," *Ebony* 9 (February 1953): 16–20, 22, 24–26, http://www.newdeal.feri.org/texts/518.htm (accessed April 14, 2003).
2. Springer, diary entry, April 25, 1957.

to death. Murray served in a leadership role in the Workers Defense League's ultimately unsuccessful campaign to save Odell Waller from electrocution.[3] Springer traces the beginning of her friendship with Murray to the organization of a silent parade protesting Waller's denial of equal justice, and also the lynchings of Willie Vinson and army private Jessie Smith, and the beating of renowned tenor Roland Hayes and his wife in Rome, Georgia.[4]

Springer depicts the Waller case and other instances of racial injustice as factors that contributed to African American frustration in supporting the war effort for a nation that denied blacks equal opportunity and treatment. She describes the part she played protesting the Red Cross's blood segregation policy and her role as executive secretary for the 1946 Madison Square Garden rally to make the wartime Fair Employment Practices Committee (FEPC) a permanently funded federal agency. In exchange for A. Philip Randolph canceling a mass march on Washington in the midst of the war, Roosevelt had issued Executive Order 8802 outlawing discrimination by the government and defense industries for the duration of the war and establishing the FEPC as the enforcement arm. Even for its limited duration, the FEPC proved to be weak. Moreover, the armed services remained segregated, and black servicemen were primarily confined to duties as laborers. It was not until 1948 that President Harry S. Truman, under pressure from Randolph and other civil rights leaders, issued an executive order mandating equal opportunity in the armed services. The order was then used to desegregate the armed forces.

In this chapter, Springer also recalls the strong support for Franklin Roosevelt's presidency among the needle trades and humorously reflects on the rivalry between ILGWU president David Dubinsky and ACWA president Sidney Hillman (1887–1946). Although these leaders came together to found the American Labor

3. Norman Thomas and Socialist labor leaders founded the Workers Defense League in 1936 to defend the legal rights of workers. See Murray Kempton, "Workers Defense League," *The New York Review of Books*, November 5, 1970, http://www.nybooks.com/articles/10773 (accessed April 14, 2003).

4. Described as a youth, Vinson was lynched on July 13, 1942, in Texarkana, Texas, for an alleged rape of a white woman, the usual justification given for lynching black males. Smith was lynched in Flagstaff, Arizona. The police beat Hayes and his wife on July 16, 1942, following an argument between Mrs. Hayes and a shoe store clerk. Georgia Governor Eugene Talmadge scoffed at protests of their mistreatment and, pledging that Georgia would uphold Jim Crow laws, advised those who did not like it to stay out of the state. TSHA [Texas State Historical Association] Online, A Digital Gateway to Texas History, "The Handbook of Texas Online," http://www.tsha.utexas.edu/handbook/online/articles/view/LL/jgll.html (accessed November 22, 2003); "Alabama, Georgia Enforce 'Jim Crow' Laws," July 23, 1942, in "U.S. News: Senate Votes Alcohol Rubber Agency Bill; Other Developments," issue date July 28, 1942, World News Archive, Facts on File World News Digest (accessed November 22, 2003). Pauli Murray, *The Autobiography of a Black Activist, Feminist, Lawyer, Priest, and Poet* (Knoxville: University of Tennessee Press, 1987), 173–75; see picture and caption in the *People's Voice* (New York), July 25, 1942.

Party as a way of bypassing corrupt Tammany Hall to support Roosevelt's reelection, they fought each other for the favor of FDR and over questions of jurisdiction in the garment trade. Their disagreements led to a split in the party, resulting in the creation by ILGWU leaders of the Liberal Party. Not until 1995 did the two needle trade unions come together to form UNITE, the Union of Needletrades, Industrial and Textile Employees.

In contrast to the rivalries of the male leaders in the garment trade, Springer produces a different image of the female activist circle. She paints warm portraits of her friends Dollie Lowther Robinson and Charlotte Adelmond, the black founders of the ACWA-affiliated laundry workers' union. Robinson held the positions of shop steward and secretary to her local before becoming educational director of the Laundry Workers Joint Board (ACWA). Robinson also would serve as secretary of the New York State Department of Labor and equal opportunity officer for New York. Springer recalls Robinson's undercover investigation of conditions in migrant labor camps during the 1950s. From 1963 to 1965 Robinson was the assistant to Esther Peterson, director of the Women's Bureau in the U.S. Department of Labor.[5] Peterson, who had previously worked for the ILGWU and the ACWA, was also Springer's friend.

Two other union women Springer discusses are Minnie Lurye Matheson (1909–1992) and fellow ILGWU business agent Jennie Silverman (c. 1909–1993). At the time of this 1990 portion of the interviews, Springer shares her thoughts regarding her recent reunion with these two women at an eightieth birthday celebration for Silverman. In 1945 Matheson became regional manager of the ILGWU at Wilkes-Barre, Pennsylvania, a state where runaway shops escaping unionization drives were settling. Both she and her brother, William Lurye, fought shops under the control of organized crime. In May 1949, when Lurye was the organizer in charge of pickets at a New York shop under the control of a partner of Albert Anastasia of Murder Inc., he was stabbed to death in a telephone booth. One hundred thousand turned out for the funeral. Will and Min's father, Max Lurye, had survived a machine-gunning in Chicago during his own days of organizing. Ill in the hospital when his son was murdered, Max died a few days later with remorse for having told Will, over Min's objections, to continue to organize despite the danger.[6]

5. Dollie Lowther Robinson, interview by Bette Craig, March 1, 1977, transcript, "The Twentieth-Century Trade Union Woman: Vehicle for Social Change," Oral History Project Program on Women and Work (Ann Arbor: University of Michigan, Bentley Historical Library).

6. Lester Velie, "The Lady and the Gangster," *Reader's Digest*, January 1957. For more information on Min Matheson, see Kenneth C. Wolensky, *Fighting for the Union Label: The Women's Garment Industry and the ILGWU in Pennsylvania* (University Park, PA: The Pennsylvania State University Press, 2002).

Educational Outings, Strikes, and Struggles for Equality

Jennie Silverman also experienced great family tragedy. Her father and brother had been killed in a 1919 pogrom along with all the other Jewish men present in their Ukrainian town. Silverman's mother then appointed her to perform the Jewish ritual of saying prayers for the dead in a synagogue in the morning and the evening for a year. By having ten-year-old Jennie perform this ritual instead of hiring an outside male, Silverman's mother was going against Jewish custom since only married women on high holy days were allowed to go to the synagogue. Seeking passage to the United States via Romania, Silverman with eleven other members of the family split into four groups for the journey in order to decrease the chances of them all being killed by either the Russians or the Romanians. After harrowing experiences they managed in the end through bribery to secure passage to the United States.[7] In the stories of her rise up the union hierarchy to her finally becoming a business agent for Local 22, Springer recalls the support she received from Randolph. She used her position not only to fight against racism of employers, workers, and union officials but also to encourage black women to take advantage of union educational opportunities in order to increase their skill level and secure better-paying jobs. Union officers supervised such training programs in cooperation with the Fashion Institute of Technology. Local 22 and the New York State Board of Education also sponsored training classes for operators at the Central High School of Needle Trades. Springer reflects on her inability to convince more black women to take advantage of these programs and views this as her own failure.

Springer also draws a colorful portrait of political leader Adam Clayton Powell Jr. (1908–1972). Powell's pastorship of Abyssinian Baptist Church, one of the largest congregations in the country, served as a base from which he launched his political career. Elected to Congress from 1945 to 1970, he was the first black congressman from the east and the first black to hold a committee chair. Named chair of the House Education and Labor Committee in 1961 he played a pivotal role in the passage of major social legislation concerned with antipoverty, wage and work standards, education, and vocational training. As chair he would take Zimmerman, Dubinsky, and AFL-CIO president George Meany to task over union discrimination. Powell had a long history of supporting the left-wing opposition to the Zimmerman slate. Although Springer greatly admired Powell, she felt ambivalent about the nature of his attacks on the Zimmerman administration. Her friend Dollie Lowther Robinson was closer to Powell, and he would later recommend her to work in the U.S. Department of Labor. A charismatic, flamboyant, and controversial character, Powell openly manipulated government finances and perks for

7. Jennie Silverman, interview by author, April 30, 1991.

his own personal pleasure while pointing out the hypocrisy of his congressional critics who engaged in similar behavior. After Congress voted to expel him, he was reelected and again excluded from the government body. The Supreme Court declared his exclusion unconstitutional. However, Powell did not regain his seniority, and he subsequently lost the Democratic primary to Charles Rangel. Powell's legacy includes his forthright challenge of segregation and discrimination in the halls of Congress and in the United States as a whole.

∾⚬∾

Let's talk about your work with Local 132.

I began as educational director of Local 132, the Plastic Button and Novelty Workers' Union, in 1943 during World War II. Local 132 had had a revolutionary change. The draft wiped out a lot of the young membership. The old men and the women were left, and others came in to replace those who went to war. I would say 75 percent of the membership was male, and they did all the trimmings for the garments. They were metal workers who made buttons, belts, buckles, and a lot of things like that. The women worked with acetone, gluing the trimmings together, putting rhinestones around buttons and all kinds of complicated things.

So when World War II comes, there was then an influx of new workers. You had refugee survivors from Hitler's death camps who had the marks on their arm. You had people coming up from the South who had never worked in a factory before and certainly had problems in their black-white relationships, both ways. People worked together who were so strange to one another's cultures. This was my first exposure to a large number of Southern workers.

In Local 132—and this was the only place I was faced with this—the owner of this waste products plant, a very big firm, was a philanthropist who worked with the prison system. He employed people just out of jail. So they could do their probation and work for this firm which made industrial cleaning rags. The firm got all of this old material, some of it from as long ago as World War I, and processed it and made industrial rags for cleaning and oiling the big machinery in plants. It was a big business making these industrial cleaning rags. As I recall, the people on probation were all black and maybe a couple of Hispanics. All told the number was not more than eight or ten.

Local 132 felt that they needed to do something rapidly to assimilate these workers who could be very antagonistic to one another. So the leaders of the union talked among themselves, and my name kept coming up. My name was known for doing various volunteer activities and representing the dressmakers. I think that my friend Julie, who was an accountant in Local 132, must have put my name in and talked with Sasha and Marty Feldman, the Local 132 manager. I was at first friends with Julie's wife, who was a secretary in the education department of Local 22. So my manager, Charles Zimmerman, was approached about having me work to put this together. Zimmerman agreed and said he would talk to me.

So he called, and I said, "Oh no, I can't do that." He went on to point out all the things I had done for the dressmakers, on the various committees. He said, "You're the chairman of the education committee here, aren't you?" I said, "That's different. This is a volunteer activity." As an educational director you are employed to put together programs and organize activities on behalf of the workers. I was scared to death, and he challenged me to accept this appointment. He said, "You aren't going to embarrass me, and I trust you and I have faith in you. You would have an opportunity to put your ideas to work in a smaller context." And I think the final thing he said to me was, "You know, I want you to get your feet wet. We want you on the staff here, but it's too big a jump right now. This is an opportunity *I* want you to accept. Here you can begin to work, and I think you'll do a good job."

He was very supportive and tried to see to it that I was given a chance to take advantage of every opportunity. That was my relationship with him. He thought I had potential. I hope I didn't deceive him. This was my first staff job. Two or three years later I came back to my own union, Local 22, and worked in the complaint department where you saw all of the ramifications of the day-to-day work of the union, and you were responsible for adjudicating all of these various problems. And in 1948 I became a business agent for the Dress Joint Board.

In Local 132 I worked closely with Marty Feldman and Sam Eisenberg. There were only five people on the staff, so we did everything together. You do everything from sweeping the floor to cleaning up the coffee cups, if it was late at night after an executive board meeting and the cleaning people had gone. The committees were very active in the union. If you were leafleting a factory that was nonunion and the shift changed at four o'clock or five o'clock in the morning, you went to leaflet at that time as the men changed shifts. Sam or Marty would pick me up and off we would go. Sam was the business agent. Many years later he became the manager. Marty was the manager of the union. He was a big, bluff man. He shouted and was quite the opposite of what I had dealt with with Sasha in Local 22. I went down and he interviewed me, and in a very strange way we hit it off right away. (*Laughs.*)

The immediate problem I faced was the integration of all these newcomers to union membership. There were refugees throughout the ILG because the ILG was instrumental in bringing people out of Nazi Germany, out of Mussolini's Italy. Very instrumental! In my own Local 22 before I went down to the Plastic Button and Novelty Workers' Union, there were those people with the numbers marked on their arms, people whose teeth were gone. They now had big silver caps pressed over their mouth because when they escaped to a refugee place, people there tried to rehabilitate them. There were centers set up where people were given health examinations, were given clothing, were given much of the essential. And many of them were brought to the United States and all over the world, Latin America. So our union was one of those that helped. The unions were *very, very, very* much involved. When they escaped to the refugee camp, there were monies from the American unions to help rehabilitate them.

Some of these folk would tell you they were brought here by ORT [Organization for Rehabilitation and Training], and they were brought here by underground. ORT was a Jewish organization which was an international relief organization, and I think it still functions. They did training and all sorts of things.[8] There were a number of international organizations helping to bring them out of the refugee centers in Germany and in Italy, in Belgium. These are some extraordinary stories. And I just happened to know a number of people who were working and had brought people out, which was extremely risky. Some of them, of course, lost their lives. In the garment workers, we tried to make sure that refugees were given employment. Many of them had some background in an industry, and they went to work in some of our shops. Others went into teaching. Others went to work doing all sorts of things.[9]

As a matter of fact, speaking of teaching, one group worked for the Workmen's Circle, which is a Jewish organization.[10] I wanted to take some courses

8. World ORT is a nonprofit, nonsectarian Jewish organization based in Switzerland with various affiliates throughout the world. ORT's international programs are aimed at promoting economic development and social justice by helping disadvantaged people gain vocational training and education. See World ORT, "Educating for Life," http://www.ort.org/asp/page.asp?id=1 (accessed April 14, 2003).

9. The ILGWU worked with the Labor Division of the Committee to Defend America, which gave support to the International Transport Workers' Federation's underground operations against the Nazis. Labor also helped the Norwegian underground forces and the French resistance movement. See David Dubinsky and A. H. Raskin, *David Dubinsky: A Life with Labor* (New York: Simon & Schuster, 1977), 244–45.

10. Founded in 1900, the Workmen's Circle/Arbeter Ring is a Jewish organization that seeks to preserve Jewish culture and promote economic and social justice. See Workmen's Circle/Arbeter Ring, "Workmen's Circle: The Center for Cultural Jewish Life," http://www.circle.org./index.htm (accessed April 14, 2003).

Educational Outings, Strikes, and Struggles for Equality

in Yiddish, which the Workmen's Circle sponsored. People who spoke Yiddish were a part of my life; I dealt with them every day. And I thought I should go beyond a couple of phrases, so I would have a greater sense of involvement and would understand some things that were happening or said. These were evening classes held in one of the high schools downtown. My name again is beguiling—Maida Springer. No one had said to these people when I registered what I looked like. These intellectuals from whatever part of Europe they came from thought that they were going to be teaching Yiddish to young American Jews who were largely English speaking. So when I turned up for this class this night, they looked at me and said (*voice raised expectantly*), "Good evening. May we help you?" I said (*voice raised expectantly*), "Yes." So I dragged it out as long as I could. Then they looked up and said, "And your name?" I said, "Maida Springer. I'm from Local 22. I'm a business agent for the dressmaker's union." "So why didn't you say so?!" (*Laughter.*) So I started with a class in Yiddish. It was a *wonderful* experience.

I left the class because there was a young man in the class that bothered me. I traveled a lot and missed some classes. He wanted to be my tutor and I did not care for that. He would answer for me, and he was very anxious that I become a very good student, and that got on my nerves. I did not want to be patronized. I'm hung up about that. Whether one was patronizing me or no, I very often assumed that the person was, and that was the end for me.

So after my first recital, when I recited a Yiddish poem, I left the class. I knew enough to manage around in my union. They used to call me, "*mein shvester,* Springer" (*laughter*), "my sister, Springer." And there was a time humorously, kiddingly, they used to say that I was a Yemenite Jew, since the Yemenites are dark.

Since there were all these refugees here before the war ended, why didn't the general American public know about their plight?

I think you may have read that in that early period refugees from Germany were on a ship [S.S. *St. Louis*] and tried to get into the United States.[11] Whatever those involvements and political reasons were, they were refused and had to go back. What I am saying to you is that I come out of a union with roots in all of Europe. So when it was ominous before Hitler and Mussolini came into power, Luigi Antonini for the Italians was saying what would hap-

11. The refugees fleeing Hitler on the S.S. *St. Louis* were prevented from landing in Florida in 1939. Afterward, four European nations took in portions of the nine hundred passengers. About one quarter of the passengers eventually died in German concentration camps. History Net, "The Tragedy of the S.S. *St. Louis*," http://history1900s.about.com/library/holocaust/aa103197.htm (accessed April 14, 2003).

pen if they came to power.[12] He said that these men were authoritarian and that they were going to be merciless. It was out of my union that we were raising money for the fight against Franco, and our young people were going to Spain to fight against Franco. So we remained in the ferment, and we knew what authoritarianism meant. They tried to tell America this, but we were talking to ourselves and not many people were listening outside of that international community. We were talking early on before Hitler had completely controlled the government. And when the Jews were being slaughtered, there was a daily concern about that. Our concern with refugees began earlier than was the official policy of the United States.

The labor movement understood. The first thing Hitler destroyed was the voice of the workers. He destroyed the labor movement in Germany. So because we were an international union and had dealt with our workers always through an international labor movement, we were aware of the problems of international labor. This interest has gone on since the 1880s, when the AF of L was a part of an international federation and unions were a part of the trade secretariats, which are international organizations of a given trade—the iron workers and the garment workers and shoe and leather workers.[13] Coming from this kind of background and as a foreigner, I had some concept of this internationalism.

What kind of activities would you as educational director organize for Local 132?

I organized weekend seminars at Hudson Shore Labor School. You would bring in lecturers from New York. You would have marshmallow roasts and square dances maybe. There are some hilarious stories in connection with organizing for Hudson Shore. As an educational director, I had no blueprint. I did not come out of the tradition of New York University and Hunter Col-

12. Italian-born Luigi Antonini (1883–1968) was manager of Local 89, the Italian dressmakers' local. He became an executive board member of Local 25 in 1914 and an ILGWU vice president in 1925. From 1934 to 1964 he served as first vice president. He was a founder of the Anti-Fascist Alliance and president of the Italian-American Labor Council. See Robert E. Lazar, "Guide to the International Ladies Garment Workers Union; Local 89; Luigi Antonini, General Secretary; Correspondence, 1919–1968," collection number 5780/023, Kheel Center for Labor-Management Documentation and Archives, Cornell University Library, http://rmc.library.cornell.edu/EAD/htmldocs/KCL05780-023.html (accessed April 14, 2003).

13. The predecessor to the ICFTU was the International Trade Union Secretariat (ITUS), established in 1903 at a conference in Dublin. At the 1913 ITUS congress in Zurich the organization reorganized into the International Federation of Trade Unions (IFTU). Some of the International Trade secretariats were associated with both the IFTU and the ICFTU. See Erhan Tuskan, "Introduction, Historical Background, Inventory of the Archives of the International Confederation of Free Trade Unions, 1949–1993," International Institute of Social History Archives, http://www.iisg.nl/archives/html/i/10751819.html (accessed April 14, 2003).

Educational Outings, Strikes, and Struggles for Equality

lege. I learned about labor within my union. Given the opportunity to be in-
novative and do it on my own, I tried all sorts of things.

In organizing educational activities, in pulling these diverse groups together, I learned that the parents of some of the women didn't want them to
participate. When we organized an educational weekend, girls of all colors
roomed together at Hudson Shore—two, three girls in a room. Some of the
parents of these young women were horrified. First, their daughters were
going to be sleeping next to a Negro woman. And two, there were going to be
Negro men—minimal. Maybe if there were going to be thirty people away
for the weekend, there may have been two Negro men who were shop chairmen. (*Chuckles.*) But families were very scared that these "niggers" were going
to be there. Here were these black people, Negroes, that their daughters were
going to be talking and laughing and eating with. These parents were Greeks,
they were Polish, they were of German extraction. These were the three that
are sharpest in my memory. Either the mothers did not or the *brothers* or the
fathers did not want daughters to be involved in a weekend activity where
you were sleeping in the same place with blacks.

So I had a public relations job. The young women, the shop chairladies,
wanted, of course, to go away on a union weekend as part of the educational
activities. A chairlady would come to me and cry and say, "I want to go to
Hudson Shore for the weekend, but my brother said or my father said or my
mother said they'd kill me if I went anywhere with niggers." The letter about
the weekend would have gone home to the family and they would have discussed it. The women who wanted to go were comfortable enough with me
not to varnish what had been said at home and the attitude.

So I was invited for dinner in a number of homes so that the family could
look me over. The parents would say let us meet this . . . I don't know what
they called me, because the daughters told their mothers, you know, I didn't
look like them. But after we talked, the parents thought I was the nicest thing
since sliced bread. (*Laughter.*) Grudgingly, the men in the family would allow
these young women to go to a weekend seminar at Hudson Shore. Talking
with these families had nothing to do with my stated duties as educational
director, but I understood the significance of going. So I went to dinner and
ate Polish food and Greek food. The Poles were predominant. The Jewish
women were a little older and their families had been exposed to enough of
the social concerns and the "radicalism" of the Jewish community, the labor
movement, so I didn't have problems there. If I went to their homes, it was
just that I was active and they wanted to meet me.

But that was a real persuasion job I had as parents asked where did the men sleep and other amazing things. Every member of the family raised questions about this weekend. Prejudice takes an extraordinary form. Among the things I learned was how important it was to be direct, to have respect for yourself, and not to let anyone disrespect you. Fortunately, I knew enough political history that I could cite simple examples of how prejudice played a part in their lives from the countries from which they came. And since I was also a foreigner, I think it was acceptable, grudgingly. Because no matter what I did, no matter what I said, I still wore this brown skin. I would go with documentation and do a little union history. Some of the men in the family were union members somewhere else.

I would also end by saying if the answer is no, if the family feels that this is something that is wrong, I would certainly stand by the family's opinion, but it would be with deep regret. And sometimes in the course of the dinner, the opinion would change to let's try. They felt their young women benefited in their activities with the union. And sometimes members of the family would attend some of these activities. We would invite them.

I think the education was mutual. I learned a great deal. Hopefully I contributed a little. This I considered a part of my responsibility, which I took very seriously. There may have been one family that invited me to dinner, that did not let their daughter go. But in almost every case, to their credit, these young women were permitted to come to Hudson Shore for these weekends. The families were satisfied with what I said. The educational process never ends, you know, never ends.

When the family was talking to you, would they specifically talk about the fact that black men were going to be there?

Yes!

And this concerned them, because they felt their daughters . . .

. . . would be at risk. They would *say* that to me, that they did not *want* their girl in a mixed place with men. So I would explain that the women would be rooming in the main building and the men were a half a mile down the road in the men's cottage. You know, they would be very honest and say their children had never been anyplace like this and they heard that black men did this, that, and the other. I said most of the men who were in jail for rape and this, that, and the other are white. But you have to be able to say this without embarrassment and to have a few of your facts. In those days, I would always go with some facts. You had to stand your ground.

My first experience of prejudice as an educational director involved a big shop chairman. I had an expert on constitutions come in and run the classes on union orientation and the contract. So the workers at these classes saw me, but the manager probably introduced the speaker because he was the head of the union. There were two or three sessions for half an hour after work. You then came to the educational director to get your union book. Everything went all right. People liked me, or didn't like me, or were shocked to see this brown woman who was the educational director. For some reason the executive board fell in love with me. We developed a very good relationship. There was one black woman on the board at the time. (*Chuckles.*) Your executive board members were part of your leadership team, the nonpaid representatives, the shop chairmen who were the liaison between the union and the employer. They kept the wheels of the industry going. These are marvelous people, these shop chairmen and shop stewards.

But early on this shop chairman, who was an older person, a molder who was highly skilled, came into my office to pick up someone's union book. He said he wanted to see Springer. My name doesn't tell you anything, nor does my voice. I was sitting at my desk in a big office all by myself, and I said, "I'm Maida Springer." He looked at me and said, "You're Springer! Puh!" Spit on the floor and walked out. This all comes with the territory.

Six months later this same man worked with me when we were planning a Christmas party for the local. You know I did all sorts of strange things. He organized a committee of shop chairmen to take a half a day off to decorate the hall for the Christmas party. He staggered their times so that their shops would not in any way suffer. So you never know. You never know. He, too, determined that I was good as sliced bread. So hours, wages, and conditions are only part of what you had to live with.

What changed him?

He was dealing with an unknown, and as far as he was concerned he did not want to deal with anyone that was not Polish or whatever he was, you know, or white. And I am sitting in a position of responsibility. This was just a matter of prejudice. If an American Southerner or an American white who was resentful of anyone with my paint job, had walked into an office and was told that you have to see me, they'd have the same attitude. They may not spit but they'd have the same attitude. There was nothing shocking about that. Not a thing shocking except that he was dirtier. (*Laughter.*) I had to go wipe up the floor. No, this was just a manifestation of prejudice.

People become accustomed to you. Work with you. Well, this is what happened to this chairman. I was therefore different. I wasn't like all those other people he hated whom he did not know. We had to deal with each other in meetings. He was out with us at five o'clock in the morning because some of the shops that had metal workers and big machines involved worked around the clock. He was a part of the union activists that would be with us if we had to issue leaflets or talk with people about the trade during the changes in shifts. He learned to work with me. It did not mean that he had any more respect for Negroes. But I was one of those he worked with and served him well, served his shop well. And that was the priority. I never misunderstood. (*Laughter.*)

You know, people become so accustomed to you, so that they forget for a minute that they are telling me something prejudiced. If you allow yourself to be seduced, to be told that you are different, you are psychologically in real trouble. Because there but for the grace of God go I, that person whom they are stereotyping and describing to me. When I was told that I was different, my blood pressure would rise, and I would become angry and illogical. It's pointless to give you examples. It was on so many levels and so trivial sometimes that it made you want to scratch.

But I must tell you a delightful story about an operator, one of my mother's overland friends. I think she was trained in Cuba and had been educated in a convent school where you learn *very* fine dressmaking and hand work. Her name is Melba Solomon.[14] As an adult she came to the United States and was working in a bridal factory and was being exploited. Through my mother I met her and we became friends. I knew she was a very fine dressmaker. She had worked in Florida.

When I was a business agent for the Dressmakers' Joint Board, many employers would call me and say, "Springer, I need an operator, I need a cleaner, I need a something." Business agents serviced a district covering twenty, thirty shops. You know the workers, their capabilities, and the price range of garments they made. You had to be a skilled operator in order to be able to take a bundle of cut-up fabrics and make a precise garment. So an employer called, and I said to him, to this contractor of very high-class dresses and gowns, "I have a *very* good operator for you, and I will send her up." I think I had once before sent him a colored operator, and he had a colored cutter—this same Carl Clark was working in his shop at this time. This is the fifties. So he said to me, "Springer, don't send me a *schwartzer* [a Yiddish word meaning black that acquired a derogatory connotation in its use in the United States]. And I said, "I don't know whether you want an operator or a shoemaker, but have it your way." He said, "Oh, Springer, I didn't mean nothing. Send her." In the industry if you were not a good dressmaker, a good worker, the employer would call you a shoemaker. (*Laughter.*) And this same employer tomorrow I would have to work with, so I could not walk out of the shop and give him some emotionally satisfying answer. So you learned the many ways of edu-

14. Melba Soloman became a price adjuster for the ILGWU in New York City.

cating the people you dealt with. (*Chuckles.*) This woman went in to work for him. She was *fast!* She was *good!* I mean, she was a first-class dressmaker. She wasn't a butcher or a shoemaker. This same man would walk past her machine with his hands behind his back, and he would say, "Look at her, her fingers. She's gold. She's got golden fingers. She's got golden fingers. Look at them." He'd take the garments up and he'd say, "Look at it. Look at this garment she makes." This same employer that told me not to send him a *schwartzer.*

So this sort of prejudice was pervasive?

Yes. But people show their prejudices in all sorts of ways. Let me give you a crazy example, which does not have to do with work per se. One of the workers in one of my shops was a very slow worker. She was a good worker. But employers want a worker who is skilled and fast. The shop committee or the employer would try to give her fewer garments, smaller bundles, and different colors which would make the difference in what you earned. If you have to change the threads for every garment and change all the trimmings, this would affect what you earned. I had to fight all of the time to ensure that she got her share of work and that the committee understood that I was adamant about this. She would come and complain. She would bring her tickets to me and show me, "Springer, look at what I earned, look at what the committee did to me!" So I would go back to the committee and say, "Look, I don't care what the employer says. She is a member of this union as you are. She is a slower worker; therefore, I don't ask you to give her special privileges, but I insist you give her a share of the good and the bad." If the employer was the one who switched the bundles of work around, I would take him to the impartial chairman.

My opposite number in management who represented the employer as I represented the workers and the union knew that this was my position, and he was a very *decent* person. You worked as a team, because in a piece-rate industry and in the needle trades, if your garments aren't shipped on time, you are out of the ballpark. So the rapidity with which the local employer delivers his garments to the manufacturer who then delivers them to the stores —Saks, Marshall Field's, Macy's—then determines how much work the local employer gets for the next season. If you don't deliver, the manufacturer is not interested in you. But this was only one worker who was slow, and the representative for management would try to talk some sense to the employer. He would say, "This is one worker. Don't discriminate against her." This was not color. She was Jewish. She was all of the right things. She was religious. But the bottom line was his profit.

Educational Outings, Strikes, and Struggles for Equality

So she became very attached to me because she was always in trouble. She lived in a room and was a single woman. At that point, everyone knew that I was a divorcée and that I had a grown son. She loved me so much and thought that I was so nice, that she thought I should get married again. And she had just the right person for me to marry, her landlord. But the only thing that was wrong with him was that he was a *goy*. He was a Christian. In her mind I represented her and her religion. A Christian would not be good for me to marry. I should marry some nice non-Christian. (*Laughs.*) I should have a Jewish husband.

I've had all kinds of crazy things said to me, *all* of the stereotypes, but the story I was telling you about Melba Solomon, we used to laugh at years later. This woman subsequently became an officer of the union with my support, retired from the union, and still goes in and works for the union. They call her in because she is proficient. She's an expert on settling prices. She's marvelous. She's one of my better stories.

I have some defeats. Young black women would come to see me about some grievance when I was working in the complaint department for the Dress Joint Board. They would come to my desk and I'd have to adjudicate the grievance with the employer. I used to say to some of them, "Look, you've been in the industry for X number of years. You're only going to get raises when we renew a contract. Go to school. You don't have to leave your job. Your union book is your passport. Go to the Needle Trades school."

They would walk away from me and say to a friend who was with them, "She's a *fool* if she thinks I'm going to take my time and go." This used to make me very sad. I have seen some of those women when I go back to New York, older with children, a broken home, looking depressed. They were no better off because they lost a job and the incremental pay and benefits they had had. Or when their shop went out of business, they could not get a comparable wage at their new place. They had to start working at lower wages, and they were still examining and cleaning dresses, running a felling machine. This has been my failure. I felt that I did not have the technique to reach them. I was lacking in something that I could not have persuaded more young women to take advantage of what was offered to them as a part of their union membership. This I have always felt sad about. But I had a few successes in addition to Melba. Yeah.

Do you remember the name of the philanthropist you talked about earlier in your experience as Local 132 educational director, who employed people on probation —or the name of his firm?

Educational Outings, Strikes, and Struggles for Equality

No, I don't. I don't want to remember the names. (*Laughs.*) The first strike I was given responsibility for was at this firm. I think this was my *real* growing experience as educational director. These were the telling experiences of a young woman who had the responsibility of developing programs. Nineteen forty-three or '44 was the year of the strike with this firm that was considered so philanthropic and hired all of these various groups—escapees from Hitler's concentration camps, blacks from the South, people recently released from prison. The owner was paying the workers thirty-five cents an hour. People wouldn't believe that today. They think you're out of your mind if you say somebody earned thirty-five cents an hour. We were asking for fifty cents an hour. When we had to take them out on strike, the firm was paying strike-breakers seventy-five cents an hour and had goons in Cadillacs bringing people to work.

I don't know who these drivers were. I knew that they hired them from somewhere in Harlem, because this firm was in Manhattan. All of the drivers were black. We've had people doing ugly things before, but they were black and white. But in this particular instance in Local 132, this firm or either Father Divine's people had gotten this group of men who drove these strike-breakers to work in private cars. They would pick the workers up at I would think a subway station or someplace nearby before they got to Vandam Street.

Most of the strikebreakers were black and had been gotten through Father Divine, and most of them were women. They were "Angels" or "Children" of Father Divine. All of the money that these Angels made went into the "heaven." Not only that, the seventy-five cents was just a temporary thing. What was more important were the people who put their life savings, their property into these heavens, people who abandoned their children and their homes and went into the Father's mission. Husbands and wives were supposed to become brothers and sisters. When they went into the mission, they had to give up the business of connubial bliss.

In this strike we were permitted to picket around the building for a specified time in the morning, at midday, and in the evening. It was a triangular building at the mouth of the Holland Tunnel, and we were permitted only twelve people—four on each side of the building. We had to keep the lines of progression straight, because the employers would call the police if we didn't keep to units of four picketers. We could not have a mass line. Therefore, I had to have some place for workers to eat and to rest and to change the pickets. We rented an empty store on Tenth Street in the dock area.

In getting food for the strikers I came into contact with having to set up a kosher and nonkosher table for the first time. The Orthodox workers, many of whom, as I told you, had come here with the marks on them having escaped from Hitler, would only eat kosher food. So I sat down with the committee and I said now you tell me what we need to do. We set up shopping committees, and we set up the people who were going to fix the food and made sure that no nonkosher person was going to be working with the kosher people. We had to set up separate tables—one for the Orthodox people, and for all the other nationalities there was a table over on the other side of the room. You had to have separate glasses and eating utensils because the Orthodox workers would not drink out of glasses of people who had eaten fish and meat and butter.

This is a part of the education that does not come in a book. You see what you are faced with and that you could lose the cohesiveness of a struggle you are in if you do not understand the social implications. They picketed together. The common objective was better wages and recognition. There was no problem with this, but if we interfered with their social institutions, we could have destroyed that struggle.

The other thing I had to learn and handle quickly was that the people who were on probation, who were out of prison and were working, could not be on picket lines or be visible in the strike. That would have broken their probation, so they had to stay away. I checked with a lawyer on this. I think Sam Eisenberg and I were handling this problem. Standing in that empty store on Tenth Street, we agreed immediately that all the men on probation would work in the office with us, stuffing envelopes and mimeographing, preparing the leaflets.

Two things happened which ended the strike. Early in the morning Marty Feldman and two other staff members would come. But after eight o'clock, I was left by myself. This was my responsibility. As we were doing our mass picketing around the building—I don't know how, I don't know who—somebody blackjacked Feldman. He was lying out in the street with the cars going quickly by him. I don't think one of the strikebreakers hit him. I think it had to be one of the people who were bringing in Father Divine's people, one of the goons. At that time I was up high on the loading platform, talking to the men who were escorting some of these women in. I had been describing to them the complaints of the workers who had been employed there—these people who were marching around picketing, this thirty-five cents an hour we had been paid, we were asking for fifty and these workers, the strikebreakers, were getting seventy-five and what was wrong about what they were doing. And so, it happened so fast. Feldman was blackjacked, and then the men held me while some women *kicked* me. And I'm not even sure if they were Angels.

But I know that they worked my legs over pretty good until somebody stopped them. I still have marks on my legs. That's also part of the price you pay.

They got Feldman up. By this time the firm calls their lawyer. I think it frightened management when Feldman was blackjacked and I was held and kicked around pretty good. They wanted this stopped, because this was a big philanthropic person. Immediately, that same morning the firm sent someone out to tell us they wanted to talk if we would stop the picketing. Fine. We did. We agreed to cut the line that morning, and I think the next day we went to talk to the lawyers and the son of the owner of the firm. I guess maybe we were on that picket line maybe a week or two.

We went back to our office and began the telephone calls to Father Divine's people. I think I had begun before, and we had gotten nowhere. After this incident, I got a phone number of one of Father Divine's people. He was not just an Angel, and I knew this man. He had been a big real estate man and a lawyer also before he joined Father Divine.[15]

Well, Feldman couldn't talk to them, because he didn't understand the language and he was getting nowhere. He would speak to a representative of these workers and say, "Mr. So-and-So, you know these people are strikebreakers." And he would get a response, "I don't understand you. The Angels, the Children are working." The representative would be talking nice and low key about the *Children*. So he said (*laughs*), "Maida, you better try." What did Feldman say? "Maybe you understand this lingo." Because whomever he talked to said that they knew that the Children didn't do anything. So I got on the phone and said that I knew that the Angels did not know who did this, and what this represented, and that we would like to come in and talk with them.

Those conversations should have been taped, talking about what the Angels and the Children didn't know. I understood that you had to speak in terms of Father Divine. You dare not call them anything but Angels when you spoke to the Father's representatives, which I did three times a day. (*Laughs*.) I gave Feldman a crash course in Father Divine language. That was difficult. When you call a representative or employer, you attempt to do a straightforward discussion. If you are angry, he's angry. But to be spoken to in nice soft tones about the Children and heaven was bewildering. Feldman would hang up and say, "Springer, what is he talking about? These people are out there killing us." We laughed about this very often after that.

15. Black lawyers who had some attachment to the Divine movement included James C. Thomas, Arthur Madison, and Ellee Lovelace. See Weisbrot, *Father Divine*, 63, 66–67.

Educational Outings, Strikes, and Struggles for Equality

They ran us around for three days. This would drive Feldman up the wall. They would give us hours like five or six o'clock in the morning to be at a mission to meet whomever. Feldman and a business agent would come for me at my house—I was living in Manhattan still then—and we would go to meet the Angel. He would never be there. We would just have missed him, or he did not spend the night at that heaven.

I don't even remember now how we finally got that sorted out. We now had a contract and we made the compromises that these Angels, these people, were going to remain. But we had a difficult time because, you know, the Angels or Children didn't want anything. They did not work for holidays and other benefits that were a part of the agreement. There were very strict rules for those in Divine's organization. They never joined the union, and they remained a little isolated and eventually left. But we could not and did not demand that the Father Diviners all be thrown out. We would not have been able to settle.

I went to the Sunday meetings of Father Divine in order to try to settle this. Father Divine could only come into New York over the weekend because there was something that they were going to hook him up for, there was some infringement. In the state of New York if he was here on Sunday night after twelve midnight or Monday morning, they could keep him here to raise questions and do something legal. So he left every Sunday evening.[16]

I went to the meetings on Sunday and watched all the food being passed and talked to whomever I was supposed to talk to there. You would sit there and watch the ritual of hundreds of people being fed. All the food was passed over Father Divine's head. We would have our meals there and wait to be spoken to by some of the leadership but not the Father himself. I met Father Divine, but I was another face in a crowd. He knew who I was. But he was too big, too influential. He did not take time with me. I was simply introduced to him on a couple of occasions, but he was in the midst of the food being blessed. He was blessing the food for the multitude! The message would be sent that I was there and wished to have an audience with whomever was involved in the strike. I may have talked with the person in question that was dealing with these workers at this waste plant. And I talked with other people, but no one who was *directly* responsible. My face became known around the Angels. Sometimes I would go by myself. But since I didn't have a car and

16. In July 1942 Divine changed his headquarters from New York to Philadelphia in order to avoid going to prison for failing to follow a court order and pay Verinda Brown, a former follower, seven thousand dollars. Ibid., 209–11.

didn't drive, I think on some occasions I had someone come with me from my community, someone that I knew who was involved in the Divine organization.

I knew some people very well who were involved with Father Divine. Some were really from their heart thinking that this was a way to salvation, and I knew a couple of hustlers for whom Father Divine was a nice gimmick. You ate a whole meal for five cents and you lived somewhere for very little and you did the minimum. I knew a couple of hustlers, and I knew also very committed people. So it balanced out.

That was quite an experience with Father Divine. So the strike must have been for a longer time than two weeks, because I tell you we went to many of the restaurants and missions. But I guess my focus was on when we had the violence. I had to be concerned with all of the nuances, this young educational director without a clue about how to do these things but on the spot having to make a decision, so that you got the best benefit and didn't hurt people. I had to grow up very fast.

Was there a reaction by the strikers to the fact that the drivers of the Children and the strikebreakers themselves were black?

No. I thought about it. We talked about it. But in none of our meetings in the storefront, that never came up. The type of workers you had here were for the first time working in a group relationship, working with black workers or with white workers. So all of these nuances did not obtain, really. The owner of the firm, this philanthropist, was a very wealthy Jewish employer, and he would give these Jewish refugees employment. Some of these folk had no skills, had nothing, and were devastated people. The black Southern workers who were recruited through some agency were workers for the first time in a factory situation. And the third group were these people on parole. So you had a *raw* group of recruits in this situation.

It's not clear to me how Father Divine became involved.

To none of us. No one ever told us that story. But somebody in the owner's office made the contacts, offered employment, and guaranteed the safety of the people. I guess if I had been wiser, I would have pursued the story and would have known, because I became on pretty good terms with some of the Divine people.

Sometime later after the strike, I took workers to a Father Divine heaven, which was near Hudson Shore Labor School. You see, Mr. Roosevelt was very much disliked by the Republicans, and so someone sold to Father Divine one of these estates that was facing the Roosevelt home across the river. The Father bought a lot of property. These homes were in the very rich Dutchess County area where there were big family mansions. Father Divine's property was walking distance from Hudson Shore. My relationship after the strike was comfortable enough that I could ask them if we could bring a delegation down to see this heaven facing Hyde Park, the Roosevelt home. You could not take pictures, but you could talk to people and you could walk around. Many people didn't believe, and particularly white workers, that the place could be orderly. This was very unusual to talk about, heavens and Father Divine. They would see how *well* the place was kept and the meals that were served and the Children.

And why did you see this as important for them?

Well, people were talking about Father Divine. I was among the few people that had had actual experience. And while this in my view was a cult, most of the people who went into Father Divine went there to change their lives into hope, and they'd given their all to the work of Father Divine. Since I was the educational director of this local union, I was able to take these workers and show them physically that people were being rehabilitated. They could see the physical presence of this place. They could see the people quietly going about their business of doing various things on the estate. Since it was always a big news story that this man had sold his big estate to Father Divine to embarrass the Roosevelts, they could then determine what they saw as against what they would read in the newspaper. It was simply a learning experience of what this religious group was doing.

Have you ever been in violent or dangerous strikes before or after this one in Local 132?

I have been in strikes where I was roughed up in Manhattan. I was threatened but never hit in the South. Overseas in Africa employers have threatened me. I'm a survivor. I didn't have sense enough to be afraid.

I came across some papers that attributed to you the term "gunka munka," which served as the strike slogan for the 1958 ILGWU strike. Did you make up that term?

No, it wasn't a term I made up. One of my friends, Evelyn Scheyer, had a place in Flemington, New Jersey, where we congregated and had weekend parties. We would roast marshmallows or grill steaks in their great big fireplace. Her husband, Dave, was a great reader. They would have readings that would include stories written by Sholem Aleichem.[17] Dave had a Jewish last

17. Born in Kiev, Sholem Yakov Rabinowitz (1859–1916) took the pen name Sholem Aleichem. Renowned for his humor, he wrote about poor and oppressed Jews in stories, plays, and novels, and helped to establish Yiddish literature. *Fiddler on the Roof* was based on sketches he wrote in *Tevye's Daughters* (1894). He wanted people to remember him by gathering together and reading his stories. See Brooks Atkinson, "Artful Simplicity of Sholom Aleichem Captured in 'Fiddler on the Roof,'" *New York Times*, October 6, 1964, in "Sholom Aleichem Network on the Worldwide Web, 1997–1999," www.sholom-aleichem.org/fsaws/Memoirs,%20Comentary,%20Reviews/nyt%20fiddler%20review.htm (accessed May 15, 2000).

Educational Outings, Strikes, and Struggles for Equality

name but he was not Jewish. In Sholem Aleichem stories the rabbi did all things. He was the lawyer and the doctor and the mender of fences. You went to the rabbi and he took care of things and advised you on various things.

So at the Madison Square Garden strike rally I was speaking about the Sholem Aleichem stories in which the rabbi took care of all of the social, economic, and political ills. When he talked about people with double standards and funny business, he would call it—I don't remember the exact term —kunkel-munkel business. That was a person that was indecent and trying to do you in. This was what I was in effect saying, that the employers were trying to do funny business to the agreement and to the workers in the industry. I thought the term was kunkel-munkel business, which got to be translated as gunka munka business. The term I used I may have misused. But the audience knew, because this was a mainly Jewish audience. All the Jewish newspapers picked it up, and English-speaking papers picked it up. The labor press. I had just come back from Africa, I think, two days before. It became a slogan. My innocent remark. Just off the plane from Africa. (*Laughter.*)

Evelyn was formerly a schoolteacher and was from the teachers' union. She was a former Lovestoneite, an intellect. She had worked in Europe. She went over with the Marshall Plan and did a lot of work in Germany. She was based in Paris. It was in her house that I always stayed on holidays when I was studying at Ruskin College in 1951 and '52. That was my base, my second home. I had a nice place to stay. I couldn't come back to the United States. I never had that kind of money. Evelyn and I had mutual friends. It was almost a family relationship. Once you knew Evelyn, you met the rest of that family. It was a very narrow circle.

My friendship with Evelyn gave me a further relationship to Eddie Welsh. Eddie's wife, Miriam [formerly Miriam Spicehandler], was Evelyn's sister. When Eddie and Miriam moved into the ILG cooperative, Eric had just then been sworn in as a law clerk to a justice of the state supreme court. Eric took their old apartment because he had to live in Manhattan in order to work. Before, I had known Eddie as this bronze Adonis at the Harlem Labor Center, and then also in small circles, people who cared about social issues. He was the pride of the intellectual radicals, and he was among the few people of color in that framework. You always were in awe of this man who went to Russia and went to other places. He was organizer par excellence. He had done yeoman work in the Panama Canal Zone. In the early 1960s he organized workers in East Africa.

You talked to Eddie Welsh all along about your experiences in Africa, I suppose.

I guess. To some degree. Among other things, you did not try to bore your friends to death because you have been suddenly a three-week expert. In that atmosphere these people were students of world history. They were strong political ideologues. So you lived in this atmosphere of constant change, the world changing after World War II, and all of the things that the labor movement was involved in and spoke to. And for some reason I drank from that fountain. I wasn't an American by birth. I had the experience of an immigrant! And almost all the people I dealt with, their parents or they were immigrants. So this atmosphere was a great education.

Were there any controversies regarding equal access to the ILGWU's cooperative housing project when they decided to build?[18]

On the part of the union, no. You know, it's big money to borrow for this real estate. I think that there was a quiet agreement that banks would not lend money unless there was some understanding that it would be limited. President Dubinsky, I am told, thanked them very much. I think he got up in a meeting and told this one. And so they raised their own money, built housing all over the place.

We began building in the forties. We were trying to educate our members on how they could apply for an apartment. We were proposing to them that they could get loans through their union's credit union to make their down payments. I was one of those who was a walking delegate, with my pamphlets and calling shop meetings. We went from shop to shop to discuss it, had experts come in talking about it. If I had a shop that I felt might be hard to convince, I would have an authority on housing within the labor movement come to make a bona fides of the material I had passed out. We had forms to register people who wanted it to take back to the credit union. I think at that time the cost was probably five hundred dollars a room. Oh, it was very exciting. It was very exciting. They were going to be *beautiful* apartments for workers. You can walk around New York City and see them now.

How much contact did you have with people in the Amalgamated Clothing Workers' union?

My best friend, Dollie Lowther Robinson, was one of the early officers of the Amalgamated Clothing Workers. Her daughter, Jan, is my godchild. Her son-in-law Melvin McCray, a man I call my big godson, is an editor for ABC.

18. The ILGWU broke ground in 1953 for the housing development at Corlears Hook on the Lower East Side after investing fifteen million dollars of its own funds. The four-building, twenty-two-story cooperatives were built in an area where many garment workers had formerly lived in slum conditions. See Dubinsky and Raskin, *David Dubinsky*, 216–17.

He also makes documentaries and is doing one on Dollie, an extraordinary woman.[19]

Miss Dollie. My mother always called her Miss Dollie. I think we first met in the Women's Trade Union League in New York City. She was much younger than myself. But because she was big, she moved around with an older crowd. Bessie Hillman, Sidney Hillman's wife, liked her very much.[20] She had also been the godmother to Dollie's daughter, Jan. When they were organizing the laundry workers, Dollie was working in a laundry. They pulled her out of the laundry and put her on staff, because I think she probably was in college at the time and they recognized her potential. They saw what a mover she was and how people responded to her. She later became the educational director of the Laundry Workers Joint Board. She went on to work on the staff of the Amalgamated Clothing Workers as a representative. As a matter of fact, she went to law school while on staff with the Amalgamated.[21] She had one of the most engaging personalities and was brilliant. She was beautiful, she was articulate, she was an absolute political animal. She *absorbed* politics.

Dollie had always gone to school. She would speak of her life in the Carolinas where she was born. She went to school in the winter and in the summer, because friends and family were all schoolteachers and her mother kept her in school. And she spent a lot of time in church programs. So she did not feel the brunt of segregation that most young blacks did because her family kept her in a cocoon. Her mother kept her away from the experiences that were prejudicial. She did not go shopping or work in someone's kitchen. Her life was in the black community.

Dollie's family came to New York when she was in high school. Her father died very early. Her mother worked and they got a home.[22] First, Dollie went

19. Melvin R. McCray is a writer, producer, and editor. His documentaries and films include *Surviving the Odds: Black Males in America; Black Panther in Exile: The Story of Pete O'Neal;* and *Looking Back: Reflections of Black Princeton Alumni.* Among his works in progress are video documentaries on Dollie Lowther Robinson, Maida Springer and Julius Nyerere, and Reverend William J. Shaw, pastor of the White Rock Baptist Church in Philadelphia, and the president of the National Baptist Convention USA, Inc.

20. Bessie Abramowitz Hillman (1889–1971) led her co-workers into a strike against Hart, Schaffner & Marx in Chicago in 1910. She went on to serve as an organizer and educator for the ACWA. See UNITE, "Women in UNITE History," http://www.uniteunion.org/research/history/womeninunite.html (accessed April 14, 2003).

21. Robinson enrolled in law school because she wanted to make contracts understandable to workers. Robinson, interview by Craig, 27.

22. Robinson's mother had been a hairdresser in the South and did some domestic work in New York. Later she took up upholstering. Robinson, interview by Craig, 12–13.

Educational Outings, Strikes, and Struggles for Equality

to Brooklyn High and then to college. Since there were limited jobs that you could get with your good education (*laughter*), she went to work in the laundry and continued to go to school.

When she left the Amalgamated, she became the secretary of labor for the State of New York. It was she who put a scarf on her head and did the survey and early reports on migrant workers in the forties and fifties. She went to work in upstate New York as a migrant worker with a camera and a tape recorder and came back and reported. After that she went on to Washington and was the assistant to Esther Peterson in the Department of Labor. When she left there and came back home to be with her daughter, she went to work for Brooklyn College in their special developmental department where she helped adults going back to college by seeing to it that they got the right kind of tutoring. There are masses of people who graduated from college as adults as a result of her efforts. I think they are going to name a scholarship or a chair in her honor at Brooklyn College.[23]

Well, that was my beloved friend Dollie Lowther Robinson. Our base was narrow in terms of the number of Negroes who were working as staff people. We all knew one another. We attended conferences together. We attended all kinds of events together. And as a result of the war, the unions were participating with the government in this wartime effort, and Dollie Robinson and I were members of the War Production Board on the same team. There were all kinds of questions that came up in terms of pricing, in terms of allocation. We really didn't make the decisions, but we were looking after labor's interests. Our input was considered useful. Labor's involvement with the War Production Board was an attempt by the government to be very inclusive and involve everybody in the war effort.

Charlotte Adelmond was another person I was close to who was out of the Laundry Workers Joint Board of the Amalgamated Clothing Workers. From what I have heard, it was Charlotte who was the moving force behind organizing the laundry workers. And Dollie Lowther came in as the highly educated, soft-spoken, both physical and mental giant. They were a pair! They were a team. Both of them were tall women and not thin women. Charlotte wore her hair in an Afro. She was a black nationalist. These kids today think they're nationalists? Shucks. They don't know. She was outspoken, outrageous.

You have to have some sense of the labor movement. We were supposed to be enemies, because they belonged to the Amalgamated and I to the ILG.

23. Brooklyn College of the City University of New York established the Dollie Robinson Memorial Scholarship.

And this was at a period when Sidney Hillman, the president of the Amalgamated Clothing Workers, and David Dubinsky, the president of the ILG, were vying for FDR's favor. Everybody who *worked* for them was either with them or "agin 'em." I was supposed to dislike everybody out of the Amalgamated. But this never happened to Dollie, it never happened to Charlotte and myself. We were like this. We were the curiosity of sections of the labor movement. I didn't care what anybody was doing, what anyone was saying, nothing or no one broke the relationship between the three of us. They tell me Mrs. Hillman would say to Dollie, "Diyah, you still with that Dubinskynic? (*Laughs.*)

Dollie and Charlotte were fierce about workers' dignity. Fierce! These people who stand over big steam tubs and ironing tables and big machines with dirty clothes going around inside had a right to personal dignity and decent wages. The workers endured great hardships in the laundry, steam rooms. Charlotte was formidable. When the shops were organized, she still would remind people that the flame was always burning, lest we forget, lest we relax our vigil, lest anybody get comfortable while someone does an under the table contract or somebody gets sloppy about their work.

Oh God, Charlotte was something to listen to, wearing her man-tailored suit—they called them that in those days—and her felt hat pulled over one eye (*chuckles*), her comfortable walking shoes. You could not miss Charlotte with her fedoras and her tweed skirts. And she could cook! I'd go over to Charlotte's house in Queens and take off my shoes. (*Laughs.*) She spoke in this sweet Trinidadian sing-song. She was lovely. One of the lost warriors. Talk about a pioneer. When she went back to Trinidad, I think she was a very sick woman, a very broken woman when she died. Oh God, strength, courage, she had it all. Nationalist to the core. Part of her undoing. This was so long ago and people couldn't accommodate that. And whether anyone said anything about it or not this made angry people who couldn't accept her vigilance, her forthrightness. She was too much for them. After Charlotte lost an election, she was out of the labor movement. Both Charlotte and Dollie were giants in the labor movement.

When I was educational director of the Plastic Button and Novelty Workers, my office was Twenty-second and Broadway, and Dollie's office with the Laundry Workers Joint Board was around the corner on Fifth Avenue. And so we'd go to lunch together and talk and go to meetings together. Do whatever we were doing. And her child, Jan, is the godchild that I run to New York for all of the time and who now has three children.

Last Sunday I saw Jan when I was in New York for the birthday celebration of Jennie Silverman. This was Jennie's eightieth birthday [1991]. We've been friends for forty-three years. Her daughter and her nephew who is now a university professor were there. Jennie helped raise him, and I went to his bar mitzvah. We shared in one another's life a great deal. She lives in the ILG housing development near the Needle Trades school. Jan and Melvin and their three children came to participate in this occasion. Bessie Hillman's daughter was there. She spoke to Jan, whom she had not seen in a long time. So it was almost a kind of international family day.

For Jennie's birthday two people were asked to come and speak. One was Minnie Lurye Matheson who was a union manager and a *fiery* union activist. And I was the other. Minnie was one of the officers of the International Ladies' Garment Workers' Union, a manager in Pennsylvania. Her brother, Willie Lurye, was murdered in New York City in a telephone booth by the gangsters who were fighting the union. So all of these people are a part of my history. We're all old and sick now. Minnie has had bypass surgery but she came. We hadn't seen one another in twenty-some years, the two of us.

Jennie came from the Ukraine and has such a history in the United States in the labor movement. She was formerly a young Communist. She was one of those young foreigners that was a Bryn Mawr summer student. Bryn Mawr did a documentary on these workers who went to the summer school there. The film was called *The Women of Summer*.[24] Jennie talked about the time arriving here in the United States from the Ukraine and about the time when all the men in her village were killed. This was before the revolution in the Soviet Union and before she had emigrated that these men were killed. She talked about how the Jews were discriminated against by the Russians. So we three women—the two of us foreigners and Minnie, who was born in Chicago —were the persons who spoke at this old-timers' affair.

Let's talk about some of your activism outside of union work. You were involved with the silent parade for Odell Waller that A. Philip Randolph asked Pauli Murray to organize. Describe that event and your relationship with Pauli Murray.

This was my introduction to Pauli Murray in the early forties. Dollie Lowther knew her before and said to me that this young college woman was organizing the silent parade. Pauli wasn't a lawyer yet, a writer, a teacher, etc. She was working for the Workers Defense League on the Odell Waller case. Waller was a young sharecropper who worked with his mother for this plantation owner. The man refused to pay his mother her share. He took all

---

24. Suzanne Bauman and Rita Heller, *The Women of Summer: An Unknown Chapter of American Social History* (Filmmakers Library, 1985), film.

of the crop. Odell Waller went to the owner of the land, and they had an altercation. Waller shot the man and he died. So Odell Waller was tried and was sentenced to the electric chair. The Workers Defense League took the case on. Pauli Murray moved across the country with Odell Waller's mother, Mother Waller, raising money and talking about Southern justice. Randolph gave Pauli space in New York City to meet, raise more money, and to talk about the case and organize a rally. In the meantime, the case is lost. Pauli has done a tremendous educational job, but the law is the law.

So after Waller's death, Randolph issued the right kind of statement. Pauli organized the silent parade. Dollie said we need to involve some young people and trade union people, so we will have a body of people to march if we have this silent parade. I was one of the persons she asked. Then we met —a group of us who had arrived that evening to participate—in one of the rooms which the Brotherhood used. There were offices and rooms available in connection with what was the 1941 aborted March on Washington. You still had the nucleus of the organization. I think we met in a private clinic of a doctor who was a part of the March on Washington group. We were in awe of all of the older people who were activists and who had helped to organize for the march. I had been one of the delegates ready to march.

I walked into this meeting with Dollie and other trade union people, and we heard this little small person with cropped hair, wearing these white sailor pants and standing on the table. She was on *fire*, talking about social injustice and Jim Crow. Pauli was, I guess, maybe size eight then.

Someone took a movie of the silent parade, but Pauli never could find it. She tried to find it years later when she was writing her autobiography, *Song in a Weary Throat*, and before that when she was writing her family biography, *Proud Shoes*. We carried a big white banner talking about "Jim Crow Has Got to Go," because the emphasis was on the issue of Jim Crow in the South. Dollie, who was tall and strapping, carried the center of the banner. Pauli was on the extreme left. I held the banner on the extreme right. We marched with that banner to Fourteenth Street, because that's where you went to rally and to talk.

I think I did not see or hear from Pauli for many years after that, because then I think she went to law school. And then for two minutes she was the assistant attorney general in California. Pauli and I knew some of the same people through the various organizations, the Workers Defense League and all of those other third-party challenging organizations. We met for the second time in 1946 when both of us were selected among ten women as "Women of the Year" by the National Council of Negro Women [NCNW]. It was a very elite group to have been included with.[25] Helen Gahagan Douglas was selected. She was the congresswoman from California whom Richard Nixon had done a *vicious* campaign on by implication and association. You know, when you said the word "Communist" in this country, all the flags went up. And Nixon concocted all kinds of things, which he did in other cases.[26]

Pauli Murray mentioned Bessie Bearden of the Housewives League as participating in the Odell Waller march. Who was she?

The artist Romare Bearden's mother.[27] I was her neighbor for a short time. She was living in this building before I arrived there. We lived on the same floor, and W. C. Handy's children or some of his relatives were next door to me.[28] The double building there on 119th, 120th had all been white. The elevator man in my building was still there. He was a German. He quit the job after the night of the [Joe] Louis/[Max] Schmeling fight. He left. But people would ask him on the elevator—we had all just moved in there, people my color—"what floor or what apartment So-and-So what floor are they on?" And he would answer, "they all look alike. I don't know." I've heard him say that. But that was a long time ago. There was not that sensitivity. (*Laughs.*)

25. On March 15, 1946, the NCNW gave Women of the Year awards to twelve outstanding women for "devotion to the public good." They included Virginia Durr, president of the National Council to Abolish the Poll Tax; Lois M. Jones, a teacher at Howard and an artist; Lieutenant Colonel Charity Adams, leader of the Negro WACS in Europe; Helen Gahagan Douglas, Democratic representative of California; Maida Springer of the AFL; Agnes Meyer, wife of publisher of the *Washington Post*; Pauli Murray, California attorney; Arenia Mallory, founder of an industrial training school in Lexington, Kentucky; J. Borden Harriman, former U.S. ambassador to Norway; Eslanda Goode Robeson, anthropologist and wife of Paul Robeson; Judge Jane Bolin, New York City Court of Domestic Relations; Dr. Catherine Lealtad, associated with United Nations Relief and Rehabilitation Administration work in Germany. See "Women of the Year," *Evening Star*, March 16, 1946 (Amistad).

26. Helen Gahagan Douglas (1900–1980) was a Broadway star in the 1920s. From 1944 to 1950 she served as a New Deal Democrat in the U.S. House of Representatives from California, representing much of Los Angeles. In her run for the Senate in 1950 her opponent Richard Nixon used a relentless barrage of red-baiting charges to undermine her. To paint her as sympathetic to Communists, he stated that she was "pink right down to her underwear." His campaign workers were even more visceral in their attack.

27. Famed artist Romare Howard Bearden (1914–1988) produced vibrant collages and paintings of African American life. He was also a songwriter. His socially prominent parents had known many of the leading talents of the Harlem Renaissance. His great-grandparents were also Duke Ellington's grandparents. Things Graphics and Fine Arts, "Bearden, Artists Bios," c. 1999, www.thingsgraphics.com/biographs/bearden.htm, and Buffalo Fine Arts Academy, "Bearden," in Education Programs, ArtStart Index, Albright Knox Art Gallery, © 2000, www.albrightknox.org/ArtStart/ASimagesA-I.htm; Bearden, "In Black-and-White: Photomontage Projections 1964," Bassett Gallery, August 23–November 16, 1977, http://users.aol.com/MenuBar/bearden/bearden.htm (accessed April 14, 2003).

28. Known as Father of the Blues, William Christopher "W. C." Handy (1873–1958) was a bandleader and a prolific publisher and songwriter. "St. Louis Blues" was his most popular song.

Educational Outings, Strikes, and Struggles for Equality

Would you tell the story of your involvement with the 1946 Madison Square Garden rally for a permanent Fair Employment Practices Committee?

Yes. During the war you'd had Executive Order 8802 to combat discrimination in industries which had government contracts. Hmm? That was limited. When the war was over, there was a challenge for a permanent FEPC. So Randolph, who was a great rally and marching man, organized a group to put together the Madison Square Garden rally for a permanent FEPC. I was asked to be released from my work with the ILG to become the executive secretary for this rally. This was one of Randolph's telephone calls to President Dubinsky and to my manager, Charles Zimmerman. When my manager approached me and said, "You know, Phil called today and he wants you to work with the committee, wants you to be the executive secretary," I said I'd die. I never raised money. I am not in public relations, or whatever we called it in those days. So he said, "Randolph believes in you." Well, I was dead in the water then. "And we are going to release you. Your salary will be paid and you will go up and talk to Randolph." I said, "Sasha, I can't do it." He said, "You can't?"

So I think it's finished, because I'm scared and I said I can't do it. I have said no from the president of the ILG on *down*. The long and short of it, I wind up at a meeting in Brother Randolph's office. I walk out of Randolph's office with six hundred dollars to rent Madison Square Garden. I think then it cost three thousand dollars. And the people who were there sitting in that meeting made all kinds of promises. Well, one of the religious groups that had a building on East Fourteenth Street said they had offices I could use. Morris Milgram,[29] the chief of the Workers Defense League, was going to lend me his best secretary, Vivian Lemon. They would continue to pay her salary. She speaks six languages and later worked for the United Nations. Crackerjack. She covered all the dumb mistakes I made. I walked out of there the executive secretary. This again was an extraordinary experience. I don't know how I didn't have a heart attack. Once having now committed myself, the managers said to me, "Maida, you know the ILG and their affiliated unions are going to support the Madison Square Garden rally." Max Delson, who was a great Socialist lawyer, was going to give us legal advice.

So this was how I got to be involved with the Madison Square Garden rally. We filled Madison Square Garden. We had a five-hundred-voice choir.

29. Morris Milgram (1916–1997) also served as president of Planned Communities, Inc., a national firm that builds planned integrated housing. Along with James Farmer he founded Fund for an OPEN Society with the mission of building racially inclusive private housing. See http://www.opensoc.org/milgram&farmer.html (accessed May 15, 2000).

Educational Outings, Strikes, and Struggles for Equality

Nobody believed it. How do you get a five-hundred-voice choir? The leader of this gospel group [Freida Louise Andrews] respected and loved, as she called him, "Mr. Randolph."[30] She worked with a number of different gospel groups and organized the choir of men and women. Many of the members were domestic workers or worked in the post office.

She also organized the members of the choir to sell tickets, provided I would come to the rehearsals and collect the money. There were nights that myself and Vivian Lemon would go to Staten Island to meetings and discussions on the rally. I would go home on the subway with a thousand dollars in my pocket because towards the end I had been to one of the last rehearsals and received the money for the tickets that all of the people in this section of the choir had sold. So I took it home and then to the office the next morning. And I wasn't afraid. Times have changed. Such a crazy thing, you know. Back then you didn't have somebody bonded who would take the money and lock it up for you. No. But I'd go home on the subway with these bags of money. What naiveté. This was cash. Nobody meeting me at the subway.

I started out with the worst blunder in the world. Max Delson alerted me to this oversight. He did a lot of work for the Brotherhood for nothing, you know, small fees. For the rally he was a volunteer to guide me through whatever the Brotherhood needed. We had to correct an oversight on the first hundred thousand or fifty thousand leaflets. I can't be accurate about the number, but it might as well have been a million. It seemed that many. This was a very simple black and white leaflet on which we were talking about employment. I used the name of a company that sounded like a John Doe. After these leaflets were printed, we discovered there was such a company with the same name I had used. And then Delson said, "Don't die." You can imagine how I felt. We had no money. I'm running up bills and I'm foraging every day. I'm raising money to keep this going. All of us are working, many as volunteers or for little money. And so a group of volunteers, college students, were brought in who were politically minded like us to block out the name of this company. You know what trying to do fifty thousand leaflets is like? That was boner number one. (*Laughs.*)

A lot of people helped make the rally possible. Bill Sutherland worked on the committee. He later moved to Africa where he married and had children. I have a book featuring pictures of Ghanaians taken by his African wife, Efua Sutherland. First, he lived in Ghana and now he lives in Tanzania and only

30. The *New York Amsterdam News*, "Leaders Still Hopeful FEPC Will Pass," March 9, 1946, reported that the choir had one thousand voices.

Educational Outings, Strikes, and Struggles for Equality

comes back to the United States occasionally. And earlier this year [1990] an organization out of Boston celebrated "Women of Courage East" which featured his sister, Muriel Sutherland Snowden, and others of us.[31] So again these were all close relationships. Bill was working for nothing, very little money. He, too, was a war resister, you know, doing all the right things. This was a part of the group that I worked with. While I was around begging, they were giving full support. It's public relations today, not begging. It has a good title today. And it's being a consultant, but I didn't know those words.

We were busy around the country. My job was in New York City putting it together and finding the money. Bill's job was working with the artists and some other folk. Anna Arnold Hedgeman, who died recently, was working out of Washington.[32] A very great woman. I knew her when she was head of the YWCA in Harlem. She was a person who was known to the activities of A. Philip Randolph. I maybe was a little in awe of her. She was on a very different level. She was an effective and strong personality. I think Dollie was probably a closer friend of hers than I. And Ben McLaurin, who was one of the officers of the Brotherhood of Sleeping Car Porters, figured very prominently. He was working closely with me on this. He's protecting the Brotherhood's interests. (*Laughs.*)

Does that give you some sense of what we were, how I got into this? The Brotherhood. A. Philip Randolph always when he picked up the phone and spoke to people in the ILG or in any union, they were prepared to support him. I do not know why it was my good fortune to have been selected to share in these experiences. I certainly needed more talent, more experience. And maybe because I didn't know, I did a lot of things out of my ignorance. If I had been very smart I would not have dared to do some of the things I did.

31. Bill Sutherland was one of the founders of the Congress of Racial Equality (CORE). In 1953 he settled in the Gold Coast (Ghana), and married Efua Theodora Morgue, a teacher and poet. He has served as private secretary to Komla Agbeli Gbedema, the first finance minister of independent Ghana. After moving to Tanganyika (Tanzania), he worked in the offices of Prime Minister Rashidi Kawawa. See Stephen Williams, review of *Guns and Gandhi in Africa*, by Bill Sutherland and Matt Meyer, *African Business* (January 2001): 42. Muriel Snowden (1916–1988) and husband Otto (d. 1996) founded Freedom House in 1949 as a community center for the Roxbury area of Boston. It also has served as an educational and career development center. For her activism she was awarded a MacArthur Award.

32. Anna Arnold Hedgeman (1899–1990) was an author, activist, and social worker. She served on the staff of the National Council of Churches and the YWCA. She also was executive secretary of the National Council for a Permanent FEPC. She was the first African American to serve in an executive post in the Federal Security Agency, a precursor to the Departments of Education and Health and Human Services. She was the first woman to have a position in a New York City mayor's cabinet, and she was one of the leaders of the 1963 March on Washington.

Educational Outings, Strikes, and Struggles for Equality

(*Laughs.*) So I've been lucky on that score. And I have had people with great faith in me.

On the day of the rally, people were lined up all the way around Eighth Avenue up to Ninth Avenue. This was the old Madison Square Garden. It was a great evening. Orson Welles, Mrs. Roosevelt, Senator [Dennis] Chavez from New Mexico were all supporting Randolph.[33] I think that was the night that Adam Powell kept the meeting overtime. Wherever he was, he was always a star. He said, "You know I'm a Baptist preacher, and you never stop a Baptist preacher." And I was having a hemorrhage because of the overtime that one would have to pay. And he just wiped that away. He wasn't interested. He wasn't paying for it.[34] He was irrepressible! Gorgeous! And intelligent! And ruthless! And way ahead of his time. And unfortunately thought that he was clever enough to challenge the white American Congress who were doing a lot of things that he did. But he would flaunt it. He would flaunt it. He was something to see, to hear, and to deal with.

Had you ever been to Abyssinian Baptist Church?

Oh, sure! I come out of that community! I *lived* in Harlem. I knew Adam. Again, it's narrow, the circle of people you know in that political community. I was among the young activists in the labor movement, so he knew me. I was not often on the same side of the ballot with Adam in some of those Labor Party and Liberal Party contests when they split. I had run for public office to my shame. I knew him as friend and foe. I was never a challenge to him really, and so there was never any confrontation. He was always able to be cordial and pleasant to me. Because beneath whatever the facade was, we were moving in the same direction and each of us in turn had our role to play.

Dollie Lowther Robinson was closer to Adam than I, but Adam and I were on first-name speaking terms. Adam Powell was closer to CIO unions than he was to the ILG. Dollie was a member of a CIO union. Adam Clayton Powell admired Dollie. They were good friends. Dollie also was a very good

33. The sponsors of the bill to make the FEPC a permanently funded federal agency were Representative Irving M. Ives and Senator Dennis Chavez. Some of those who spoke and who were in attendance at the rally included Secretary of Labor Lewis B. Schwellenbach, Eleanor Roosevelt, Senator Chavez, former mayor La Guardia, Republican Wayne Morse of Oregon, film stars Orson Welles and Helen Hayes, choreographer Katherine Dunham, Matthew Woll of the AFL, secretary-treasurer of CIO James B. Carey, Milton Webster of the Brotherhood of Sleeping Car Porters, and NAACP leader Roy Wilkins. See *New York Amsterdam News*, "Leaders Still Hopeful FBPC Will Pass," March 9, 1946.

34. Powell gained a reputation at rallies of ignoring time constraints and falsely promising to pay for any overtime costs. See Charles V. Hamilton, *Adam Clayton Powell, Jr.: The Political Biography of an American Dilemma* (New York: Macmillan Publishing Co., Inc., 1992), 146.

Educational Outings, Strikes, and Struggles for Equality

friend of the woman who was really in charge of Adam Clayton Powell's office [Maxine Dargans]. Dollie was very busy with Adam and she was in his office all the time. Dollie was much more a political animal and was very, very bright, and so she knew a great deal about the internal machinery of Adam Clayton Powell's office, and she was very proud of him. And I respected Adam Clayton Powell and was very ambivalent about him.

Did you and Dollie ever talk about your ambivalence toward him?

No, no, no. That was a given. She knew why. My ambivalence arose because I wished that Adam Powell and my union source were on better terms.

The only time Adam embraced me (*laughter*) was when he wanted to make a show, when President Meany was entertaining in Geneva. Mr. Meany was giving a grand cocktail party, and Adam, who was there, had not been invited. The AFL-CIO did not think very highly of Adam. He did not conform, and he challenged the labor movement about many of their policies. So he wasn't a popular person. (*Laughs.*) Adam came striding into the reception, wearing a short evening jacket—you know the way some wear them in the tropics—with a red cummerbund and black silk-striped pants. I was standing welcoming guests. Normally, he would have said hello and passed by me. But this evening he was effusive. He walks over to me, "Oh Maida, oh, oh . . ." and made a big fuss. (*Laughter.*) And Mr. Meany was looking at me and looking at Adam. He was doing this for cause; he was a showman par excellence. After he had made the rounds and everyone had seen him talking so much to me, he left. He had a *presence* that filled the room. My husband Jim [James Horace Kemp] was very much like that. When he walked into a room, he *dominated* it. Adam was it. You knew everybody. And you couldn't have been in that early political community without knowing Adam.

This cocktail party was at a time when Adam was chairman of the House Labor Committee and was challenging the labor movement, including the garment workers. He worked with Herbie Hill, the labor secretary for the NAACP and a white man, who was hostile to many unions, including the ILG. And so at that point, labor was under attack from the House Labor Committee. So it tells you that there could not have been a very loving feeling.

But he showed up uninvited, huh?

Well he was a congressman! And he was in Geneva! And, what?! He stayed around just long enough to make everybody uncomfortable and went on to do whatever else he was doing. No, he was larger than life. Larger than life. He was something to see and hear—to hear him speak and watch him shake his six foot four frame, walk across the stage, his gesticulations, his eating the audience, taking them with him, was something to see.

I take it that he and Meany didn't speak.

Of course he said good evening. No, no, he spoke. And I imagine President Meany looked very shocked. (*Laughter.*) I imagine so. I never looked back.

Why did you say that you ran for public office to your shame?

Well they *promised me* that I couldn't win the primary, but they had to have a name and they wanted a union name. I'm a community person. I'm a union officer, the education director of a very small local. They wanted somebody who was an activist, so they twisted my arms, and I said yes. I had to lose it, they said. Then those people organized committees, they rang doorbells, and I won the primary. I really nearly collapsed! So that's why I say I never intended to run for public office. I *believed them* when they said I'd lose the primary. That was a real misadventure. They knew I couldn't win the election, but it was a political plus for me to run. You put up a stalking-horse. Well, I was one.[35]

I never belonged to a major political party until I moved to Chicago and had married Jim. I was always a member of some third party because I didn't like the Republicans, I didn't like the Democrats. But in Chicago there was nothing for me to belong to, and I was married to a die-hard, in-house Democrat. But in New York City, you dabbled around.

Did you have an accident after the rally for a permanent FEPC?

I fell down the stairs. I don't remember whether it was after that rally or after a rally for President Truman's reelection that I fell down the stairs. People were saying this, that, and the other about Truman. And I said as far as I'm concerned no white American could really serve my interest, because what we suffer, we suffer as a result of kinds of legislation and unspoken things that were done. I talked about housing, talked about jobs. But I said this man will be no worse than others, and I will take a chance and work for him. We filled the Garden. I wasn't the executive secretary, but I worked in the community. I raised money. And, I don't remember after which one of these rallies I fell down the stairs. I broke my ribs. When you break your ribs, all they do is band you up. My mother was so frightened, she pretended she didn't know me. She was paralyzed with fright by the time the ambulance came. I had a good healing body. I don't know what I have now.

35. Springer ran on the American Labor Party ticket for the Twenty-first District seat of the New York State Assembly.

Educational Outings, Strikes, and Struggles for Equality

4

The International Affairs Arena

Maida Springer's foray into international affairs transpired against the backdrop of racial exclusion in the nation's capital and rivalry between the two major U.S. labor federations. In 1945 she was celebrated as the "first Negro woman" to represent the U.S. labor movement abroad due to her appointment as a member of a four-woman exchange delegation to England to observe wartime conditions. Her appointment made her into a symbol of ILGWU liberalism and represented the capacity of the U.S. government for improved race relations. However, Springer narrates how the racism she experienced in the nation's capital during preparatory meetings for the trip nearly induced her to withdraw. This discrimination included exclusion from one of the nation's premier hotels, the Statler, where the other delegates stayed.[1] During this period there were no hotels in Washington open to blacks. Upon the delegates' return from England Secretary of Labor Frances Perkins presided over an international reception for them and their British counterparts at the same hotel. Although Springer was one of the honored speakers, she still could not stay at the hotel.

Instead of staying at the Statler, Springer stayed at Council House, the residence of Mary McLeod Bethune (1875–1955) and headquarters of the National Council of Negro Women, which Bethune founded in 1935. An educator, Bethune also founded what became Bethune-Cookman College in Florida. Forming a close friendship with Eleanor Roosevelt through their service in the network of women's clubs, Bethune was appointed by the Roosevelt administration to the directorship of the Negro Division of the National Youth Administration, the highest federal office to be held by a black woman at that time. Springer describes how Bethune profoundly influenced the way she learned to deal with racism.

With her appointment Springer also became an important symbol in the struggle between the AFL and the CIO involving issues of Communism and equality

1. Bought by Hilton Corporation in 1975, the Statler building is now the Capitol Hilton.

on the domestic front and internationally. The rival Congress of Industrial Organizations (CIO) formed in 1938 after the craft-oriented AFL two years earlier had expelled eight unions belonging to its Committee for Industrial Organization for pressing industrial organizing. Although the ILGWU was one of the expelled unions, the leaders declined to join the more progressive CIO because they opposed the establishment of a permanent rival federation and Communist influence within the CIO, and they also had personal differences with CIO head John L. Lewis.[2] In 1940 the union rejoined the AFL. Although Randolph supported the goals of the CIO unions, he elected to keep the Brotherhood of Sleeping Car Porters within the AFL to fight against racism. Fifteen years later, the ILGWU would play an instrumental role in the merger of the two federations into the AFL-CIO and Randolph would become a vice president. The rivalries continued between AFL and CIO leaders, however, and would affect Maida Springer's international work.

Springer relates the tensions between her and the other delegates that arose from racial prejudice, level of experience, and AFL and CIO rivalry. The CIO delegates were Grace Woods Blackett of Local 50 of the United Auto Workers (UAW) and Anne Murkovitch of Branch 16 of the American Federation of Hosiery Workers, CIO. The AFL delegate was Julia O'Connor Parker (1890–1972) of the Telephone Operators' Department of the International Brotherhood of Electrical Workers (IBEW). Parker had helped to organize telephone operators in the 1910s and was president throughout the department's existence. The telephone operators had a predominantly Irish American membership and was the first national union controlled and run by women.[3] Springer describes the process by which she and Parker moved from mutual suspicion to friendship.

Springer also recalls the anxiety AFL leaders expressed about her appointment. They may have believed that this young, relatively inexperienced black woman would further undermine the AFL's standing among world labor by not being able to handle questions about the AFL's anti-Communist foreign policy. This fear proved unfounded as most observers were interested in her because of her representation as a "Negro First" and not as an exponent of AFL ideology. At that time the AFL was the only major national labor center in the world refusing to

2. John Llewellyn Lewis (1880–1969) was head of the United Mine Workers (UMW) for forty years. During this period the mine workers were the highest paid of the major industries and gained the first employer-financed health care and retirement plans. U.S. Department of Labor, "Honorees, the Labor Hall of Fame, History and Resources, About DOL," http://www.dol.gov/dol/oasam/public/programs/laborhall/evd.htm (accessed January 15, 2002).

3. Stephen H. Norwood, *Labor's Flaming Youth: Telephone Operators and Worker Militancy, 1878–1923* (Urbana: University of Illinois Press, 1990), 2, 139, 150–51.

The International Affairs Arena

support the establishment of the World Federation of Trade Unions (WFTU). The major objection the AFL had to the WFTU was the inclusion of unions from Communist countries. Two consecutive conferences, in London and in Paris, would establish the WFTU in 1945. Four years later the non-Communist labor centers would leave the WFTU and with the AFL form the International Confederation of Free Trade Unions (ICFTU). However, in 1945 the AFL was isolated on the point of WFTU formation. The labor delegates' arrival was slated for the weeks following the closure of the London conference.

Springer outlines how the agenda of her trip expanded once she reached England. She was introduced to the pan-African network of African and Caribbean leaders who were formulating strategies for independence. As part of this effort, they were planning the Fifth Pan-African Congress, which would take place in Manchester, England, in October 1945 to coincide with the Paris meeting for the WFTU formation. Springer's initial contacts were with Una Marson, George Padmore, Ras Makonnen, and Jomo Kenyatta. She recalls the leadership of Una Marson in bringing together politically minded soldiers from the Caribbean. Marson (1905–1965) was a poet, playwright, and journalist. After coming to England in 1932, she became secretary to the League of Coloured People and editor of its journal. She also served as Ethiopian Emperor Haile Selassie's private secretary during his exile in England. In 1938 she began working for the BBC World Service; she met Springer in this capacity.[4]

Padmore (1901–1959), née Malcolm Ivan Meredith Nurse, would serve as Springer's mentor as he brought her into the inner circles of the pan-African movement. Born in Trinidad, he attended school at Fisk and Howard Universities and joined the Communist Party, where he quickly rose to become head of the Negro Bureau of the Profintern (the Red International of Labor Unions). Padmore used his position to build a global network of black labor and political activists. After he broke with the Communist International, accusing the leaders of downgrading anticolonial work in exchange for closer alliances with Western powers following the rise of Hitler, he continued to build this network. Settling in England, he worked closely with Ras Makonnen.

Born in British Guiana (now Guyana), Ras Makonnen, née Thomas R. Griffiths (1912–1978), came to the United States in the 1930s and worked at a black YMCA in Texas before moving on to Howard, Lincoln, and Cornell Universities. Afterward, Makonnen spent a year and a half at the Danish Royal Agricultural College in Copenhagen and studied the cooperative movement. He was deported to Eng-

4. Margaret Busby, ed., *Daughters of Africa: An International Anthology of Words and Writings by Women of African Descent from the Ancient Egyptian to the Present* (London: Jonathan Cape, 1992), 221.

land after making remarks which suggested that, in their trading practices, the Danes were aiding the Italians in their war to colonize Ethiopia. After settling in Manchester, he helped to finance pan-African publications and movements through the proceeds of restaurants he owned. Both he and Padmore counseled Kwame Nkrumah in the years before independence, and they moved to independent Ghana in 1957, whereupon Padmore became Nkrumah's adviser on African affairs.[5] Makonnen helped to run the Ideological Institute at Winneba, the Workers and Builders Brigade, and the African Affairs Center.

Kwame Nkrumah (1909–1972) gained a number of degrees from Lincoln University and the University of Pennsylvania before going to England to serve as joint secretary with Padmore of the Fifth Pan-African Congress. In 1947 he returned to Ghana and became the leader of the independence movement. He was the foremost exponent of a political union of African states. He was overthrown in a military coup in 1966. After the coup, Makonnen settled in Kenya, welcomed by his old friend Jomo Kenyatta.

Springer recounts how her meeting with Jomo Kenyatta (c.1893–1978) in one of Makonnen's restaurants during this wartime trip played a role in her decision to use her labor connections to promote African independence. Returning to Kenya in 1946, Kenyatta became the leader of the political organization, the Kenya African Union. In 1952 colonial officials used the pretext of the primarily Gikuyu-led uprising (coined Mau Mau) to arrest him. Imprisoned and detained until 1961, he became independent Kenya's first head of state.

As Springer constantly points out in the interviews, the circle of people who were involved in social activism and left-wing political work was small. Padmore, Makonnen, and Jay Lovestone all knew one another before they met Springer. However, Springer did not know of their connections with Lovestone until much later. Makonnen had met Jay Lovestone in 1932 in his New York office on Forty-second Street while trying to track down Padmore. After having read *The Life and Struggles of the Negro Toilers*, he suspected that the author Padmore was the man he had known at Howard University as Malcolm Nurse. Also during this period, Makonnen spent his summers teaching at Brookwood Labor College and became familiar with ILGWU workers and leaders such as Mark Starr (1894–1985) and Frank Crosswaith.[6]

Upon coming to England Springer notes her surprise at Padmore's depth of knowledge about the ILGWU and its leaders, including Starr. The British-born Starr had participated in an Office of War Information mission of educators to

5. See Kenneth King, ed., *Ras Makonnen: Pan-Africanism from Within* (New York: Oxford University Press, 1973).
6. Ibid., 90, 102.

The International Affairs Arena

Britain the year before Springer had gone. Before coming to the United States in 1928, he started working at age thirteen as a hod carrier, then later taught miners in Wales and lost a campaign for Parliament on the Labor Party ticket. He served as ILGWU educational director from 1935 to 1960 and taught at Bryn Mawr Summer School for Women Workers. In 1943 Mayor Fiorello La Guardia nominated Starr, who was deemed the only qualified candidate, for the position of first director of adult education for New York City. However, the Board of Education rejected him, citing his labor activism as a reason for disqualification.[7] In the early 1960s Starr would do some educational work in Tanganyika during Springer's activist period there.

Springer describes her renewed contact with Padmore and new connections with other pan-Africanists when she again traveled to Europe in 1951, first to observe workers' education in Scandinavia for two months and then to attend Oxford's Ruskin College for nine months. Ruskin College was established in 1899 to provide a standard university education for working-class people so that they could better serve their communities and organizations, including trade unions. In her relations with Africans and Caribbeans Springer recalls the vibrancy with which discussions about independence were infused. She also relates her sense of outrage at the paternalistic treatment she received from a small group of her British associates at Ruskin College, who were resentful of the post–World War II change in the balance of world power away from England and toward the United States. While in Sweden, Springer stayed with her old friends Esther and Oliver Peterson. The Petersons lived in Sweden and Belgium from 1948 to 1957 where Oliver served as labor attaché. While they were in Brussels, Esther worked for the ICFTU. Oliver later became the labor adviser in the African Affairs Office of the U.S. Department of State.

After returning to the United States, Springer expanded and consolidated her connections with African political and labor leaders who traveled to the country seeking support from the United Nations or U.S. groups for political or labor causes. She describes how her home in Brooklyn became a refuge and meeting place for African travelers and recounts how her mother Adina Stewart Carrington became a beloved figure in African labor and nationalist circles. Springer discusses the activism of three men with whom she developed close relationships: Julius Nyerere, Maynard Mpangala, and Tom Mboya.

Much loved by Tanzanians and known as *Mwalimu* (Swahili for "teacher"), Julius Kambarage Nyerere (1922–1999) led Tanganyika (now Tanzania) to independence in 1961. During his rule he also helped lead the fight against apartheid and ordered a successful military overthrow of the brutal dictator Idi Amin of

7. Matthew L. Wald, "Mark Starr of Garment Union," *New York Times*, April 28, 1985.

Uganda. In 1985 Nyerere became one of the few African heads of state to leave power voluntarily. Maynard Mpangala, the assistant general secretary of the newly organized Tanganyika Federation of Labor, first told Springer about Nyerere when he met her in 1956.

Thomas Joseph Mboya, the general secretary of the Kenya Federation of Labor, represented another of Springer's links with East Africa. She recalls first meeting him on August 15, 1956, his twenty-sixth birthday, as he arrived in New York under the auspices of the American Committee on Africa.[8] On this first trip to the United States, he stayed in Springer's home. Five years later Springer and her mother would attend his wedding to Pamela Odede, the daughter of Walter Odede, who served seven years in detention without trial during the period that the colonial government had declared a state of emergency in response to the Mau Mau rebellion. In 1962 Mboya became Kenya's minister of labor in the transitional government before independence was instituted in late 1963. Afterward, he served first as minister for justice and constitutional affairs and then minister of economic planning and development. An able and talented and shrewd politician, Mboya incurred the wrath of rivals. Seen as a successor to Kenyatta, he was assassinated on July 5, 1969.

༄

I came across a newspaper article about the ILGWU in 1949 that covered the work of three blacks in the labor movement: you, Mabel Durham-Fuller, and Arthur Boyer. However, the article highlighted you, calling you the pride of the ILGWU, and there was a picture of you as well.

Really!

Yes. (*Laughter.*) Were you aware that you were thought of as the pride of the ILGWU?

I knew that Sasha Zimmerman had very strong views about me. Encouraged me. That I was the pride of the ILG, I did not know, in those days. I think when I went to England during World War II that, of course, had to be extraordinary.

Do you recall how you were chosen to go on this labor exchange trip?

I will never know the real facts of how I was chosen. The AF of L was told they could select two women from the federation membership. And the same

8. The American Committee on Africa was formed in 1953. It interpreted for a U.S. audience the momentous events occurring in Africa, promoted African movements for self-government, and supported Africans studying in the United States. See George Houser, *No One Can Stop the Rain: Glimpses of Africa's Liberation Struggle* (New York: Pilgrim Press, 1989).

The International Affairs Arena

went for the CIO. The garment workers was one of the unions selected for choosing a woman. And the IBEW was the other union selected. I am aware that I was not the first choice. A woman vice president, I believe, was chosen from the ILG, but I think she had some very serious problem—I learned this many years later—and could not go. The ILG then had to select a second person out of its membership of 440,000. (*Laughs.*) The rumor was the ILG has 440,000 members, 90 percent of them are women, why did they have to pick this one? This caused a great deal of concern. It was DD's [David Dubinsky] coup. And for whatever it is worth, we four labor women on this mission were not going to resolve serious social issues. Actually, it was a goodwill tour, a wartime measure, and a symbol of all of the investment and cooperation among the Allies. This trip was put out of all context of what a "hands across the sea" trip would mean. It gained great importance because of my paint job. (*Laughs.*) And for whatever reason, President Dubinsky said that I was the person. So the politics of that I don't know about. The union continued to feel that my representation served *them* well, that I was a credible representative. My participation in this trip was a great to-do in New York City at the time. Ooh! And the Negro press played it up, and the *New York Times* carried a piece on it. The [*Chicago*] *Tribune*.

My AF of L counterpart, Julia O'Connor Parker, was extremely perturbed that she was going to have to be the colleague of a Negro woman. So much so that to appease her, it was arranged for her to meet me in New York City at a hotel. So she came up for a weekend, and I went down to the hotel to meet her on this Saturday evening, feeling very hostile. My feeling was who was she that she had to determine whether she would like to be my colleague or no. The International Ladies' Garment Workers' Union had determined to appoint me.

I think the AF of L had a queasy stomach about my selection also, and for complicated reasons. I say they had a queasy stomach because an AF of L delegation from Washington came to New York to look at me (*laughs*) and to listen to me at some function that Dubinsky gave prior to my going away. I understand that they went away feeling more comfortable. I was told that Dubinsky said (*imitating his voice*), "Don't worry about Springer. She knows her way around the political world." This was an important mission to them, and they did not want some inexperienced person who could be twisted around someone's fingers.

So I think they questioned Dubinsky's wisdom in this and for selecting a Negro woman. Race had something to do with that. They could not deny him the *right* to select me, nor did they try. But who had ever heard of a national union sending some black woman somewhere to represent the labor movement? Their concern in the first place was that I was young, and I looked younger than my age. I was an officer of a small local union, the Plastic Button and Novelty Workers. You're talking about power. And even though this was a goodwill delegation and you were not making any important decisions, you left a *présence*. The AF of L and CIO were very hard-nosed people. They lived in a world of all men. They would understand a Julia O'Connor Parker. She was there with Gompers for the discussions of the League of Nations, and she was a political warhorse. I was not. And you throw in my color for good measure. Never leave that out. (*Chuckles*.)

So I went down and I met Julia O'Connor and we talked. I don't know what she thought after that. But I think our discussion was as two women workers, one an experienced leader. She was an old, *experienced* woman. She was probably in her fifties at the time. And by my standards, fifty was old. Now that I'm eighty, I don't know what I think is old. (*Laughs*.)[9] But she was *formidable* to talk to, and she cut through niceties and went directly to what she wanted to talk about, trade unions. She was attempting to test me. I knew my business about New York trade unions and about the work of the ILG. And as an officer of a small union, I knew that work. I knew about strikes, and I knew about struggles around wages, hours, and conditions of service. She could hardly challenge me on any of that. Hardly. (*Laughs*.)

So I went to visit her with every confidence and intended to quarrel with her, but we never came to that. We talked as two people who represented working people. She, the experienced person internationally, also. The only place I had been was Panama. She, of course, was very conversant with the politics of the labor movement, the broader context of problems and jealousies in regard to the CIO, which was considered the young avant-garde group. So in that context, she saw our duty was to hold our own and to work at being the most effective representatives that we could be. And so we established an accommodation, not friendship. That was my meeting with Julia O'Connor Parker, who became such a dear friend that when she died, I was out of the country and her daughter tried every way to reach me. When I came back home, my mother had the message left by Julia's daughter about her death.[10]

So you had kept in contact after the trip?

Absolutely. We exchanged cards and we would meet. If there was a meeting somewhere, which she was participating in, she would let me know. And

9. This part of the interview took place on September 15, 1990.
10. Parker's daughter, Sally Parker, was active in the American Federation of Teachers for many years.

if I was going to be attending, we would have a chance to meet, or if I was going into Washington we would meet. She, I think, retired very soon because, as I say, she was in her fifties then. Yes, we became fast friends.

You once stated that the AFL was considered conservative compared with the CIO.

Conservative, yes. The focus was that the AF of L was the old reactionary one. The CIO had the name for the militant and the young, and they had organized these mass unions with all these black folks and different kind of people coming into it. The CIO grew out of the Committee for Industrial Organization, which was an AF of L committee. The committee's recommendations on broad-based industrial organization were not acceptable to the Executive Council of the AF of L. Within the AF of L, there were the more tightly knit craft unions, and they threw out these unions that wanted mass organization and challenged for it. The mine workers, the steel workers, the United Auto Workers, the United Electrical Workers, all said that they would not stand on a cracked base anymore. So they stayed out and formed the Congress of Industrial Organizations. It maintained the same initials but a different name.

My union was thrown out because they supported the CIO's recommendations. We never joined the CIO when it formed a separate organization. I came from a union where we were among the people always up in the front doing all sorts of things. I happened to be a member of a union for fifty some years.[11] They didn't have a white membership and a black membership or an auxiliary membership. I was a garment worker. I paid the same dues, got the same kind of opportunities based on my own *will* to participate, moved into the structure of my union. So there we are. I belong to an AF of L union.

The AF of L position was that the formation of the CIO was dual unionism, and that created a conflict of interest. So, in this context, of course, the AF of L was conservative. It still had a lot of unions that thought of a more narrowly based structured organization and did not think about the great masses of workers that came about as a result of expansion of industry and the wartime efforts. So there was a very sharp division on how you *looked* at development, and the AF of L had a politically narrow base by CIO standards.

The sharpest division internationally between the AF of L and CIO happened when the AF of L refused to join the World Federation of Trade Unions [WFTU]. This was the high point of their disagreement. During World War II

11. This part of the interview was conducted on October 17, 1990.

the CIO joined this new international world body, which was led by the Communist Party unions. The British trade unions and European unions also were members. The AF of L's contention was that a government-run organization was not a free trade union. There was no freedom of association because the government controlled that union. The workers in the trade unions in the Soviet Union were government operatives; they had no voice. So there was a very sharp political and psychological division.

I heard one of the CIO's leaders from the electrical workers admit at a public meeting that the Soviet unions had no voice. But the CIO unions were members of the WFTU for the reason that they would work to transform the leadership's ideas about representation from the inside. That among the things that they hoped to do in working in the WFTU was to help change the methods, the ideas of how a union functions. The CIO's position was much more to the left of the AF of L. And while the CIO was anti-Communist domestically, they felt that belonging to such a world federation at that time could mean that they could help to shape and to forge an industrial workers' movement that was much more broadly based, involving the other world trade unions and the United States.

Well, they found that they could not work with the structure like that because they were dealing directly with a government body in terms of the representation. The president of the union, the head of the factory, you know, he was a member of the government body. In due course, out of the disillusionment of the CIO unions and some of the European unions with the WFTU, was born the International Confederation of Free Trade Unions, the ICFTU. You have to be very old to be a part of that history. (*Laughs.*) But there was always a very strong relationship in many unions in Europe and in Great Britain with Communist unions.

And *always* the CIO had a more flexible position than the AF of L, even when they were merged federations. So I think that ought to be clear. (*Laughs.*) The hierarchy of the AF of L was adamant about international politics. You were either Communist or you were not a Communist. These were real conflicts, terrible conflicts, ideological conflicts both domestically and particularly internationally. So after the 1955 merger the compromises had to be fought out bitterly within the structure of the AFL-CIO. The auto workers would maintain many things that they would do in a very separate way. So there is no denying that there was conflict. Lord, this is history, you know, making you scratch your head and go way back. Because, you see, I was there. I was a part of all that transition.

The International Affairs Arena

Coming from my ideological group, I believed that the WFTU could not serve the cause of the workers. I guess I had listened enough and I had thought about it. And don't forget my background with a husband who had such a dim view of the labor movement. (*Laughs.*) We did not discuss the WFTU or anything like that, no. I think he was so anti much of what was happening here that he didn't even take into question the WFTU. He did not challenge me or question me about going on this trip. I think he felt I was already lost on this question of the labor movement. But supportive, always.

How did you come to stay with Mary McLeod Bethune at her residence in Washington, DC, when you were being briefed for the trip?

I stayed at Bethune House as a guest of the National Council of Negro Women because Washington in 1945 was a very highly racist town. We were fighting a war for democracy everywhere and black soldiers were going to die for it, but I could not stay in a hotel with a delegation sponsored by the Office of War Information of the federal government. If I had known about the segregation I would face, I would never have gone to DC. To be treated like that when I was going on an overseas trip for the Office of War Information! And I was selected, one of four people in the United States to go! Had I known that this might have been one of the conditions, *no*, I wouldn't have gone. I was too young and too warm-blooded to have accepted anything like this in advance. No, I did not know that. (*Laughs.*) And it wasn't put to me that way when I was leaving that I was going to be the guest of the National Council of Negro Women because of segregation. The fact behind that came a little later. My three colleagues stayed at the hotel that did not give me admission at that time.

I had met Mary McLeod Bethune in groups when I was one of a hundred people. But personally for the first time I met her in January 1945, when she welcomed me to the Bethune House. I think I was a member of the National Council of Negro Women but had no active working relationship. The National Council of Negro Women was an organization that you would be very proud to belong to. And under ordinary circumstances to have been invited to be the guest of Dr. Bethune was a great honor. OK, so here was how my personality got very split on that. The evening that I arrived late, someone from Dr. Bethune's staff welcomed me to her residence and headquarters of her organization. It's a beautiful old mansion, very elegant, very nice. So there was the bittersweet. I had a sense that there was something I was not being told. And the bitter truth came the following day.

The next morning I was due to be in a meeting with the head of an international relief organization. We were meeting, I think, with former Governor

Herbert Lehman.[12] I walked out to take a taxi, and it was freezing, dreadfully cold, and *no* taxi would pick me up. I was not aware of this. The Western Union man was delivering telegrams in their brown cars and kept driving around and around and around, and I'm still standing on the corner waiting. I don't know *anything* about transportation. I don't know where to go to take a bus or anything. Finally the young white driver came over to where I was shivering and asked me where I was going. I gave him the address, and he said, "Don't you know it is not easy, you won't be picked up." He told me the white cabs would not pick me up, and there were very few black drivers and jitneys. So he drove me to the building where I was to go.

There was a coffee shop next door to this building, and I went in and sat on the stool to get a cup of coffee. My teeth were chattering. I sat there and no one came to ask me for my order. Other people came, and they got their coffee and donuts. It was a greasy spoon. It was a very ordinary coffee shop. Finally, someone came over to me, a porter with his mop, and he said, "Us don't serve colored in here." By that time I was nearly apoplectic.

So I collected myself and went upstairs to the meeting out of my mind, out of control. I was late, of course, and indicated what happened to me and wanted to go home right away. (*Laughs.*) Well, a telephone call was made to Dr. Bethune. And as a result of that incident I had a chauffeur-driven limousine that took my three colleagues and myself wherever we wanted to go. They'd picked me up first and we went all over the city for whatever days of discussion that we had. They didn't call it briefing then. We met with *every* government agency, with the congressmen, the senators. Here we are, just taken out of our little cocoon, our unions, and we were given some political history, the wartime history, background information. So that was my introduction to Washington, DC. (*Chuckles.*)

That night, Mrs. Bethune—she probably was told that I was less than polite the rest of the day in the office at that meeting—called me into her sitting room and gave me tea or chocolate and pound cake, and you know you're in for something. She lectured me gently. In effect, she said that I did not have the right to the luxury of popping off and wanting to go back to New York. That this was an extraordinary opportunity to go "abroad," as she said, learn

12. Springer was attempting to get to the first briefing session for the trip, which was held in the United Nations Relief and Rehabilitation Administration (UNRRA) office. In 1943 Herbert Henry Lehman (1878–1963) became the director of the UNRRA, which was established to give aid to people in countries the Allies liberated. He had previously served as governor of New York (1932–1942). Later he served in the U.S. Senate (1949–1956), where he opposed McCarthyism.

about the conditions and the problems and meet people and come back and report to the Council, report to my union and my colleagues. She said *that* was my right; *that* was my duty!

Well, when that dear lady got through talking to me, I felt like a worm. I thought that I had picked up a cab and pushed it against the wall and done some horrible thing. It was a very great lesson for me in terms of what you do to achieve things you want, or what you make of your resentment, your disagreement with how you're being treated, that you never won anything by running. In effect, what she was telling me was that I was running. I was taking the easy way out. It was quite an occasion. I ate that cake and drank that tea or cocoa, and I crawled back to my room. I had to have a deep conversation with myself. (*Laughter.*) A great one had done it to me.

Fortunately, for the rest of her years, I was able to be among those that she called her labor women. Dollie Lowther was one in the small group of trade union women that was active in Council. I am told—I never heard Dr. Bethune say this—that whenever something was going on that affected women workers, she would say, "Call my labor women." (*Laughs.*) It was very nice to know that she felt that we would have that competence and effectiveness and commitment to Council. I think one of the things that really enamored me to Council was my feeling that the National Council of Negro Women was an all-embracing organization and attempted to reach women in all walks of life. This was one of my fascinations for Council. For most other women's organizations, you either had to be out of the university, out of a lodge, or you were an activist in a church. But Dr. Bethune spread her umbrella open very wide to reach us all. She knew that it was important that working women should be a part of the National Council. So, I have said very special thanks to Council for looking at the role of the working woman.[13]

Dr. Bethune was a woman revered, a woman looked to for her capabilities. Few other women had her access. How many women were on a telephone communication basis, constantly, with the White House? With Mrs. Roosevelt? With cabinet officers? It was she who made it possible for the inclusion of black women in the female counterpart to the CCC. But I think the white women of conscience who shared Mrs. Bethune's view were amenable to the idea of how you involved and how you open the doors for all women, in-

13. In 1950 Springer and Dollie Lowther Robinson co-chaired "Women Workers—Their Gains and Goals," the first session of a three-day conference sponsored by the NCNW, entitled "Women Looking Forward toward Peace and Security." Pauline Newman also participated in the conference. See Hazel Garland, "Labor, Youth Session Highlight Three-Day Meeting," name of newspaper and date missing (Amistad).

cluding black women. I don't know any other women with influence like that, so Mrs. Bethune was one apart, and the only thing that I knew was that she was revered. If Ma Bethune said, "This is the way you go," I do not think anyone in those days would have dared challenge her.

How did she address you?

Maida—I was down here on the floor; Mrs. Bethune was up here in the sky—but with respect. She would call us daughters, too. For example, there were occasions if she thought you were moving too slowly, you weren't doing something, she would say, "Come along, daughter." But generally in conversation, she would call me Maida. I do not want to blow this out of proportion. I was not a part of Mrs. Bethune's inner circle. I was someone known to her, someone that she thought was a young woman with a future, a young woman who could make a contribution in the work of Council.

How did you get to London for this exchange trip?

By boat. It took perhaps seventeen days. We went from Halifax in Canada. This was unknown territory. I was being sent on assignment during wartime. After I got over being frightened about it, I was very pleased I had been selected. But I was terrified. You couldn't tell anybody where you were. Terror! Terror! No one was to know what we were traveling on, how we were traveling. Our families could not be told. And we did not know. The ships were being strafed and the German submarines were bombing or damaging the ships.

I remember Owen and Eric as they saw me off on the train to go to Washington for the briefing. Owen knew I was scared silly. So he and Eric just stood there and he just held my hand. I am sure he told me some comforting words. Got on the train, went to Washington (*claps hands*), did X number of days in briefing, got on another train and went to Canada. Still didn't know where I was going. We left on an Italian ship, which had been impounded by the United States government and was the commodore of the convoy. It was a convoy of many, many ships, although I never saw the whole convoy. There were some airplane carriers in the convoy, and sometimes you could see the planes as they would take off and getting back. But no one told you anything.

The ship we were to leave on developed some kind of trouble. It was rumored that since this was an Italian vessel, it did not take well to cold water. So there were some leakage repairs. I saw rescues at sea. The worst thing I saw was when an engineer on our boat had his finger cut off. There was a little boat to take him to the hospital ship, and the swell in the ocean that these two big vessels made left you with this extraordinary impression that this tiny little boat would never get over to the hospital. But it did.

The International Affairs Arena

We had to be instructed on how to go over the side of the ship into our lifeboats because we lost ships all the time. You would hear by the grapevine about a loss, because it was a small ship. We were told a ship had been lost in the night, and that the submarines had gotten it. It would be supposedly a secret, but we were the commodore of the convoy, so things got whispered around. We could never have any open discussion. We practiced every day, twice a day, the procedures for getting in the lifeboats. We all wore jackets that had all of our identification in it. I had crocheted a big pocket, and I put various documents saying who I was in it. I guess down in Davy Jones's locker I wanted to be assured that the sharks knew.

All of us had hilarious stories about when, three days out at sea, it was thought that we were going to be hit. Since we practiced in the daytime, this caused confusion when the alarm signal came one night for us to go up to our stations. When the bells rang and we went to our stations, we were told we could go and pick up (*hits hand on table to indicate speed*) something in our rooms and get back to our stations. I took a brown felt hat—beret—and a bottle of perfume. I did not know I took that. We went up in the dark to find our way. I was so paralyzed with fright I couldn't move my feet to step up to go up to the gangplank. When the all-clear came, that it wasn't our ship that was hit, we went back and found that many of us had done some crazy things. But I think I came out with top honors that night. A brown felt hat and perfume. I think I took gloves, also. When I was young, I wore gloves and hats. So we all sat and laughed, and all of us, I guess, had big shots of brandy when it was all over that night.

Did you get to know your colleagues a little better on the ship over?

On the ship, yes. They didn't like me, and I didn't like them. It was mutual. Myself and Julia O'Connor per force were together. We talked with one another more. There was a *surface* politeness, and, of course, each of us had a different set of experiences as union representatives. All of us were officers of a union. One woman was from the hosiery workers out of Massachusetts. Another was from the United Auto Workers. And Julia O'Connor was from the telephone workers, and I from the garment workers. So, we had a body of experience that we could speak about and have an interchange. So, on that level, we were fine. We were together for months, and I got to know them very well. On shipboard I roomed with them. There were twenty-three people on board.

Were there any other black people on the ship?

No! In 1945? Doing what? (*Laughing*.)

Did you stay in the same hotel with your colleagues when you got to London?

Oh, yes. The accommodations were mind-boggling in London. Generally in many places, we all had separate rooms. In London at one of the hotels, we had an enormous suite, and I think two women stayed in the suite, or three of them. We all met; we did everything in the suite. Always in rural areas, very nice accommodations; in bigger cities, fantastic accommodations. I had never been in fancy hotels like that before in my life. (*Laughs.*)

There was a very big American staff in England, and *everything* was done to maintain the solidarity and the feeling of cooperation. This exchange was one of those "hands across the sea" efforts. The United States was considered the godfather or godmother to the war effort before they entered the war, and the American labor movement was dropping vans of money and support into the war effort. I think one of those pictures you saw was of the Merchant Seamen's Club. This is one of the things that the ILG had contributed its money to, to build a recreation place for all of the Allied seaman.[14] I presented on behalf of the ILG a letter and money to a women's hostel which one of the ILG unions was supporting on behalf of the trade union war effort. This was an effort to support recreational facilities for the women in the war. The whole *nation* was at war in England. From one minute to the other you didn't know whether your city or your village was going to be bombed out. This was not a game. You heard the V-2's coming over, and you could see the sky light up, and you'd see a place bombed out. The V-2's did not respect anything or anyplace or anybody.

And when did you first start seeing black people in England? Was that almost immediately?

Oh, yes. Black Americans who were staff people overseas knew I was coming. I saw people in the Red Cross and the YWCA. But by the time we arrived, the newspapers were full of our presence, and always they said that there were two women representing the AF of L, one of whom was an American Negro. Not just two women representing the AF of L.

One person I met in England who was very involved with the Caribbean was a Jamaican named Una Marson. She was a writer and was working for the BBC. Her book of poetry [*Heights and Depths*] is somewhere on these

---

14. Before the United States entered the war, the ILGWU had founded the Merchant Navy Club with a gift of seventy-five thousand dollars. Ernest Bevin, the British foreign minister, opened the club. See Eric Hawkins, "The ILGWU Merchant Navy Club in London," *Chicago Sun*, August 12, 1942; reprinted in Leon Stein, ed., *Out of the Sweatshop: The Struggle for Industrial Democracy* (New York: Quadrangle/New York Times Book Co., 1977), 252–53.

shelves. It was with her that I made my first international broadcast. When you fill out a dossier for overseas, they know everything about you. And since it was written in my dossier that I was born in Panama, I was asked by the BBC to do some broadcasts to the Caribbean for the whole "hands across the sea" effort. Since there were all of these Caribbean soldiers fighting this war and going through England, there were broadcasts to the islands. So it was Una who was the person in charge of the underground broadcasts six floors below the earth somewhere near Winston Churchill's offices. I didn't know that then. I've read that since.

I met a large number of Caribbean soldiers in England. Una lived in a blown-out building. Half of the building had been blown away. She would shop in the markets and find vegetables and codfish and things that were not rationed and cook West Indian food. England is a kind of international center. Its universities attract people from all over the world. So late at night we —whomever was off duty—would meet in her bombed-out place, and she would cook, and we would eat and talk. Somebody who knew the dark streets would get me back to my hotel, because there were no lights except the little lights down on the sidewalk. But I spent a lot of interesting time listening to the soldiers from the islands. (*Sighs.*) Had I been a writer, to have documented that would really make your discussion here very pertinent. The soldiers saw the war as giving them a chance to come out of their country. They had no illusions about what they were doing, and for the most part— because I think Una was very selective about the people she invited—these were men who had a vision of the future, and they were looking to the day when they were going to have a country, not a colonial dependency. So it was very good talk at night. Very explosive talk! (*Laughs.*) Had they been heard, they would all have been court-martialed.

That's some of what we did. This was not a part of my official duties there. I performed all of the duties. I went to all the meetings. I drank all the toasts with all of my British colleagues. But by this time between George Padmore and Una Marson, I had a whole different agenda also.

It was at a public meeting that I first met the acid-tongued writer and empire basher, George Padmore. I think we were in one of General Eisenhower's war rooms, where they were giving us a picture of the war effort, a very cursory thing in a big assembly room. Every newspaper reporter was there, asking us all of the foolish questions that they ask people who have no information. (*Laughs.*) You know, you're there two days, and they ask, "How do you assess the war effort?" and "What do you think of the workers?" George Padmore sent a note up to the platform, asking me did I have some time, because he would like to speak with me. I immediately wrote back and indicated the hotel where I was staying and that I would be there in the afternoon. So that began our relationship. I knew of him before.

He had very positive feelings—and I didn't know why then—about the ILG. Padmore had the reports of many Caribbean people who had come to the United States and become members of the garment workers. I did not know at the time that he knew Mark Starr. Mark Starr was a Socialist who had come from Britain. In the United States he became the educational director of the ILG. I did not know at the time that I met George Padmore that he knew Lovestone. There was *never* any conversation about him knowing Lovestone. Well, I didn't know, so the question never arose. But Padmore was so knowledgeable about things in America that I was a welcome person.

Did you talk to George Padmore about the WFTU, or did he discuss it with you at all?

Not much. He had another issue, the Pan-African Congress. I knew about the Pan-African Congress in Manchester that Padmore was planning in terms of the NAACP's involvement.[15] Therefore, Padmore was very interested to talk to me about what I knew about the Congress and other things. After we met and had tea, I guess he made the judgment that I had some possibilities. (*Laughs.*) He said to me, "Let me see your itinerary," and I showed it to him. He then gave me letters of introduction to people in the areas where I was going. He said, "Good, you are going to Manchester." Wrote a note and gave me Makonnen's telephone number, and when I got to Manchester I called immediately. That was my introduction to Ras Makonnen, whose book you saw with his notation to me when I saw him in Kenya in 1977.[16] Padmore's letter of introduction introduced me to *that* world of the African people who were doing various things. And *this* is how I was invited to meet African leaders based in England, of which Jomo Kenyatta was one.

I had just missed meeting Kwame Nkrumah. But subsequently ten years later, I met him. By that time the Padmores and I are very close friends. We are writing to each other, and I am traveling back and forth. Whenever I'm

15. On March 4, 1945, Makonnen, Padmore, and Peter Milliard invited delegates from British West Africa and the British Caribbean to meet in Manchester to plan the Fifth Pan-African Congress for October of that year. See Imanuel Geiss, *The Pan-African Movement: A History of Pan-Africanism in America, Europe and Africa* (New York: Africana Publishing Co., 1974), 389–90.
16. King, *Ras Makonnen.*

in Europe, I always see the Padmores. George is usually at the airport to meet me. We developed a real bond. At that point he was, of course, talking to me about what he saw as the future for Africa, which he was contributing to, because much of what went on was cooked in his kitchen (*laughs*), his book-lined kitchen. George Padmore, I considered, was my Ph.D. education without going to a university for it. In a half hour we would sit down and over a cup of tea and cognac he would—not discuss with me, because I wouldn't have known what I was discussing—but he would *lay out to me* part of the history of what he called "empire." What his presentation of the historical facts gave to me, one would have had to spend a semester in school getting the lectures. So he was a great educator, and he didn't have a problem proselytizing me. I was a very *willing* subject. If it was thought that I could be a friend in court, in terms of what Africans saw as part of their moving towards independence, George gave me the blessing, I guess. He was among the thinkers and the movers and the organizers.

I met Jomo Kenyatta at Ras Makonnen's restaurant in Manchester. In this building he had this very profitable restaurant downstairs, and he had a big area upstairs where all of the African activities went on. He was financing a lot of things dealing with Africa because his restaurants—he had more than one—were moneymakers. For the African independence movement, he was one of the movers.[17] On the evening when I was in Manchester, Makonnen told me about a meeting upstairs in this restaurant and invited all of my colleagues because he couldn't invite me by myself. I think maybe one of them came. But I know I had a chance to meet Jomo Kenyatta and to talk one on one with him. He raised various questions with me about the American working class. What did they know about the fight to end colonialism? I said I wasn't sure I could answer that, but I was going to sure try to find out. And I guess I've been trying ever since. (*Laughs.*)

If I still have some of those old diaries, I may have a note saying who else was there. But I'm not a good note taker, and I think I was so overwhelmed by Jomo Kenyatta that I may have given only a cursory mention to a lot of very important people, men who were making history.

Did you think that you would have a chance to come back again and visit the Padmores and become more involved?

No. I had a hope that perhaps at some point I would be able to travel more

17. Makonnen established five restaurants. For a time Jomo Kenyatta was in charge of the Cosmopolitan, and Padmore helped with the running of the Belle Étoile (ibid., 135–39).

freely and go back to England when my son was out of school. But in no way did I think I would be involved in international affairs in the way that it developed in 1945. I surely didn't think that. After a letter of introduction from Padmore and you meet the Ras Makonnens and you've met some other folk whose names at the moment are escaping me, you kept contact. Later, I met Dorothy, George Padmore's wife. I had been seeing George Padmore for a long time back and forth but had not yet been to his home. He would talk about Dorothy, and then finally we met. So after that he would say, "Maida, Dorothy thinks"—he was very nasal (*imitates his speech*)—"that you should come and do this, that, and the other with us. We're having these people over." And I would say, "George, I can just listen." (*Laughs.*) I would just take a cab. And it was a home I was very welcome in.

What would you say were the experiences of the Padmores as an interracial couple in Britain?

I can only talk of the Padmores as an interracial couple within the context that I saw them, and that was within this warm familial relationship of the revolutionaries, black and white supporters. I never saw them outside of that. I think I became aware of some problems when they moved to Ghana where both of them were outsiders. I don't care what contribution George made, which was considerable. And Dorothy was a member of that inner circle. There were tensions.[18]

Ras Makonnen stated that a number of black and Indian students in London felt it was a "revolutionary act to get their own back on Europe by seducing white women," and that "these apparently intelligent students . . . felt that by getting a bastard child they could solve the problem of imperialism."[19] Can you comment on that?

He's telling the truth. I cannot speak of it in any intimate way as Ras Makonnen would, because this is something he dealt with, with his colleagues. I knew some of the women, who were the typists, who ran all of the dirty errands, and who were always at meetings and making speeches and raising money and being the handmaiden to a lot of these men. They were Socialists. I know some of the men, who were not using the women, but really loved them. And if they could have, they would have married these women

---

18. Dorothy Padmore had been visiting W. E. B. Du Bois and his wife, Shirley Graham, in New York when George Padmore died. She continued to live in Ghana until her death in 1964 from a heart attack. See Makonnen's observations of the strong antiforeign sentiment that developed within Ghanaian government circles in ibid., 255, 259, 277–83; Du Bois, "The Spectator: George Padmore's Life," *National Guardian*, October 12, 1959.

19. King, *Ras Makonnen*, 147.

and gone back to their countries with them. A few did, like Joe Appiah, and the head of the government in Botswana, formerly Bechuanaland, Seretse Khama, and one or two others.[20] But the feeling about independence and marrying within the African context was very strong. This was not only true of Africa, it was true of any group. There are some cultures where the families mourn if you marry outside of that culture.[21]

Did you see Ras Makonnen when he lived in Ghana after independence?

Oh, yes. He was very busy with training programs, and feeding hundreds and hundreds of people, and various youth programs, things that the Ghana government was doing. Like George, he was very close to Dr. Nkrumah. He married a Ghanaian woman subsequently and they had two sons. I met one teenage son years later, I recall, in Kenya.

The details of how Makonnen got to Kenya after Nkrumah was overthrown I do not remember.[22] Jomo Kenyatta wrote to the Ghana government advising them that Makonnen was welcomed in Kenya and that they wanted him as a citizen of Kenya. Of all the countries, Kenya was the strongest in support of Makonnen because he was very close to Mzee [Kenyatta; "Mzee" is a title of respect for an older man]. As a matter of fact, he probably organized the

20. From a noted Ashanti family, Joseph Emmanuel Appiah (1918–1990) studied law in England where he met Peggy Cripps, who was the daughter of Sir Stafford Cripps, the Labor Chancellor of the Exchequer. They married in 1953. The scholar Anthony Appiah is their son. Joe Appiah was Krame Nkrumah's personal representative in London before independence. After joining the Nkrumah opposition, he was jailed under the Preventative Detention Act in 1961 and 1962. Later, he served as chair of the Justice Party, an opposition group, as president of the Ghana Bar Association, and as Ghana's representative at the UN. Eric Pace, "Joe Appiah Is Dead; Ghanaian Politician and Ex-Envoy, 71," *New York Times*, July 12, 1990, section D, p. 20.

In 1948 Patrick Gordon-Walker, a member of the Labor government, was behind banishing Khama (1921–1980), chief designate of the Bamangwata people of Bechuanaland, in response to him marrying Ruth Williams, a white woman. They had a civil ceremony when all the Anglican churches in London agreed with the government not to marry them. In 1956 the British government let them return as private citizens. Khama became president of Botswana in 1966. See Reuters, "Sir Seretse Khama Dies at Age 59: President of Botswana Since 1966," *New York Times*, July 13, 1980, section 1, part 2, p. 34; George Padmore, *Pan-Africanism or Communism? The Coming Struggle for Africa* (1956; repr., New York: Doubleday, 1971), 146.

21. Kim Marie Vaz found in her research that Nigerians made no distinctions between black and white foreign wives. They were both viewed as foreign. Vaz, "Social Conformity and Social Resistance: Women's Perspective on 'Women's Place,'" in *Oral Narrative Research with Black Women*, ed. Kim Marie Vaz, 223–49 (Thousand Oaks, CA: Sage Publications, 1997), 228.

22. Springer wrote Jay Lovestone in 1977 saying that she had seen Makonnen in Kenya and that the story of what happened after Nkrumah's overthrow was incredible. Springer to Lovestone, October 7, 1977, "Springer Kemp," box 708, LP.

The International Affairs Arena

money for Jomo Kenyatta to return to Kenya, because Ras Makonnen was a prosperous businessman.[23]

You spent some time with Esther Peterson in Sweden when you were studying the Scandinavian labor movement in the summer of 1951. What was your relationship like with her then and before?

Esther Peterson and I were great friends. (*Laughs.*) She worked for the Amalgamated Clothing Workers, which was then called the men's industry in the needle trades. She was, I think, the educational director of the Amalgamated Clothing Workers at the time when I was the educational director of the Plastic Button and Novelty Workers' Union. Dollie Robinson was educational director of the Laundry Workers Joint Board. Because we were all union people, we all belonged to the Women's Trade Union League and to all kinds of other things that were labor oriented.

By the time I got a scholarship to study workers' education in Denmark and Sweden, Esther and her husband, Oliver, and I were *wonderful*, intimate, *warm* family friends. One of Esther's sons is named Eric, not because of my son, Eric, but because they are Scandinavians in background. At that time Oliver was labor attaché to Sweden. They warmly welcomed me and hosted me, and I stayed in their home for part of the time. There was a committee in the United States, the American Scandinavian Foundation, that selected me that year to go.

You were involved in some controversy on the trip.

In Sweden there developed a controversy about what newspapers alleged I had said. Esther traveled with me to the meetings that the women held and could verify that I didn't say the things that the newspapers alleged. The issue of conflict there was that in this wonderful egalitarian society where they had day care for children of working mothers and all kinds of adjustments in favor of the aged, men and women received different wages for the same work. There was a training wage so that a boy could come in as an apprentice at sixteen; and in a couple of years, he would earn more than perhaps the woman that helped to train him.

Well, the women in Sweden were challenging that and were discussing it with the trade union women. These women were the journalists and teachers who were inveighing against this differential. I certainly was aware enough

23. Makonnen, who asserted he was always ready in his life to go anywhere to help with the cause of African liberation, remarked on his isolation in Kenya in King, *Ras Makonnen*, 283. Apart from the homes of Eliud Mathu, Peter Mbiyu Koinange, and sometimes Kenyatta, he was not invited into Kenyan homes because of ethnic divides of communities.

not to get into that pitfall. But they needed a platform to be provocative about their challenge. So on one occasion I was invited to a very swell affair where we had a talk and an exchange of view. After that it was alleged that I said I pitied the women workers of Sweden because of the wage differential, which I never said. But this got a lot of newspaper publicity. So Oliver and Esther then invited about a hundred labor leaders to their home to try to straighten this out. I was being used (*chuckles*) as the stalking horse.

Oliver and Esther had enough credibility in the country to help. They got the newspaper people, who had taken literary license and said what they wanted to say, to admit that I had not said that I pitied the women workers. But that's like a refutation in our newspaper. The headlines say you did something, and the apology is in the obituary page. Same difference.

So they were upset with you?

But for God's sake, if you read articles in the press that this visitor has become an expert on the labor conditions in your country after forty-eight hours, of course you're upset. You're annoyed. And worse that she pitied the women of Sweden. At the moment I don't recall the details of what I said. But I had *never* responded by saying anything about a difference in the wages, that it was terrible. I simply stated what happened in the United States. I talked about women's work from the Conestoga times, and the adjustments that we have had to make in industrial development. You can make a difference in earning power by all kinds of methods. If you don't have a wage differential, you could structure the work so that there are certain jobs women don't have.

You went to Ruskin College afterwards. Why did you want to attend Ruskin?

I had done a lot of traveling. I'd represented the American labor movement on many occasions and always I felt that I needed to know more and have a broader base. Now, being a curious person and one who was taken into the training processes of the movement and coming as I did from somewhere else, a foreigner, I had a concern, an interest. All of this to say that it was almost a natural development. And so I asked for and took a leave of absence to go to school for a year in England. Lester Granger and Judge Sadie Alexander and some other folks raised the money privately, and I was given a National Urban League Fellowship to study at Ruskin. That's how I got there. (*Laughs.*) So I spent nine months, the school year, at Oxford University's Ruskin College.[24]

24. Future New York governor and U.S. Vice President Nelson Rockefeller (1908–1979) also supported Springer for this trip.

Sadie Tanner Mosell Alexander (1898–1989) came from a distinguished family that included Paul Robeson, Bishop Benjamin Tucker, and the artist Henry Ossawa Tanner. She was a "first" in many fields. She was the first black woman to graduate from the University of

I stayed at Ruskin College residence. It was a student hostel [Headington hostel]. I guess there must have been eighteen, twenty women in the building I was in. I had a private room. Some women had large rooms together. They were very pleasant, very decent accommodations. It had been an old farmhouse, which was made into a residence. We were just outside of Oxford proper. There were many women studying, but only a few trade union women. I was a curiosity as a black woman from an American labor union. There were a couple of African men, one from Ghana. In those days, *most* of the people who studied at Oxford were West Africans. East Africans, I did not meet then. I later learned of the people who were studying in Scotland, a number of East Africans.

My social life was with my colleagues at the college, a couple of people I liked and they liked me, and a number of Africans. And since I was interested in colonial history, I took the lectures at Rhodes House, so there you met a lot of Africans. And I participated in the Oxford community events. I went to the Oxford debating society. I was never a debater, but you listened to great oratory. And you realized when you sat in on Parliament what that training meant, because you never see a parliamentarian with notes. Years later I recognized the kind of British training that I saw when Africans debated on their feet with never a note and would go from one subject to the other. It's *marvelous* training ground. I never mastered it. (*Laughs.*)

The first time I went to Africa in 1955, I met two of them who had studied at Oxford during that time. They were *right* there to greet me, to take me through the hoops. They were in the ministry of labor in Ghana and had been sent to Oxford to study. Ben Essumen was at Ruskin, but he lived in the town at the main men's hostel in Oxford. The other one, Richard Quarshie, was a senior labor officer in Ghana when he was sent to England to study. I worked with Richard Quarshie as a volunteer at the airport and doing other things for the Ghana independence celebration in 1957. Back then through Richard Quarshie I met Alex Quaison-Sackey. Later he became the ambassador to the United Nations after Ghana's independence. And he was, I think, one time a president of the UN. He did not go to Ruskin. He was reading law in

Pennsylvania Law School (her father had been the first black to graduate), to pass the bar in the state of Pennsylvania, and to serve as a national president of a black women's sorority (Delta Sigma Theta). She missed by a day becoming the first black woman to earn a Ph.D. A prominent civil rights activist who served on President Harry S Truman's Commission on Civil Rights, she also served as secretary to the National Urban League. In 1981, under President Jimmy Carter, she chaired the White House Conference on Aging. See "Sadie T. M. Alexander, 91, Dies; Lawyer and Civil Rights Advocate," *New York Times*, November 3, 1989.

London when I met him.[25] John Tettegah did not go to Oxford in my time. I met him in 1955 in Ghana when he was the secretary-general of the Trades Union Congress. He was barely in his twenties.

Well they were all *so* young. Oh mercy. *No one* was older than me, no one except [Leopold] Senghor of Senegal and Jomo Kenyatta of Kenya.[26] Africa was a young world, and even the Americans who were participants in that early period were all people much younger. If you looked at me in those days, I didn't look my age but I was the old lady in Africa. And it was generally known. And you see so many people who had been here, they'd been to my house, they'd seen my son. So everybody knew that I was Mama Maida and that I was an old woman.

George Padmore was in London at the time you were studying at Ruskin?

Oh, yes. And whenever I would be on, as they say, "a sticky wicket," I would see him. That's an English expression meaning a difficulty. And I think that in my tutorial I did not do well. I wasn't able to answer and I was embarrassed and I maybe was nearly crying. I wanted to learn about international affairs and the labor movement, but I was more interested personally in colonial development. So I went to a lot of those lectures and read and sometimes neglected my tutorials on the labor issues. I would take myself off to London and spend the weekend there and talk to George, particularly, and Dorothy, generally. And he would go over to his bookshelf and take a few books—some of the books I have here like *Africa, Britain's Third Empire*—and he would sit down and talk to me, and I would make notes. (*Laughs.*) No, he was a liberal education. From 1945 until his *death*, we were good family friends.

George Padmore lived in Camden Town. It's a good train ride from Oxford. It was in Padmore's house that I met Eric Williams, who became the prime minister of Trinidad. I didn't know him in the United States when he was teaching at Howard, but I met him when he was writing some papers, I think, before going back to Trinidad to start the campaign for independence.[27] You

25. Quaison-Sackey received an education at Exeter, Oxford, and the London School of Economics. From 1959 until 1965 he served as Ghanaian representative in the UN and also as the ambassador to Cuba and Mexico. From 1964 to 1965 he served as the first African president of the UN General Assembly. And from 1965 until the 1966 coup he served as the foreign minister of Ghana. In 1978 Colonel Acheampong appointed him ambassador to the United States. See Daniel Miles McFarland, ed., *Historical Dictionary of Ghana*, African Historical Dictionaries, no. 39 (Metuchen, NJ: Scarecrow Press, 1985), 151.

26. Leopold Sedar Senghor (1906–2001), the poet and scholar, was one of the founders of the Negritude movement, a word he coined. He also was the first African to earn a doctorate degree from a French university, the first president of independent Senegal ruling from 1960 until 1980, and the first African leader to voluntarily give up power.

27. Trinidad and Tobago became independent in 1962. Eric Williams (1911–1981) served as prime minister of the country until his death.

The International Affairs Arena

know, meeting these people was very exciting stuff. (*Laughs.*) So this house was my laboratory and it was my university. Just walking down the streets, walking down Marble Arch in London with George was an event. You were learning something all the time. Yeah. I'm very indebted to George Padmore. I was very privileged to have been included in that company.

How did people of African descent fit in with the environment of Ruskin, with the English people?

Well, the English people had been dealing with blacks forever, and this was in the fifties. Blacks had been over there fighting, had been over there all during the war. There wasn't a large problem. The newspapers would say when they had ads for rooms, "No Africans." (*Laughs.*) They didn't have to do what we do. They didn't have to have any subterfuge. They just said they didn't want any Africans living in their house. The second industry at Oxford was renting rooms to people who did not live in the university proper. There was always the undercurrent of this discrimination, but Africans, West Indians moved around easily.[28]

I probably had more trouble because I came from the country that was the big brother. The United States had been the great member of the alliance that helped to win the war and save Britain. Nobody likes you for that after a while. I had my problems and sometimes I won, sometimes I lost. Sometimes I had issues with my young Socialist friends, not the ones who had some real understanding, but a certain minimal group, the ones who were snide, not decent. They were in the labor movement and were all on scholarship at Ruskin. When they asked you about American Negroes, they were being sarcastic and attempted to make you feel that you were privileged to be in their country, because in your country you were so disadvantaged. I would never take that.

I have had a young man say to me (*speaking with a haughty British accent*) "that wasn't I very glad I was here in England" (*mockingly breathes in*), "so that I would not be faced as I was in the United States with *lynchings*." And I then went on to (*speaking in mock British accent*) "*give him*" some British history about where my father came from and that West Indian background. I wanted him to tell me the policies of the British in the colonies. *Then* talk to me about the United States. That usually made people quite quiet. (*Laughs.*) And I would go further and say, "Tell me about Stepney and Shorditch." These were seaports where the relationships were very mean and bad and where there were a lot of blacks who were seamen. Britain was a trading nation, and

28. See King, *Ras Makonnen,* for Makonnen's comments about racial hostility in England (141, 163).

The International Affairs Arena

they would bring the raw material back from their colonies in the great trading ships. And many of these seamen from Africa and the Caribbean did not go back. Many of them had relationships with women, and they had children who were called (*speaks with British accent*) "half caste."[29] This did not make for a comfortable relationship, particularly when times were bad. The prejudices were there. So I held my own.

I learned a lot of things and unlearned a lot of things, because you had a chance to learn since, really, you weren't a visitor anymore. You were in-house. I learned at a labor college you could be patronized. Here is the epitome of intellectual exchange of a social philosophy. I learned a good deal about snobbery. I didn't learn how to stop being angry and answer intelligently. My British-trained African friends were good. Oh, they were good. I needed to stay around another year to have some of their skill.

Africans would ask about American Negroes, but they were more generous than anyone else because they asked for information and really for an exchange of views. The discussions went on and on and on. Well, these were scholars. You know how you people like to talk and stay up all night and change and fix the world, to have all of the probabilities—what if, what if, what if, what if. And since this was just after World War II, we were still fixing the world. But the emphasis for most Africans was *not* what was happening to American Negroes. They were concerned with what *they* were about in terms of a change in the system of government, colonial domination. This was the dominant discussion.

In 1945, you *cannot* bring hundreds and thousands of black men to come to fight for freedom and democracy for which they would be jailed if they *spoke about it* in their country. So World War II turned the equation upside down in terms of the colonies. It is in these days hard to describe the ferment in the preindependence period. All kinds of the movements were happening after World War II and there was a ferment about African independence. Don't forget, India got independence in 1948! (*Laughs.*) And there was a big surge in parts of Asia. Africa coming along with Ghana's independence in 1957. The Portuguese and French were challenged by their African colonies for independence. Liberia, of course, was very old and was not considered

29. Makonnen, ibid., reported that black soldiers in Britain fathered hundreds of "illegitimate" children. In response to this situation he helped to found an orphanage for these children after World War II ended and also tried to find homes for them in the United States. The Daughters of the American Revolution reacted by lobbying for a bill prohibiting children fathered by black men from entering the United States. Makonnen believed that the DAR feared that black fathers might marry the English and Italian mothers and bring them to the States (143).

part of the colonial Africa. Liberia and Ethiopia were independent countries. Ethiopia had been through its Italian syndrome.[30] No. The whole ferment was changed, and I think it was becoming very difficult for this tiny little island of Britain to control so much of other parts of the world.

The emphasis, the night discussions were not about Americans and what was happening to American Negroes. That was a minute part of what was happening. Americans were American citizens, and they were having problems. You had to fight to change it. And we could discuss it on that level. "What was the NAACP doing?" Every African knew about the NAACP and some of the women's organizations. Since I was a member of the National Council of Negro Women, there was a great deal of discussion about that. "What did this women's group do?" It was *wonderful* discussion.

I read in some of your papers that you once told some European labor representatives during a conversation about Indian independence that Africans would be fighting for their rights as well. And they laughed at you and said maybe North Africans but not Africans south of the Sahara.

This was in France. I think I had just been to Denmark and Sweden looking at their very impressive workers' education program. This was kind of just general conversation. And that's all that was. People were not tuned in. Some people were not as ready for black Africa as perhaps they should have been.

When did you first meet Julius Nyerere?

I first met Dr. Nyerere in 1956. A young trade unionist named Maynard Mpangala was attending an international labor seminar in Mexico, and he had been told he had a few days to be in New York City. Of course, there was no money available for him. I was asked to meet with him. I told him that I had an old house in Brooklyn, a mother who liked people and cooked a lot, and two manual typewriters (*laughter*), and that he was welcomed. And my young trade union colleague in this discussion said, "You know, our leader, our teacher is going to be the father of our country. He's going to win independence for us, but we need education. Help us. Help our teacher to find scholarships." Julius Nyerere was a schoolteacher.

---

30. Liberia was founded by the American Colonization Society in 1821 as a place to colonize Northern blacks and ex-slaves of the South. Americo-Liberians ruled the country and greatly oppressed indigenous Africans. United States financial and political interests in Liberia helped to keep it free from European colonization. Ethiopia beat Italy at the 1896 Battle of Adwa and managed to stay independent until Benito Mussolini's invasion succeeded in conquering the country in 1936. Italy was pushed out of the country in 1941 and Emperor Haile Selassie was returned to the throne.

In due course, Mpangala got the message of our conversation to Dr. Nyerere, who was going to the UN as a petitioner.[31] I was going to a meeting in one of those assembly rooms at the UN. I guess both of us had been described to one another. So as we walked toward one another—I was moving from one end and Dr. Nyerere was moving from another—he said, "You're Maida Springer." And I said, "You're Julius Nyerere." That's how we met. He was going to an important meeting and I was going to some noisemaking thing that I was involved in, some protest involving Africa. Dr. Horace Mann Bond, who was the president of Lincoln, was at one of the meetings at the UN.[32] So I said to Dr. Nyerere that this is a man who cares about education in Africa, and he's among the first persons you should meet.

I did not follow what happened after that. But when you make one introduction, a hundred things may flow from that. Once Dr. Nyerere was heard, he was off and running. All sorts of people and organizations were deeply concerned about improving educational opportunities. Certainly the Catholic Church in the United States was, because you had the missions in Tanganyika. Dr. Nyerere was educated in Catholic schools. He *taught* in a Catholic school. So he came here with all kinds of credentials.

How were you first put in touch with Maynard Mpangala?

If you're involved in international trade union activities, there is a network. It is assumed that if you have something to *give* or contribute, you do it, whether it is providing a place to stay or having information run off on a mimeograph machine. All of us who worked in this area contributed what we could. I was a business agent in New York, so everybody was calling me on the telephone. I had a thirteen-and-a-half-room house, an old brownstone, nothing grand or special, but an old house with space and a backyard. Only a few of us lived in it, my mother, myself, and my son. Eric was always away at school, but his space was there. We had a big freezer in the pantry. And my mother loved to cook and loved to pontificate and explain everything. My home was not officially on the international circuit. It was officially so in connection with my work, you know, your nine-to-five or -six arrangements. All after-five events and the people who stayed at my home as a result of meeting me in my office or at the UN were personal things that you elected to do.

31. In December 1956 Nyerere addressed the UN Fourth Committee. Bowing to British request, the U.S. government restricted Nyerere's movements to a few blocks near the United Nations. Houser, *No One Can Stop the Rain*, 66.

32. Horace Mann Bond (1904–1972) was the first alumnus and the first black to become president of Lincoln University. He pursued policies favorable to the enrollment of Africans. Civil rights activist Julian Bond is his son.

Your spirit and that person's spirit or that group connected, and they would meet at your home.

I think one time I think I had the *whole* Ghanaian delegation in my backyard. Dollie [Lowther Robinson] use to tell the story. She would say, "my daughter"—you know this little girl, Jan— "gets invited to all of this. Maida doesn't invite me." (*Laughs.*) Oh, she was there but she was in the kitchen with my mother. Ako Adjei was at Eric's wedding.[33] He was my guest, and I went to the wedding in the Ghanaian embassy car. Later they were going to pour libation and entertain the bride and groom, do a Ghanaian wedding ceremony. But Eric and Cecile didn't know that. They had already gotten on a plane and left for Europe. (*Laughs.*) The Ghanaians were going to surprise us.

Did your local have a lot of contact with the United Nations?

An extreme amount. You must remember all of the terrible things that were happening in Europe. Surviving leaders from Italy, Germany, Spain, these places and many others I have not mentioned visited the International Ladies' Garment Workers' Union. David Dubinsky was *deeply* committed internationally, personally, and trade-union-wise. So they were very supportive of any group, NGOs—nongovernmental organizations—that had a resource they wanted to share with people from overseas at the UN. There were times that you would think that I was a member of some group at the UN because I spent a lot of time there. My union encouraged working part-time, overtime (*laughs*), provided you did all that you had to do in representing the members of your union. I think when the State Department brought groups over and scheduled them in New York, we regularly were asked to do X, Y, and Z to host groups. They would have luncheons, they would have evening meetings, they would come to the executive board meetings to see what we did. We showed them whatever we were doing in the course of that day.

These were labor, government, political delegations. If the State Department asked us—we were not taking the political side—we would do those things that would be supportive. Similarly, we did this for American educators, for many of the universities in this country. They would have programs to bring a delegation of college students to see what workers do in the course of a day. They would learn about piecework, wages, hours. And we had a

33. Eric and Cecile Springer were married in Brooklyn, New York, on October 25, 1958. Adjei was a longtime political associate of Nkrumah's, serving in his government as Ghanaian minister of justice. They both had attended Lincoln University. In 1962 Adjei was arrested on charges of conspiring to assassinate Nkrumah, who kept him in jail after he was acquitted. Adjei was released following the 1966 coup. See McFarland, *Historical Dictionary of Ghana*, 71.

seven-hour day. There were many surprises for these delegations, the kinds of things that unions did on behalf of their dues payers. You know, vacation resorts! Housing. Clinics. Scholarships for their children. I think the Amalgamated, our sister union, was the pioneer in housing and banking. They began *long, long* before the ILG. We were the pioneers in some other things. A labor union, a workers' group, doing this out of their members' dues and investments. One of the things that was particularly effective with foreign trade union leaders was an exposure to our projects. This was my emphasis with African leaders. Yes. The workers in the United States were very, very anxious to be supportive of the new worlds.

I would like to talk with you about meeting Tom Mboya.

Oh, please. I'd love that. Tom was invited to the United States by the American Committee on Africa. It was very deeply involved in what was happening in Africa. I was not officially a member of the American Committee on Africa, but they knew that they could call on me and that I was actively involved in what they were doing. So I agreed that after Tom's arrival and after he spoke at a meeting that had been put together, he would go home with me. I had a little broken-down Ford, which I didn't drive. A friend of mine, the Reverend Dr. Pauli Murray—she wasn't a reverend then—drove this little beat-up Ford. (*Laughs.*) When the meeting was over, we took Tom to Brooklyn to my mother. And she fell in love with him immediately. Tom would sit in the backyard writing notes and doing other things, and she would take him a glass of cold milk and something to snack on. Oh, she loved Tom. Serious young man.

After coming to the United States, of course, everywhere Tom went, he caught on like fire. He was this soft face, beautiful black young man, very black young man, whose mind was like a sharp sword. He could cut through a lot of verbiage and red tape and foolish questions and answer directly to the point, draw you out. Oh, he was wonderful. He was the then general secretary of the Kenya Federation of Labor. He was here talking to the American labor movement.

One meeting was with myself, Jay Lovestone, Irving Brown, and maybe another person, discussing with Tom what it was he needed. It was an exploratory discussion over dinner this Saturday evening in a Chinese restaurant on Third Avenue. He told us about the mass detentions, the plight of Jomo Kenyatta in detention, and the curfew they lived under.

Some of his hosts then arranged for him to go to Unity House, because the AFL-CIO Executive Council was meeting there, to speak with the American labor movement about the problems of the workers. It was a beautiful place to meet. Unity House was the ILGWU's summer home, a vacation center. There was a dining room that seated two thousand, cottages for guests. It was the union's Las Vegas without gambling, and it had decent rates.[34] So he met the Executive Council people and spoke there and, you know (*snaps fingers*), lightning struck and it was wonderful.

Tom was trying to secure two things. One, he said that there needed to be a workers' center. President Meany and the Executive Council saw the validity of such a project. The Kenyan labor movement was under fire, under extreme pressure. And the second was to secure educational opportunities. Kamau Mwangi was the first student he sent to study here, and he stayed at my house.[35] He was a Kikuyu, and Tom thought it was important to present a different image of them from that of the colonialists.

Then other things, small things I arranged for Tom. I arranged for him to meet with some other folk, so the conversations could go on about the things that he was interested in. The African community was under siege and they were under all kinds of restrictions. You had to be off the street by nine o'clock in the evening. Most of the top leadership of the Kenya Federation of Labor were Kikuyus and were in detention, and this twenty-two- or twenty-three-year-old Tom had taken the reins of that union and held it together. So Tom was off and running.

The Kikuyus were considered the strongest tribe in Kenya. And they were the ones that were placed in preventive detention en masse during those days of what was called Mau Mau. The Kikuyus were the people trying to build schools and teach their people. The Kikuyus also had green thumbs. By law, no Africans in Kenya could borrow more than five pounds from a bank in order to work their land. This was about fifteen dollars. And the Kikuyus were challenging these restrictions. These actions were deliberate on the part of the colonial government to make Africans work for the big farms of white

34. Unity House grew out of the efforts of Local 25, out of which Local 22 was later formed, to provide a vacation spot for workers. In 1915 the local rented a house in Pine Hill, New York, for such use. Four years later the ILGWU bought the Old Forest Park Hotel Resort on one thousand acres of land in the Pocono Mountains of Pennsylvania and named it Unity House. Declining union strength led to its demise; it closed in 1989. For more information on Unity House, see Kenneth C. Wolensky, *Fighting for the Union Label: The Women's Garment Industry and the ILGWU in Pennsylvania* (University Park, PA: The Pennsylvania State University Press, 2002).

35. Mwangi was a political science and economics major at Ohio Wesleyan University. Among the many African visitors, he was a favorite of Springer's mother. Stewart agreed to let Mwangi, whom Springer describes as a fine artist, and his colleagues paint a map of Africa in the cemented center of her backyard. Subsequent visitors from West and Central Africa argued that the representation of their countries was too small.

settlers. Europeans came and were loaned money for seed and given great plots of land. These farms could maintain cheap labor and low standards and be prosperous.

Tom Mboya came under a lot of fire because of his relationship with the American labor union.

This is true. In my view I would say this was generated in part by the British TUC (*claps hands*) against whomever they did not like—many in the AFL-CIO. They did not like George Meany. They would say that these activities were involved in politics. But how do you work for change nonpolitically?

How did Mboya handle that type of situation?

Well, by the time Tom became a minister, he was on very shaky ground. You know, as a minister he did not have a strong relationship with the labor movement then. People remained his friends. I was always treated courteously. But he moved away from us. And I would mislead you if I told you otherwise.

What was your relationship like with Tom Mboya's family?

His younger brother, Alphonse Okuku, was in and out of my place in Washington. Well, there were a lot of people who stayed in my apartment. If I was out of town, my secretary Violet Lewis had the key and had a list of people who could stay there. Alphonse Okuku was on a study tour here. My mother and I went to Africa in late 1961 for Tom's wedding and for the independence celebrations of Tanzania. Tom brought Pamela to our home in Brooklyn while she was in college in America and said to my mother—Nobody talked to me! They always talked to my mother—"Mama, I'm going to marry this girl when she finishes school."[36] In due course she graduated, went back home, and worked. I have a picture somewhere around here of us going to the wedding. Tom by this time is a minister, and he's being respected and doing everything all over the country. No, Tom was my second son. We corresponded a lot in those early days.

My mother and I were in East Africa for about four months. We stayed longer than expected because I had to have exploratory surgery. It was nothing that was fatal. But my mother and the labor attaché [Seymour "Cy" Chalfin] and a group of Africans walked into the hospital as they were wheel-

36. The former Pamela Odede, who studied at Western College for Women in Oxford, Ohio, held one of the forty scholarships Mboya secured for Kenyans while on tour in the United States. See David Goldsworthy, *Tom Mboya: The Man Kenya Wanted to Forget* (New York: Africana Publishing Co., 1982), 93, 120.

ing me into the operating room with all the bottles over my head.[37] I was unconscious. My mother carried on terribly. She stretched out on the floor. She thought I was dead, and they'd killed me. The young Africans bent down and told her that she must not make Mama Maida ashamed. Fortunately, she was in the Aga Khan hospital, so that her carrying on was accepted. It was all right. (*Laughs.*) No one was going to be offended. They simply wanted to help her and tell her that it wasn't serious, but they just had to do a test. The next day the labor attaché and the boys all told me how my mother behaved. You know, she didn't have anyone else. I was her only child. And here she was in a strange country. And they're moving me on a stretcher into the operating room.

Do you want to talk about how you ended up at the Aga Khan hospital?

Oh my. Very simple. The surgeon in charge was an English doctor, a very learned man on tropical diseases. The assumption was that I had developed some tropical disease. Something was eating my insides. The one hospital where all of the services were available was the European hospital.[38] Both the specialist and my local doctor had been there for a couple of years. I said that I would not go there. They were appalled at my behavior. And again my mother had reason to say if she had had me in a hospital, she would disown me, because she said, you know, they can kill you. They can slip the knife on you. So I told her I can die once only, but I would not go to the European hospital for them to mistreat any Africans who might come to see me. Tom Mboya, they wouldn't dare. But other Africans who had their torn jackets on they just felt they could mistreat. And I said if I know that any African coming to the European hospital was mistreated—I said normally they won't let them in there anyway, but since I am there, they would have to let them come to see me—I said I would pull all the tubes out of me; I would break all the furniture. And you know, I was unreasonable but I did not go. I went to the brand-new Aga Khan hospital where I was welcomed and I was happy.

37. Chalfin was formerly the labor attaché at the U.S. Embassy in Ghana. Also present at the hospital at this time were labor leaders Anselmi Karumba, Fred Kubai, and Maynard Mpangala. While Springer was in the hospital, Karumba, who was from the Kenyan garment workers, held a union meeting there for domestic workers. Springer speculated in her diary that the meeting was ending because she was overhearing the workers singing "Solidarity Forever" in English and Swahili. Springer, diary entries, January 23 and 24, 1962.

38. During the early part of her trip Springer was under the care of Dr. Haddock at the Ocean Road Hospital in Tanganyika. In Kenya she was under the care of diagnostician Dr. F. A. Thompson and surgical specialist Dr. Wilfred Barber. Springer, diary entries, January 2 and 22, 1962.

The International Affairs Arena

And I had just met the Aga Khan sometime before that when he came to East Africa. He was a very, very young man.[39]

My mother's relationships with Africans were so good that I could have gone home.[40] (*Laughs.*) And the only concern they would have had, is Mama Maida going to be able to follow through on A, B, and C agenda. Insofar as charm, my mother had it. She shared their interests and had a sense of awareness of what they had and didn't have. Her own mother as a young woman in Panama was an entrepreneur, had the tinsmith build her a big baking oven. My mother was wonderful with the women and just generally wonderful with everybody.

We met Fred Kubai and his wife when we went to Africa. Fred had been in detention. He was a top labor leader and a Kikuyu, so he was jailed with Kenyatta and all of the other high-profile Kikuyus. His wife was threatened, but she maintained the farm and she was a manager par excellence and kept the fires going. My mother and Mrs. Kubai got along like bread and cheese. There was a community of interests. I was nice and I was in the labor movement and I was going to be doing something and I was involved with her husband, but she was in love with my mother. They understood one another. When I was ill and I'd had surgery, *every day* Fred Kubai's wife brought fresh vegetables and fruit to the house we were living in. It is through Fred Kubai and particularly his wife that we became involved in the Indian community they knew.

A funnier side to that, through the Kubais we met this wealthy Indian family. They had magnificent soirees, a film room where they showed films, and the wife grew *beautiful* flowers. My mother had a green thumb. Her eyes just fluttered. So they gave my mother all kinds of seeds to plant when she returned home. I did not know this. My mother tied a big bandeau around

39. The Aga Khan is the honorific title given to the leader of the Shia Imamai Ismaili Muslims. In 1957, at the age of twenty, Prince Karim Al-Husayni Aga Khan IV interrupted his studies at Harvard University to assume his new duties as the forty-ninth Imam upon the death of his grandfather, the Aga Khan III. Enthronement ceremonies were held in Dar-es-Salaam, Nairobi, and Kampala just as Springer arrived in East Africa in connection with the AFL-CIO scholarship program. See Shah Karim Al-Husseini, Ismaili History, First Ismaili Electronic Library and Database, http://ismaili.net/html/ (accessed November 22, 2003).

40. Among the many people who entertained Adina Stewart were Tom and Pamela Mboya and Peter Mbiyu Koinange, son of Senior Chief Koinange. Koinange's sister, Grace Wanjiku, married Jomo Kenyatta in 1946. In 1960 British Colonial Secretary Iain Macleod and others had waged what later turned out to be an unsuccessful attempt to prevent Koinange from participating in a conference to consider Kenya's constitutional status by stating that he was wanted in Kenya in connection with Mau Mau. Following independence, Koinange served in a number of ministerial posts.

her with these seeds. She did not say a word until she realized that we might be searched in U.S. customs. And first of all my luggage was overweight, but that you could pay for. They came to the airport to see us off with all sorts of gifts you shouldn't have on the plane. (*Laughs.*) They brought her fine embroidery, they brought baskets of fruit and much more. But she never said a word about these seeds until we were on line for customs. And then she told me about these seeds. No, that was a shock. And I told her that there are all sorts of strange things that can happen to a person who is in the workers' movement because of strikes and other things, but I did not think I would go to jail because my mother had illegal seeds. (*Laughs.*) Well, my mother found one of the examiners was Spanish speaking. So they greeted one another and she told him about where she came from in Panama, and he came from some place close to there. And we sailed through customs with my mother's seeds and too much luggage.

5

African Policy Conflicts within the International Confederation of Free Trade Unions

In 1955 Maida Springer visited the Gold Coast (now Ghana) as the only woman to attend a three-week seminar sponsored by the International Confederation of Free Trade Unions (ICFTU).[1] Her second trip was as an observer to the first ICFTU African Regional Conference, held again in Ghana in 1957. Afterward she traveled to East Africa before returning to Ghana for the March 6 independence celebrations. Her third trip to the continent placed her in East Africa in the fall of 1957 where she served as the special representative for what turned out to be the ill-fated AFL-CIO Scholarship Program for African Trade Unionists. Her job was to help facilitate the selection of eight to ten scholarship recipients to attend the Harvard Labor Management Industrial Relations Center.

Springer relates the astonishment that her European colleagues expressed during the 1955 ICFTU seminar when they realized the extent of her insider status in African political circles. During the time of the seminar she met Kwame Nkrumah, who served as leader of the Gold Coast's Convention People's Party. The party's nonviolent "positive action" campaign, which made use of boycotts, strikes, civil disobedience, and noncooperation, had landed Nkrumah in jail in 1948 and again in 1950. While in jail he was elected to the Legislative Assembly in February 1951 and then was released to assume the position of the leader of government and business. In 1952 he became prime minister.

On her trips to East Africa Springer was embraced by workers, political leaders, and ordinary Africans. In addition to building a deeper friendship with Julius Nyerere, leader of the Tanganyika African National Union (TANU), Springer became close to Rashidi Mfaume Kawawa, who served as the first head of the Tanganyika Federation of Labor (TFL). In 1958 he won a seat in the Legislative

---

1. Labor delegates from seventeen countries of Africa, Asia, Europe, and the Western Hemisphere were in attendance at the 1955 ICFTU seminar. The agenda focused on working and living conditions of agricultural workers and problems of trade union organization and administration.

Council (LEGCO) and two years later became vice president of TANU. Since independence Kawawa's posts have included second vice president, minister for defense and national service, prime minister, and secretary-general and vice chair of Chama Cha Mapinduzi (CCM, Revolutionary Party), the successor to TANU. Although he retired in 1992, he was appointed chair of the CCM's Board of Trustees in 1997.[2]

Springer also began a friendship with Bibi (a term of respect used to address women) Titi Mohamed (c. 1925–2000). As the first woman and the sixteenth person to join TANU, Bibi Titi played a major role in drawing in the female membership and building the nationalist movement. With the female membership of TANU in 1955 greater than the male, women's activism served as an impetus to men joining. Bibi Titi became a LEGCO member in 1960 and served as junior minister of Labor and Community Development. Two years after her 1967 resignation from the TANU executive committee due to health problems, she faced serious political problems. Charged along with six others with involvement in an alleged plot to overthrow the government, Bibi Titi was given a sentence of life in prison. Two years later, Nyerere pardoned her, and subsequently her property was restored. She remained a strong political force in her country until her death.[3]

Springer relates how these friendships and others helped to sustain her and keep her focused on her mission as special representative for the scholarship program during her three-month stay in the region. She remarks on the outright hostility that colonial officials, her British Trades Union Congress (TUC) colleagues, and many in the broader ICFTU expressed toward her presence. The Kenyan colonial government's state of emergency in reaction to the Mau Mau uprising affected all of East Africa and did not bode well for her reception.[4] Under the emergency, which lasted from 1952 until the end of 1959, the Gikuyu, in particular, were subjected on a mass scale to suffering and torture. Africans in general had to abide by a curfew.

Springer notes how her relationships with African labor caused the profitable

2. See "Tanzania's Ruling Party Secretariat Gets New Leaders," Xinhua News Agency (Dar es Salaam, Tanzania), November 15, 1997, item no. 1115156, http://www.chinaonline.com/refer/ministry_profiles/co1041767.asp. Xinhua News Agency is China's state news agency under the State Council.

3. See Susan Geiger, *TANU Women: Gender and Culture in the Making of Tanganyikan Nationalism, 1955–1965* (Portsmouth, NH: Heinemann, 1997).

4. The colonial government killed thousands, arrested well over 100,000, and arbitrarily placed tens of thousands without trial in detention camps where many died under atrocious conditions. By 1954 those labeled Mau Mau had killed 1,186 people, of whom 24 were Europeans, 17 Asians, and 1,145 Africans. See Joseph Wershba, "Tom Mboya: Voice of the New Africa," *New York Post*, April 19, 1959; and Mboya, "Land Question—Key to Kenya Strife," *International Free Trade Union News* 11 (December 1956).

sisal industry to view her presence as a threat.[5] She bitterly recalls the negative references to her in newspapers, particularly the article "Wind in the Sisal: A Busy Time for the Law," published in the *Tanganyika Weekly News*. It stated, "That busy little American Negress who has done so much both in cash and in kind for Kenya's Federation of Labor, Mrs. Maida Springer, is active now in Tanganyika on a new 'goodwill mission.'"[6] Colonial sympathizers pointed to the widespread corruption and connections to organized crime in the International Brotherhood of Teamsters (IBT) to discredit the AFL-CIO by portraying the federation as a whole as corrupt. The AFL-CIO expelled the IBT following the probes of the union's activities by a Senate investigating committee.[7]

The rivalries between AFL and CIO leaders also complicated Springer's activism. Although the two federations had merged in 1955, the competition and policy differences continuously plagued the federation and, as Springer recounts, wreaked havoc on her African programs and projects. Her association with Jay Lovestone may have impeded CIO leaders Walter and Victor Reuther from seeking her expertise in the field of African labor relations and led them to ally with European leaders against the appeals of African leaders.

Springer recalls the policy battles that the AFL leaders had with ICFTU and CIO leaders over U.S. labor activity on the continent. The ICFTU, with eventual CIO support, argued against Africans studying abroad in favor of "on-the-spot training" confined to Africa. Taking Africans outside the continent to advanced industrial societies, they argued, would make them, though presumably not other groups, discontented with their lot and ultimately prove a wasteful expenditure. They held that AFL-CIO assistance in general was counterproductive because it inhibited Africans from becoming self-reliant. In this, too, they treated Africans with a double standard. They criticized the AFL-CIO's decision to give a $35,000 grant to the Kenya Federation of Labor to help build a labor center. However, two years earlier in 1955, when the CIO gave the Israeli labor movement, Histadrut, $100,000 for the same purpose, there was no outcry.[8]

5. For more information on Springer's role in agricultural organizing in East Africa, see Yevette Richards, *Maida Springer: Pan-Africanist and International Labor Leader* (Pittsburgh: University of Pittsburgh Press, 2000), 139–41.

6. The paper is dated November 15, 1957, 60/23, Lovestone files.

7. The Senate Select Committee on Improper Activities in the Labor or Management Field was under the chair of John L. McClellan, who chose Robert Kennedy as chief counsel. Dave Beck, IBT president, was sent to prison in 1958 and his successor, Jimmy Hoffa (1913–1975?), was sent in 1967. In 1975 Hoffa mysteriously disappeared. It is largely believed that organized crime forces murdered him. Various IBT leaders have been prosecuted from 1957 into the 1990s for corruption. The IBT rejoined the AFL in 1988.

8. Victor Reuther to Jacob H. Oldenbroek (ICFTU general secretary), August 21, 1955, AFL-CIO Reel 1, Microfilm on the ICFTU African Labor College, International Institute for Social History, Amsterdam, The Netherlands.

Ultimately, AFL leaders agreed to curtail the scholarship program and to desist from future independent activity in Africa. Three Africans already chosen for the program by the time of the compromise were allowed to attend the renowned Harvard center along with eleven trade unionists from the United States, eight from Europe, and one each from the Philippines, Peru, and Thailand.[9] In exchange for AFL-CIO cooperation, the ICFTU agreed to establish the ICFTU African Labor College in Kampala, Uganda. Kampala College counted among its objectives training organizers and officials and training trade union teachers to administer rank-and-file training programs. Milton Obote's government forced its closure in 1968.

Springer recalls the activism of African American George McCray, who served as an instructor at the school. An employee of the Illinois State Employment Agency, McCray had served as president of Chicago's CIO Local 1006 of the Government and Civic Employees Organizing Committee (later changed after the merger to the American Federation of State, County and Municipal Employees [AFSCME]). He also had served as chair of the Pan-African Labor Council of the CIO. While teaching workers' education in Ghana in early 1958, on leave from his job, McCray became close to many African labor and nationalist leaders. He served as instructor at the Ugandan school longer than any non-African. The school's goal of having an all-African staff was accomplished by 1965 when he left the college for a position with the AFL-CIO's newly established African-American Labor Center. He reportedly remained in Africa for the rest of his life.

Springer speaks in more detail about her relationship with Kenyan leader Tom Mboya. As a service to the Kenyan labor movement, she worked to secure a tripartite agreement in 1963 with the AFL-CIO, Neue Heimat (New Home Town, the German Federation of Labor's housing development), and the Kenyan government to build low-income housing for workers near Nairobi. Neue Heimat started after World War II as a union-owned firm building low-rent housing for millions of German workers and became the largest housing developer in Europe.[10] Springer describes an unsettling meeting that she and a Neue Heimat representative had with Mboya, who was sustaining heavy attacks in Kenyan political circles. Disheartened by the interactions of this meeting and faced with a growing responsibility to her aging family members, Springer began to rethink the effectiveness of her activism in Africa.

9. Dishan William Kiwanuka, "Report on the African Trade Union Program Sponsored by the AFL-CIO" [1958] (Amistad).

10. More recently the DGB (German Federation of Labor) decided to sell Neue Heimat and other business ventures because of a long-running financial scandal plaguing the enterprise. See David Goodhart, "W. German Unions Pulling Out of Industry," *Financial Times* (London), May 29, 1990, section I, p. 4.

African Policy Conflicts within the ICFTU

F. E. [Francis Edward] Tachie-Menson was responsible for your first trip to Africa. Talk about your relationship with him.

F. E. Tachie-Menson had been the president of the Gold Coast [later Ghana] TUC early on. He was a very low-key, yet jolly man and was in the ministry of labor. I first met him in 1955 on his trip to the United States. Well, if you were an African in those early days and you were in the labor union and if you were in New York City, willy-nilly, you were going to be sent to my office. Tachie-Menson then requested of the ICFTU my presence at the ICFTU international seminar in Accra in 1955. The communication that I read thirty years later was that he was interested in organization of women. His plea to the ICFTU was that here was this black American lady who in effect could be a role model in talking to women who were moving into the workforce in Ghana.[11] So they passed the communication around to the Americans who were one of the large members of the ICFTU. And it came to pass that I was invited, I was asked. For their sins, I think ICFTU officials regretted it.[12]

North Africans were at that meeting, and a great labor leader from Tunisia [Farhat Hachid] had just been murdered.[13] So we all had a time of silence in respect of this labor leader. That was something you would not forget. It was my first such conference, and the earnestness of the men attending that conference—I was the only woman (*chuckles*)—impressed me very much. It was doubly impressive for the reason that most of the black Africans had gotten much of their training from correspondence courses. So that told me that their desire for education was such, that they studied very hard. The level of the discussions was very high. It was a challenge for those of us who thought we were hot stuff. (*Laughs.*) It was very impressive. And, of course, we were hosted by the soon to be independent government of Ghana.

11. Tachie-Menson, who also served as a government minister, helped to arrange Springer's first visit to Africa. He first met her earlier in 1955 during her U.S. tour under the auspices of the State Department's International Education Exchange Program. See Tachie-Menson to Oldenbroek, September 2, 1955, 4/17 (Brown files).

12. Springer responds in this way because African labor leaders after meeting her looked to her for support because they considered the ICFTU paternalistic.

13. Three years later the anniversary of Farhat Hachid's death would fall during the All-African People's Conference, where he was again remembered with a moment of silence. Springer, "Observations on the All-African People's Conference held in Accra, Ghana, December 5–13, 1958, and Its Trade Union Implications," 14/12/11 (ILGWU Archives).

And I had my own special arrangements. Through my London friends notice had been sent out that I was coming. It was George Padmore who gave me a letter of introduction to meet Dr. Nkrumah. I don't know what he said in the letter, but the evening after my arrival, Kojo Botsio, who was to become the foreign minister, was in my hotel.[14] He had driven to meet me with the flags flying on his car. This had everybody's eyes popping and mine, *too*. That was very exciting and very important to a neophyte in African politics. This attention made some of the leaders of the ICFTU *very* curious. (*Laughing.*) They didn't know my connections, so it was a surprise. They wondered how does she know these African government leaders?

Whatever Padmore said, evidently, was positive, because Kojo Botsio had an invitation for me to come to dinner at his home. I guess he wanted to look me over to see whether Dr. Nkrumah should pay any attention to me. (*Laughs.*) Ah, yes. I went to Kojo Botsio's home and talked with him and others. There were just a few of us. His wife was hostess. His talk with me was to sound me out, I guess. This was my first intimate glimpse into high protocol. There was no serious talk. This dinner was a social occasion.

And then after that, of course, I was invited to meet Kwame Nkrumah who was then prime minister. It was a brief meeting of welcoming. It may have been on this occasion that I took to him a greeting from the president of the seafarers' union. Years ago when he was here in the United States, he had been a member of the seafarers' union. He had had summer jobs while he was in the university.[15]

A couple of years later I had lunch with him at State House. This was before independence. He wanted to talk to me about the union. And he wanted to talk to me about my work. There were one or two other persons at the luncheon. There could be a witness to the discussion if he wanted. He wanted to hear what this woman had to say. I was in a peculiar position in any case. A woman, in the labor movement, and black.

14. Kojo Botsio (d. 2001) met Kwame Nkrumah in London in 1945 and helped found the Gold Coast Convention People's Party. Botsio served as the first general secretary. After independence he served in a variety of ministerial posts. Although he was out of favor with the Nkrumah government from 1961 to 1963, he was with Nkrumah when he died in Rumania in April 1972. He later was detained by the regime of Ignatius Kutu Acheampong, who ruled Ghana from 1972 to 1978. Before his death Botsio helped to establish the latest Nkrumaist political party, also called the Convention People's Party. See "A Statesman Is Gone," *Africa News*, February 27, 2001.

15. Kwame Nkrumah lived in the United States from 1935 to 1945. While attending Lincoln University, he worked in the summers on a ship until World War II started. He rose from dishwasher to waiter and then messenger, the highest position a black crew member could attain. See Yuri Smertin, *Kwame Nkrumah* (New York: International Publishers, 1987), 14–15.

What sort of tensions were there between African trade unions and the ICFTU during the colonial period?

Well, before I tell you about the tensions, let me speak about what was positive. The International Confederation of Free Trade Unions was that body of fifty-seven unions worldwide that were a part of the free labor movement, the "anti-Communist" group of trade unions. Within that group you had the countries with large colonial dependencies. For example, the British Trades Union Congress was a member of the ICFTU. The Belgian trade unions were a part of the ICFTU. Part of the French trade unions belonged. In France there were a number of divisions. You also had a group of unions belonging to a Christian federation [The International Federation of Christian Trade Unions, founded 1920] and a group of unions belonging to the World Federation of Trade Unions, which was the Communist-bloc trade union federation, the Eastern bloc.

When the trade unions in these African countries organized a sector of the labor force, that made them a part of the International Confederation of Free Trade Unions because of their relationship to the mother country—to Britain, to France, to Belgium—whose trade unions were members of the ICFTU. Therefore, there were opportunities for these men to go to these countries and be given scholarships to study in these countries. It also afforded them the occasion and opportunity to travel abroad beyond those countries to the United States, because we were members in the ICFTU. We didn't have any colonies.

When you met in international conferences, these men, who were delegated from their African countries to be a part of the ICFTU delegation, would raise all sorts of questions about colonialism and independence and where did the trade union movement stand on these things. The American trade unions were home free. They could speak sharply about colonialism and the end of colonialism, which, of course, annoyed (*chuckles*) their European counterparts. While the Europeans wanted all trade unions to be free, it was an irritant to have the American labor movement aggressively out there. And Philip Randolph and George Meany were among the chief challengers. When Philip Randolph spoke as a vice president of the AFL-CIO, why, the African trade unionists would bring the house down.[16]

So the problems of the African trade unions were in the context that they were a part of the colonial government which the Africans were challenging.

16. African delegates met Randolph's speech denouncing colonialism before the 1957 ICFTU Congress in Tunis, Tunisia, with great cheer. It was entitled "The Meaning of Human Rights" (MSK PP).

African Policy Conflicts within the ICFTU

So there had to be irritation because while the Europeans believed in free-dom of association, they didn't want you *insulting* their countries about colo-nialism. They said that was going to go and hmm, mm, mm, mm [indicating other such platitudes], but national pride was hurt. (*Chuckles.*)

During the colonial period, how much autonomy did African trade unionists have over their labor movement?

Very little. The unions were very small except for the mine workers and railway workers because a lot of labor was needed to extract materials to send out to these European countries. Under the law any group—if I remember the legislation—of five or seven people could get together to form a union. A group like that has no strength, no organization. Secondly, in many parts of the country where you had ethnic differences, there could be problems. For example, with the mine workers it was easy to get someone to be a leader who would bring in members of his tribe. And the governing European coun-try then would tacitly agree. With that sort of organization you could really not develop much strength, because you then had a tribal basis for employ-ment. And people would begin to be antagonized not as much about the conditions under which they worked but about their tribal relationships. It was as though in the United States you had poor blacks and poor whites suf-fering, but the white employer could always point out to the white worker— even though he was starving also—that he was superior to that black worker. I don't have to pay you much more, just a little more. The technique was somewhat the same. The employers used whatever circumstances there are to limit challenges for improved conditions and increased wages. Nothing was written in stone, but they simply utilized what made it possible for you to do very little for the working class. But people overcame that and began *to see* that their focus had to be on the challenge to the employer and the chal-lenge to the government. The government had a more direct input because the major industries reflected the government's needs—coal, oil, gold, and diamonds. (*Chuckles.*) All that good stuff.

In your diary you mentioned that you were going to meet with J. A. Rogers on October 5, 1957, just before going to Africa for the American Trade Union Schol-arship Program.

Oh what an experience that always was. You know, you can just drink in the things that people say to you who are so full of the history. They are talk-ing about what you have never read. You had to begin with Lesson 101. I was very fortunate in those days to have so many people take time to open my ears to help me to understand. They thought I was a good candidate because I had a family background . . . my mother was *passionate* about Africa. That he knew. Everybody knew everybody. He knew that my mother had been a Garveyite and that I had grown up in those early days in Garvey Hall sitting with my mother, drinking in what the Garveyites were saying. So they were interested in me for that reason. Not that I did anything special. (*Laughs.*) He was a very, very controversial and famous writer in the black community, and he was a historian. Before I met him he had written a piece about local people and one was about me—I was a union officer. He wrote pieces about personalities. And then we had mutual friends, and then I met him. He gave me a set of almost all of his books. Some of them I still have. Others people have taken away.[17]

How did this American Trade Union Scholarship Program for Africa come about in 1957, and how were you picked to administer it?[18]

I had been in some countries in Africa, had spent a year at Ruskin College, and had listened to many Africans. And I had some very strong views about Africa. The AFL-CIO Executive Council wanted to know the best way to advance the trade union activities now that Africans were moving toward independence. This particular scholarship project was a subject of discussions within the AFL-CIO council. I wrote a little memorandum on that program. A. Philip Randolph, a vice president of the AFL-CIO, had a very strong voice on the council. He was a supporter 100 percent. He said we should do it, and we should do it now. The council resolved that they would sponsor the program. So all of the wheels got in motion.

The prime movers among the council for this program were A. Philip Randolph, Walter Reuther, and, of course, Mr. Meany. Mr. Meany has been given a great deal of harsh treatment, and he was a conservative, but from where I sat he was a man of principle. There were the classic incidents like the argument that George Meany and Philip Randolph had, when Meany asked who gave you the authority to speak for all black workers? But these two men respected one another. What was said then was not really how they functioned and worked together.[19] For the years that I worked for the AFL-CIO, Mr. Meany never was hostile about any request that I made.

There was only one time he refused my request flatly. A group of young trade unionists from an African country wanted the AFL-CIO to build a little

17. Maida Springer, in J. A. Rogers, "Your History," *Pittsburgh Courier*, April 19, 1952 (MSK PP). For another observation of J. A. Rogers, see Kenneth King, ed., *Ras Makonnen: Pan-Africanism from Within* (New York: Oxford University Press, 1973), 84–85.
18. For details on the AFL-CIO scholarship program, see Richards, *Maida Springer*, 130–51.
19. Jervis Anderson, *A. Philip Randolph: A Biographical Portrait* (Berkeley and Los Angeles: University of California Press, 1972), also asserts that despite their clash, Meany and Randolph respected one another (304).

hotel for their federation. They said their union people who came in from the country needed some place to stay, and the hotel could be commercially viable. But of course it couldn't be. I really didn't want to raise the request with Mr. Meany because I knew it had a poor chance of being accepted. But I tried for the group. He raised his eyebrows as we talked about it. He said among the things that the AFL-CIO does not do, we're not building commercial buildings (*laughing*) for unions anywhere. If they want to do it and have the money, OK. The AFL-CIO built a lot of buildings here, but we had the money for it, and we were not asking anybody. But everything else I ever sent—and I sent memorandums all the time—was considered.

My discussions about the scholarship program were with many AFL-CIO leaders. My argument had been that until the young African learns to sit across the bargaining table with an employer, not as a supplicant or an inferior, but as one who has the knowledge to talk about contracts and agreements, the trade unions would not be strong. The young trade unionist has to know something about international agreements and be able to speak on that level. He has to know the course to pursue, whether it is in East Africa or in some other country, so that he can evaluate intelligently. He has to *know* about all of these things, to know what the dockworkers are doing and be able to have an exchange of view. If he had this training for six months or nine months, he would go home with instruments that could serve his country and serve the labor movement. This was my simplistic approach.[20]

My second point of view in favor of the program was this. I was not a part of the leadership of the AFL-CIO, but I could just go and shout and say what I observed, since I was going back and forth to Africa all the time. I said that the exposure outside of their countries would be so meaningful for the Africans and that I disliked the custom of the British TUC and other European delegations coming to Africa for three weeks, holding a seminar, and then leaving and going back to their country. As useful as that might be, I did not think it was sufficient training. I felt that the trade union leadership was so young and so weak that they needed something with more bite in it and which would give them greater exposure and confidence. And this was the first step, the scholarship program.

Harvard had a trade union scholarship program, but they had never had Africans. The intention, I think, was to begin with ten or twelve scholarships. I was to have an office in Africa in order to facilitate the administration of the program. So I opened an office in Dar es Salaam.

20. Springer responds in this manner because a lot of opposition to the program soon developed in the United States and in Europe.

I was interviewed in London on the way to do the scholarship program. I told George Padmore the people I had seen and the buildings I had been in. George then explained to me whom I had seen, what their connections were. The equivalent of a CIA official was a person who had interviewed me. George then made it a point to take me first to the Ghana embassy and to other places and explained to me about protocol. He took me around London and gave me a liberal education on what I could expect when I got to Africa. The scholarship program had created a furor in British government circles. So George told me this is why they wanted to see you, because he had it all at his fingertips. He helped me not to stub my toes as much as I would have, I am sure.

Well, the program didn't last long, and it offended a whole lot of people in the international community and raised a great storm in the United States. At a late date, I think, just before I left the country for Tanganyika, there were people who felt that we ought to wait. There were some people who had such views that it was too hastily put together. I wasn't at the AFL-CIO convention that decided to stop the program.[21] I was still in East Africa. At that convention I think the Teamsters were thrown out of the AFL-CIO because of their alleged bad connections. But that convention was a turning point in terms of African relationships.

The program was killed, withdrawn with the proviso that a trade union residential school with lecturers from the International Confederation of Free Trade Unions be built in Africa. This was the compromise. And again choices had to be made as to where it would be built and who would be on staff. I am very glad that my small voice in this helped to see that the college was built in Uganda. So for all of English-speaking Africa, you had this beautiful center, the ICFTU African Labor College in Kampala, Uganda, for many years. It had three-month or six-month programs for trade unionists. I was never a participant in the school, but that was all right. Africa attained the Uganda school, so I have no quarrel with that compromise. It had African teachers. One was from Kenya, an economist. There were people from Sweden, people from the UK and other places. There was an American from Chicago, George McCray, who was African to his toenails. (*Laughter.*)[22]

21. The AFL-CIO convention took place in Atlantic City, New Jersey, in early December 1957.
22. In this portion of an early interview Springer downplays her extreme disappointment over the scholarship program's curtailment. For more information regarding the ICFTU African Labor College, see Richards, *Maida Springer*, 147, 148, 151–56, 192, 255.

Before George McCray worked at the ICFTU African Labor College, I knew of him rather generally as someone who was a committed person, very active in the labor movement in Chicago. And then he came into the international arena. He moved out of AFSCME and worked in Africa. Any likable person and interesting person, someone with talent and caring about the African experience like George McCray, would be a must. So here was this black man with this long history. I think I was told that his family was involved in the Garvey movement. This was unusual. I thought only New Yorkers (*laughs*) were Garveyites and Caribbean people.

Africans felt very strongly about the college and who should run it and felt very strongly that they had been done a disservice when the scholarship program was canceled. George was welcomed at the college. And they had some particular feelings about me. They thought I was for real and a person *really* concerned about education, about opportunity for Africans.

How was Dar es Salaam chosen as your center for the 1957 scholarship program?

Oh, we talked about it and thought about it. My feeling was this, and people concurred with it. We knew a lot about West Africa. We didn't know a great deal about East and Central and South Africa, where the heat and the fire was going to be. If the program was located in East Africa, it would help to bring a greater focus to that area and a greater opportunity for the people there, because East Africans had not had the educational advantages and exposure that West Africans had.

What was your reception like when you arrived in Dar es Salaam?

If I had not been old and had a fairly steady head on me and conscious of what the colonial office would do to me in terms of sabotage, I would have been giddy, out of my mind beyond belief, because there was constant harassment. But there was a lovingness, there was a welcoming, that was almost like a religion from the African community. Whenever I arrived at the airport, there was a big commotion. (*Laughs.*) On this occasion the colonial government was making a fuss, because the taxi drivers wanted to greet me. The taxi drivers in a tradition of welcome put small branches of trees with green leaves on the hoods or sides of their cars to welcome me. They wanted to do something special. They were going to take their lunch hour or some time off to come en masse to the airport to greet their "Mama Maida," when the government told them that they would be treated harshly, that they couldn't do that, and that their employers didn't want them to do it. So what the *askaris*, the police, did on that occasion was to rim the airport with sandbags and guns. (*Speaking softly.*) When I came out of customs and everybody was . . . (*softly imitates cheering*). I was quietly told, this is for you, the police and the

African Policy Conflicts within the ICFTU

sandbags. They made it appear as if I were going to make a riot.[23] No one would rent me a place to stay.

I read in your letters to the States that when you first came there to start the scholarship program, you stayed in a place where chiefs and government officials usually stayed. There were no hotel rooms available because of the coronation of the Aga Khan that was then taking place.[24]

The hotels had space. They wouldn't give me a room. By then the government had frightened them so that it was a negative to rent to me. Before they knew me, the name "Maida Springer" could have led them to believe I was an English woman. But now Maida Springer was "that busy Negress from the United States."[25] Finally, they agreed to let a man who had just built a building rent the building to me provided he would keep tabs on me. The union, the Tanganyika Federation of Labor, had their headquarters downstairs and I lived upstairs. (*Wistfully.*) So much crammed in so short of time.

So I was not liked by the local government. In the first place, I was the guest of the trade union movement of Tanganyika. Number two, I was in contact, in friendly relations with TANU. TANU was challenging the government. Julius Nyerere, the president of TANU, was the man that they were calling the (*with a British accent*) "irresponsible agitator." So I was an irritant to the colonial government because I was positive and cared about what was happening and was hoping that Tanganyika was a part of the future for independence.

In your letters you said that it was good for the community that you occupied the building you did in Tanganyika.

Sure. The building is in the heart of the African community on [22] Wanyamwezi Street in Dar es Salaam. I said it was good for the community because the TFL had office space and my house was open. You may see some pictures somewhere around here with children wearing silly hats. This was

23. About two hundred trade unionists and friends, including Julius Nyerere, welcomed Springer at the airport on October 18, 1957. For more on the reactions of colonial governments to Springer's presence, see ibid., 134–39. Springer recorded (diary entry, October 18, 1957) that she had been subjected to a rigorous customs search in Dar es Salaam for forbidden literature and other goods.

24. In a letter written to Jennie Silverman dated October 27, 1957, Springer stated that her temporary stay in this place was a feat, considering the "disquiet with which the project has been regarded" (MSK PP). Springer arrived in Dar es Salaam the day before the coronation ceremony of the Aga Khan, which was attended by thirty thousand Ismailis. See Shah Karim Al-Husseini, Ismaili History, First Ismaili Electronic Library and Database, http://ismaili.net/html/ (accessed November 22, 2003).

25. Quote is from "Wind in the Sisal: A Busy Time for the Law," Tanganyika *Weekly News*, November 15, 1957.

a Christmas party on the roof of my house. We were sitting on those chairs that the woodworkers built and serving the children sweets and cake and samosas and something to drink. Of course, I was green. I was living in a Muslim community, in a non-Christian community, a mixed community, and I had a Christmas party. I called it a Christmas party, but if I had called it something else, it would have been wonderful still.

People realized that this is Bibi Maida. That's what I mean by it was good for the community, that I was not exclusive. I did not go to live somewhere fancy—not even fancy but away from the African community. I did not go to live in the white oceanfront houses. I'm not living in a hotel. I'm living in the midst of the African community. I go to the *sekoni*, to the market, to buy my vegetables and meat and fish. And I insisted on doing that myself, because many in the community didn't think that I should be busy with shopping. But I said, "How will I learn?" So I would go with Mzee Hemb, who guarded the building where I lived.

The woodworkers and carpenters had a meeting, and they said for Bibi Maida they must make the furniture for her apartment. The building had a courtyard, and the unemployed carpenters set up their tools and worked there. I think they made at least four dozen chairs without a nail. They were built with pegs and were for the roof of my house where you gave sundowners and entertained. The only thing that was bought was the bed, because I had to have some place to sleep right away. But everything else was made by the woodworkers and carpenters' union of Tanganyika—my eating tables, my worktables, the table in my office. To see before your eyes every day the work they had accomplished was amazing. The men who were employed would work in the evening as long as there was light.

You had known the TFL assistant general secretary Maynard Mpangala since his 1956 trip to the United States.

Yes. He was like my young son, and his family became part of my life. He was working for no money. They all did not have enough food, and you would attempt to do little, little things to be helpful. I had great affection, very warm feelings for Maynard and his family. They were a part of my family in East Africa in Tanganyika. I saw him every day except when he had to go off and organize somewhere else. But I saw him; I saw them all, all the time. This was my life. I didn't have anybody else. I didn't know anybody else.

The government did everything to make you uncomfortable while at the same time being very charming on the surface. For about a month many mornings I had to report to the principal immigration officer, and he would say (*with a British accent*), "Mrs. Springer, *it is* not clear what you mean by" whatever it was I had written on my itinerary.[26] In three months in order to help facilitate the selection of trade unionists, I was going to travel first to Uganda, then Kenya, and then to the Sudan and then across the continent, west. That first part of the itinerary I gave them, I submit, was too simple; it was too clear-cut. My commas were evidently in the wrong place or something, because often they would *send* someone over to say that, "The principal immigration officer would like to see Mrs. Springer at nine o'clock." You get up early in the morning. So I would go over and explain whatever was requested.

Part of the reason they did this was to make me angry and blow up and be insulting. I never did. I'd go and say, "Yes sir. I assume it's my fault. I probably was not clear. And this is what I mean. And I will be back on . . ." I had to have visas that allowed me to come back and forth from countries.

And then somebody in the government became a friend and whispered around, "Tell Maida not to get angry. We'll sort this out. We're working at upsetting her, but I am so pleased at the way she has behaved." But had that man in the government been faced with that story, he would have had to deny it. But he became a friend, remained in Tanzania, and I think he became a Tanzanian citizen. He became a minister in the government and was helpful in many ways. I think it was he who finally made it possible for me to stay somewhere, in this chief's house, until I could get my own place.

I also had to meet with government officials. You stated your purpose. I did a memorandum. That, too, was too brief and too simplistic. Always. Always. You met with the government, went to their offices. They would ask, "How long are you going to be here?" And I, "For X months. I want six months renewable." I had a little card, which said that I am Maida Springer, representative of the AFL-CIO, and that my federation is a member of the International Confederation of *Free Trade Unions*. I told them that I was here to visit with my colleagues to discuss educational opportunities and some training opportunities, and that the trade union federations had made requests and asked that we come. I said the AFL-CIO is giving scholarships, which will be granted based on the selection of the trade union federation of each country. One person is to be sent from each country. The AFL-CIO will be responsible for all the expenses. We hope the people come back to serve their country. And I would be glad to answer questions.

OK? You stated that. Nobody believed you. But you stated your purpose

26. The name of the principal immigration officer was S. C. Sinclair. As an example of Springer's experience with the British ability to be polite in their harassment, Sinclair ended a letter to her by writing, "I am, Madam, Your Obedient Servant, S. C. Sinclair." November 9, 1957 (Amistad).

and you were telling the truth. You have to envision that a colonial government is not interested in giving up its trusteeship or its colony. Even someone as minor as a trade union representative, not the president of the union or a treasurer or a secretary but some staff person who is not British and who is American, is going to be resented. You're resented *doubly* if you wear my *paint job* because they make an assumption that the Africans are going to empathize with me and I with them. In addition, I come into the country from the American labor movement which has a reputation of being anticolonial. For openers, that's negative. Your association is with those people who are struggling for independence. So if you put these things together, you don't have to ask how they feel about you.

I would go to these sundowners in the white community and listen to the people who came there. They would chide me about (*with British accent*) "*what my people are doing, what those boys are doing*" [referring to African trade unionists]. These sundowners are cocktail parties after five. The LEGCO [Legislative Council] would recess, because it was hot in the afternoon, and they did not come back until the sun began to go down. Then they wore their cummerbunds. And then after that somebody was always having a sundowner. I would put on a clean skirt, a clean dress. Mrs. Springer was always invited to the sundowners to see what Mrs. Springer was going to say, so that maybe they could ship her out of the country the next day.

Sometimes the government was giving sundowners. It was a way of entertainment. This was the social life of the community. You didn't have a lot of theaters. You didn't have a big playhouse. So there were a lot of local things that you did. And sundowners, cocktail parties—and this is still true in Washington. It's true in every capital—where the political wheeling and dealing and conversations happened. You don't learn a lot in the speeches people make. You don't learn sitting across from them in the conference room. But you learn a lot of things at sundowners. So I always went. (*Small laugh.*) And fortunately for me I was always able to manage and hold my own and not say things that would create problems for me the next day. They would allege I did or said something sometimes, but never at a sundowner. They'd say I secretly talked to somebody and promised them money or threatened them.

You didn't have ambassadors before independence. There were liaison officers. And the United States consul in Tanganyika [Robert L. Ware] was *very* hostile and would tell me that he knew what Julius Nyerere was thinking by the way his cook behaved a morning after Nyerere gave speeches to ten thousand people at a meeting. (*High-pitched, incredulous voice.*) *Not only did he tell me that, but he said it so very publicly!* So I said to him one day, "Have you ever met the president of TANU? Have you ever asked him for a cup of tea or called him to your office to talk, just to have a discussion?" He said, "No." "Then how do you know what he thinks?" He said by his cook. The attitude told you. I said, "What you need to think about is those young Africans who are clerks in these offices, who watch you all go home to eat your lunch with all of these African people serving you. At lunchtime these young Africans, wearing a clean shirt and khaki pants, go and sit on the beach with nothing to eat because the salary is so poor they can't afford lunch." And while I never raised my voice, I was very serious about what I was saying. I was furious. Well, he never invited me to his office after that.

I think shortly sometime after that he and Julius Nyerere did meet. And I think I talked to him publicly sometime after that. He admitted that Julius Nyerere was a man to meet and was very different from his impression. His impression came from listening to all of his white British counterparts. And perhaps to some African that was saying to them what they wanted to hear, that was anti-TANU.

Would Africans come to some of these sundowners that were given by the settlers?

Oh yes, oh sure, oh yes. Local chiefs, schoolteachers, people who have some little minor government post. Yes! And they would always engage Mrs. Springer in conversation, the Africans and the Europeans. You knew that you were *bait*, and unless you were prepared for that you wouldn't go. If you think you could handle yourself, you'd move right through it. Keep smiling.

What is the background to the story about the wife of Tanganyika's Governor Twining refusing to let you speak before their branch of the International Council of Women, an organization to which you also belonged?

Yes. The background of that story is this. Zainy Jamal was this wonderful community woman, very well educated, and a high-caste Indian. Her husband, Amir Jamal, was very active with TANU politics and was in the first cabinet after independence.[27] He remained in the country, but his life with Zainy was subsequently broken up.

---

27. Amir Habib Jamal was first elected to LEGCO in 1958 and was appointed unofficial minister for Urban Local Government and Works. After independence he held several ministerial portfolios and government positions until at least 1992 when he was ambassador to the United Nations in Geneva. In 1988 he became the first African to chair the council of the Geneva-based General Agreement on Tariffs and Trade (GATT). See Chakravarthi Raghavan, "Trade: First-Ever African to Chair GATT Council in 1988," *International Press Service*, December 4, 1987.

Zainy, the wife of the governor of Tanganyika,[28] and I all belonged to the same international women's organization, the International Council of Women. As I began to move around the international world, people thought that belonging to this organization would give me some small security. So I should have been welcomed. But the governor's wife simply *refused* to have me presented at their national center—they had a building or a hall. She told Zainy that I would not be permitted to speak there because I was considered a person who supported the point of view of the labor movement, the Tanganyika Federation of Labor, and of the political instrument, TANU, the Tanganyika African National Union.

Now, I hadn't done anything or taken any position, but I knew these people, and I worked with the labor movement. This was what my responsibility was within the *legal* context of participation with the unions that were a part of this umbrella of unions belonging to the International Confederation of Free Trade Unions. But I was not the kind of American person that a colonial government could look kindly on. I looked like every other African. I supported projects that I thought would be important, like trade union education for Africans in another country, so that they would come back and be more constructive and more intelligent and better able to bargain with the employer, and not just be hostile for hostile's sake. You are grieving, but you need to know how to grieve. This is all I was trying to do. But I was considered a very bad person for that by the colonial government. There was even one newspaper that went so far as to say, "Mrs. Springer wears a silk glove with a mailed fist." It wasn't true. My very presence created hostility with the colonial government.

After the governor's wife told Mrs. Jamal that I could not be received in their national center, a group of largely Indian women—because they were kind of the movers—invited me to talk to them, have an exchange, a coffee in the morning.[29] And Mrs. Jamal opened her home, which was very beautiful and large. She invited a very great Indian instrumentalist and his troupe, who were coming through Tanganyika, to perform. I've forgotten his name. So she made this a social occasion. It was an occasion to welcome him and hear him play and sing and an occasion for me to talk with the women.

28. Sir Edward Francis Twining (c. 1899–1968) was the governor of Tanganyika from 1949 to 1958. See "Deaths: Lord Twining," Facts on File World News Digest, August 9, 1967, FACTS.com, http://www.2facts.com (accessed November 22, 2003).

29. Springer recorded that there were twenty-five present, seventeen Asians and about nine Europeans. See diary entry, December 18, 1957 (MSK PP).

I spent maybe five, ten minutes having an exchange of views with the women who had the courage to come, because their coming may have meant that they could not participate in whatever the governor's wife had for Indian and African women. They would be quietly shut out. And the governor's wife, I think, threatened the women, that it would be made difficult for some of them who were looking for offices. So they took a great risk to spend a social morning with me.

What I said to them that morning—I had to be very careful with my words —was this. I spoke about the history of American women. I gave them a description of the things that women had not been able to win and the courage they required. I talked about the period from colonial times and the development of America where women rode the Conestoga wagons. I described what a Conestoga was, a covered wagon. It was used in the opening of territory in the United States. Women then knew how to use a rifle, they had babies, they cooked, and they wove the cloth. I talked about how women had always worked hard. That life was not easy.

I had researched my notes and was very careful, because the only thing I could do was to create problems for my African friends and Indian friends. I would get on the plane and go, be gone. And I was deeply aware of that, deeply conscious! Therefore you never find any documents in which I made speeches against this, that, and the other. I don't think you have found such, and you would have found it. They would have been very glad to indicate in all of the notes and such their anti–Maida Springer things.

I said in my speaking that I couldn't talk to them about Tanganyika women. I didn't know that much about Tanganyika women, but I could make a comparison of the struggle that the women in the United States had had, you know in getting the vote and the rest of it. That I could do and dared anyone to challenge me. This is the background of that story. So the story came out in the papers following that, that "Mrs. Springer wears silk gloves with a mailed fist." You know, people who used to wear armor used to have this, a mailed fist. What they were really saying was that I was really clever about what it was I said or did at this party.

The government sent somebody, the wife of the chief of police, to listen and take notes, because she was a member of the organization. They couldn't stop Zainy from having the meeting at her house, so the wife of the chief of police came, and I was very correct. She could not report that I had said anything in defamation of the country or anything that would put me in jail. If I had said anything untoward, the organization would have been in trouble and they would have attempted to lift my passport. Oh, those were rough times. They didn't fool around. And everyone was *so polite*. (*Muffled laughter*.)

There were these newspaper stories about me, saying things like we are watching that "little busy American Negress from the AFL-CIO." This is how I was described. And the colonial authorities said I was a demagogue, a Communist. So President Meany just sent a letter at some point which simply said that I represented the AFL-CIO. I was not a demagogue. I wasn't a Communist. I wasn't, I wasn't. That was all. You're out there all by yourself, and it was good to know that the AFL-CIO would send letters backing you and indicate, "This woman represents the AFL-CIO!" I was a union representative, and I tried to keep many people abreast of what was happening because I wanted their support. I wrote people in my union, the ILG, because I was on loan to the AFL-CIO. I still had to maintain my relationship with my union, my home base, a union to which I still pay dues.

You were in on some negotiations between the Eastern Province Plantation Workers' Union and the Sisal Growers' Association. The employers stated that they didn't want the sisal workers to be muddled in any way with politics.

Well, this was true of every single issue in every single union. All the industrial and agricultural owners wanted to do was to force the unions not to have a political point of view. This was true generally all over Africa, certainly East Africa. The employers, who gave workers meal and oil and next to no money, said that outsiders were being irresponsible. They said to the workers, you are with us and they will go home. They felt politics should not be involved in their business. That would weaken unions to not have a point of view. They said, "These people are spoiling you. They're trying to make you political." That was all that was involved there. And I just sat and listened to the negotiations, when the plantation workers invited me. I was not making any decisions or comments. My comments would be with my people in my house (*laughs*) after or before.

Did you witness any strikes while you were in Tanganyika?

I witnessed the attempts at a strike. The dockworkers in Tanga threatened to strike and went on strike.[30] At that time I think we were in the midst of the

30. The first and most powerful labor unions in Tanganyika were the dockworkers and stevedores. The settlement talks in Tanga included union recognition and workers' problems, but excluded discussions of wages. See diary entry, December 2, 1957; A. P. Ndoe (general secretary of the Tanga Port Stevedores and Dockworkers Union), "Union's Report," December 21, 1957; and Ndoe, "Secretary's Report over the Alleged Illegal Dock Strike in Tanga, January 1, 1958" (MSK PP).

third national conference of the Tanganyika Federation of Labor [November 25–28, 1957]. It was quite young. And we adjourned the conference so that the general secretary of the union, Rashidi Kawawa, and myself could go to Tanga and talk to the dockworkers and beseech them to come off the strike because there was a feeling that the strike put me in jeopardy in terms of being able to remain in the country. The assumption always would be that I had something to do with it, or either was advising them. It may not have been the case, but we were led to believe that I would be held responsible for the strike.

So we flew to Tanga, and I did everything but get on my knees, because they were tough men, the dockworkers. And it was a very bold question. The dockworkers were threatening some drastic actions. Rashidi Kawawa said, "The trade union wants Sister Maida to stay. Your grievances are right, but there are ways that we can do this. Do you want her to stay?" And so we were told that the men agreed to end the strike. They would negotiate, and we could go on back to Dar es Salaam and continue the conference. The dockworkers' representatives were at the conference anyway. Oh, yes! They were troublesome days.

And the brewery workers didn't go on strike. They said we won't drink beer. Now, you know, you drink large bottles of beer. You don't drink little bottles like they drink here. And the white community drank beer modestly, but they made their money on the beer that the Africans drank. The community didn't drink beer, either. That was fantastic. The brewery workers won their point. My memory is dim on this, but they were able to negotiate whatever pay they were after. They succeeded.[31]

You told me earlier that you had wanted to live in Tanzania. Could you expound a little bit on that?

By 1959 I had been to most of the English-speaking countries in Africa and two or three of the French-speaking countries. I felt that whatever small contribution I could make, I could make it in a setting in East Africa. When I'm speaking of East Africa, I'm thinking particularly of Kenya and Tanganyika. The countries that were very beautiful and I liked and enjoyed were Kenya, Tanganyika, and Uganda. Kenya and Uganda were wonderful, but

31. Kawawa and Mpangala wrote Springer of the beer boycott throughout all of Tanganyika that happened after her departure and was proceeded by a strike. The government had Kawawa arrested on charges of intimidation because of the TFL support of the boycott. Workers, whose wages were substantially below the minimum cost of living standards, demanded a wage increase based on the Government Statistical Department minimum cost of living report. Mpangala to Springer, April 24, 1958, and Kawawa to Springer, May 13, 1958 (MSK PP).

there was a greater (*claps hands*) bustle in those places. And, of course, Kenya is a big tourist country. It has become since independence a city of high-rises and all kinds of fast moving. You don't get that sense in Tanganyika. I didn't get it there in the fifties. I've just come back from there; I don't get that sense now. I found Tanganyika a place that perhaps temperamentally suited me. There was a pace of the people that appealed to me. Though I am a city-bred person, I am temperamentally suited to a slower-paced environment.

I have here a little East African coffeepot. (*Shows it to interviewer.*) The boys used to sell the bitter coffee drunk by Muslims using the larger coffeepots. The boys walk along the street clicking the pot. You get tiny cups and you come out and you buy for pennies, coffee. This little small one I treasure because the elders of Tanzania gave that to me in 1957.

(*Reading inscription.*) "To Mrs. Maida Springer from TANU elders, Dar es Salaam, Tanganyika, 12/6/57." So that's June 12, 1957, according to the British ordering.

And with that they sent an elephant hunting gun, which had been used by a man named Chom Wanyewe. Mbutta Milando translated for me from Swahili and told me that as a young man, Chom Wanyewe had traveled all over Tanganyika under the Germans.[32] He was considered an elephant boy. He knew uncharted places, which he was able to relate to them. That the elders thought that as a woman I was serious enough that they would welcome me and honor me in this way touched me. I was given this elephant hunting gun—which I think hangs in my son's study at his home—along with this coffeepot and some other things. They thought that because this woman who is our sister is here we will honor her. So I treasure this.

I'd like to ask you about some of these pictures. This is a picture of you with about seven or eight men in Tanganyika. Can just tell me who they are?

Yes. The very old man in the front holding his jacket is Mzee Hemb. He was the man that was selected to be the guard of my residence and the offices where I was going to live and work on Wanyamwezi Street. The young man standing directly behind me, tall, is Patrick Mandawa. He was my secretary, and he was the young man selected by the Tanganyika Federation of Labor to come to the United States for the African scholarship program.[33] The per-

32. Julius Nyerere brought the gifts to Springer when he came to the United States in June 1957 as a petitioner before the UN Trusteeship Council. See chapter 10 for more discussion of Milando, who served as publicity secretary of the Tanganyika African National Union

33. The scholarship recipients were Arthur Aggrey Ochwada, assistant general secretary of the Kenya Federation of Labor (KFL) and the head of the Building and Construction Workers' Union; Percival Patrick Mandawa, the press and research officer and education secretary for the TFL; and Dishan William Kiwanuka of the Posts and Telegraphs Union in Uganda.

son standing right next to me, who was the then general secretary of the Tanganyika Federation of Labor, is Rashidi Kawawa. He is now the second in command in the political party of Tanzania. He has been in several ministries, and he's really a very powerful man now. I have forgotten the names of some of the others that are there. One was the driver of the car that I used. And these were other local union officers and an elder who was standing beside Mzee Hemb. They considered themselves part of my little guardian group to see that I was not harmed or harassed. It was a very loving relationship.

Here is a picture of a pretty good-sized delegation meeting greeting you at the airport in 1957.

(*Laughs wistfully.*) Yes. These are union members. These are domestic workers. They are the clerical workers. The officers of the union. You know, Sister Maida couldn't arrive in Tanganyika and not be welcomed. And with the then colonial hostility, they would make it a point to be at the airport when I arrived so that their presence would be helpful. The domestic workers told me, "You are our sister. You are our mother. So we women have to be with you." One or two of them worked at the house with me because there were economic problems. You had unemployment, and they needed jobs. And they thought here was an American sister who had come to work with the federation and give us some positive things.

Did people on your plane know this big delegation was for you?

Oh, of course not. These were people coming home, coming from England for vacations and the rest of it. Some of them, if they were government officials' wives, would look at me askance, because the assumption was I was an outsider. Some of them knew my face. When I would get off the plane, all of the porters would rush to me and say, "Bibi Maida! *Habari? Karibu,*" to welcome me.

Here's a picture of a big TANU rally that took place during your first trip to Tanganyika in January 1957.

This was at the place that we called Mwazi Moja, One Coconut. It was a big open field. And what you see here was Dr. Nyerere reporting on his mission to the United Nations.[34] And the very dark square that you see are all the

34. The mass meeting of fifty thousand Africans at Mwazi Moja to hear Nyerere speak of his UN mission, his search for scholarships, and to answer the anti-TANU editorials in the *Tanganyika Standard* happened on January 27, 1957. In response to Nyerere's popularity and his success in gaining international attention, the government closed eleven TANU branches and banned Nyerere from speaking. The ban lasted from February to September 1957. Springer, memorandum on Tanganyika, January 31, 1957, and "Newsman's Diary of the Week," *Sunday News*, January 27, 1957, both in 60/23 (Lovestone files); diary entry, January 27, 1957 (MSK PP).

African Policy Conflicts within the ICFTU

Muslim women with their black coverings on, their *bai buis*. On that occasion, I'm in here somewhere on the platform with a committee of TANU, a committee of trade union people, as we listen to Dr. Nyerere report *without a note* for hours standing there. It rained. The sun shone. The clouds came. And the only upset person in all of that was myself. *No one* moved a muscle! I was upset because I didn't want my hair to get wet (*laughter*), because it would shrink and other such ridiculous things. But the feeling of the people in a meeting like that was like a religious experience. And the Muslim women would all be together.

Well, it would be understood that when Bibi Titi and the Muslim women of TANU came, they would congregate. There was no problem. There was no question. That's a wonderful picture. Bibi Titi organized the Muslim women. She believed in TANU. She believed in the independence of her country. This work for independence was a very unlikely thing for a Muslim woman to be engaged in. But she was a great force, traveled up and down the country, working to organize the Muslim women. She was a strong woman, Bibi Titi Mohamed.

During this same visit to East Africa you wrote in your diary that you were invited to the ship of the *kabaka* [king] of Buganda for further conversations about politics and unions.[35]

Oh, yes. He was going to do whatever sporting people do, shooting and the yachting thing. I don't remember those details, but he was the friend of some of the people I knew, Julius Nyerere and his entourage. And so this occasion was not just to talk to me; he was going to talk to his friends. So this American was there, and he was courteous and I was invited to join. The *kabaka* was most gracious — well, you are impressed with meeting, I guess, one could say a monarch — and very gentle, very down to earth and had a knowledge of all kinds of things that one talked about. And while I was a strange piece of woman in the labor movement, he accepted that with grace and treated me as a person who had some substance and with whom he could converse about politics. He treated me *very* well.

35. Popularly known as King Freddie, the *kabaka* was Sir Edward Frederick William Walugembe Mutebi Luwangula Mutesa II (c. 1924–1969), the leader of the largest ethnic group in Uganda, the Baganda. The British favored the Baganda over other ethnic groups. This divide and rule tactic helped to perpetuate ethnic conflicts during colonialism and afterward. In an effort to exert greater control over the Baganda, the British exiled the *kabaka* in 1953. However, they were forced to restore him to his position in 1955. Milton Obote deposed him in 1966, forcing him into exile again. See "The Buganda Agreement, 1955," in History, The Buganda Home Page, www.buganda.com/back1955.htm (accessed May 4, 2003).

African Policy Conflicts within the ICFTU

During your second trip to East Africa in the fall of 1957 for the scholarship program, you wrote letters home stating that you and Tom Mboya while in Uganda helped glue the labor movement together there.

They were very fragmented. They were having all kinds of internal dissension, and we were offering the Harvard trade union scholarship. I said that I refused to talk to people who didn't talk to one another, and that it was their labor movement, and I would not know whom to talk to if I could not speak to a leadership which could have some consensus. They agreed that that was correct, and they caucused among themselves. They respected Tom very much. Tom had either preceded me or on occasion Tom went with me, but this scholarship program was something that the labor movement could rally around. So this was a positive contributing factor for uniting the Uganda trade union movement. That I considered at the time an accomplishment.

I don't remember the quarrel. This is, you know, the kind of ego rivalry that all of these unions were involved in. The two large unions were the railway workers and the postal and telegraph workers. All of the others were little, tiny, fragmented, small, small groups. I don't know whether there was jealousy, because these big boys wanted to dominate the trade union federation. And personalities, *very* strong personalities. Some of them, even after they agreed to unity, insisted that they must come and talk to me personally before we had the meeting. So in the hotel every half hour on the hour another representative from some union would talk their point of view to me. And if that would make for some cohesion, the least I could do was to listen. (*Laughs.*)

In one of your letters you wrote about a party for Tom Mboya in Uganda attended by mostly university students and a few non-African professors.[36] Do you recall what university this was?

Oh, sure. It was Makerere. There was only one university. (*Laughing.*) This was for *all* of East Africa, *all* of East Africa. It was the only place that Africans went to study, so you can imagine the competition. Whatever professors came to the party had to be courageous. These were the people who supported the independence of Africa, who supported the rights of the trade union movement. And so these men and a few women who would show their face had a great deal of courage. It is difficult to accept that, sitting in the United States.

You talked about the Special Branch being at the party and one of them asking you to dance. (*Springer laughs.*) I guess he wanted to get information out of you.

Of course! The assumption was that you were so stupid or that you knew

36. The party was held at the Mengo Garden, an African-owned association. A local band played American jazz. Springer to Dollie Lowther Robinson, December 7, 1957 (MSK PP).

some dreadful thing that you could tell them, and they could come back and hassle you even more for. Yes. And you knew, you *absolutely* knew who they were. And if you didn't know, someone had said to you, "Bibi, *hapana*." You know, "My sister, look out. This is the secret police!" Who were not secret. Everybody knew who they were. And we knew all the small people that they paid for information, and some of these poor people couldn't read or write. And the more clever ones, the educated ones, the secret police had to give them something to do. (*Laughs.*)[37]

Sometimes we would do devilish things. We would say publicly that we were going in this direction, and they would get on motorbikes to follow us, and then we'd move in another direction. We had some fun with it, too. You had to have a sense of humor or else you would go mad. You could not be isolated like that without a sense of humor. After a meeting was over, you went back into your house or back into your hotel, and you did not know what was going to happen. You knew when your room was searched. So you did have to have a sense of humor and had to be lighthearted about this and accept this situation because your friends were under the gun. I could get my return ticket and return home. But the reason you needed to be circumspect and not have a big mouth and think that you're talking brave and showing these people was that when you got on the plane and left, your colleagues were there to face whatever. So with this situation one had to try to be intelligent.

I have seen some horrible things. And I have been chased off the street like a wet rat. When there was a curfew [due to the state of emergency]—and I look like every other African—the authorities demanded to know what I was doing on the street, because at nine o'clock you had to be off the street. I would say I've just come in off the plane and I'm trying to find something to eat. The dining room restaurant in the little hotel I was in was closed. The little Indian restaurants were still open. So I'd show my passport and be virtually escorted to my hotel. This was in Kenya. And sometimes I had been at a meeting that Tom Mboya had organized where I talked to my trade union colleagues. And it was getting to be nine o'clock when Tom started organizing pools of people to get everybody back to the places where they lived, so that there would not be trouble with the police.

So I have witnessed a lot of hostility. I was told in no uncertain terms in

37. The secret police did not always get their facts straight. Tom Mboya arrived in Uganda on a Thursday and Springer met him there on Saturday. Before she left for Uganda she was in a hotel in Nairobi, Kenya, when she heard a radio broadcast in which the police said she had arrived in Uganda that Friday night. The police had demanded that the hotel keeper in Uganda confirm her arrival. Springer to George [T. Brown, AFL-CIO director of international affairs], December 2, 1957; and Springer to Robinson, December 7, 1957 (MSK PP).

African Policy Conflicts within the ICFTU

Uganda by a half-drunk—I'll just say European—that I was here and discussing things and making trouble with Africans. He said that I was doing things here that I could not do in the United States, and I was getting my frustrations out. This was a man I did not know. I was sitting at a bar waiting for someone and having a drink. And he just walked over to me—my name and face were known everywhere—and said, "Oh, yes. You're Maida Springer from the United States," and then would go on a tirade of abuse. So that, you expected.[38]

Once, I looked at newspaper headlines in Kenya, which said that I was there with blood money from the trade union movement in the United States, from the Teamsters. The Teamsters didn't have a thing to do with what I was doing. We were trying to help Tom build a trade union center because Africans couldn't meet anywhere. And the discussions that led to the first $35,000 for the trade union building, Solidarity House, was held at Unity House in the United States when Tom Mboya was here.[39]

I was given the task of following that up by having discussions about the building with Tom, after he had spoken with the council and met with A. Philip Randolph. It was decided that we would ask the workers in the union to do something called "shilling a brick." It would be a token. The workers earned very little and didn't have money, so this would give them a sense of participation, and $35,000 wasn't enough to build the union center. Other international unions had not come into this program. "Shilling a brick" meant that workers would pay a shilling for each brick that went into this prospective union home. I did a memorandum on this and went to Kenya.

Tom walked me through the labyrinth of all of the people that needed to be spoken to about how this would be done. I went with him to all the responsible departments of the colonial government. They were all polite and didn't want to hear me (*laughs*) at all, because here was this American trade unionist from this terrible American labor movement. And on top of this, I was a woman and I was *black*, and therefore I would empathize with the workers in Kenya. So I was called everything, a demagogue, and was accused of bringing blood money.[40]

38. Springer later noted that the bartender, who was from Zanzibar, wanted to hit the man for having insulting her. But she talked him out of it by pointing out to him that he would then have a hard time finding another job in East Africa.

39. In the fall of 1956 Mboya met with AFL-CIO Executive Council members Meany, Walter Reuther, David Dubinsky, and A. Philip Randolph.

40. Upon arrival in East Africa Springer immediately made appointments with department heads concerned with the functions of labor. She recorded that she received pointed questions. Springer to Stolt, November 7, 1957 (MSK PP).

African Policy Conflicts within the ICFTU

Then the AFL-CIO sent its vice president, A. Philip Randolph, to Kenya to present $35,000 to the Kenya Federation of Labor from the first William Green Memorial Fund [summer 1957]. Of course, fortunately, it became an international program. The various international unions around the world—the Scandinavians, who were always wonderful, and the British and others—contributed money to build Solidarity House. This union center, I am pleased about having had something to do with. The motivation was there in the American labor movement. And Tom was his own best salesman.

So, if these were wrong approaches, I didn't know any better. And if I had to do it over again under the same circumstances, I hope I would be more intelligent and even stronger in my pursuit to share with the workers of Africa the feeling of solidarity beyond their beleaguered borders. If that is my sin, I accept that.[41] As a staff person committed to what was happening in Africa, I was able to put the small nuts and bolts together and helped with programming. I was commuting back and forth to Africa all the time. So it's in that context, having shared in those experiences, I consider certainly broadened my education, and it was a privilege to have known such people.

But I have witnessed a lot of hostility by the colonial governments. Unless you have a strong back and a weak mind you don't engage in this work. (*Laughter.*) Because only someone with a very weak mind would take on some of the stuff that you have to do completely alone. You get off that plane and walk into a country whose native language you don't know well. You know greeting words only, and you are so busy that you don't take the time to grasp and learn the language, which one should do. Conveniently, everyone you deal with on a certain level is English-speaking. I do not like to dwell on whatever the hardships were of being alone and isolated, able to have your passport lifted for any trivial reason in order to have you thrown out of the country. This you lived with day and night.

Accepting that, you move on from there to the rewards, which are intangibles. The rewards have been in sharing interests and occasionally being able to put together something positive. You were able to get a scholarship here. You were able to give a whole community a sense of caring, that over there these Americans were caring about what happened to you.

Once there was an incident. I was sitting in my office attending grievances with the impartial chairman about wages, hours, and conditions of service, when I got a cable from Tanganyika for help. It said however many hundreds

41. Springer responds in this way because of the criticism of the settler press that the AFL-CIO was using the blood money of the Teamsters to build this center and criticism from the British TUC that the AFL-CIO was acting unilaterally.

African Policy Conflicts within the ICFTU

of workers [five thousand] had just been *sacked*. This was the Princess Margaret incident. She was visiting in East Africa. You know, the royal family goes and looks at their colonies and their trusteeships. There was some incident at the hotel where she was staying. My memory is dim at this point. The chef, who was the shop steward, put his sharp knives down and walked out. All the workers walked out. So it was called the Princess Margaret incident and you had a great tumult going on there. Then management said good, all right, *poof*, and everybody was fired. Many of them lived in the compound owned by either the hotel owners or the government. So these people were thrown out of their lodgings.[42]

I got this cable, and without knowing all the details I started talking and telephoning. I had no authority, but I'd talk to people. I was exercised. First, I called Sasha Zimmerman. I called Jay Lovestone, who was in international affairs and was concerned about world politics. I had listened to him many times, and I knew that I had a responsive ear. I called Philip Randolph, the chief, who was going to an executive council meeting in Washington. It was suggested—I don't know by which one of these men—that I do a memorandum explaining what was happening in Tanganyika, and it would be presented at this meeting in Washington. So I did. And then I got a telephone call in my office saying, "Maida, breathe easy. The council has agreed to send . . ." —I think it was twenty-five hundred dollars or whatever, but that was a lot of money then—"to the Tanganyika Federation of Labor." I was able to send a cable to the general secretary, Rashidi Kawawa—you may find a copy of that cable here—"Help is coming. Maida" [June 1957]. It meant again that beyond the borders of Tanganyika, white and black workers' representatives cared. What were we talking about? Really pennies, which meant that these people, who had to pay rent on their houses or who were thrown out of employer-owned housing, would have some sense of the American labor movement's concern about the plight of this young African trade union federation.

Those were wonderful days. People listened to you and cared about your opinion. Those have been my rewards. (*Very softly.*) Those kinds of incidents where the American labor movement helped and having the respect and friendship of a lot of people in Africa have been my rewards. Little people.

42. The incident known as the Princess Margaret incident was so called because it happened in connection with the visit to Tanganyika of Queen Elizabeth's sister in early December 1956. The strike over abysmally low wages and poor work conditions was precipitated by the Kinondoni Hostel's firing of the highly respected shop steward because he interceded on behalf of four workers who were fired on allegations of being inebriated while working at a party in connection with Princess Margaret's visit. For more information, see Richards, *Maida Springer*, 124–26.

African Policy Conflicts within the ICFTU

I've had people in Africa angry at me because the workers' organization that I represented could not support the things that they were doing—workers got locked up, the trade union movement became part and parcel of the political party. I disagreed with the priorities. The wages and hours of the trade union movement were not a priority. The labor movement represented the second core leadership after the intellectuals in the independence movements. And after independence the leadership of the labor movement was siphoned off into the government. But they had to make decisions for their country, and the standards of industrialized society did not reflect their interests. The trade union movement was seen to be a privileged group. As an American trade unionist, I couldn't support the locking up of the principal officers of unions. You disagreed with them. But you remained friends, and you maintained the respect of a lot of people.

I have been *bloodied, battered, misunderstood*. Made a lot of mistakes. Done dumb things like with the housing proposal for Kenya. I told you this was bad negotiation on my part, bad representation. You never negotiate that way. I just *wanted* it so badly. I was ready to suggest that the labor movement would stand a possible loss because I was so consumed with wanting this housing project for Kenyan workers. If something happened and they could not be paid back, it was going to be such a small thing that the American labor movement could lose in terms of its investment. I didn't say that. No, I'm not crazy enough to say that, but I did not negotiate with all of the hardness that a labor organizer should have. I accepted very minimal guarantees for the investment of money that was due American workers.

You once told me that Tom Mboya was one of those who alerted you to the need for housing?

Absolutely. He taught me so many things, this young man. He would say, I am taking you for a drive and a walk through X, Y, or Z community. We went various places. He said housing is deplorable. We can't afford decent housing. We would not be loaned money. He began talking to me about housing on behalf of the working class, the people of Africa, most of whom were workers. Tom Mboya was one of those who went the whole round. He looked at trade union housing in New York, trade union housing in Detroit, the UAWs. He had seen what labor had done in Germany and other places. He looked at housing *wherever* and at whatever programs unions were doing. He was so moved by this. I think he started talking to me about housing by 1959. And then when I joined full-time the staff of AFL-CIO, he talked to me seriously. (*Laughter.*)

Tom was never lazy with ideas. He had a fertile brain. I think he knew I was a good listener, and I respected what he had to say. I respected his view of the future of an independent Kenya where Africans would be treated like the citizens they were. Africans would become the leaders, whether it was business or government or education, whatever. Yes, and so as he walked me through these dirt patches and these little tiny houses, he said, Maida, we must do better, we must do more, we can't do it ourselves alone. We need the help of the international labor movement. I listened. And so I said yes, I will go back and talk. But I am afraid it wasn't good enough. I was not good enough; it just fell apart somewhere.

I came back and did a memorandum to President Meany and reported that Tom had said this was a need. Indeed I would say this was a need wherever one could go in Africa. But it was very important that we should attempt to be supportive of Kenya, because this young man was so sound. President Meany then had a few of the people who managed labor affairs on housing sit down with me. He was present. I said my little say, and they raised questions.

Then after a trip to Africa, I stated to President Meany that the leaders of the German Federation of Labor were interested in this. All of these countries in Europe were looking at ways to support things that were going on in Africa, in terms of investment, in terms of looking to the future. The German Federation of Labor said they would come in as a partner to build housing in Kenya if the American labor movement would be a partner. They would do the building, and the Kenya government and trade union movement would be involved. This would be a tripartite agreement.

So we had to talk about it. First I said to the DGB [German Federation of Labor], "I don't know what I'm talking about. It may not relate, but I need to look at some of what you do." The people in the Neue Heimat, the housing development for the DGB said, "You're right. Come to Germany." President Meany was listening and supported the idea that I go back, and I could engage in some discussion. Two, that I could go to Germany and look at their housing. I had not been to Germany for that reason before, but I knew something about post–World War II. In 1951, 1952, when I was at Oxford, the house I stayed in, in Paris, my friend Evelyn Scheyer was one of the American government officials who was one of the authorities on housing and was working with the German federation. So I had some awareness, while I didn't have a lot of factual knowledge. So I go to Germany. I look, and I'm thrilled and excited, upset. I see the potential of building this urban housing. I see the kind of rebuilding done after the devastation of World War II. The German Federation of Labor had done a remarkable job. They had set up cooperatives and had built all kinds of housing. But I was upset because I knew that the same kind of base was not there in Kenya. Looking at the miracle I wondered how can this be translated.[43]

I come back, and I do a small memorandum for the AFL-CIO on this proposal, saying who was involved and stating my hope for the participation of the AFL-CIO. President Meany said, "You got my blessing. Go. Get on the next plane." Before I left, there were some cursory discussions with people who were involved with investment in housing in the AFL-CIO, because we do a lot of housing in the United States. But this was still just my conversation. I go to Kenya for negotiations. The representative from Neue Heimat [Herbert Weisskampf] comes, and we sit with the Briton who is head of the housing authority of Kenya and who was a very hard-nosed negotiator. I guess it's maybe just before independence. My head was soft on anything that had to do with Africa, and I *loved* Tom Mboya dearly. I think he was either the same age or maybe a couple of years older than Eric. I would have gone to hell and back to have successfully gotten something he wanted.

Tom was a minister, and I felt that he was so busy and so involved in some immediate things that his input was not a priority, and he did not need to sit in on these discussions. So I negotiated. What I'm saying to you was that I was ill suited for that. I allowed those negotiations to go on and accepted certain conditions that I brought back to the United States labor movement that were bad. What I accepted in the negotiations was that for X number of years the AFL-CIO would put up X number of dollars on housing, and those details were OK. What was not good was that I said you couldn't guarantee that a government would be in place or that there would not be a change of government. There had to be guarantees like this as part of the conditions of getting the money at this low interest. There had to be a guarantee that it would be repaid. Both the Germans and the Americans wanted these guarantees. I don't remember the details now, because I was so angry with myself that those documents I never (*claps hands*) kept. I threw them away. I was a bad negotiator on this because I negotiated on my felt need for the Kenya citizens and on behalf of the Kenya labor movement. The negotiations for Solidarity House and the Institute of Tailoring and Cutting were good. But these negoti-

43. In January 1963 Springer traveled to Germany where she observed the housing projects of the labor movement. The following month she attended the meeting in Kenya with Weisskampf, Nairobi's city treasurer A. W. Kemp, the assistant city treasurer, and the director of Social Services and Housing. The AFL-CIO and Neue Heimat agreed to provide a loan of 134,000 pounds each to the city council for the cost of building 287 homes. Springer, "Summary of Conclusions Arising from the Meeting Held in the City Treasurer's Office, Nairobi on the 26th February 1963" (MSK PP); see Springer to Mboya, December 20, 1962, 10/19, and housing project documents in 11/1 (Country files).

African Policy Conflicts within the ICFTU

ations for urban housing, flats, maybe five or ten miles outside of Nairobi, were done very badly by me, I submit.

You want to tell me about an unsettling incident you had with Mboya.[44]

Tom could not come to that meeting with the Kenya housing people, the Neue Heimat representative, and myself. We were to meet with him after. I tell you this story because I have kept it locked inside of me for a long time; it has been so terribly painful. When we left the conference with our notes and we went, myself and this German official, to Tom's office, I thought that he treated us rather short. I was embarrassed because so much effort had been put into it, and this German housing labor official was so enthusiastic and had so many good ideas. It was so wonderful that I thought that even on an extremely busy day that he would have taken some time. I didn't understand why the minister had treated us coolly. I didn't have that kind of relationship with Tom. I think that the level of acceptance I had and my respect for what he envisioned for his country was such that I would have done handsprings to be supportive and to bring back a positive report of what I believed he was about. I felt very badly about that occasion. But I came back and reported to President Meany and the housing people whatever details there were on terms of housing, not anything about my personal feelings or my uneasiness.

At that point I felt I needed to do a review, a mental review, of where I was going with my concerns about Africa. Maybe I wasn't doing enough, maybe I didn't know enough, maybe it was time—I had been seriously ill twice—and maybe it was time. In addition, my family problems were becoming more demanding. I had an aged stepfather whom I *loved*. As I told you many times, I thought my mother's second husband was an angel. He was many years older than my mother. We had recently brought my grandmother to the United States, and she was a responsibility for my mother and for me. I didn't live in New York. I lived in Washington, DC, and when I retired moved to Chicago. I had a big house in Brooklyn, an old house. And my grandmother stayed there with my mother. Eric and I were, you know, her buttressing support on this. My son was a young married man with his own career in the legal profession. I also had a marriage that required that I be in the United States sometimes and that I have other priorities besides the African labor movement and African independence.[45] So you looked at all of those things, and I knew that I couldn't make arbitrary decisions that only suited me personally.

44. This part of the interview took place ten years later than the portion above, on February 13, 1999.
45. Springer married James Kemp in 1965.

African Policy Conflicts within the ICFTU

I am fortunate, having a very small, narrow family, a family that is loving and respectful and compassionate. My mother during her last five years was sick. During a visit with me while I was living in Chicago, she was hospitalized. My son did not want me to be alone when her illness was discussed. He was growing and building in his profession. He was on some serious legal case and flew from wherever he was and had a taxi waiting at the airport to drive him to the hospital and come to a conference about my mother's condition. He would leave that meeting, get back in the taxi, go back to the airport, and fly back to wherever he was. I'm very fortunate.

So I knew then, I began to feel the need for some kind of decision. One of the important things that I faced was that I would kill myself at the pace that I was going, crowding a year's work into three or four months. Coming back, working like a donkey in the United States, and then rushing off, preparing something else. I began to feel that it was too fast, too much.[46] And I perhaps couldn't give it my best and maybe didn't give all . . . you needed more than your heart. I had some limited talents (*laughter*), but you needed more than your heart. Physically, I was breaking down and I knew that, and there had to be some considerations plus my unease about the meeting with Tom.

There was nothing ever otherwise in his attitude toward me. For example, after I resigned from the AFL-CIO, Tom would keep in contact. Whenever Tom was going to be in the United States or Canada, he would make sure that he got a note to me. And I would meet him for a brief moment, a greeting, a welcome. I have spent a couple of hours at the airport when his plane was delayed, waiting for him and listening to the reporters wile away the time and saying very little to them. And always the greeting from Tom was warm. "Maida, how are you? How are things going on now that you are doing . . . ? Will you be coming back for a visit? Pamela said so and so. The kids are so and so." But I always had this disquiet as to what it was, the pressure he was under, what it was that he was so cool that time. As gracious as Tom was. The way I knew that he could juggle sixteen things and never seem to miss a beat. I was troubled about the seeming disinterest in the housing conference.

I knew some of what was going on. Some, some, some. Tom's work to find dozens of scholarships for African students all over the United States is legendary as well as the funding to charter a plane to bring the students to Africa,

<hr />

46. Years later, when Springer decided to consult for the AALC, Violet Lewis (Porter), her secretary during her years with the International Affairs Department, expressed the hope that she would take it easy, since she had known her in the past to work too hard. Porter to Springer, June 12, 1980 (MSK PP).

the airlift. He was aided in the project by some high-profile black Americans.[47] The still partial government over there would resent that, the old colonial government. Some of the people who benefited by it, either they individually or members of their family, resented it. This Tom is doing too much. The kind of access that he had and respect around the world. And then, I am sure, that there were small power plays within the country. Power is such a strong motive for various kinds of behavior.

I knew the kind of pressure he was under, and there were those who promoted the feeling that he was too Western. Anti-American sentiments. Or people were thinking that they could get great opportunities also and rival Tom in some other ways. I was aware of this. And therefore when I felt so badly about the meeting at his office, I knew this pressure he was under. This was the only time from the moment I met Tom until my last meeting that I ever had any reason to be doubting or questioning, only time.

His American connections were alleged to be a demonic CIA plot to undermine Kenyan independence. You showed me an essay alleging that I was bag lady for Tom, that I worked with him with the CIA.[48] As far as CIA activities with Tom, about Tom, or even general conversations, I never, never had any. The envy and hostility that Tom Mboya endured he did not deserve. His constant concern was for the good of his country.

Do you think that by this time, perhaps, he saw the housing project as it was constituted as a possible liability?

No! No! This was very positive and being discussed officially very quietly. And for whatever reason that he did not give it his attention, it was only in the exploratory stage. This was not something you had the press about and the rest of it. No. This was still only in the discussion stage, showing there were people who were interested. You could speak to a Kenya government who had to listen to you, and they were giving you advice and suggesting areas to build.

The reason I belabor this—I have not talked much about my unhappiness —is because of what happened the last time I saw Tom. Sometime after I resigned, I went back to Kenya for the African-American Labor Center. At that

47. For details on the airlift and Mboya's political struggles, see Richards, *Maida Springer*, 199–204, 209–15, 256–59.
48. Based upon assertions the *People's News Service* made in 1978, Barry Cohen alleged that Springer served as the CIA contact officer for Mboya. After Springer first read the essay that I had given her, she retorted that the only truth to the charge was the spelling of her and Mboya's names. Cohen, "The CIA and African Trade Unions," in *Dirty Work 2: The CIA in Africa*, ed. Ellen Ray, William Schaap, Karl Van Meter, and Louis Wolf, 70–79 (London: Zed Press, 1980), 75.

African Policy Conflicts within the ICFTU

time one of the locals of the ILGWU was presenting new equipment, some new machinery for the school which I had helped to put together in '63. So I said yes, I would present the material on behalf of the ILGWU. I was going to be doing some other things there, too.

When I got into the airport, Alphonse Okuku, Tom Mboya's younger brother, was there. I was surprised. Tom's a member of Parliament, etc. And Alphonse said, "Maida, Tom wants to talk to you, and I am to bring you from the airport to his house." I had just taken a seventeen-hour flight. I was so exhausted and probably partly ill, that I suggested that he give me at least two hours. I would go to the hotel, wash, and stretch out for an hour or two. Two hours exactly later, he came back to the hotel for me. He said Tom says he has to go to a ministerial meeting. He is meeting all of the ministers at the airport and they are going . . . I don't remember the place now. I think these were ministers from Kenya, Tanzania, Uganda, and maybe someplace else. I remember surely those three.

When we got to the airport, the ministers from these other countries said to me, "Ah ha, Mama Maida, you come and you have not told us. You are mistreating us." And with that kind of kidding and jollity, we went to the private lounge for the ministers. Tom and I never had a chance to have a conversation of any kind. He just came over to me and said, "Maida, walk with me," as they were leaving. I walked with him to the plane. And he just put his hands on my shoulders and just said to me, good-bye and I will see you. I will let you know when I am back in the States. That was the last time I ever saw him because he was assassinated after that.

It's one of the things that has kept me up nights, has worried me. For some time after his assassination, I was to do a piece for our labor news and I couldn't do it. I couldn't face it. It took a very long time before I could do it. Maybe it will release me now, now that I am saying this to you. I keep asking myself why didn't I go, no matter how tired? It bothers me that I did not go to his home, that I wanted to go to the hotel and be quiet and bathe and rest myself for two hours. I could have bathed in his house. I could have changed my clothes. Pamela would have put me to bed. Oh, I have worried myself for years as to why I did not. I was very tired and feeling sick. I have been tired before.

But two hours on the dot Alphonse was there. I have never asked Pamela, and I wouldn't. And she never volunteered anything. I don't know whether she knew. I had all kinds of conjectures. Maybe he was going to explain this and that and the other to me. He was going to tell me something. I'll never know. I'll never know, but maybe this will release me.

African Policy Conflicts within the ICFTU

Your cousin Scottie [Clarence Scott] told me a story about Tom Mboya's assassination. He told me that he had a dream the night before, that Tom came to him and told him to tell Maida they are trying to get me.

You never told me this! Oh, my goodness!

And then he told you, and of course you were upset.

Oh, that was the constant, that they were trying to get him. But I am amazed that you say Scottie told you that. Let me tell you what happened on another occasion. I owe Scottie a debt of gratitude. Scottie lived across town from us in Brooklyn. My mother fell ill and was on the floor unconscious in our home in Brooklyn, and he found her and saved her life. He said that Mr. Carrington, my mother's husband who was dead, wouldn't let him sleep and kept pulling his toes—and he believed all of those things—and that he got out of bed—this was about three or four o'clock in the morning—and went to our house on Macon Street. He called our house and couldn't get an answer. So he got dressed at that hour in the morning, and he took the bus across town to our house.

The doors were all open, upstairs and downstairs, because my mother had seen people out. She had had dinner for Kamau, whom you met, and a group of men he had brought with him.[49] I think Kamau was getting ready to go home. He was going to be working in the Kenya government. I think he was a distant relative of Jomo Kenyatta. People believe what they believe. But Scott said that Mr. Carrington pulled his toes (*laughs*) and he got up. And he found my mother unconscious, lying on the street floor downstairs. So he called another one of our young friends who also had come to the United States because my mother had told them, "Come to the United States. (*Laughter.*) My daughter will help you." Her aunt came and then her aunt brought her. They then called me in Chicago where I was living. By the time I got on the plane to come to New York, my mother had had very serious surgery. When my mother woke up, she had had surgery; she had had a colostomy.

I don't believe in old wives tales, or old men's tales for that matter, but these stories makes me wonder if there are some things stranger than we know. This is the second time for Scottie. He told you about the story of Tom, and he called me to tell me that my mother had been taken to the hospital. The young people had just left. (*Softly.*) I don't know. I don't know. Very strange things happened.

49. I met Kamau Mwangi in East Africa in 1991 when I was a guest of Maida Springer while she was on a three-month vacation there.

African Policy Conflicts within the ICFTU

Did you ever speak to Jomo Kenyatta about Tom Mboya?

Not about Tom. I had not seen him since 1945. The only conversation I had with Jomo Kenyatta after independence was when I asked for an audience. I didn't think he would remember me or anything, but he laughed and he said, "You are not a small girl now." He had asked me back in 1945 in Manchester, England, "Young girl, what does the American working class know about the fight against colonialism?" After then I had seen him in a crowd in Kenya. And of course I was sitting in the stands on independence night crying with joy as Prime Minister Jomo Kenyatta with his fly whisk strode across the tarmac waving to the people. But to be in his office as prime minister and to speak with him was this one time. And he laughed.

6

The All-African People's Conference and the International Labor Affiliation Dispute

The dissension that developed among African trade unions over the issue of affiliation with non-African internationals, most notably the International Confederation of Free Trade Unions, forms the bulk of Maida Springer's discussion of African events surrounding the coming of independence. Interspersed with conversation revealing the headiness with which she viewed independence are remarks demonstrating the pain of separation from friends and allies brought about by irreconcilable differences in policy between Western labor and African governments. The foreign and domestic policies of the U.S. government also resonated with how she assessed her role in Africa.

Shackled by a bipolar view of the world into Communist and anti-Communist camps, the U.S. government projected an ambivalent stance against colonialism, which in turn set the tone for the scornful treatment Springer received at the hands of U.S. consular personnel in territories like the Belgian Congo and Southern Rhodesia. In the Congo they were concerned that Springer would upset the delicate balance they were trying to strike between the colonial power and African nationalists. Pushed by Soviet anticolonial policy and fearing the loss of influence in an independent Congo, the United States promoted support for private investment and some educational and technical programs in the country. However, sensitivity to Brussels' outrage over these limited overtures led the U.S. State Department to ban African Americans from traveling to the Congo, downsize its consul staff, and end the English classes the same year Springer had a transit stop in the territory. Springer recalls that the U.S. consulate attempted to circumscribe her activities during her short stay. In the fight against Communism, U.S. relations with NATO allies took precedence over giving support to African aspirations for self-determination.[1]

---

1. Jonathan E. Helmreich, "U.S. Foreign Policy and the Belgian Congo in the 1950s," *The Historian* 58 (Winter 1996): 315–29.

In connection with her travels between the Congo and Ghana for the 1958 All-African People's Conference (AAPC), Springer speaks of the Briton Michael Scott (1907–1983), an Anglican priest known for his sense of humor and for his relentless opposition to South African policies. With the African leadership prohibited from traveling, Scott in 1949 petitioned the United Nations on behalf of the national claims of Africans of South-West Africa (now Namibia) for independence. As a result of Germany's defeat in World War I, its colony South-West Africa was put under the League of Nations' mandate system to be administered by South Africa. After the founding of the United Nations in 1945, South Africa refused to hand over the mandate to the Trusteeship Council and moved to incorporate the territory as a fifth province in the Union of South Africa. After Scott was banned from returning to his missionary post in South Africa in 1952 because of his activism, he helped to establish the Africa Bureau in London as a forum to advance justice for Africans and particularly for Namibians. As part of the antiapartheid struggle, he continued to lobby the UN, particularly on behalf of the Hereros of South-West Africa. The Germans massacred about 80 percent of the Herero people in a war in the early 1900s, after which the Hereros and other Africans continued to suffer victimization at the hands of the South African government. Scott attended the AAPC as a representative of Herero chief Hosea Kutako.[2]

In contrast to her reception in the repressive Congo, Springer had good relations with U.S. embassy personnel in the newly independent nation of Ghana, where the question of alienating a colonial power was then moot. Her description of her excellent relations with Africans at the AAPC, however, are tempered by her reflections on the resultant discord germinated at the conference over the question of international affiliation of African trade union centers. Along with George McCray and white American Irving Brown (1911–1989), she helped to diffuse a situation that might have led to the immediate disaffiliation of African unions from the ICFTU.

Like Springer, McCray and Brown engendered the respect of many Africans. Brown, a son of a Teamsters leader, graduated from New York University in 1932 with an economics degree. He organized for a predecessor of the UAW and for the AFL before becoming field representative for the AFL and later the AFL-CIO from 1945 to 1962. He was instrumental in fighting Communist unions in Europe

2. Ralph Bunche gave assistance to Scott's efforts to speak before the UN. See John Grigg, "A Very Practical Faith," *The Times* (London), August 14, 1992, features section; George Houser, *No One Can Stop the Rain: Glimpses of Africa's Liberation Struggle* (New York: Pilgrim Press, 1989), 111; Kenneth King, ed., *Ras Makonnen: Pan-Africanism from Within* (New York: Oxford University Press, 1973), 192; Springer to Bayard Rustin, November 10, 1982 (MSK PP).

and gathering support for the Marshall Plan among labor unions. By the late 1950s, however, he was committing more time to Africa. He became head of the ICFTU United Nations office in 1962, head of the AFL-CIO's African-American Labor Center in 1965, AFL-CIO European representative in 1973, head of the AFL-CIO International Affairs Department from 1982 to 1986, and for the last three years of his life, senior adviser to AFL-CIO president Lane Kirkland.[3]

Springer explains how the diminishing status of the West and the ICFTU, nevertheless, began to compromise her effectiveness in Africa. Under pressure from Kwame Nkrumah following the AAPC, the Ghana Trades Union Congress (Ghana TUC) joined with francophone Africa's Union Générale des Travailleurs d'Afrique Noire (UGTAN) and labor unions from Nigeria and the United Arab Republic in calling for the formation of an autonomous African labor international whose affiliates would have no formal ties to outside internationals.

Springer's remarks indicate that she understood the reasons for the turn of some African nations away from the West. The case of Guinea provided one example. Following Guinea's vote in September 1958 for independence and against membership in a French commonwealth of nations, France broke off relations and destroyed whatever equipment they could not remove from the country. With Western nations remaining indifferent to Guinea's plight, Ghana reached out to the country by forming the Ghana-Guinea Union and approving a significant financial aid package. The union, which would not become fully realized, represented the first step toward Nkrumah's vision of a united Africa.

By 1962 the African labor movement split into two rival internationals; the All-African Trade Union Federation (AATUF) opposed outside affiliation while the African Trade Union Confederation (ATUC) allowed individual affiliates to decide. In 1964 Tanganyika, the country to which Springer felt most attuned, brought about the disaffiliation of the national labor center from the ICFTU, following an attempted coup involving some labor leaders. Reorganized and renamed as the National Union of Tanganyikan Workers (NUTA), the new labor structure, following the pattern for unions in the new African states, became part of the apparatus of the political party. Not until 1973 was the pan-African labor split resolved with the founding of the Organization of African Trade Union Unity (OATUU), which proclaimed against outside affiliation.

The language Springer uses during her discussion of these momentous events alternates between her perception of herself as an insider and an outsider on the African scene. She also had hoped that the structure of the trade unions after in-

<hr />

3. "Irving Brown, 77, U.S. Specialist on International Labor Movement," *The New York Times*, February 11, 1989.

dependence would eventually change. These portions of the interviews took place before the realization of changes as a result of the end of the cold war. Starting in 1991 many African labor centers became independent of their governments and flocked to the ICFTU. And OATUU no longer serves as a force against outside affiliation.

Although Springer opposed African disaffiliation from the ICFTU and the growing undemocratic practices of African nations, she was sympathetic to the plight of these newly independent countries in their quest to overcome the legacy of colonialism. She relates how these sympathies became a source of discord with her friend Pauli Murray. Their strong disagreements included differences over how they viewed their African heritage and the politics of African governments. Murray, who at Springer's urging had accepted a position at the newly established Ghana School of Law, came to oppose Nkrumah as a dictator. Just before she left Ghana, she and another U.S. lawyer, Keith Highet, secretly helped Nkrumah's longtime political opponent, Joseph B. Danquah, build a case against the Preventative Detention Act under which eight opposition leaders had been arrested. Danquah, a founder of the political organization, the United Gold Coast Convention (UGCC), had made it possible for Nkrumah to become general secretary of the party in 1947. Two years later Nkrumah formed the Convention People's Party. For his opposition to Nkrumah's policies, Danquah was arrested. Released in 1962, he was rearrested in 1964 and accused of connections to an assassination plot on Nkrumah. Danquah died in prison a year later.

A more difficult question for Springer was reconciling her activism with the widespread belief among Africans that the U.S. government was engaged in nefarious activities that involved the assassination of Congolese leader Patrice Lumumba. It was later confirmed that the CIA had attempted to assassinate Lumumba because of cold war concerns for independent Congo and its mineral resources. However, forces loyal to the opposition movement in the Katanga region of the Congo murdered him first, but with U.S. complicity.

Within the context of the labor affiliation struggle, Springer reports her conflicting feelings in advocating democratic ideals that did not apply to the lives of blacks in the United States and which were not universally practiced by all AFL-CIO affiliates. The famous clash at the 1959 AFL-CIO convention in San Francisco between A. Philip Randolph and George Meany over the pace of civil rights reform illustrated the problems and contradictions that blacks faced within organized labor. Springer's disillusionment with the record of civil rights in the United States led her to consider moving permanently to Africa.

As Springer came up against roadblocks in working through Western unions for African labor development, she began to view Israel, founded in 1948 under

UN auspices, as a viable partner for Africa. Her relations with prominent Israeli political and labor leaders included Foreign Minister Golda Meir. Meir forged a policy of building strong relationships with African nations, reflecting Israel's need for allies in a region where Arab countries were working for its elimination. For many prominent pan-Africanists in the late 1950s the founding of Israel as a homeland for scattered and oppressed Jews resonated with feelings about African struggles for independence. The displacement and dispersion out of Israel of a significant portion of the Palestinian population during military conflicts between Israel and Arab countries and Israel's seizure of some of the land the UN had proposed for a Palestinian state did not gain widespread attention among pan-Africanists. However, the 1967 Arab-Israeli war did. Springer recalls the war as a turning point in Israel's African relations. Egypt and other North African countries by this time were exerting more power within the pan-African movement. As a result of the war Israel began its occupation of the Palestinians in the conquered Arab territory and began to build settlements there despite UN Security Council Resolution 242 calling for Israeli withdrawal.[4]

Springer reveals how another UN resolution concerning Israel scuttled her plans to have the ILGWU, with its largely Jewish leadership, work with Mali, a predominantly Muslim country, in the establishment of a day care center under the direction of the Mali labor movement. In response to the continued occupation of Palestinian territories, the UN General Assembly in 1975 passed Resolution 3379 equating Zionism with racism. Springer found herself in a situation that again reflects how larger political issues had a detrimental impact on her goals. It also reflects her uneasiness with her role in difficult political situations. In 1991 the UN General Assembly revoked the resolution; however, the debate over Zionism and racism remains a hotly contested issue.[5]

Springer's work in Mali to establish a day care center was part of her larger work as drought program coordinator for the African-American Labor Center. The drought in the Sahel, a semiarid region of Africa south of the Sahara desert, began in 1968, but the world did not recognize it as a disaster for two years. Lasting until 1985 the drought brought on one of the world's worst periods of starvation.

4. Following a second Arab-Israeli war in 1973 most African nations broke off relations with Israel. Israelis and Arabs refer to the 1963 and 1973 wars by different names. Israelis refer to them, respectively, as the Six Day War and the Yom Kippur War while the Arabs refer to them as the Setback and the Ramadan War.

5. Secretary of State Colin Powell, in agreement with President George W. Bush, decided against leading a high-ranking delegation to attend the United Nations World Conference on Racism held in Durban, South Africa, in 2001. The administration downgraded its support for the conference because of moves within the conference to equate Zionism with racism and to call for reparations for slavery.

The All-African People's Conference

Of the five countries where Springer worked, Mali was one of the most seriously affected by the drought. Three U.S. unions were to share in the support of the day care center, and U.S. graduate students and medical personnel were to participate in the program. Future plans for the center included training the mostly female rural workers who were streaming into the workforce, and adding nutritionists and nurses to the staff.[6]

☙❧

What groups or what people do you think really made the independence struggles work?

Well, let's see now. I attended the independence celebrations of Ghana, Nigeria, Kenya, Tanganyika, the Gambia. So in these five I actively saw the change in governments. In Ghana you had an educated elite. This group had formed what they called the United Gold Coast Convention movement or the Gold Coast Convention Party. And then this brash, American-educated Kwame Nkrumah was invited back to Ghana to stimulate. The United Gold Coast Convention had been moving politely and saying please and petitioning. When Dr. Nkrumah came back, there were big outdoor rallies and he had sound trucks. He added the element of street corner politics that was known in America. The same thing was true everywhere, that Africans wanted an opportunity to rule themselves. They didn't want to be in their own country, where 95, 98 percent of the population was the native citizenry, and have to face all of these places with signs saying that you could not enter. The jobs were so limited; they would bring somebody from Britain for you to teach them that job which you could not hold. And your salary was poor.

On the Gold Coast and in Nigeria you had a larger educated elite than you had in East and Central Africa. That made a difference in that this elite had a large administrative responsibility. You didn't have a settler community to administer government affairs totally such as you had in Kenya and Tanganyika and in Northern and Southern Rhodesia. In West Africa there was this sense of we know, we have it, and we are going to be independent. We are not in the same category as East Africans, you know, under the same restrictions. This was the feeling, but the bottom line is they were all part of the colonial empire, whether it was Portugal, whether it was France, whether it was Britain. Just worse in some areas. And in Ghana and Nigeria there used

6. Springer to William Ross (ILGWU vice president), February 24, 1974, and to Mattie Jackson (ILGWU vice president), August 10, 1975 (Amistad).

to be a story that the reason the British could not settle in these countries was because of the tsetse fly.[7] It was a kind of running joke. And, of course, South Africa's structure was different. They were not a colony. They fought the Boer War and became an independent entity. And Namibia, which just became independent, had been a German colony before World War I. The South African government was supposed to administer it after that as a trust territory but would not report on it to the United Nations and *treated it* as its colony.[8] So the aggressive elite, the higher percentage of trained Africans on the west coast as against the more limited-educated group on the east coast and Central Africa was for me the great difference in the independence movements.

The work with no money, the spirit of the people, the market women of West Africa and how they raised money to build community action and a party boggles the mind. The market women were the independent entrepreneurs. They sold cloth. They sold food. They had their little *shambas* (small farms). They were independent! So they always had ways that they could help put money together and support whatever they wanted to support. And there were such masses of them. These women had trucks that were put to use. They could create masses, bodies in meetings, and they would exercise the interest of their slower-moving sisters. So I give the market women in West Africa a great deal of credit toward the independence of those countries. They're the unsung heroines.

I think as long as I live I will still be moved by the night of independence in Ghana on March 6, 1957, when the British flag came down and the Ghanaian flag went up. We were in a very dark and great, great, great outdoor place, and the lights were dim, when Kwame Nkrumah and the ministers of an independent Ghana came and stood on the platform clothed in

7. The tsetse fly's presence in some African regions made it difficult for European colonialists to engage in large-scale ranching and agricultural pursuits. As a bloodsucker the fly acts as a vector, transporting disease-carrying parasites to humans and animals. Trypanosomiasis, commonly known as sleeping sickness or nagana, is one of the diseases. According to the World Health Organization, sixty million people in Africa are at risk from infection. In some regions sleeping sickness is the leading cause of death, ahead of HIV/AIDS, although it is curable in its earliest stages. See Naututu Okhoya, "Eradicating Tsetse Flies from Africa," *Africa Recovery*, April 22, 2003; and University of Leicester, "Course BS2024: Microbiology II, Trypanosomiasis," http://www-micro.msb.le.ac.uk/224/Trypano.html (accessed February 26, 2003).

8. Although the Afrikaners lost the Anglo-Boer War (1899–1901) to England, they became independent in 1910. South Africa's long history of racist treatment of Africans and other nonwhites culminated with the imposition of apartheid in 1948 when the National Party won an electoral victory. More on South Africa follows in chapter 9. This portion of the interview was done on July 2, 1990. More on Namibia follows in chapter 9.

The All-African People's Conference

their striped jail clothes and hats.[9] That is an experience that though staged gave me goosebumps. People acted as though they had one voice. I was standing beside Philip Randolph, and on the other side of me was Ras Makonnen. And I wept like a baby on that evening.

To have seen planeloads of people come from all over the world for that was exciting. Some of the same persons who said it could never happen you saw bowing and scraping before *a chief, His Excellency, PM*, and other such officials. It gives you an awareness of human nature to view this. They respected power and what the power could perhaps do for them, like keep them in the country so they didn't have to go back to their country, to wherever they came from. (*Laughter.*) If they were able to stay, their wives could still have a house full of servants—a nursemaid for the children and a gardener and a cook and a chauffeur. They couldn't have that where they came from. They had it in Africa. In addition, the diamonds and the gold and bauxite in this mineral-rich, still poor Africa are the things that come to your mind when you speak of Africa and the independence movements.

These countries had a right to challenge for independence. And I guess, for England, holding onto all these places was becoming a burden. A *little* tiny country like England ruling "Inja" [India]. (*Laughs.*) Holland had a great big archipelago [Indonesia]. No. These people had the right to challenge. They had a right to have independence. They had a right to make their mistakes. You got me on a bad subject, you know. I don't know any objective people, but I'm not one of them. I hear people say they are objective, but they're objective about their point of view that they're putting forward.

You wrote in your diary in 1957 that you got on a flight in the Congo that had originated in South Africa. Why did you remember that flight?

Oh, yes. Well, I was on my way to Ghana independence from East Africa, and a South African delegation was coming, too. I had never been to South Africa at this point. In my view the only reason they would come is to hope that it would be so disastrous that they could make fun of this independent government. On that transit flight was the Reverend Michael Scott, whom I knew from the UN. I had first met him when he was presenting the case of the Hereros in South-West Africa in those days, now Namibia. Everybody

9. Independence was celebrated at the Old Polo Grounds, an area that was formerly used primarily by colonialists. At independence Nkrumah made the now famous statement, "We again rededicate ourselves in the struggle to emancipate other countries in Africa, for our independence is meaningless unless it is linked up with the total liberation of the African continent." The Kwame Nkrumah Mausoleum has since been established at the Old Polo Grounds. See "Nkrumah, Legendary African Personalities, African Unification Front," http://www.africanfront.com/b-names.php (accessed May 4, 2003).

The All-African People's Conference

knew everybody. You were in small groups and you were trying to raise money and you were trying to interest people.

On this flight I foolishly did not take off my shoes or put on slippers. I had a beautiful pair of lizard shoes on and sat there all night on the plane. So my feet were swollen. The shoes had a strap across and a button and I could not get them off. And it was remarkable because my seat companion, this South African *man*, got down on his knees and twisted this strap and got it off the button, so I could take my shoes off. And this man, my seat companion all night, was helping me. He was a different person in a different atmosphere. He was behaving like a person, helping someone in distress. And Reverend Michael Scott said (*laughs*) that this is a story that ought to be told, because I'd be someone they would lock up if I went near a white man in South Africa. So we just made a joke of it.

Tell me about your experiences in the Congo.

Before independence I was just in transit from East Africa when I stopped in the Congo. In those days you'd have two days before the next plane was available to go wherever you were going. When I was there on my way to Ghana for the independence celebrations, I went to the American consulate — it wasn't an embassy yet — to register, to do the official things, to pay my respects, to let them know I was there. I was doing nothing that I was ashamed of or afraid of. Whoever was in charge of the American consulate did not want me to talk to anybody in the Congo. When I checked in, I said, "I'm Maida Springer." And he said, "Oh, yes. We know you're here." (*Chuckles.*) "Please be a good tourist." I wasn't bothering anybody. People were coming to me and trying to make *contact* with me. People knew I was there. The grapevine is fantastic. Fantastic.

According to your diary, a Mr. Bunsey [probably Gilbert E. Bursley][10] of the U.S. consulate in the Congo told you that there was a reluctance on the part of the people in the Congo to let Africans study outside the Congo because they feared Belgian and U.S. influence.

Belgian? Well, the Belgians weren't permitting many Congolese to study abroad. What I recall was that the consul said, "Maida, be a good tourist. Go to the market. Look at things. Buy curios." He was in effect saying to me

10. From 1955 to 1957 Gilbert E. Bursley served as the American consul and public affairs officer in charge of the United States Information Agencies Program in the Belgian Congo, French Equatorial Africa, Ruanda Urundi, Cameroons, and Angola. In his public career, Bursley also served as a military officer, UN observer, and a Michigan state legislator. James F. Green was the consul general. Diary entry, February 27, 1957 (MSK PP); "Gilbert E. Bursley," biographical information, University of Michigan News Service, January 1965 (Ann Arbor: University of Michigan, Bentley Historical Library).

don't interfere. He was warning me to be a good tourist, get back on the plane, and go on to Ghana. They wanted me do whatever and not be political, because they were having problems. The U.S. consulate wanted to develop programs to teach English and other things. They were having a difficult time trying to develop these basic type of classes. Nothing is a secret. I guess he knew that someone wanted to talk to me.

Whenever I went back to my room, the young steward, the person that they had as the emissary, would come to me and say that somebody was downstairs who knew that I'm a missionary and wanted to talk to me. It took a day before it dawned on me that this was just somebody's way of getting a message to me. They knew I wasn't a missionary. "Pardon, vous-êtes Madame Springer?" "Oui." "Vous êtes missionaire." "Non, je suis syndicalist." I said, "No, I'm not a missionary." "Oh, Madame. Oh, Madame. S'il vous plâit?" I wasn't functioning quickly. And then they sent people who spoke some English, to try to make me understand that they didn't want to socialize with me. (*Laughs.*) By the time the third person came, I got the message. Between my bad French understanding and their limited English, we got our act together. Some of the most extraordinary things happen to you as an outsider with people trying to get you to do something, to listen. I wasn't exactly unaware of the difficult situation in the Congo. So once accepting that someone was trying to give me a message, I then agreed to go down.

So then I went down the stairs to this big open terrace restaurant and sat down. And somebody came and had coffee and croissants with me. An English-speaking person. White. It was somebody from one of the religious groups. There was no suspicion with someone sitting there drinking coffee with me. I don't know if he came with someone who was a nonwhite. There may have been three people sitting down having coffee and I'm listening.[11] Extraordinary experiences. And of course the consul knew it.

There was suspicion of the U.S. consulate even giving these classes?

Of course! Of course! Of course!

You were quite a threat.

Imagine! Imagine! Quite a threat. Imagine. Very simple things. There wasn't a political party, there wasn't anything. On another occasion I was given a white paper to take out of the country. That document was saying what conditions the Africans were living under, detailing the problems in the Congo,

11. According to the February 27, 1957, entry in Springer's diary, two Congolese gentlemen visited her in the evening at the Hotel Regina. One was a doctor and the other was employed at the Mpare Import House. They showed her embroidery as a ruse while they explained the conditions of workers.

The All-African People's Conference

the lack of education, the problems in the mines, etc. Subsequently that document was widely published. The Belgian government felt that no Congolese could have written that paper, so they blamed (*laughs*) the Catholic missionaries. But I had been given a copy of this paper. "Take it outside. Let somebody see it. This is what we're living under." Nothing subversive, except if you want *change* and think you are entitled to some of the fruits of your labor in your rich country. *That's* subversive. And I was given this by no trade unionist but by people who just said, "Please. You're an American. You're going outside. Take it!" I don't remember who I gave it to, but I came back and delivered it to some African-oriented committee.

Nothing was secret. Maida Springer arrived somewhere. The grapevine works. Both politically and in government circles. And of course there was a great deal of distrust at anything that "outsiders" were doing. I had a history already from the scholarship program [October–December 1957]. And the news spread that this Maida Springer would come here trying to start trouble also, to encourage people, to talk to the Africans.

Once in the Congo I had been with Dr. Nyerere in a taxi. He was in transit on his way to Ghana. I don't know if this was a fact, but I was told subsequently that the taxi driver was asked what did that American talk about? And the taxi driver told them, "Je ne sais pas. Parlaient anglais constament." I only spoke English, and he didn't understand what I was saying.

There were all kinds of nuances that made you suspect if you were in a country and you were considered opposed to the policies of that government. The American labor movement was anticolonial, so that put a mark on you right away. The Congo was a very complex and troubled business and there are many ugly things that I think happened in there which, if you have read, it was alleged that Americans were involved in.

Did Patrice Lumumba's assassination affect your relations in Africa?

Yes. To many there was the assumption that the United States was implicated in Patrice Lumumba's death. And never mind what I was saying or attempting to do with the labor unions. No, it was difficult! Couldn't explain Patrice Lumumba's death. I couldn't. People smarter than I maybe explained it. I couldn't. I couldn't. I could not accept assertions of U.S. complicity. If I had, I would have raised questions within myself about my role in Africa.

What are your impressions of Patrice Lumumba?

Well, Patrice Lumumba, in my view, did not live long enough for fulfillment of whether he was a bad person or was a good person. I start with the judgment that he was a good person who was challenging. As far as I note, he did *nothing* wrong. He wasn't in that kind of authority long enough for me to pass judgment. I don't think he lived long enough to really prove himself. He was cut down very early. I think I was somewhere in Africa when he was assassinated. I was very sorry. Congo, big country, the potential in the Congo. I wish I could be . . . just take it in life's stride, but the African experience for me was very personal.

Later there were two or three things I was interested in in the Congo. Government missions brought some leaders of the trade union movement here to the United States to discuss opportunities for educational programs with an eye toward down the line arranging a French-speaking program. I think this was during the Kennedy administration. They brought them to have an *échange de vue*. We talked of health programs for workers and other services that might be offered. Since my French wasn't that good, I was not as good a facilitator in the Congo. So my efforts there were not as strong as they could have been. But I am still well remembered in the Congo. (*Chuckles.*) There is an article floating around here, which I guess was written the third or fourth time I was in the Congo. I had just arrived that day and the newspaper article described me as an ancient trade unionist from the United States. (*Laughs.*)

The other thing I was interested in later was the refugee problem in the Congo, the Portuguese problem. The people who were fleeing from Angola and Mozambique were being housed in refugee camps in the Congo.[12] By this time the Congo is independent and the AFL-CIO is trying to be supportive. And I at some point developed a program of working with a union to send a shipping container of clothing and supplies that could be used in the Congo. Something went very wrong. Somewhere along the line I think that container got opened. I believe they got half rocks (*chuckles*), I am told.[13] I was interested in a health program in the Congo, also. Preliminary work was done, but it did not come to fruition. So there were these discussions about things one wanted to share and to do.

12. Unlike other European colonial powers, the Portuguese authoritarian regime of António Salazar tightened its grip on its African territories in the early 1960s rather than accept the inevitable march toward independence. African nationalists began guerilla wars against Portugal in Angola in 1961 and in Mozambique in 1964. After the Lisbon regime was overthrown in 1974, Portugal granted independence to its colonies in 1975. Long, brutal civil wars that became ensnarled in international cold war politics then plagued Angola and Mozambique. Cease-fires came to Angola in 2002 and to Mozambique in 1992.

13. Jewel Frierson and other officers of Local 194 of the Retail, Wholesale and Department Store Union of Chicago, and the National Council of Negro Women gave support to Springer's work on behalf of Angolan refugees fleeing the war with Portugal. See "Maida, U.S. Unions Send Clothing to Exiled Angolans," *AALC Reporter* 7 (July–August 1972).

Let's talk about your impressions of the 1958 All-African People's Conference in Ghana.

Some of the people who came to the All-African People's Conference were there with a price on their head. You know, we had somehow sneaked them out of the country. Money was raised all over the place to bring these Africans to Accra. I *even* raised money. George Padmore wrote to me or either called me in New York and said, "Maida, you know we are having trade union chaps here from East Africa. We do not have a lot of money, and we are trying to make sure that they are all here. We expect you to come and find money to help *your* (*laughs*) trade union colleagues. What can you do about it? Can you talk to your colleagues?" So I raised a few dollars to make sure that fares could be paid, but I said on one condition. I knew that when I got there, they would have upon a big bulletin board the names of the people who were raising money and who had done things to bring some of the delegations there. So I said, "I do not want any praise for this; I didn't raise the money. People in the labor movement in the United States believed in what you are doing, and so it must be anonymous."[14]

It was an incredible conference. Ghana was the place that was vibrant and was pulling together all of the people from Africa. What was significant was that Africans from east, west, north, and south were meeting for the first time! Some of them could have culture shock. They were so different from other Africans in terms of the approach, in terms of their language, in terms of attitudes. But the common denominator was that they were meeting in an African country—the prime minister, an African; the African cabinet welcoming them; *all* of the arrangements, the eating and living facilities, were made by the African government of Ghana, their host. Now if that isn't enough to turn your head and turn you upside down, I don't know what will. *This* was as incredible as the Berlin Wall coming down or even more so, because people from all over the continent were meeting together and sharing problems, aspirations, and talking about an African community of support for one another. This had never happened on this continent before. *Couldn't* have happened without an independent Ghana. There were other independent countries, a couple of them. But *none* of them could have pulled that off. Ghana, Nkrumah's showmanship, Nkrumah's belief in himself as the leader of Africa made it possible. These were extraordinary times to be a part of. But you were so involved in it that you didn't realize what a history-making event you were a part of.

One of the most extraordinary experiences involved a speaker from the

14. For more on the All-African People's Conference, see Richards, *Maida Springer*, 176–86.

United Arab Republic. And this is an amusing story. We did not—I say we, because I felt so deeply involved and a part of the conference—we did not have simultaneous interpretation. There wasn't money enough, people enough to do all that needed to be done. So people were translating from the platform. The Egyptian delegation spoke in French. One of my colleagues, Irving Brown, the archenemy (*laughs*) in terms of some of the challenges that came up, was asked by some of the Ghanaians to be a translator. Irving Brown is a famous name in international affairs, not just in Africa but all over. He was the AFL-CIO European representative, *deeply* involved in international affairs and based in Paris. So he stood on the platform interpreting what was being said in French. And this particular man, very high in the Egyptian government, who spoke English fluently, didn't like the way Irving translated something he said. So he walked across the stage (*laughs*) and he said (*with an Egyptian accent*), "No, no, Mr. Irving Brown." These are some of the subtleties.[15]

I couldn't be a delegate because this was the All-African People's Conference. But the Ghanaians asked me to be a volunteer, to work at the conference center and receive the applications and process them. I was admitting the delegates, looking at the credentials, helping people with information, and doing whatever I was asked to do. I saw various people who came in. And, of course, my French would put me in jail but would not take me out. My French still is poor. When I would run into difficulty, I would have to call someone to help me because the French that is spoken to you is so fluent and so rapid that you become lost. I would have to get Irving or some French-speaking person to help. Patrice Lumumba was one of the delegates signing in. That was the only time I met him. It was a very quick encounter. People were trying to get to meetings and we were trying to process them through.

So here I am a volunteer working in this sensitive position for the conference trying to be very careful, because you didn't know who was who and which government had sent in spies. Some people wanted my help in getting into the conference. A couple of the Americans were there because they had a big embassy in Accra. So some of the lower echelon people said to me, "Maida, can you get me in as an observer?" (*Laughs.*) At that time, still, my rating was high in Ghana. I hadn't become an enemy, yet.

15. In a report Springer wrote after the conference, she remarked, "Irving Brown did a sterling job as part-time interpreter. The significance of this is that the personnel of the conference sanctioned his activity despite his known affiliation with the unpopular ICFTU. One can only conclude that Irving's presence as representative of President Meany and the American labor movement outweighed other factors. His general friendliness and usefulness with the delegations was very effective." "Observations on the All-African People's Conference," 14/12/11 (ILGWU Archives).

I was known, I had been there before, and I had been a volunteer at the airport for the independence celebrations. One of my friends, Richard Quarshie, who was going to be in foreign affairs and a minister, had asked me to do this since they were short-handed. (*Laughs.*) Ah, those were crazy times. Everything was so new and so full of optimism. We were so thrilled to see men and women doing their jobs as leaders of the government, leaders in various places in their country, who could not have entered segregated places before, who saw the signs come down. Places in the country with 95 percent of the population black, but Africans could not enter. That leaves incredible impressions on you, extraordinary impressions. I have seen that. And I would think that there were many whites representing the colonial government who resented me. They had attacked me and said things about me. I didn't mind that. For once in my life I was somewhere I had the right paint job. I empathized with the people in Africa. I was not objective. I couldn't be objective! Very few people in the world are. They are objective to what suits their purposes.

But you name it, they were there. From everywhere. Oh, my God! Ooh! I still get goosebumps when I think of the All-African People's Conference and reflect now on the significance of it. At that time I knew it was important, thought it was important that so many Africans from all over the continent for the first time were meeting.

You told me earlier that there were few women there. Do you recall any of the women or any discussion about women at this conference?

Oh sure. There was lots of discussion. Well, the women, particularly the French-speaking women, were on fire! The French-speaking women were from Guinea, from Senegal, and from a few other countries. I do not remember any English-speaking African women, except the Ghanaian women, being outstanding and extremely vocal. They talked about the conditions of the country, the problems that women face, the things that men have to face up to so that the women would be entirely included in the future independence of their country, the social problems that women face, the difficulties. They were burning questions, and these women raised them all. Education, employment, religious and marriage customs. They talked about the whole spectrum. Every country with its own difficulties and tribal cultures. And they annoyed some of the African men. (*Laughs.*) So they didn't get off easy. The women didn't have it all their own way. But the women talked.[16]

It wasn't pervasive, but there were men who just couldn't quite cope with

16. See speech by Mrs. Martha Ouandie, representative of the Kamerun Women Democratic Union, 3/5 (Brown files).

the articulateness of the women. There were a couple of instances when they tried to shout them down in some of the small committee meetings, which I did not attend. And I listened to some of the things the men said as they talked. Because they considered me nonfemale, they would say anything in my presence. (*Laughs.*) They would voice their annoyance in this context, "But then what we have to fight now is colonialism. These other things cannot be our priority. They have an undertone that will be dealt with when we are free." This was the best face I could put on what some of the men were saying.

Yes, they considered me nonfemale. Number one, my age always—not the way I looked, but everybody knew I was old—made a difference. Many of these people were young people in their twenties. I was a person who had some sort of "status" in the United States as "labor leader," a woman alone, moving around the world, being able to speak on behalf of the American labor movement to my colleagues in Africa. This gave me a certain role, a certain standing. So they would say, "You understand the difficulties we face; we must fight colonialism first." It is in this context that I'm saying that they could say to me and discuss with me what they considered the broader implications of the fight for independence.

And what would the women say to you?

Nothing. Women didn't pay much attention to me. In small groups they would individually speak to you and ask you about this and the other. But remember, you are talking about the All-African People's Conference. What *these* women were there for was to state their case to the men at the conference, to be in the committee meetings. I had no voice. I couldn't do anything for them within the context, the change that they wanted their men to look at. I was an observer. I did not sit in their closed meetings. So, the women didn't come to me in any large groups. That would come years later when trade union women were emerging in the labor movement. But this was the world political movement that women were attending. I was not an important factor in that, and I couldn't mislead you and tell you I was. (*Laughs.*)

Now, the *men* thought I was an important factor, because they could get some concessions, some support, some understanding. I could help move an agenda. The women knew that they had to work with the men, who may be the leaders of tomorrow. They were very clear on that. And these African men were from their country, from their tribe. The women didn't have any mistake about their priorities. So that's what I'm trying to get across to you. Not that the women didn't like me, or this or that or the other. No! Their priority was to challenge the men for greater inclusion.

The All-African People's Conference

And what happened after independence? You said these men said the first problem was the colonial problem.

Oh, I can't answer that. After independence every country that went their way had six thousand different problems that they had to deal with. But in Africa, in almost *every* country without exception, the women formed the bulk of that movement that raised money, that formed the warm bodies that made the presence in the cause of independence. So I can only share this with you in terms of what I saw and what I felt and my perception of this. There weren't a lot of us that lived through that time and saw much of it. I was one of them.

Some trade unionists at the conference were angry at the ICFTU and wanted to pull out.

Yes. Many of them did afterwards. The All-African People's Conference was not a trade union conference. It was a conference about independence. It was a conference about the changes in Africa. And because these countries were still under colonial rule, the trade union movement came in for its share of very sharp criticism and hostility. Out of that conference you had the beginning of the discussions of being nonaligned.

The nonaligned movement was about not being affiliated with either the ICFTU or the WFTU.

Well, that was eyewash. The nonaligned movement, in my view, was recently emerging from colonialism to independence and trying to move away from whatever they considered colonial. And they didn't want to be in a position of being under the constriction of being anti anything. So there was both in Asia and in Africa a nonaligned movement. But you had all over Africa the nonaligned groups quietly ask you as a representative of the AFL-CIO to do this, that, or the other for them. Then the African countries developed their own international organization of trade union federations within this nonaligned group, and they worked closely with the Scandinavians, with the Germans on individual projects, and with the Soviet Union.

So I suppose nonalignment was a heated debate at the conference.

I would say that that was the understatement of the day. Of course, people are *passionate* and they're *angry*. You have your own world forum, so you denounce everything and everybody, even the things you support. Here was the ICFTU, which made it possible for you to do a number of things that you could not do before. As a part of your colonial past, the ICFTU made it possible for you to travel, meet with your colleagues, but they were still your masters. And *this* was what Africans were talking about, the organizations, nations that they felt were still dominating them. So all the groups that they belonged to in the past, they denounced as reactionary.

The All-African People's Conference

I understood the nonaligned position. I could not be as vehement about it as the people who were under this colonial hegemony. I understood it. I thought, like anything else, much of it went to extremes. So beyond understanding it, I never closed my eyes or closed the door on my friends, those who wanted to remain my friends, when many people I knew took a sharp position and considered me an enemy and an outsider. And I accepted that. It hurt, but I accepted it.

What are your impressions of Kwame Nkrumah's rule in Ghana?

Let me say that I have at least three kinds of feelings about his rule in Ghana. One, what he did in leading the political instrument that brought independence to Ghana thrilled me right down to my toes. There was great excitement and joy at the independence of Ghana. Nkrumah while living in the United States had membership in the seafarers' union. So this all boded very well for relationships between the trade unionists in Ghana and the government of Ghana.

Oh, let me tell you about my weakness. When the government began to change the structure of the labor movement in Ghana, it should have been to me more ominous than it was. You had a very large number of very tiny unions, fragmented unions, and maybe one or two potentially large unions, the miners and dockworkers. And I felt that amalgamating a number of these unions to make a smaller number of unions was not a bad thing.[17] That's number two.

Number three. When the government made the unions a part of the political party, the Convention People's Party, that was ominous. The leadership of the union became ambassadors and held other government posts. Then you had the development of the All-African Trade Union Federation [AATUF] and later the Organization of African Trade Union Unity [OATUU], which showed a hostility to Western labor organizations which had been supported before. That left me very distraught and upset because I had placed a great deal of credence in the Ghana Trades Union Congress leading the way with a number of unions, helping them.

What happened was a kind of turnabout. There was a hostility and an anti-American feeling, anti everything that was a part of the Western labor movement. And there was no way in the world that I could be anti-Western

17. In 1956 the Ghana TUC began to restructure the trade union movement by replacing the craft and house unions, numbering more than one hundred, with national industrial unions. The ICFTU opposed sections of the 1958 Industrial Relations Act, stating that too much power over unions was given to the government. In 1962 Ghana made some amendments to the act following a complaint filed by the ICFTU against Ghana's treatment of workers. See Wogu Ananaba, *The Trade Union Movement in Africa: Promise and Performance* (New York: St. Martin's Press, 1979), 9–12.

The All-African People's Conference

trade unions. I had lived with what had been constructive and positive with regard to the relationship of the American labor movement and the trade union movement of Ghana. This was deliberate action and left me certainly among the unwelcome people in Ghana. This was the government acting, not an independent action of the labor union, because the Ghana TUC was now a part of the CPP. All of the various actions taken, whether it was against ATUC [African Trade Union Confederation] or whatever, was anti-Western, and there was almost open warfare.

I could not but be *very* sad, because I had *great* hopes and *liked* Dr. Nkrumah very much, was charmed by the way he treated trade unionists when they came to Africa. At independence an American delegation came to Ghana and wanted to meet with Dr. Nkrumah. His schedule was so tight and difficult, but I spoke with John Tettegah or other leaders of the TUC, and it was arranged. This was the kind of positive relationship that I had. So for me it was a sad time when the Ghana TUC and the government's position became so anti-American.

Certainly the French government's behavior toward Sékou Touré was *enough* to make *that* government anti-Western. They ripped the telephones out in Guinea.[18] They left the country almost barren. They were so angry with Sékou Touré because Guinea voted for immediate independence. There was discussion at the time of the All-African People's Conference of Ghana and Guinea unifying. Let me tell you what happened on the occasion for Guinea to get the loan for twenty-eight million dollars from Ghana. You had to go through the Parliament to get the loan, and for the third reading Dr. Nkrumah had Madame Sékou Touré sit in the Parliament. She didn't say anything. She didn't make a speech. But as the debate went on, here was this beautiful, silent woman representing her husband. I want to tell you that Madame Touré sitting there was very impressive. The act went through. But the united effort was not successful.

Did you feel conflict within yourself in carrying out any of the policies of the AFL-CIO in Africa?

No, I don't think I had a problem. Everything was so new and so fresh. I never asked anyone in Africa for their membership in or whether they were a member of the Communist Party or no. That's number one. I never had any ideological rifts with the Africans I was dealing with. The time came when many of them in their countries became a part of the nonaligned group,

18. Ahmed Sékou Touré (1922–1984) became head of the postal workers' union in 1945 and a member of the French National Assembly in 1956 before becoming president of Guinea from 1958 to 1984. His rule increasingly relied on repression, and his international alliances were with the Soviet bloc until 1978.

OATUU. I was out of that stream. We were not going to be participating. I think I would have had conflict had I been living and working in Africa when the divisions became sharper and sharper.

I felt very bad about some of the things that got terribly warped and misunderstood, but there it was. Trade unions were incorporated into one-party states, and they withdrew from international affiliations. The Western world couldn't accept anything but freedom of association. This created ambivalence for me. I tried hard for Africans to maintain their relationships within the ICFTU. They did not have to accept how unions operated in other countries, but they could adapt what they found useful. But the West couldn't be in the shoes of Africans. All the Africans had dealt with were the wrong things from the colonial powers or whoever was trying to purify them now. I thought that somewhere down the line that this type of structure, trade union incorporation into the national governments, would have to change. I wanted to believe that this was only inexperience and a transition. I was weak enough in my head at one time to believe that perhaps you had to make this kind of sacrifice. But that was emotional and illogical. (*Chuckles.*) I think that basically the governments wanted to do everything at once and some things suffered.

I had some emotional problems, not because I was asked to do anything that I disagreed with, but because I saw the drift between my colleagues in Africa and my colleagues in the United States, the hardening of the arteries. And when you would find articles written in the *Free Trade Union News* about the AFL-CIO challenging Kwame Nkrumah, when Ghana then had a one-party state and the unions were completely absorbed within the political instrument, those things made a difference. And when certain people were jailed, you had both the ICFTU and the American labor movement speaking out against the swallowing of the labor movement so that it was not an independent voice. And the Ghana TUC became very hostile to the American labor movement and to the ICFTU.[19]

What happened when those unions, which were within the government, weren't hostile to the American labor movement?

It didn't matter whether they were hostile to the American labor movement or no. The government policy was X! You did what your government

19. The AFL-CIO criticized Nkrumah's suppression of the Sekondi-Takoradi strike. Since Sekondi had a history of opposition to Nkrumah's rule, there is evidence that the violence associated with the strike was partly motivated by his political opposition. See "Support Ghana Strikers," *AFL-CIO Free Trade Union News* 16 (October 1961); "The Strikes in Ghana: What Are the Facts?" *AFL-CIO Free Trade Union News* 17 (May 1962); and "Ghana's Descent to Dictatorship," *AFL-CIO Free Trade Union News* 19 (April 1964); Paul Gray, *Unions and Leaders in Ghana: A Model of Labor and Development* (New York: Conch Magazine Ltd., 1981), 27–28, 108–9.

The All-African People's Conference

wanted done or else you went into exile. What your country was saying was that you wanted unity in the country and that you can't build the country without the unity of everybody, and that you don't strike, and you don't ask for more money, because you are not a separate entity. You are a member of this country and the union is a part of the political party. If you understand that's a part of the structure, that's what you support. You don't have to live with this union outside. No matter what you believe in, you're going to support your country, or either leave the country, go into exile, or go to jail. Very simple. Any union that became a government union—it doesn't matter what the AFL-CIO would say—that union then had to represent its government. So what anybody else said didn't make any difference to them, because then they were part of whatever unions around the world had the same point of view that they had.

Did you have trade unionists come and talk to you when they felt that they couldn't speak independently from the government for their trade union?

Yes. I had many people talk to me, little people, because the top folk were ministers of labor, they were other cabinet ministers, or held other positions. And there were those who now, as a part of the government, would condemn anything that I would have to say, talking about freedom of association and the rest of it, because we were then talking about unity. You were talking about nation building.

So had you tried to talk to people about this?

No. Whom could I talk to? I could not go to the government. All the people I talked to were little people.

I have a letter here that one minister of labor for Tanzania wrote to me, in which he said I was considered family and friend and reproached me.[20] He said this because I had said to him in Geneva that the American labor movement in those days was not contributing workers' money to build some structure that he was requesting.[21] The principal thing was at *this* point the

20. Michael Marshall Mongray Kamaliza was president of the Tanganyika Federation of Labor from 1960 to 1962. In 1963 he was appointed minister for health and labor. In 1965 he became vice president of AATUF. From 1964 until 1969 he was appointed general secretary of NUTA. In 1969 he was arrested along with Bibi Titi Mohamed and five others and charged with plotting to overthrow the government. He was given a ten-year prison sentence. See "Bibi Titi and the Treason Trials of 1970," *East African*, November 10–16, 1999, features section, http://www.nationaudio.com/News/EastAfrican/081199/Features/PA3.html (accessed February 24, 2003), reproduced from *Tanzania: The Story of Julius Nyerere*, © JRA Bailey, Mkuki wa Nyota Publishers, Dar-es-Salaam; Fountain Publishers, Kampala; Laura S. Kurtz, *Historical Dictionary of Tanzania*, African Historical Dictionaries, no. 15. (Metuchen, NJ: Scarecrow Press, 1978), 83–84, 213.

21. The structure to which Springer is referring is housing for workers. See Richards, *Maida Springer*, 252–53.

The All-African People's Conference

AFL-CIO was not building buildings for unions. That was their position. I think I must have said that to him, but there was certainly misunderstanding in what I was saying. When he went home, he had the impression that because their union was now a part of the government, the American labor movement, of which I was the spokesman at that point on Africa, would not be interested in doing anything for his federation.

The labor structure in Tanzania would have limited the relationship between the Tanzanian labor movement and the American labor movement. But we had not discussed that. We were talking about buildings. We were talking about a methodology, what one represented. It was a very bad conversation, because we never got to finish it. And to this day I regret that. This was a country that I would have cut my tongue out before I said or did anything derogatory. But I think unless you were wholeheartedly in support of whatever, you were considered negative and that you were not for nation building. So, you know, this tormented me.

Did you and Pauli Murray resolve your strong differences in opinions about Ghana? Or were you at odds?

Always! Always! Always! To begin with, Pauli Murray was a 301 percent American. We always had a difference of opinion, because I told her I come from a different cultural context. Pauli was a sharp critic of all of the undemocratic practices in the United States and all of the injustices that black people were victims of. In Pauli's case I will say "colored people," because all of her family is mixed. Her position was that she could not isolate herself from a heritage that she had nothing to do with forming. She was mixed black and white and Indian. So we always had a difference.[22]

My passionate feeling about Africa she certainly did not share. She was too coolheaded and intellectually searching and was unwilling to make any compromises for undemocratic practices in Africa. So we never agreed, but we never lost the friendship. Somewhere in these documents you may run across a letter I wrote to Dr. Nkrumah, when she was applying to teach law in Ghana, which said that Pauli Murray is this kind of a lawyer.[23] You know the book that she and the South African put together on Ghana law. It's right behind you.[24]

When Pauli went to teach at the law school, she was not a critic of Ghana,

22. For more information on Murray's experiences in Africa, see Richards, *Maida Springer*, 206–8, and Pauli Murray, *The Autobiography of a Black Activist, Feminist, Lawyer, Priest, and Poet* (Knoxville: University of Tennessee Press, 1987), 318–43.

23. Springer to Ambassador Ako Adjei, February 13, 1960, and Springer to Nkrumah, February 25, 1959 (MSK PP).

24. Springer points out Pauli Murray and Leslie Rubin, *The Constitution and Government of Ghana* (London: Sweet and Maxwell, 1961).

The All-African People's Conference

or else I do not think she would have gone. Her criticisms developed later. She was supporting privately the opposition. She personally befriended Dr. Danquah, who was later jailed. I shared some of the views she had, and I was very pained by some of the things that were happening in Ghana. In due course, if Pauli had stayed she would have been persona non grata and sent out of this country.

Only minimally was Pauli a problem for my relationships in Ghana. I only was in Ghana once while Pauli was there, and I did not see any of the leading people. I was on my way somewhere else. I think I spent a night or two there. I did not try to see Nkrumah. It was made clear to me in some circles that Professor Murray was overly critical. However, Dr. Murray was thought of so highly that the Ghanaian government asked her to go to do some legal, technical work involving the Congo because she was an American and because she was a lawyer and because she had bona fides. They seconded her to help with this tough, sensitive problem in the Congo.[25] And she did this willingly. So we all do contradictory things. At that point it wasn't only Pauli but the American labor movement that was on bad paper [negative relations with Ghana government]. I thought foolishly that I had enough credit that I would not be affected by it.

Do you think that the hard-line anti-Communist philosophy of the AFL-CIO could cause contradictions in its anticolonial program?

Cause suspicion. Yes, I think it could cause conflict. I think it could. There are all kinds of reasons for the suspicion. No matter what the AFL-CIO was saying or doing, there were many unresolved problems in the United States in the American labor movement. So you can take that as a part of your challenge to the AFL-CIO. In an imperfect world, of course, you could do that. One of the big things that had a refrain all over the world was what happened at the 1959 convention, when the demand was made that the AFL-CIO punish intransigent unions. People wanted the unions to be integrated and not have separate locals. Meany, in exasperation, I think, said to Vice President Randolph who the hell gave you the responsibility to speak on behalf of Negro workers? Or some statement like that. Books have been written about this *all* over the world. This is an immediate contradiction.[26]

But I know one of the black unions out of Chicago, whose head talked to

25. Murray does not mention this incident in her autobiography.
26. Meany met Randolph's insistence that the AFL-CIO punish discriminating affiliates with the rhetorical challenge, "Who the hell appointed you as the guardian of all the Negroes in America?" The official report of convention proceedings did not include the profanity. *Proceedings of the AFL-CIO Constitutional Convention*, vol. 1 (1959), 485; Jervis Anderson, *A. Philip Randolph: A Biographical Portrait* (Berkeley and Los Angeles: University of California Press, 1972), 302.

me about it. They were opposed to Philip Randolph's challenge that all of these unions should be integrated. The black musicians didn't want to be integrated by anybody. They had a good building. They had done all this organizing by themselves. And they thought that the white unions in Chicago were not up to the standard that they were, and they would get swallowed up if they integrated.[27] They were *angry* with Randolph. A number of other unions had written—maybe not as sharply—to Meany and said we don't support what Randolph is doing. That same evening after that convention discussion on the platform, Meany and Randolph were sitting talking to one another and doing what they did normally. No. There were many, many contradictions. Many!

Let me tell you the degree to which Africans had the news of the civil rights movement. The European press and the British press publicized all of the various things that were happening. World interest. I would get off the plane and hear of this news, of Autherine Lucy, James Meredith, Medgar Evers. I think one very sharp one was when young Emmett Till was murdered.[28] I was in

27. In her oral history study, Diane D. Turner, "Reconstructing the History of Musicians' Protective Union Local 274 through Oral Narrative Method," in *Oral Narrative Research with Black Women*, ed. Kim Marie Vaz, 177–96 (Thousand Oaks, CA: Sage Publications, 1997), noted the opposition of black musicians to the integration of their local unions. References on pp. 179–80, 191; Anderson, *A. Philip Randolph*, 304.

28. In 1956 Autherine Lucy (Foster) became the first black admitted to the University of Alabama at Tuscaloosa. Violence and intimidation from thousands of whites protesting her admission forced her to flee the university. After the courts ordered her readmitted, the Board of Trustees expelled her. Decades later she was readmitted and earned a master's degree in the early 1990s. Her portrait now hangs in the student union building. See "Autherine Lucy Foster to Visit, Lecture at UA," University of Alabama home page, http://graduate.ua.edu/news/nov2002/foster20021111.html (accessed May 4, 2003).

In 1962 James Meredith became the first black to attend the University of Mississippi. On two separate occasions Governor Ross Barnett and Lieutenant Governor Paul Johnson blocked Meredith's registration by standing in the doorway. Two students were killed during the race riots that followed. In 1966 Meredith was shot in Mississippi as he led a march to encourage blacks to vote. He recovered and later completed the march with Martin Luther King Jr. and other prominent leaders joining him. In 1989 he accepted a position in the office of North Carolina U.S. Senator Jesse Helms, who often used race-baiting techniques to solidify his white support.

Medgar Wylie Evers (1925–1963) became the first NAACP field secretary for Mississippi. He supported James Meredith's admission into the University of Mississippi, worked on behalf of voting rights, and investigated the numerous crimes against blacks, including those against Emmett Till. Evers was gunned down by white supremacist Byron De La Beckwith. Although De La Beckwith bragged of the murder, an all-white jury failed to reach a verdict against him in two trials in the 1960s. Finally in 1994 he was convicted.

Fourteen-year-old Emmett Till, who was from Chicago, was viciously murdered in Mississippi while visiting relatives in August 1955. Unaware of the dangers in his action, he made a flirtatious remark to Carolyn Bryant, a white woman, on a dare from his young friends. Soon after the husband, Roy Bryant, and his brother-in-law, J. W. Milam, were acquitted of murder, they sold the story of how and why they murdered Till to *Look* magazine.

The All-African People's Conference

Africa but was going from one place to the other, and the news was just very hot. You could not deal with the business at hand of your program and what you were there for until you had discussed these issues of the South and the brutality of white Americans on black Americans. *Any* city that you went into in Africa, whites and blacks were going to attack you personally. The people you worked with talked in broader terms, you know, "What is this policy in America?" You were talking about the whole Southern situation. You didn't have the right to vote. No, you never had a moment's peace. And all the whites that you dealt with considered that it was a feast. There wasn't a discussion without it, no matter how gentle or how polite. (*Speaking with a British accent.*) "The Americans . . . There seems to be quite a controversy. Have you seen the latest news, Mrs. Springer? Were you in America? Where were you when this happened?"

I don't think I ever apologized for what was happening. Possibly I tried to escape by pointing out, stupidly, that I am a naturalized American citizen, and I was not from the South, was not brought up in the South. But I made sure I said that the colonialists had very little to chortle about. And since I knew a little bit of colonial history, I would cite examples of chapter and verse. They were South African. Every country I was in. East Africa (*laughs*), 99 percent black population in one country with big signs saying that you can't go in here and you can't go in there. So I don't think I did badly. It wasn't the United States alone that had these policies. And Belgium. The brutality. I just finished reading something about the Belgian Congo and the brutality there, what they did to the Africans who worked in the mines. So, I didn't do badly. (*Laughs.*) It forced me to be conversant with world history and with slavery, and in a negative way it contributed to my education.

With Africans I didn't fare as well, because I could not challenge them. But I would say simply as a matter of world history that the United States in its profession of the democratic ideal was a long way from it. So I was treated in the main kindly. There were hostilities and shoutings from some occasional groups, but we could discuss this and talk about it as long as I was not an apologist. I tried not to be. They were warm days. Ooh! Ooh! (*Laughter.*)

How can you be in another person's country, trying to relate to the workers and to the political system there about the workers in America, when you have all kinds of problems? You have unions in the United States that made black workers second-class citizens or wouldn't admit them at all. So you had all of that to contend with. And as you perhaps know, the Europeans and Africans and Asians know a great deal more about us and our history and particularly our negative policies than we know about Europe and Africa. They're

The All-African People's Conference

230

much better at history. They're taught more than we are. So I had few dull moments (*laughs*) in the sixties and during the heat of the renewed civil rights movement about American policy.

There always was a civil rights movement. We stand on so many shoulders in the United States, but memories are always short and it's the immediate next thing that is remembered. Today, many youngsters know the name Martin Luther King. What it stands for, they don't know. James Meredith and a lot of people who were so crucial, they don't know a thing about. Walter White. W. E. B. Du Bois certainly was the father of the quest for equality in changing the system. We don't know! The library is full of books about it now. And white Americans know, and what they know they're not going to discuss with us very much, except those few scholars. But the things are there for us. We don't do enough. So you and that 10 percent, the young scholars, you've got a big job on your shoulders. Believe me! Because if you don't know who you are, what you came from, you are in trouble. And if you think your role model is only the last basketball player or football player, and what is important are Nike sneakers, football shorts, football jerseys, that is not what we are about. I'm finished. (*Laughter.*)

How did you feel about this conflict you were in, in Africa during the civil rights movement? How did you keep your faith or your stamina to continue in your work?

Very often I didn't think I ever wanted to come back to the United States. (*Laughter.*) But I was so emotionally involved in the history of this country and that this was the be-all, the mecca for people who were oppressed all over the world, so I had a split mentality on this. I thought it was important for young Africans to come to the United States, to maintain contact with the United States, to be trained here, in order to have a comparison. They could have exposure to other cultures. So I always had a divided feeling about the United States but was unwavering in my belief that we should do everything we could to raise the standards for the working class in Africa. The intellectuals, the elite, were going to get scholarships and were going to go off to Europe and maybe would *never* come back to their country or come back in small numbers. Very often they would not come back, because there would be enticements and restraints.

For me independence was something that was intertwined with the workers' life. And I was not passionately hostile to the labor movement's involvement in government because in most all of the young governments the labor movement, as young as it was and immature as it was, was the second strong force in the building of a political instrument. The danger, of course, was that the independent government, having swallowed the labor movement, absorbed it as it had taken its leadership, then enforced rather unpleasant things on the working class. So, you see, I had all kinds of tortured feelings about postindependence, but *always* I felt that the African citizen should have every opportunity to come to the United States. Disagree with us, quarrel with us, but it was an exposure that I thought would be important.

On the labor side, my passion about educational training for Africans was very basic. The company you work for is Ta Ta Ta Flour Company, Limited. The only thing you know is that that company says that they can't pay you anything and will sack you, will fire you, if you say the conditions are impossible and so on. If you don't even know how to write a letter to quarrel about something you don't like, you are immediately ignored. If you can't arrive at a point where you can speak to the employer and understand more about the industry, then you can't settle your grievance. But with this greater exposure you could have access — because you are a part of the international labor movement — to documents and records from other labor unions in different parts of the world that have contracts with the same employer. You have more leverage because they could give you financial reports, what the spread is, and what the wages are. This is a part of the necessary education to make you more effective in raising the standards for workers, because most of these industries were foreign-owned and you needed to know something about who they were and what they had. And we're not talking now of upgrading wages based on the United States or Europe, but you're talking about getting wages measurable to the economy of this country and the profit coming out of this big, giant flour mill or sugar estate. The worker in country X in Africa may be paid one-tenth of what the worker in England or the United States or Germany is paid. You needed to have a relationship with the labor leadership in that foreign country where the industry originates. Hence the need for an international organization like the ICFTU, the International Confederation of Free Trade Unions, like the tripartite ILO, which is the International Labor Organization and the only instrument of the League of Nations that survived. (*Laughs.*)

As it stands now, we are called the "global factory" because you can't touch anything that is made in one country. There are very few things made in the United States. You can go to Mauritius where there are knitting mills. Sri Lanka. Very few electrical things are made in the United States. This is what I'm talking about. Having some sense of what you are dealing with, so that you are operating from awareness. So just as the big companies have their old boy networks, you begin to develop one through your international affiliation. You can't take a person who has never discussed finances—the budget and bookkeeping, keeping accounts—and send them to a negotiation session or even send them to an employer to present or discuss a grievance. This is from the point of view of my trade union head.

I learned about the world of double, triple, and quadruple standards. Countries have economies that are deliberately structured to maintain a subservient and submissive underclass. I have seen teenage girls with pock-marked faces because of the acids they were using.[29] Oh, yes, they say they have protective devices and health facilities but the girls don't use it. *Baloney*.

How did you meet Golda Meir?

Oh, Golda Meir I would have met in group functions in the United States. Jewish women were organizing all kinds of events to raise money for programs in Israel. So it was in that connection that I met her.

You were invited by her to spend nine months in Israel after the All-African People's Conference. Didn't you go?

No, no, no, no. I never got around to that.[30] What I would have done then was go into the *ulpan*, which is intensive training in Hebrew. I would have done that for a reason, which Prime Minister Meir knew about, and that was in connection with Africa. She was very involved in what was happening in Africa. I went with her to two openings in Kenya of health centers and training centers for women that Israel was supporting. My idea at the time was that if I spent nine months in Israel learning some of the techniques in their system of the *kibbutz* and the *moshav*, it could be replicated in Africa with the needed changes.[31] As I moved around Israel, I saw their techniques as having great possibilities because this country was small. It was a desert. They made flowers grow. They made food grow. I was very excited about Israel. The Israeli people and I and people around Africa had lots of conversation. But, of course, that blew up after the '67 war. Most of Africa then denounced

29. Springer is speaking of her experiences in Indonesia in the late 1970s.
30. Due to the stress of her work on behalf of African labor, Springer became ill and had to take a leave of absence for nine months.
31. The kibbutz and moshav represent different kinds of cooperative settlements. In a kibbutz (cooperative society), all the members live, eat, and work together and market their labor products collectively. The money received is used collectively according to need. Moshavs are agricultural settlements in which families live separately. Depending on the type of moshav, there are different kinds of cooperative arrangements. See Adjingboru A. Syme, *Ghanaians Salute to Israel: The Story of the Ghana Youth Delegation to Israel* (Accra, Ghana: Guinea Press Ltd., 1957), 20–25.

The All-African People's Conference

Israel and supported the positions of the Middle East. Israeli embassies were closed down. But in those early days it was a *wonderful*, positive relationship between Israel and the new African governments.

While you were attending the All-African People's Conference you wrote in your diary about Israeli and African relations. You remarked that "Israelis have an Arab and other assimilation problem in their country that leaves something to be desired." Did you have any thoughts about the Palestinian question at that time?

At that time, no, I did not. Some countries were beginning to question their Israeli relations.

You also stated that "Israelis in the United Nations have not been exactly vocal on some issues in South Africa and yet they are the only non-African country Western in outlook and philosophy that [have with] Africans . . . mutual respect and attempts at understanding."[32]

If I wrote it then, that's the way I felt. There were so many things that I thought good that Israel was offering to share with Africans. First of all, they had just become a country in 1948. They had been wanderers all over the world, and I came from a working culture that was very involved in Israel. So my feeling was that there should be no blemish on Israel's relations. Nothing should happen that you should have to question the Israelis. I thought that whatever was to be done, the Israelis ought to be pure in heart. That was my point of view.

In 1975 you wrote a letter to William Ross, manager of the ILGWU Philadelphia Joint Board, saying that the American unions would no longer sponsor a child care center to be built in Bamako, the capital of Mali, and this was partly in response to the United Nations resolution equating Zionism with racism. What was the connection between that resolution and building this child care center?[33]

William Ross was very supportive of *anything* I was doing. This personal letter you have seen that I wrote to him was a limited explanation to a wider problem. I was talking to a friend out of my own desperation. The discussions of the child care center started with people in the UNTM, the Union Nationale des Travailleurs du Mali. Dr. Mamadou Dembele was then the

32. Diary entry, November 19, 1958 (MSK PP).

33. In 1963 Ross's union had given Springer ten thousand dollars to start the Institute of Tailoring and Cutting in Kenya. The letter informed Ross, who was also an ILGWU vice president, that Patrick J. O'Farrell (AALC executive director) had advised the secretary-general of the national union of workers in Mali that the U.S. unions could not build the child care center because of the passage of the UN resolution. The AFL-CIO sent their views on the resolution to all ambassadors of the UN. See Springer Kemp to Ross, December 30, 1975 (MSK PP); see also Springer Kemp to Ross, February 24, 1974, and Springer Kemp to Mattie Jackson (ILGWU vice president), August 10, 1975 (both in Amistad).

president of the UNTM, and because he was a doctor he put a great deal of emphasis on the need for health care as he looked toward the future. The building for this child care center would also house a medical clinic and a training school to help the mothers gain skills for employment. In the long run these health clinics could be replicated in small ways to serve rural communities. Dr. Dembele had come to the United States and had made such a good case for this need. I had gone to the executive board of the union and had begun negotiations, discussions with them about a child care center in Bamako. And so this is the history behind that.

There were a lot of political overtones to work through to make this child care center a success. The project was on delicate grounds from the beginning partly because Communism of the French, Chinese, and Soviet variety was still prevalent in Mali government and trade union circles. However, no matter what the politics or relations, the AALC [African-American Labor Center] provided to the UNTM through the years medical supplies, maintenance for ambulances, and educational activities. Many of the funds for this aid were raised by U.S. unions.

As a result of the fallout over the UN resolution, the project was finished. Seventy-two countries, including Mali with its large Muslim population, voted for the UN resolution. Israeli relations were very ugly with most African countries. If Zionism is equated with racism, and the position of these countries at the UN was to remove themselves from all relationships where Jews speak in support of the Jewish nation of Israel, you have a bad political situation. I am asking the Jewish leadership of a union to help with the project, and American unions in general had close relations with Israel. And if a government said we do not want the support of anyone who supports Israel, what choice do you have. This child care center was to be a cooperative venture with U.S. unions, some U.S. health professionals, the Mali government, and the UNTM. This was the political position that one was in.

7

The Cost of the Cold War on
AFL-CIO Programs and African Unity

In the United States Maida Springer was considered a resource on Africa by many in education, labor, and government. Harold R. Isaacs (1910–1986), who served as a World War II correspondent for *Newsweek* magazine, authored several books on China and Southeast Asia, and taught at the Center for International Studies at the Massachusetts Institute of Technology, was among those who wanted to tap into Springer's expertise. He wrote her, "Almost everybody I do interview sooner or later gets around to saying: 'You must talk to Maida Springer.'" He and his wife, Viola, would spend time in Ghana monitoring the Crossroads Africa project, a precursor to the Peace Corps.[1]

Many African nationalists also counted Springer as a valuable resource and ally. In this chapter Springer recalls her activism in the British settler colony of Southern Rhodesia (now Zimbabwe). She supported African nationalists and labor leaders who struggled against the imposition of the Central African Federation, which lasted from 1953 to 1963. Britain instituted the federation of Southern Rhodesia with the territories of Northern Rhodesia (now Zambia) and Nyasaland (now Malawi) in order to better exploit its labor and resources.

Springer speaks of (Murray William) Kanyama Chiume's struggles against the Central African Federation and against the autocratic rule of Malawi's first independence leader and Africa's longest ruling dictator, Dr. Hastings Kamuzu Banda. Chiume was one of the architects of the independence struggle in East Africa, and he and others had invited Banda back from England to lead the fight against the federation. In 1956 Chiume received the largest number of votes among the five Africans who swept all the African seats in a limited Legislative Council election in Nyasaland. In 1961 he became minister of education, social development, and information. On Independence Day in 1964 he became minister for foreign

---

1. Pauli Murray, *The Autobiography of a Black Activist, Feminist, Lawyer, Priest, and Poet* (Knoxville: University of Tennessee Press, 1987), 414; Isaacs to Springer, July 15, 1958 (MSK PP).

affairs. Banda then fired Chiume and two other ministers within weeks of independence. For many years it was illegal to even possess photographs of the exministers. Chiume went into exile in Tanzania. As the national chairman of the Congress for the Second Republic of Malawi, Chiume was an important figure in the struggle against Banda. At the time of this interview with Springer, Banda was still in power. With the end of the cold war, international pressure from the West and a strong opposition movement led to multiparty elections in 1994, which Banda lost. He died in 1997.

Springer discusses the effect of the cold war on Southern Africa, including the AFL-CIO's anti-Communist policies. Within two years of her introduction to Southern Rhodesian labor leaders, many of those who had supported labor head Reuben Jamela began to turn against him. Among them was Charles Mudundo Pasipanodya, head of the garment workers' union, who was a participant in the 1961 labor scholarship program Springer had designed. He returned to Southern Rhodesia to find that some of the garment union leaders had joined a rival national center. Months later he broke away from Jamela's national center and formed yet another national center. The succession of splits in the labor movement reflected power rivalries, ethnic divides, differences over the issue of international labor affiliation and the relationship of the labor movement to the liberation movement, and the intrigues of the white minority regime that benefited from the disunity. The documentation of the period shows that in response to the appeal of competing factions for aid and support against their rivals, Springer often urged them to unify.[2] Unity, however, remained elusive as labor leaders either aligned unions with rival liberation movements or professed a desire to remain independent.

The cold war has colored how critics of AFL-CIO policy perceived Springer's activism. The main split that reflected on her standing was between Jamela and Joshua Mqabuko Nyongolo Nkomo (1917–1999), nationalist leader of the Zimbabwe African People's Union (ZAPU) and a one-time general secretary of the Rhodesian Railways African Employees Association. Although supportive of the liberation movement, Jamela continued the policy of the Southern Rhodesian Trades Union Congress of staying independent from the liberation movement. Differences over this stance were a factor in the fracturing of the labor movement. Recalling her relationship with Nkomo, Springer reflects on other possible causes of the divide between them.

Nkomo and his nationalist rival, Robert Gabriel Mugabe, leader of the Zimbabwe African National Union (ZANU), spent ten years in prisons and detention

2. For more details on the Southern Rhodesian labor struggle, see Richards, *Maida Springer*, 216–21, 226–33.

The Cost of the Cold War

camps under Ian Smith's white minority regime.[3] After being released in 1974 they united in a guerilla war against the regime. The war, along with UN sanctions, led to independence in 1980. Through his party's electoral victory Mugabe became prime minister. Nkomo's party was brought into a coalition government, but two years later Nkomo was forced out, precipitating violence along ethnic lines. In 1987 Nkomo was brought back into a unity government and served as vice president until his death. However, Mugabe maintained a tight reign on the levers of power as he increasingly became more autocratic.[4]

Springer also reflects on her relationship with John Kofi Barka Tettegah. In 1954 Tettegah became head of the trade union movement in Ghana (then called the Gold Coast). Springer's close relationship with him began to change following the split in the pan-African labor movement over the issue of ICFTU affiliation. Tettegah helped lead the movement for disaffiliation, and from 1965 to 1966 he served as the secretary-general of the All-African Trade Union Federation [AATUF]. Imprisoned after the overthrow of Nkrumah, he has since served under a number of posts, including ambassador to Zimbabwe. More recently he has served as Ghana's high commissioner in Nigeria.

Labor projects that Springer helped to implement in Africa and a 1961 educational program she designed for African workers to study in the United States are also the subject of this chapter. The six-month program included six weeks of classroom work, meetings with various groups, and work within a local union. The courses included the history of the United States and the structure of the U.S. government, labor in politics, studies of collective agreements and union welfare plans, trade union principles, accounting, basic administration, and audiovisual techniques. The students met with trade unionists, members of the AFL-CIO national office, officials from the U.S. Department of Labor, and community organizations.[5]

Springer expounds on the reasons she centered her efforts in Africa on raising the skill level of workers. She traces her years of struggle with the London-based International Textile and Garment Workers' Federation to implement programs designed to help African garment workers pass government trade tests. Without their aid she was successful in establishing in 1963 the Institute of Tailoring and Cutting in Kenya. In Nigeria in 1965 Springer helped set up the Motor Drivers'

3. R. Kent Rasmussen, ed., *Historical Dictionary of Rhodesia/Zimbabwe*, African Historical Dictionaries, no. 18 (Metuchen, NJ: Scarecrow Press, 1979), 232–33.

4. "Nkomo, Joshua," Encyclopedia Britannica Online, http://search.eb.com/eb/article?eu=57393 (accessed February 28, 2003).

5. *Justice*, August 15, 1961; Springer to Matthew Schoenwald, September 19, 1961, 22/8/2, and Springer to Charles Zimmerman, March 17, 1961, 47/1/10 (ILGWU Archives).

School, the mission of which was to teach rudimentary auto mechanics and to make traveling safer by improving driving skills. The school was administered entirely by union officers and represented the sole labor training center and only union-to-union project in the entire country.

Springer ends the chapter by discussing President Lyndon Johnson's consideration of her for an appointment as the first black woman ambassador, a post she did not want. The one who would hold that distinction was Patricia Roberts Harris (1924–1985), who became ambassador to Luxembourg in 1965. Harris graduated summa cum laude from Howard University in 1945 and first in her class from George Washington University Law School in 1960. Under President Jimmy Carter she became the first African American woman cabinet member, serving in three positions, first as secretary for Housing and Urban Development, and later as secretary for Health, Education and Welfare, and Health and Human Services. Springer explains the role Harris played in helping her to change her initial impressions of Johnson as a Southerner. At the 1964 Democratic National Convention Harris gave the speech seconding the nomination of Johnson for president.

∽✵∽

What was your experience with the people struggling against the Central African Federation?

In the federation there was Northern Rhodesia, which is now Zambia; Southern Rhodesia, which is now Zimbabwe; and Nyasaland, which is now Malawi. The miners of Northern Rhodesia had the component of a very strong union. The "component," I'm saying, because this was *still* under the colonial rule in the Central African Federation, and there were all sorts of problems. One of the first things I was asked in my meetings with those people there was if there was a possibility of putting together a training program. The concerns that I raised with the American labor movement were about how much I felt there was a need for the African labor movement to be able to *confront* management in a more *rational* way and not just be angry. They needed to have some facts at hand and know how to write the right kinds of letters and learn how to negotiate. This was important that they learn these things because negotiations were with the big government, the big company against the very pained workers with very little experience. The miners, of course, and the railway workers had the best organized unions and the best potential to train people. So I was very anxious to work with members of the trade union federation. And this involved not just working with trade union people, but people who were opposed to the colonial government at the time.

The Cost of the Cold War

239

One of the persons you met in Tanzania last year,[6] Kanyama Chiume, I think related to you that I made it possible for him to have printed in the *Free Trade Union News* [an AFL-CIO publication] an article he had written which described the conditions of the workers, the conditions of the people under the federation, and the *terrible* political situation that they were in. Writing this article was a way of getting the facts beyond the narrow gate. This infuriated the colonial government at the time. This was in 1960. They were so annoyed with this that they wrote to President Meany. They said misinformation was given to the AFL-CIO. They said that they had this terrible Communist [Springer] who (*laughs*) was going around helping to incite horrible feelings and incite the people of the country to riot and worse. In this instance this was the colonial government of Nyasaland speaking, but Kanyama Chiume had written the article about the whole Central African Federation. So I was not on friendly terms with the federation. They took a poor view of me. This article and others about Africa were printed in the *Free Trade Union News* with the support of the AFL-CIO.[7]

So it is Kanyama Chiume of Malawi who was the activist and the political person in that period. He is still speaking out truthfully about the problems that they have now in Malawi, and this is speaking against the wrongs of a black regime. So he does not discriminate. If it's evil, he speaks against it. (*Laughs.*) I think that ought to be made clear.

On one occasion when I went to Southern Rhodesia, now Zimbabwe, I arrived with confirmed reservations. My name did not ring a bell with the person who accepted the reservations. When we arrived and they saw me, the reservations were lost. It was a mistake, because no black person could live in that hotel. I was with a white colleague, Irving Brown. Both of our rooms had been reserved, but they chucked us both out. (*Laughs.*) Irving was going to spend a few days there and then go on to what he was doing, while I was going to remain. There was one hotel that permitted people of color to stay, so we both went there.

The American consulate took a very poor view of my visit to Southern Rhodesia and the meetings I had with the Southern Rhodesian trade unionists. In fact, I was described to the American labor officer in his office as this awful person. I was stirring up trouble and I was talking anticolonialism. I won't say exactly what they called me, but the general thing that they call black people was bête noire, black beast. I was described as a very bad person.

6. For three weeks in the spring of 1991 I visited Springer in East Africa during her three-month visit there.

7. For more on this conflict, see Richards, *Maida Springer*, 216, 329.

The Cost of the Cold War

So the American labor officer said he didn't think I would bite him. His name is Jack Dupont. He was curious about this creature they talked about, so he came around to the hotel and met Irving and myself. He had taken the trouble to meet, under all sorts of circumstances, the trade unionists in that country. He was a great resource, an absolute walking encyclopedia. He had some documentation on the laws and knew something about a lot of personalities. He had done his homework. Evidently he was very serious about his responsibility, and he looked at both sides of the equation and saw the inequities. He said I can help you to reach some of the people. We had our connections to labor people that we were to see. But Jack Dupont had a more intimate day-to-day relationship that was very broad. We have been friends all these many years. He was with the State Department as a foreign service officer. He left the foreign service, I think, shortly, some years later.[8]

The personnel in the U.S. consulate called you bad names?

Oh, other people called me names also. Listen, I can understand. I do not respect or accept it, but I understand their position. They are in a country and deal with the leadership of the country, so they will be annoyed with anyone who comes in the country with a different view. I didn't even have to say anything. My presence as an American labor representative suggested that I was going to be anti whatever the government of Southern Rhodesia was about. The fact that it required a civil war for I don't know how many years before the independence of Southern Rhodesia came a few years ago tells its own story.[9] The fact that a white worker doing the same job as a black worker received five times more in salary tells its own story. My very presence reflected hostility to that kind of equation. And if the American government was building their relationship with the status quo, then I, representing the American labor movement, would be an annoyance. It was not a personal thing. I was messing with the status quo.

Did you feel afraid there?

No. I am a fatalist, and I took the position that whatever happened to me, particularly in Africa, if my time had come, that would have been it. You had anxieties, of course! But I did not have a sense of fear or else I wouldn't do it. I could stay in the United States and work and not be exposed to that.

You wrote about meeting with a group of labor leaders who explained that all the real leaders were in jail. Do you remember who were among that group?

8. Canadian-born John (Jack) M. Dupont was the labor attaché in the U.S. consulate when Springer and Brown traveled to Southern Rhodesia in 1957.
9. African nationalists who had opposed the Central African Federation and white minority rule were met with imprisonment, banishment, and exile.

The Cost of the Cold War

[Reuben] Jamela, [Knight] Maripe, [Ignatius T.] Chigwendere, I think.[10] You know time is hard on the memory. But we met some people from the railway unions. I think Knight Maripe had been a member of the railway workers' union. He was a writer, a newspaperman, and had a mind like a steel trap. If you spoke to Knight tonight, and you say, I am not clear on so-and-so and I don't know about legislation. And he would give you a documentary the next day and *pieces* of legislation. So I am always amused when I hear that I was uninformed. The *Economist* and all of them have said that I was a demagogue. No. I had good teachers. Well, Knight was a first-class brain being choked by a system that would eventually destroy him. I think he did work for the ICFTU for a while, but I think his spirit had been broken, something inside of him was gone. I liked Knight Maripe.

Josiah Maluleke was in prison when I first went to Southern Rhodesia. I think some of our people were sending him reading materials which a lot of it, I guess, he never got, because the government would not permit him to receive it. I have read in some of the things that you have researched that Jay Lovestone had corresponded with him and some others.[11] I met him, of course, later, but he really got turned around. Ahhh! Have to be there to see what those men lived with. See how potential is destroyed. To see how people were made to feel inhuman. It bothers me to *think* about it even now.

In an article I showed you, you were accused of splitting the Southern Rhodesia labor movement.[12]

I am not guilty *ever* of wanting to split a labor movement. In the first place, I didn't have that kind of clout or authority. What I was trying to do with the backing of the AFL-CIO was to help to open a door for those men, because it was all men I dealt with. I did not know any women very active in the labor movement because the basic industries were the railways and other industries in which women did not play a large part. If a black and a white worked at the same job, for the black the wages were five times less. Now why would I want to be a participant in trying to split anything? The politics of it, one gets caught up in, inadvertently. No matter what you do. If you are not with

10. Knight Maripe was a journalist for the African newspaper, the *Daily News*, and a former labor leader of the railway workers. He helped Brown and Springer locate four African labor leaders, including Reuben Jamela. Ignatius T. Chigwendere, from the garment workers union, would become the roving publicity secretary for the African Trade Union Congress, the rival labor center that broke away from Jamela's organization.

11. For more on Josiah Maluleke's relations with the AFL-CIO, see ibid., 216–21, 226–33.

12. Barry Cohen, "The CIA and African Trade Unions," in *Dirty Work 2: The CIA in Africa*, ed. Ellen Ray, William Schaap, Karl Van Meter, and Louis Wolf (London: Zed Press, 1980), 74–75.

me, you're against me. Our concern was to be as supportive to the African labor movement as possible. Sides were chosen.

They requested simple things. They may have heard about my efforts for the tailors' school [Kenya's Institute of Tailoring and Cutting]. As a result of some of the conversations I had in the Rhodesias, I came back and worked for the 1961 training program. We were trying to show that if these workers or these leaders were armed, given a base of some security and a way to better negotiate, then maybe there was a chance, maybe there was a hope that down the line there would be a change in the country. It was too long in coming. And I think Southern Rhodesia was one of the most complex and politically destroying experiences for the Africans involved, because there was a rumor factory going. Some expected a miracle from what you could get outside the country. There were some things that were going on in Communist countries *in support* of the unions. Now you can't tell anybody—and why should one so far away—to turn away from someone that's helping you. But the situation got tortured and mixed up. Too many people doing too many things and conflicting one another. You've read the documents; you know how internally so many of these leaders destroyed one another. But they got their act together finally.

The article states that you helped to split the trade union movement by delivering money to Reuben Jamela.

Not true. Not a word of it is true. I never gave Reuben Jamela ten cents. And in your book I suppose you don't have to answer to that, because it's something I never did. You arrive at the point that you don't deny these things, because a man convinced against his will is of the same opinion *still*. What I *did* do, what the unions asked of me, was to bring delegates to the United States for the 1961 training course. There wasn't a person I *ever* dealt with who was brought to the United States for training, whether it was the Harvard trade union scholarship in the fifties or the later scholarships, that did not reflect what the African trade union movement was attempting to do. But in those days you accepted all of the things that you were accused of as a part of the price you paid for what you were doing. Whatever I have been accused of, I will have to accept that, because you had to have opposition to what you were doing—right, left, and in the center. And if you don't have the stomach for that you should stay home.

I would sometimes go to bed at night in my hotel and *weep* because I was weak enough and vulnerable enough to say, Is this what I am? Is this what I represent? And the next morning I went into a colonial government office and had to state what it was I was doing. Or I met opposition with my colleagues or Africans, who were involved in whatever politics they were, whether it was with the Soviet Union, the Christian Federation [International Federation of Christian Trade Unions (IFCTU)], or even the ICFTU with some of those who may have taken a dim view of what the Americans were doing.

I met opposition from some in the ICFTU because I was representing the AFL-CIO in some projects that were bilateral, since it seemed to be taking too long to wait for the various governing bodies in the ICFTU to decide to support them. Prime example: the garment workers' school in Kenya. And this is true of a lot of things. I was only one small person getting the backing of the union to do these things after trying to do it through the normal processes. This is true with the 1957 Harvard trade union project. They chopped my head off in three or four months and ended it. So the price you pay for being this stooge and that stooge and taking money from God knows who all, that's a part of the game, and that's a price you pay.

I still get emotional about this because I did not look at this as part of the overall larger politics. I was looking at independence. My view was that you were attempting to structure opportunities for African trade unionists to improve their skills so that at some point down the line, as independence became a reality, they could contribute something positive to that society. Beneath the lawyers and the doctors and the political scientists, what do you do about the masses? What do you do about finding some way of doing pilot projects to show what can be done for the people, who do not have university education, and to contribute to the stability of independence? *That* was my shtick. And I would fight anybody on that and don't care what they call me. I still feel the same way.

The person who was then extremely active and with whom I dealt was Reuben Jamela. He was the leader of what we thought was the Southern Rhodesia labor movement. There were a number of factions. The man who was a very strong man and who was fighting hard for independence, challenging the Southern Rhodesian government, was formerly of the railway workers, Joshua Nkomo. There was great, great, great hostility between Reuben Jamela and Joshua Nkomo. Whatever divisions there were, I went into a country in which these were the men who were the leaders. I felt there was only one labor federation. My concern was to help to strengthen the leader of the labor movement, Reuben Jamela. I knew Reuben Jamela very well, and it was from his federation that Charles Pasipanodya, who was president of the tailors' union, was selected as a delegate to come to the United States in that 1961 program.[13]

13. For more on Pasipanodya, see Richards, *Maida Springer*, 227–33.

The Cost of the Cold War

There were a bunch of political parties and trade unions in Southern Rhodesia. For whatever reason, I was not close to Joshua Nkomo. He thought I was anti whatever he was doing in terms of the resistance movement. I certainly could not be an effective part of the resistance movement to the government of the Central African Federation. For example, as a representative of the American labor movement, I would not be helping to finance a political party by using labor funds. There were some awkward feelings. Not that I was supporting anything that the government was doing, but there were some clashes in the labor movement with the different groups. And evidently in his view I was not an active supporter, trade-union-wise, to what he was doing politically. That's why I'm saying I was not considered Joshua's comrade. And I can't explain it any better than that. God knows I was a supporter of change in the government of the Central African Federation and had an ardent wish for the breakup of the federation, or else I would not have dared suggest articles against the federation be written [in the *Free Trade Union News*]. But I was not fortunate in having an understanding with him, for which I am sorry. I evidently was not skillful enough to make the point of view of my support. And there was a lot of that kind of friction in Africa because of all of the ideology business.

My feeling is that we knew one another, but we were not close. I never seriously worked with him. He was out of the country. He was politicking, building his fences to become the leader of the political movement. The country many years later won independence and Nkomo did not become the president. There was a bitter feud between rival groups that had nothing to do with trade unions. In due course there became a joint effort, and they made peace, and Joshua Nkomo is now in the government. But Joshua had better relationships with some people in the International Affairs Department. I just happened not to be the person he trusted. It may very well be because I was a woman. I had no quarrel with Joshua Nkomo, so the division was not my choice.

Guilty of breaking the labor movement? No. I saw too much in Africa of the colonial government's fight to destroy a workers' movement and to maintain inequality so that black Africans remained always the have-nots to have been consciously guilty of undermining a workers' movement. Whatever they say my sins are, it was never conscious on my part. Whatever their internal divisions, it was not my fault. Given the politics of the time, given colonialism at the time, and I am from the United States and I belong to the anti-Communist bloc of the international labor movement, the lines got very garbled and you couldn't draw them. We were supporting unions, which we said had to have a democratic process. The semantics, I think, got a lot in the way.

I could only be *very*, very sad because so many good people were lost within the internal politics of the African trade union movement and political movement. I've met intelligent, bright, *brave*, committed people. (*Softly*). I did those things that we were asked to do to support the labor movement. I did not do anything to build a political movement. This was not my function. Maybe some other people did. I was too low on the totem pole for that. (*Laughs*.) All I was was an international labor representative. I guess there's some focus on me because I was the only woman who was by herself, moving around the world, meeting and doing for the labor movement.

Would saying somebody was Communist or there's a Communist fight and we need help be a good argument for Africans to use to persuade the AFL-CIO to give money or provide support?

I want to tell you something. That old man in the AFL-CIO, George Meany, would hardly give anybody money because he said he was anti-Communist. (*Laughing*.) No, that's too easy. That is absolutely too easy. It is not unthinkable that if proven you were challenging whatever the internal politics was—I was never asked to do it—that the AFL-CIO would give somebody money because they were anti-Communist. Who am I to swear that it was never done. I couldn't. But it hardly would be the basis for giving money. It would have to be something other than that, because anybody . . . On Monday you're anti-Communist and on Tuesday you're anti-Catholic and on Wednesday you're anticolonialist and the United States represents colonialism. No. No. They were very, very difficult days. The same person you loved on Monday, you said they were the most vicious person the next day.

Let me give you an example: John Tettegah. John came to the United States in 1955 for the first time. We traveled on the same plane together. He was a delegate to the ICFTU conference. In my home John came. He was living at the Commodore with the rest of the delegation. But he was so young and far removed from the interests of these older white delegates and maybe a couple of Indians, so I asked my son to be involved, to see to it that John Tettegah—he may have been then general secretary of the Ghana Trades Union Congress—meet young people, college age, discuss with them. John considered me, "This is my mother" (*said with his accent*).

Later on, when the ideological position became *tough*, John would send a message to me in the morning that he was someplace else, in Kumasi or somewhere, and that he wanted to see me and talk to me. And he would say, "You are my mother." In the evening the next day he wrote a *scurrilous* article about all of the horrible things I represented. This was a part of the "hot-cold war" in Ghana and Guinea and some of the countries that were considered to be ideologically supporting the Soviet Union policies. Those things happened. But in the morning John would put his arm around me and say, "I love her. She's my mother. I'm going to send my wife to the United States so that she can be with you." And in the evening . . . There are books written on all of the terrible things I did to the Ghana TUC or all over Africa by John Tettegah. I never had a conversation with him *once* in my life discussing ideological purity. Never. Never.

When the [1957] Harvard course was closed down, John and others wanted to put together a boycott and start some kind of pressure movement that I had to be brought back to Africa straightaway.[14] So you have to accept a great deal of what you read with a sense of the time and the politics of the time. And I can't answer to that more than to say the cold war played a great part, and I think that in Africa the cold war was used by Africans. They played both ends against the middle. Quite honestly. (*Laughs.*)

As I have said to you before and will say again, I have the first time to say to any trade union group in Africa, you either are anti-Communist or the AFL-CIO will not support you. *That,* I have the first time to do. But in terms of the general policy, in terms of some of the speeches made in Europe, the AFL-CIO was anti-Communist. If I am vilified on that account—the policy of the AFL-CIO was anti-Communist—that's a fact. Then you had the development of the nonaligned trade union federation [AATUF], which said they would have nothing to do with the AFL-CIO. The emerging politics of Africa. Yeah. You have to pay for that. (*Laughs.*) You paid your dues for that.

Some of the African unions had gone gung ho about their brotherhood with comrade this and comrade that and some of the things that the Soviet Union was doing in Africa. What I understood was that Africans wore everybody's ideology and religion very lightly. But there was a sharp feeling against the West, and African leadership felt that they had a great deal in common with the Soviet Union *if* for no other reason than the Soviet Union had never been a colonial power in their country. And the Soviet Union was offering scholarships whether you're qualified or no, were offering all kinds of things. These scholarships were handed out freely for study in the Soviet Union or one of the satellites. So this had to be balm in Gilead. I understand that.

What would you consider some of your successes in Africa? What things do you look back on with satisfaction?

14. For African reaction to the curtailment of the scholarship program, see ibid., 148–51.

I don't think I was ever satisfied with anything. Whatever you envision, you came short of the mark. But to have championed for a training school for tailors in Kenya was a reward. The effort to put the Institute of Tailoring and Cutting together began with people coming up the back stairs of a cheap hotel I was in and begging me to ask the unions in the United States for help. "We would be able to train our people better and challenge the legislation, which now limits their opportunities to even earn the minimum wage." Anselmi W. Karumba, the head of the tailors' union for years, said "Maida, this is what we are faced with. No matter how skillful an African is, if we can't pass the oral English test, you can't be upgraded." I lived with this for years. And as I began to look at the community, I wanted to participate in developing a training program so that we could train young women, give them a basic skill, train the young people who were running from the villages and coming into the urban community. This training would help solve the frustrations and problems that arise with that movement.[15]

So beginning in 1957, as I looked at Kenya—looking at the social changes to come in the country and the work toward independence—I thought that an institute should make it possible for the Kenyan garment union to train a number of young women in the needle trades. I came back to the United States and drove everybody who would listen to me crazy to the degree that President Dubinsky said to me, "Springer, you're always coming with your unilateral things."

By 1960 I was on the International Affairs staff of the AFL-CIO. I spoke with President Dubinsky about my garment workers' agenda. I told him that President Meany had said that if I can get the support of the ILGWU, the International Affairs Department would make me available to develop this program for the Kenya Tailors and Textile Workers Union. DD then replied, "Maida, I don't want to do this. We belong to the International Confederation of Free Trade Unions, and we also belong to the trade secretariat, the Garment Workers' Federation.[16] I support your idea, and if you will do a memorandum on this question, I will have Vice President Kreindler"—because we were big dues payers in the garment and textile workers' trade secretariat —"take it and present it. Will that suit you?" I said, "Yes, sir." (*Laughs.*)

So I presented the memorandum to the ILG I think the next morning. And whenever the Garment Workers' Federation met, Charles Kreindler presented

15. For more on the Institute of Tailoring and Cutting, see ibid., 233–39.
16. The name of the international trade secretariat was the International Textile and Garment Workers' Federation. It was later renamed the International Textile, Garment, and Leather Workers' Federation.

it to them, and they decided to set up a commission to look into it. That was the end of it. President Meany had said as a part of this memorandum that if the Garment Workers' Federation would contribute to the special fund, the AFL-CIO would make it possible for this to be funded as an international activity. But it was not considered, and I knew it was deadweight.

As a result of the proposal being iced, President Dubinsky couldn't answer me anymore. We did everything we were supposed to do, and nothing happened. I kept on nagging him. I said I'd like to talk to some of our ILG people to see if they will make a contribution if you now feel it is OK since nothing is happening with it in the trade secretariat. He said, "All right, all right, all right." He approved it, reluctantly, and said, "If you can raise the money, OK. You have my word. You can go ahead. Go talk to anybody in the ILG if you want. If anybody hears you and gives you any money to develop the program, go ahead." So I went to William Ross and the Philadelphia Joint Board and spoke to them. They gave me the first ten thousand dollars to begin the Institute of Tailoring and Cutting, which you see there [a brochure on the table]. *This* is how that school started. It was 1963 before we got this school in Kenya.

In the mid-1960s Patrick O'Farrell became the director of the African-American Labor Center and remained director until his retirement in the mid-nineties. As director he was responsible for labor training programs over most of Africa, including the Institute of Tailoring and Cutting. He made possible the longevity of the institute by being supportive of a number of activities there. For example, a fashion show was developed from the Institute. The show was so creative that it became known throughout black Africa. Bill Grant, a designer from New York and an adviser to the Institute, created the fashions that were sewn by the students in the Institute. Pat could see that the Institute had tremendous results and soon made scholarships available for the African teachers to attend the Fashion Institute of Technology in New York, located in the heart of the garment district. After an academic year of study, these teachers all returned to the Institute of Tailoring and Cutting. The Institute's continued existence is due in large measure to the support of the African-American Labor Center and Pat O'Farrell.

I am told that the ICFTU now operates a large center in Mombassa. And since the struggle for all of these years, now the international labor movement is involved in the Institute of Tailoring and Cutting. But what was so successful about it was that the French-speaking African countries liked the idea so well that they developed a similar program [The Regional Institute of Tailoring and Cutting]. The discussions about setting up this program were in Dakar, and I went to state my point of view. The government of Senegal had already agreed. The government made a building possible and students were selected from all of the French-speaking countries to train for the needle industry. *That* I considered a big success. That I considered important.

Let's talk about the 1961 trade union course you developed.

In a conference a number of African leaders had made a statement saying we know we have a future in terms of the leadership of our country. We are going to be independent. But we need to be able to do X, Y, and Z. We need to be able to confront the employer and be able to negotiate and have the tools for negotiation. I was on the staff of the Department of International Affairs, and I came back with this proposal, having talked to Africans in a number of places. So I structured this training course in New York City. The International Ladies' Garment Workers' Union had had their own training college to train union officers at its headquarters at 1710 Broadway. And when that was discontinued, the training center was still there. I asked President Dubinsky if I might use that facility, and I guess he agreed with President Meany. President Meany said I could go ahead and do this if I got the concurrence of the ILG. So the AFL-CIO paid whatever they needed to pay to bring people here. They footed all the bills, their housing and some remuneration for them here and a stipend for organizing when they went home.

The delegation included a woman from Northern Rhodesia from the mine workers' union [Joyce Chanda], a man from Southern Rhodesia [Charles Pasipanodya], a man from Kenya [Anselmi Karumba], two women from Nigeria [Atim Williamson and Folake Johnson], and one woman from Tanzania [Flora Manjonde]. They had a structured classroom program for two months, two months working in a union factory, and two months traveling and meeting union people.

The ILG furnished and paid for all of the teaching facilities. *All* of the unions in New York City that we needed just cooperated without a question. Specialists were there to teach you. There were instructions on public speaking, reading contracts, writing letters on behalf of the workers to employers and government officials, people with whom they might have contractual relations or working relations. And at the end of the period the delegates were all given certificates. The unions in New York supported me by seeing to it that Karumba and Pasipanodya were placed in factories, because they are first-class tailors.

Oh, that was a terrible time sometimes. (*Laughs.*) One of the Nigerian women [Folake Johnson] had an aneurysm, and I was frightened out of my wits, because if it had been fatal, there would be a blemish on us that we had not cared for her properly. It would be thought that the Americans had done something terrible. The AFL-CIO was responsible for all the hospitaliza-tion. Fortunately, she was young and it came out all right and she could fin-ish her course. When she went back to Nigeria, she became very prominent in work and labor. She was so good that management, I think, took her over at some point. (*Laughs.*)

None of these people I had known before except Karumba. They were se-lected by their unions. The schoolteacher out of Tanzania, who was elected by her union, is now the senior labor officer in Tanzania. I just missed her when I was there. She had just gone on holiday and left a note saying she was sorry. So all of these people went back and served their organization. Some fell away later on.

It was my program and I did it without having all of the technical and social work knowledge, I guess, that I needed to have. I had not worked out where to go beyond this beginning. But I was so determined to help the unions prepare for whatever they saw as their future. Maybe I missed a lot of beats. But no one had a better blueprint than I had. (*Laughs.*) And I asked for all the advice. I had the *best* instructors you could get. The ILG gave their staff. I wanted them to come to the United States for the reason that there was a greater sense of freedom and ease and an opportunity to have a cross cultural experience and get away from the pressures of whatever they were under in their country. And I was interested in women always, because I thought their opportunities were so limited.

There's a funny story connected with the delegate from Northern Rhodesia and that program. The delegates flew from Lusaka to London on their way to the United States. She was so frightened in London of this white commu-nity, what they might do to her, because coming from Northern Rhodesia she expected to be treated in a bad way. The American labor attaché in London called me because this woman was refusing to come out of her room and get on the plane. She was so *terrified*. I assured her that I would be at the airport to welcome her. When she returned to Northern Rhodesia, she worked for the miners' union in the copper belt. Then I lost track of her.

Donkey's years later in the seventies when I am in what is now Zambia, I met this young woman who had participated in the program. I got a tele-phone call from her. She said I would like to take you to dinner. I would like to see you. You did this, this, and this for me. Changed my life. I now have my own business. I have a boutique. I go to London to shop two or three times a year. When she came to my hotel, she was sitting in a red open-top sports car. (*Laughs.*) She rode me around, took me to her boutique. And she insisted on having a couple of things made for me in her boutique overnight.

The Cost of the Cold War

What was your role in setting up the Motor Drivers' School in Nigeria?

I had been in and out of Nigeria. [Ezekiel O. A.] Odeyemi, who was the general secretary of the motor drivers' union, on more than one occasion when I was in Nigeria kept emphasizing the need for training the motor drivers so that they could know better about driving, about road signs, about safety. Also there needed to be a way to teach motor drivers more English because the signs in Nigeria were in English and the accident rate was very high.[17]

I do not think they talked to me alone about this problem. I think Odeyemi spoke to anybody who would listen. But he got my ear a great deal. And the then general secretary of the TUC of Nigeria, Lawrence Borha, when he was in the United States, kept talking to me about it. I went to Rudy Faupl from the machinist union, and I think I asked him if his union could make a contribution to indicate this kind of goodwill, to help the Nigerian motor drivers strengthen what they were trying to do. They were trying to open a little school on their own in a very limited way. And it began for me with Faupl's union saying yes and giving me a contribution, which was then sent on. And then some other people were involved who began to work and develop a motor drivers' school. Later a delegation from Nigeria was here or I was there, and they *really* went to work on me. We began to look at this school.

After the Nigerian women came to the United States in that 1961 training program, Lawrence Borha and other officials of the TUC of Nigeria wrote Mr. Meany requesting my presence in Nigeria in support of various programs. In due course Mr. Meany said yes, this project is important. It's a good idea. As he said with other ideas I supported, if you can put it together, you are available for the time to go and do it.

The bottom line of this project was that we would work with a black college or university in the United States, which had a technical school. That school would send someone to Nigeria to work with the union as a teacher and running the program. All kinds of other things got tangled up in between, but Irving and I did go to Hampton University, and we interviewed a person and someone was selected. Then it became a big program with AALC [African-American Labor Center] funding very soon after that. But it all started with a special need that the union had.

17. Ezekiel O. A. Odeyemi, who was also an MP and general secretary of the Nigerian Motor Drivers' Union and Allied Transportation Workers, served as the school's director. For more about the Nigerian Motor Drivers' School, see ibid., 239–41.

The Cost of the Cold War

There have been and still are differences among different ethnic groups in Africa. What experiences have you had in general with those sorts of differences?

You're taking me away from the labor movement. (*Laughs.*)

(*Laughing.*) Well, I'm sure it happened within the labor movement, because some of these labor unions are made up of one ethnic group.

And this was consciously done by the colonial governments. Repeat your question to me. I was trying to duck it (*laughs*), but I won't.

What experience have you had with ethnic rivalries? You can pick any place in Africa, something that stands out.

Nigeria. The northerners were mostly Muslim [Hausa]. The easterners were called the hustlers. They benefited and accepted training and education, and they became the administrators. The Ibos. There were very strong differences for many, many years. The people who practiced Islam, until recently, were isolated. You studied the Qur'an and you did not study Western ways. This was *bound* to create tribal differences, *bound* to create differences. For me, the Ibos and the northern Islamic peoples represented the sharpest division, which was one of the things that developed the civil war in Nigeria.[18]

I borrowed a car in Nigeria in 1964. I was living in Lagos. And this was just before what was to have been an election. The politics was very, very hard and sharp. Well, they were burning up the election boxes. It was a very tough two days before the election. The car I was in had a western Nigeria license plate. And as the driver was taking me back to my flat near the airport, some people tried to turn my car over and burn me and the car up.[19] The young driver had great facility. He was my permanent driver and helper. He got out of the car as they were shaking the car and he told them, "This is our sister. She's here to help us. We have borrowed this car." Well, this was my closest shave, probably my closest shave. (*Chuckles.*) They were about to torch the car and me. The politics at that period was *very* tough, *very* tough.

In addition to George McCray, another African American named Howard Robinson began working for the ICFTU around 1963. Did you know him?

Yes. I think he was out of some union in New Jersey. I first met him when someone sent him to talk to me because, I imagine, they were then considering involving him in international affairs. You see, part of the sin of the

18. With Igbos living in the northern Hausa area of Nigeria being attacked on a massive scale, the Igbo who lived principally in southeastern Nigeria tried to form a secessionist state of Biafra. The Nigerian-Biafran War (1967–1970) ended the attempt at secession. A mass starvation of Igbos occurred during the course of the war.

19. The men who were about to attack Springer were Igbos. The western Nigerians were mainly represented by the Yoruba.

The Cost of the Cold War

(*laughs*) American labor movement was that they had all of these black people who were intelligent and officers in their unions. And that was bad and that was wrong that you were sending these people so that Africans could look at them and say, Ah! Ah hah! These people represent blacks and whites, not just black workers. No place else in the world could say that very much. Despite all of the inequities of the social system, the political system in this country, this was a real plus.[20]

Howard came to New York and talked to me before he ever went to Africa, just a general conversation about conditions in Africa work.[21] It was obvious he was being considered and that he was interested. But everyone played their cards close to their vest. I had nothing to hide and I shared whatever experiences I had and was happy to see this happening. At that time I did not know that I would ever be further seriously involved in Africa. I was old, and I came from a very political union, a very large union, one of the largest in the country. And so this is the union's name, and my name was one that everyone knew because I had gone to England in 1945. That combination of things, not that I was anything special, made it possible for me to know a lot of people.

You knew Harold Snell, a black man who had been in the labor movement at one point and then joined the United States Agency for International Development in Kenya.[22]

Yes! Harold Snell came out of the Red Caps. Most of those guys were well educated, and I think he was an officer of the Red Caps.[23] So, when they began to expand the role of the labor movement, working and moving abroad, Harold was a natural.

Patricia Roberts Harris served in several government posts. How did you get to know her?

Patricia Harris was a name I knew, a young person who was very bright and very able. She was a member of Delta Sigma Theta sorority and had a staff position there. I first knew Pat Roberts through mutual friends, one of whom was Pauli Murray. Patricia went to Howard with Pauli. I knew her better after I moved to Washington. As a matter of fact, the apartment that I

20. Springer responds in this way because a number of Europeans resented the African American presence on the African continent.

21. According to Springer's diary entry, she had a long discussion with Howard Robinson on March 21, 1962.

22. Snell knew Jim Kemp and was also friendly with A. Philip Randolph. He wrote Springer from Kenya about the work of Bill Grant at the Institute of Tailoring and Cutting. Grant's fashion show and display at the Kinshasa fair attracted a lot of attention. Snell to Springer Kemp, August 14, 1969. Springer Kemp to Snell, September 17, 1969 (MSK PP).

23. The International Brotherhood of Red Caps was a union of railway station porters, renamed in 1940 the United Transport Service Employees of America.

The Cost of the Cold War

moved into, Pat and her husband [William B. Harris] had formerly lived there.[24] I found that out one day when they drove me home on an occasion when we were at the same function. They laughed about it. I think that Howard University owned the property.

You once wrote that Pat Harris helped you change your mind about Lyndon John-son as a Southerner when he became president. You wrote that at that point you were in midst of your anti-Americanism because of the violence against blacks in the South.

We were talking politics because what else do you talk about in Wash-ington? I gave my profound views on Lyndon Johnson (*said with humor*). I thought that this man from the South was probably a deep, deep Southern racist. And she said, you're wrong. She said something to the effect that I needed to take a second look, and she listed some reasons why. She really changed my views. After he became president he was making revolutions. He brought up these women from Texas, Barbara Jordan and Azie Taylor Mor-ton. Barbara Jordan was such an asset, a voice and intellect. We were just so pleased and thrilled with the work she was doing. And Azie Taylor was a part of that political mentoring that Lyndon Johnson did. Dollie [Lowther Robin-son] knew Azie Taylor quite well, and so she passed muster and we were sup-portive of Azie. When Azie became the treasurer under President Carter, I came in from wherever I was for the occasion. She wrote me a note afterward. We were all there. This was a very precious time. I did not know Barbara Jordan in the way I did Azie. Barbara Jordan, of course, came to the National Council of Negro Women functions. So I knew her more as somebody I was just kind of in awe of. But I was not in her circle.

Harris became the first African American woman to hold an ambassadorship in 1965. A year earlier, *Jet* magazine stated that you were being considered as a candi-date. Would you comment on this?

There was no question about Patricia Roberts Harris getting the position. Oh, what can I comment about this, except that it terrified me. But it titil-lated my mother. I was living in Washington, and people called my mother in Brooklyn and told her, "Maida's going to be an ambassador," because she didn't read *Jet*. So she called my office, and I said, "Mama, I have just called the magazine and they're going to make a retraction. I don't want to be an ambassador." And my mother's response to me was, "May, do you think you are smarter than the president of the United States?" I said, "No, I don't think so, but you want to be the ambassador's mother." (*Laughs.*)

24. On Patricia Harris's friendship with Pauli Murray, see Murray, *The Autobiography of a Black Activist*, 202, 353–54. Springer's apartment address was 1712 Sixteenth Street NW, Wash-ington, DC. William B. Harris was an administrative law judge with the Federal Maritime Commission.

The Cost of the Cold War

It was known that President Johnson was thinking of a black ambassador, and people thought for Africa at that moment.[25] An emissary was sent to feel me out and ask me about this. He came to my office. This came out of the blue and came as a shock to me. I was soon on my way to Geneva to the ILO, and I asked for a meeting with President Meany when he arrived there. I was upset about this. I wanted to dispel this, because I could have been cooking around as people do, trying to set a groundswell to be asked to be something. I said to President Meany that I just want you to know that there are occasions when people want to do certain things and leaks go out and they are finding, checking their resources. That's not my case. I'm not putting out any feelers or any leaks. This is no trial balloon. I do not want to be given a letter of recommendation. I don't want to be an ambassador." And he said, "Maida, I know. I know that you are not promoting this."

But let me tell you the background of why I was so adamant. I knew something about the diplomatic resentment of the foreign service personnel, who would see someone made an ambassador and they were not moved up through the rank. I would get massacred. And secondly, Africa was not high on the totem pole. It was not a very high priority in the United States. This is my view. And if I am wrong, somewhere there's somebody who will forgive me. I had seen people in Africa who held "high State Department posts" frustrated when they sent information back and things that they needed an opinion on or a decision on. If you had an issue and a problem and you needed an immediate answer, it could get filed in file thirteen [meaning the trash can]. This again is my feeling about where the black principal officer for an African country in terms of the State Department stood. The urgent requests from the African country, in my biased view, were not part of the priority.

And I didn't have the education for it, and I had no clout. I was not the head of a union. I was a staff employee, a paid employee of the AFL-CIO. I had no diplomatic experience. I did not have an organization. So if things were not moved and I did not get answers, I had nobody who could go on the Hill [Capitol Hill] and talk to somebody who would listen, or who could get on the phone and get an answer or a response from somebody in the State Department. For me, that was the nuts and bolts of it. I didn't have a dime. So I didn't have all of the things that you think a diplomat, an ambassador, has, like money to entertain, to add to the lifestyle and your support of programs in a country. I had none of that. And my vanity didn't range to stupidity.

25. For negative reactions of some Ghanaians to the 1965 ambassadorial appointment of an African American, former Peace Corps official and UN representative Franklin H. Williams, see Kenneth King, ed., *Ras Makonnen: Pan-Africanism from Within* (New York: Oxford University Press, 1973), 278–80.

The Cost of the Cold War

8

Labor and Civil Rights

Maida Springer chronicles the changes in her personal life and the reorientation of her labor activism toward the domestic front. Her marriage in 1965 to James Horace Kemp (1912–1983), her desire to give more attention to her aging family members, and concerns she had about her role in Africa contributed to her decision to resign from the AFL-CIO Department of International Affairs. In the late 1970s, Springer separated from Kemp due to their strong differences in personality. However, they did not divorce, and they remained in friendly contact with each other.

To support himself as he attended John Marshall Law School in Chicago in the 1930s, Kemp owned a newsstand on the South Side where he helped to organize newsstand dealers, reputedly using baseball bats to help settle struggles. When discrimination prevented him from securing employment as a lawyer, Kemp became a policeman.[1] From 1940 he served as the business representative for Local 73 of the General Service Employees' Union, and from 1946 he was president of Local 189 of the Building Service Employees' Union, which he helped to organize. An executive board member of the Chicago Federation of Labor, he also held many positions in the national NAACP and served as NAACP national president the last year of his life. Springer portrays Kemp as a source of irritation to the white AFL-CIO leadership because of his unwavering criticisms of union discrimination. The pressure he put on labor led some whites to criticize him for wanting to make the labor movement into a civil rights organization. A commanding person standing six feet four, he was known as Big Jim.

Another irritant to the labor movement was Adam Clayton Powell Jr., chair of the House Committee on Education and Labor. In connection with his committee's investigation of union discrimination in the garment industry and in the

---

1. Kemp's father had suffered a similar predicament when the family moved to Chicago in 1929. A master tailor, he could only secure employment as a janitor. See "James Kemp is Dead at 71; Held NAACP Presidency," *New York Times*, December 9, 1983, and "James Horace Kemp," *Chicago Tribune*, December 7, 1983.

ILGWU, a fact-finding subcommittee traveled to New York in August 1962 to hold hearings. Springer discusses the nature of union discrimination and also comments on the contentious relationship between NAACP labor secretary Herbert Hill, who served as a special consultant to the committee, and the ILGWU leadership. Rancor between Hill and Charles Zimmerman, who served as chair of the AFL-CIO Civil Rights Committee, openly began as early as 1958. It is ironic that, since both men are Jewish, the conflict between the NAACP and the AFL-CIO which ensued was characterized as a rising war between Negroes and Jews.[2]

Springer also looks at issues of race as they pertained to organizing in the South, where she worked with Martin J. Morand, who was appointed to the southeast district by David Dubinsky in 1964. Morand and Springer first met in 1961 when as ILGWU manager in Harrisburg, Pennsylvania, he hired some of the African college students from her AFL-CIO summer jobs program.[3] Springer recalls how sectional divides and racism in the South were impediments to organizing. Her suggestions for overcoming these serious problems sometimes reflected her trademark humor. At a March 2000 celebration for Springer in Pittsburgh, Morand recalled how Springer found a solution to the problem of segregated bathrooms at one plant in the South. When some union officers asked her how to go about desegregating them, she advised them to turn the water off in the white bathroom and let nature take its course.

Morand was forced out of his position in 1969 under Dubinsky's successor, Louis Stulburg, who accused him of turning his union over to the civil rights movement. Morand's charge that Stulburg was a racist most likely contributed to his dismissal.[4] Under Stulburg's tenure Springer left the ILGWU. After her stint as an organizer, she worked to strengthen the trade union movement within black

2. See 47/1/9 (ILGWU Archives); and Charles Zimmerman, interview by Miles Gavin, May 8, 1979, AFL-CIO Oral History Interview no. 1 (AFL-CIO merger), George Meany Center for Labor Studies Oral History Project, George Meany Memorial Archives, New York.

3. Martin J. Morand grew up in the Amalgamated Clothing Workers' cooperative houses in the Bronx and graduated from the New York State School of Industrial and Labor Relations of Cornell University in 1948. After his work with the ILGWU from 1948 to 1969, he worked with the AFL-CIO at their staff training institute; with the American Federation of State, County and Municipal Employees as an educational director; and with the National Education Association as a higher education organizer. In 1971 he organized a Pennsylvania faculty union and served as executive director of that group until 1976. He then established the Labor Relations Masters at Indiana University of Pennsylvania and the Pennsylvania Center for the Study of Labor Relations. He retired in 1999.

4. Born in Poland, Stulburg (1901–1977) became a business agent for the cutters' union, Local 10, in 1929. He later served as ILGWU assistant executive secretary and as a vice president before becoming in 1959 general secretary-treasurer. Stulberg served as ILGWU president from 1966 to 1975. Martin Morand to Herbert Hill, May 15, 1989 (MSK PP); Yevette Richards, e-mail communication with Martin Morand, April 15, 2003.

communities as midwest director of the A. Philip Randolph Institute (APRI), a position she held for three years in Chicago. An organization of black trade unionists dedicated to the pursuit of racial equality and economic justice, APRI promotes voter education, registration, and participation in elections. Since the ILGWU continued to pay Springer's salary while she worked for APRI, she decided to resign her position in 1972 when she was accused of working full-time on the congressional campaign of Paul Douglas. Due to legal constraints the ILGWU did not allow its staff to work on individual campaigns. Springer's commentary demonstrates the extent of her determination to extract herself from any position in which she felt her work was not respected.

Springer reflects in this chapter on the civil rights struggles of the early 1960s including the 1963 March on Washington for Jobs and Freedom for which Martin Luther King Jr. gave his landmark "I Have a Dream" speech. Conceived by Springer's longtime mentor and friend, A. Philip Randolph, the march represented the culmination of his attempts to garner national attention to the African American struggle for economic and political justice on the one-hundred-year anniversary of the Emancipation Proclamation. Springer describes Bayard Rustin's (1912–1987) indispensable role in putting the march together. This master tactician and longtime political associate of Randolph's had put together the logistics of a number of civil rights marches, helped organize the 1956 Montgomery Bus Boycott, and along with Randolph founded APRI in 1965. The march served as an impetus for getting the 1964 Civil Rights Act and the 1965 Voting Rights Act passed through Congress.

Springer was slated to introduce to the assembled marchers a delegation of Guinean labor leaders that she was hosting in the United States. However, time constraints and a delay in their arrival prevented her from following through on this. Still, this labor delegation had the opportunity to observe this historic event from the platform and to meet a number of noted political and civil rights leaders, including Ralph Johnson Bunche (1904–1971), who served as U.S. undersecretary for special political affairs at the United Nations. In 1950 he was the first African American to win a Nobel Peace Prize for his UN work on peacekeeping in the Middle East.[5] Also present at the march was Dorothy Height, president of the National Council of Negro Women (NCNW). Under Height's leadership,

5. Valedictorian of his high school and college, Bunche graduated summa cum laude from the UCLA in 1927. Entering graduate school at Harvard University, he became the first African American to earn a Ph.D. in political science. His dissertation on French colonialism was awarded the Toppan Prize in 1934 for outstanding doctoral thesis in the social sciences. He also did postgraduate work on African colonialism. "Biography, Ralph Bunche," The Nobel Peace Prize—Laureates, Nobel e-Museum, http://www.nobel.se/peace/laureates/ (accessed December 10, 2003).

the NCNW was the only woman's organization in the early 1960s committed to the civil rights movements.[6]

A longtime member of the NCNW and a vice president from 1970 to 1974, Springer got NCNW support for her African projects and traveled to the South in support of some of their programs. Through these programs Springer met Fannie Lou Hamer (1917–1977). As a Mississippi sharecropper Hamer joined with the Student Nonviolent Coordinating Committee (SNCC) to organize voter registration for blacks. For her efforts she was arrested several times and on one occasion beaten so severely she suffered permanent injury. In 1964 she led the Mississippi Freedom Democratic Party (MFDP) in challenging the seats of the all-white Mississippi delegation at the Democratic convention. President Lyndon Johnson interrupted her live television appeal for support before the credentials committee by holding an impromptu news conference. The MFDP refused the compromise that gave them only two seats at large. Springer describes meetings she had with Hamer as a member of small NCNW delegations traveling to the South. The purpose of the trips was to review the cooperative livestock program that the NCNW supported in Bolivar and Sunflower Counties dating back to 1966. Springer once stated that the NCNW was perhaps the foremost leader of the volunteer organizations in the fight against hunger in the United States.[7]

⤫

How did you meet your second husband, James Kemp?

(*Chuckles.*) Well. He knew me by name. And I knew him by name, because David Sullivan, the president of his union, the Service Employees International Union [SEIU], would talk to me about this man from Chicago who was such an aggressive man and who would do things that made him unhappy. Dave and I were friends in New York. Well, I didn't know Jim from a load of coal, but Dave knew him very well, and I first heard of Jim through him.

Dave's office was near, and his union and mine were very strong advocates of one another. As a matter of fact, when the building service employ-

6. Dorothy Height has served as an advocate for black women and families in a number of capacities. She has worked on the national staff of the YMCA, served as president of Delta Sigma Theta Sorority, and presided over the National Council of Negro Women from 1957 to 1998. Through the NCNW she helped institute Black Family Reunion, which has become an annual celebration in a number of urban centers.

7. International Luncheon—Life Member's Guild, National Council of Negro Women, April 30, 1983 (MSK PP); Springer Kemp to Bert Seidman (AFL-CIO Department of Social Security), May 1, 1975 (Amistad).

Labor and Civil Rights

ees could not get a contract signed from the real estate people, they went on strike. They serviced all of the office buildings in Manhattan. I guess this must have been the late thirties, early forties. I wasn't the officer of a union yet. In the building where I was working, we would not go to work because of the strike. And I was one of those on the committee delegated to go walk up — I'm working on the seventeenth floor — seventeen flights of stairs to inform the employer that we were not coming to work. We were not scabbing on the SEIU. Well, the building service employees got the contract. (*Laughs.*)

When I became an officer of the union and I was very involved in all kinds of things on Africa, I would see Dave very often. Adam Powell was chairman of the labor committee and was eating the labor movement without salt. Jim invited one of Adam's staff people (*chuckles*) to speak at a union convention or some meeting in Chicago. And when Dave Sullivan heard, well, immediately he knew what the speech said. He nearly had apoplexy. We were sitting on the platform in some meeting, during the intermission. He said to me, "Springer, you know Jimmy Kemp?" I said "No, who's he?" And so he went on to say that oh, he wished I knew Jimmy Kemp, a helluva good guy, strong man, but he has a way of his own, and he just had this man come to Chicago and make this terrible speech. (*Laughs.*) So I say it with humor because I don't know how many years later, I married this guy. Before I ever knew Jim, I knew he was giving people apoplexy.

I told Jim that story, and then he gave me his side, because Dave did not tell me what was involved. Dave's conflict was this. Jim was a terrific, standup union guy and he would take the world on all by himself. He would be a majority of one. But by the same token he was a majority of one about something he felt strongly about that could embarrass the labor leadership. He thought you talk about civil rights and you talk this, but it's not true. And he would challenge you. So, he embarrassed them about a lot of things.

So I knew Jim Kemp by name. And he knew me by name. We'd been at the same conventions but had never seen one another. Then I was on the staff of the AFL-CIO Department of International Affairs and I was attending a meeting in Washington. There were six people of color at this meeting. One man was a friend of mine who I think was a vice president of the service employees' union out of New York. And there was the minister whom I did not know. You had a rabbi and a priest and a black minister. It was an ecumenical thing. They were talking about international affairs, the state of Israel, and a lot of things. It was very new. After the meeting, I was hugging Tom, the man I knew from New York, and we were talking and saying hello. And this giant of a man walks over to Tom and says to him (*in a very jovial tone*),

"How are you, old buddy." He wasn't an old buddy of his at all. (*Laughs.*) And, "Will you join me for a drink?" and "May I be introduced?"

He was looking down on you like that as he was speaking to your friend?

Yeah, because he was six four. I'm five four. (*Laughs.*) Then he said, "I have my daughter here as a graduation present. She's just graduated from high school, and I expect her back. Friends have taken her out." And then we said thank you very much and had a drink.

The next day I had a telephone call in my office and was invited out to have dinner with this man. I don't think I could go that day. And so I had dinner with him subsequently. He was a jazz buff and he knew every musician and he knew, you know, everybody in the world. So I went to my first nightclub in Washington, because the things I was involved with didn't take me to nightclubs. I was busy with all of the diplomatic hocus-pocus that was going on and learning my way about my job. I was a single woman. I would never go to such places by myself. OK. It was a very nice evening. He talked very charmingly, and we began having conversations.

Every occasion that he could find, he'd get back to Washington. If they were having a dogcatcher's something and the AFL-CIO was involved in some way and I was going to be involved, he was going to be present. He would come to Washington very often. But I did not know that he hated Washington. Later on, his staff told me, "We didn't know what came over Jimmy." You know, Washington made him sweat. It was too steamy. He didn't like Washington people. But suddenly Washington became a very nice place.

And if they, the NAACP or Urban League, were having a convention, and I would have an African delegation, I would have to introduce them. I think the first one was an Urban League convention in Philadelphia. Jim was as large as life, and he lived as large as life. He always had a big suite and entertained a lot of people. And so he would call me and say, "Miss Springer, I hear that you're going to be at the convention with your Africans." (*Laughs.*) "I see on the agenda of the convention . . ." And he would invite all of my crew to a party in his place. On this occasion, they were going back by bus to New York. I had a six-month or a nine-month course going on, and they had to get back to New York to be in class the next morning with the ILG, which had made it possible for me to have this program. And so our relationship began that way.

Jim would tell stories later about the Africans who came over. Of course, they met the labor movement people. Jim was a mover and a shaker, and they would meet him. He said of every African that came to Chicago, "The first thing they would holler is 'Sister Maida.'" And he said, "Of course, I would extend myself. They hollered 'Sister Maida.'" (*Laughs.*)

He was a very, very, very gregarious and charming, very handsome man, very difficult man, very strong, very strong. He would support me in my projects. There is one particular case I remember involving a young man [Kwaku Baah] who was a law student here from Ghana. The Reverend Dr. Pauli Murray knew him, and it was her project to get him here.[8] She had been a lecturer in the Ghana School of Law, which she helped to put together. And she was in deep trouble there, talking her democratic principles and challenging. As a lawyer, you think and you question everything. Well, there were a number of bright students, including this one particularly whom I got involved with. We raised money for him to get here. He was going to go to school in Chicago [Northwestern University]. So, of course, he came to see me. In due course, he got married to an American girl. He's going to school, but things are tough. He came to my house. I said, "You help me sort these papers out." And I put a few dollars his way. He was shivering. And his shoes . . . He had walked because he did not have money for car fare. So I got on the phone, and I called my dear husband. And I said, "Jim, you have a lot of cashmere sweaters that you do not wear and they're too small for you. May I give some of these things and some of those heavy socks that you do not wear?" *Well*, I think without taking a breath, he shouted at me for a couple of minutes to the top of his lungs. He said, "You bring them to eat my food, to drink my whiskey" (*laughs*), and something else I did. "Now you want me to give them my clothes." He's in his office shouting, and so I didn't say anything. When he got through shouting, I said, "May I have the things?" He said, "Damn it, yes!" Then he hung up the phone. Bam! (*Laughs.*) That was Jim Kemp. What I did not know was that this gave him extreme pleasure to be supportive. But he told me once, "Among the things I will not let you do is take my grumbling privileges away," because I would take advantage of him because of my small size. So he had to be difficult with me. He was supportive

8. Right before Kwaku Baah's departure from Ghana to the United States, he was slated for arrest due to his role in aiding Joseph Danquah in the defense of eight political prisoners arrested under the Preventative Detention Act during Kwame Nkrumah's rule. After the coup against Nkrumah, he returned to Ghana. He became a minister under the government of Dr. Kofi Abrefa Busia and an MP in 1980. Most recently he has served as vice chairman of the National Democratic Congress. See Murray, *The Autobiography of a Black Activist, Feminist, Lawyer, Priest, and Poet* (Knoxville: University of Tennessee Press, 1987), 318–47; "Kwaku Baah Praises Busia, Danquah . . . Chastises NPP," *Ghanaian Chronicle*, November 7, 2000, AllAfrica Inc., Africa News Service, Global News Wire (accessed March 2, 2003).

about anything I was doing, but he would always complain. (*Laughs.*) Always complain.

While he told me he was not a strong advocate of all of this African business, there was never an occasion that I asked him to be supportive that he wasn't, as was the case when I was working on a trade union summer jobs program through the AFL-CIO. He would go to the Chicago Federation of Labor, of which he was a strong member, and he would read the letter he had just gotten from Sister Springer from the International Affairs Department of the AFL-CIO. He would say, "I think we should support this program." He would get on the phone and would talk to a few of the unions, and thereby I would get people placed in Chicago.

I worked with unions across the country helping African college students, not trade unionists, to work in the labor movement, summer jobs. Some were hard-working jobs. Others were working with the staff, learning about the labor movement. My feeling about that was that if this potential leadership for the future had some greater awareness of the workers' problems, then the workers would not have as tough a time with the political leaders as did the American worker whom I knew and the European worker about whom I'd read. In the back of my head, this was my motive. President Meany okayed it, and I drafted a letter under his signature to many unions around the country. I worked with an Africa group in New York, and that was a creditable piece of work. We had problems, because some of my brothers (*laughs*) created problems.[9] To my everlasting happiness, not one woman whom I ever placed created problems for me or the labor movement. (*Laughs.*)

One woman [Ms. Babin] was so good. She's an economist from Sierra Leone. The Communication Workers of America were doing President Meany a favor when they took this woman I sent over. They put her to work on some minimal jobs, you know, not to her abilities. And then she found some incorrect tabulations, some mistakes in a contract they had just settled, or some months earlier. She pointed this out, corrected this problem, and just presented it with a memo. *Well* (*laughs*), she was the fair-haired girl of the CWA.[10]

My secretary, Violet Lewis, was a Sierra Leonean. She had a master's in

9. Springer is referring to their penchant for flirting with women, particularly white women, who worked in union offices. This flirtation often created tension.

10. Babin served as economic research assistant for the CWA's research department. The error she found in the base year figures completely changed the productivity figures for the telephone industry. See Springer, "Summer Jobs of African Students," *AFL-CIO Free Trade Union News* 17 (December 1962).

Labor and Civil Rights

business administration. But, of course, you work with whatever you can get. Somebody recommended her to me. So we looked at one another and said, well, I like you and you like me. Later she married, and I kept track of them. When I was in Ghana at one time, her husband was the ambassador. And he said, "Tonight I am going to cook for you." So there are vignettes of very good, healthy relationships, friendships that one shares over the years.[11]

What was James Kemp's relationship with Meany?

Mr. Meany did not know Jim. He only knew him by reputation, this obstreperous guy. I think Mr. Meany's annoyance with Jim came from this. Jim was a member of the Chicago Federation of Labor and whatever he didn't like he would let you know. The federation votes yea. Jim would say, "Let the record show that I voted no." (*Chuckles.*) So Mr. Meany got a lot of these reports about Big Jim. And then it turns out here we have Maida Springer who is blah, blah, blah. For God's sake, with all the people in the world, she goes and marries this outrageous Chicagoan. (*Laughs.*)

You shrug your shoulders.

No. The die was cast. That was my decision. That he was outrageous I knew by that time. We married in 1965.

Before you met James Kemp, did you ever think that you would remarry?

No. Never! Never! No. I never thought that.

So, why did you decide to remarry?

A variety of things. I was in a different work, nationally and internationally. I had to make some personal choices. I was a divorced woman, moving around the world. There were all kinds of hazards and pitfalls as a single woman. In addition, James Kemp was an extremely attractive man. In my wildest dreams I would never have thought I would marry someone like him. (*Laughter.*) There were two great things that attracted me to him. One, he was aggressive, a lawyer by education, believed in being a majority of one. He would take a position in opposition to everybody else in the room and he would stand up alone to defend it. He didn't ask anybody. If he was a friend, he would go down the line with you. Two, the history of his family in the NAACP. He was a *strong* advocate for the NAACP. His parents' home in the

11. According to Springer's diary entry for June 10, 1962, Violet Lewis was assigned to her as a secretary. Lewis had gotten an MBA from a Southern college but had not yet found employment. After Lewis married she became Violet Porter. Her husband served in the Sierra Leonean diplomatic corps, including as an ambassador to Russia and to Ghana. Violet Porter later represented her country at the International Labor Organization (ILO) in Switzerland and served as a labor officer in the Sierra Leonean government. Porter to Springer, June 12, 1980 (MSK PP).

South was one of the way stations for blacks who could not stay in hotels, the leaders of the NAACP. Across the country there were homes where they could stay as a kind of bed and breakfast. Jim was very active and very supportive, a fund-raiser, par excellence, a mover within the NAACP leadership circles.

Do you recall any contests or struggles in the NAACP that he participated in?

Well, there were always contests. You know, it's power. Whenever you get more than three people together, you are going to find a yea and a nay. But his concern was for the good of the NAACP. One struggle that stands out for me concerned who would become chairman of the board after Robert Ming had died. Robert Ming was a lawyer and also a personal friend. Jim was very anxious that this woman, Margaret Bush Wilson, who was a lawyer also, be the chairman of the board.[12] She was very active in the movement, and they were part of a nucleus. This is one of the ways, I am telling you, he would stand up in an audience and be a majority of one, to state his case and champion whomever. He was a wonderful guy, if you were in a struggle, to be your supporter. This I admired very much about him.

Can you explain more about your limitations as a single woman moving around in the world?

Well, I think this would be true particularly in those days when women were not as accepted. They are not entirely so now. But it was strange. Here was this woman moving around, with colleagues in Africa, as an officer of the International Affairs Department of the AFL-CIO. African leaders, for the most part, welcomed this. But you were almost sometimes dancing on the end of a needle because the emphasis was that Africans should stay out of politics. How do you effect social change if you are not involved in some way in politics? And the second cadre of the leadership in Africa was the limited labor movement of Africa. The unions were small. There are all kinds of problems, you know, the work that you were doing, and you are a single

12. William Robert Ming had also been part of the group of renowned law professors at Howard University in the 1940s and 1950s who successfully argued civil rights cases before the Supreme Court and who provided training for the future generation of civil rights lawyers, including Pauli Murray. See Murray, *The Autobiography of a Black Activist,* 182. Following Margaret Bush Wilson's election in 1975 as the first female chair of the NAACP Board of Directors, she declined to view her position as a win for the women's movement. Ironically, she lost her reelection bid to the sixty-four-member Board of Directors, coming in ninth after James Kemp in a field of ten candidates for the eight open positions. Kemp had died after the ballots were sent out but before the votes were counted, causing Wilson to declare that she had lost to a dead man. A wrenching and debilitating battle then ensued within the NAACP board, which had its roots in a long-simmering power struggle between Wilson and NAACP executive director Benjamin Lawson Hooks. See Sheila Rule, "Ex-Chair of NAACP Says She May Sue the Board," *New York Times,* January 10, 1984, section B, p. 8.

woman. I did not look my age in those days. Among others things, I was still the oldest person among labor leaders, people in Africa. Both the political leaders and particularly the labor leaders were very young. So I became known as a Mama Maida. And there was this running joke in Africa, particularly in East Africa. There were young men who respected me and wanted my support, but they called me Brother Maida. You've read some of the correspondence. I don't know why (*laughter*), but I was Dear Brother Maida.

Any single woman faces these problems. That was pretty universal, whether you were black, whether you were white. What is it they called it? The glass ceiling that women were trying to break in the United States. That was part of the reason behind the creation of an organization like NOW, like CLUW [Coalition of Labor Union Women] in the labor movement.[13] Women in the labor movement remained a part of the AFL-CIO but set up a structure which eventually became quite accepted. These problems were universal. They didn't pick on me. (*Laughs.*)

Did you think that a married woman would be respected or looked at in a different way than a single woman would be?

Yes. I assume so generally, because this was the concept I had nationally in the United States and overseas. I was doing something in an unusual field for the times. Not so now. And the majority of the workers, the people you were talking to and sharing experiences with, were male. Women were not a large part of the workforce. I did not know this until quite recently. The person who requested my presence for my first trip to Africa did so because he wanted support for the women in West Africa. It was felt that my presence as a woman from the United States would encourage other women who were moving into the workforce to become union members. In Africa women were not a part of the large industrial complex, but they were in the Western part of the world.

You did a pamphlet, "Pioneers of Negro Leadership," that featured labor pioneers in Chicago like James Kemp. In some of the papers I read the pamphlet wasn't accepted as well as you would have liked in labor circles, including the AFL-CIO. What do you think limited its acceptance?

Well, "Pioneers of Negro Leadership" was talking about black labor leaders of an older generation in the Chicago labor movement. All of these men that

13. Formed in 1974, CLUW's objectives include promotion of affirmative action in the workplace, organizing women and increasing their leadership in the union movement, and promoting women's involvement in the political process. See CLUW mission statement, "Coalition of Labor Union Women," http://www.cluw.org/about.html (accessed April 29, 2003).

were featured came up through the ranks and were leaders of their unions. The unions included the Brotherhood of Sleeping Car Porters, the Amalgamated Butcher Workmen, the musicians, and a few others. The history of the Chicago labor movement was, I think, so important that we should talk about it. A. Philip Randolph wrote the preface to it, and I was so foolishly modest that I think somewhere down the bottom of a line somewhere I indicated that I was the editor of it. I think there were those who didn't take strongly to it because it was talking only about black labor leaders and we were then at a high point of talking about the integrated labor movement. I was talking about history.

They thought it had a nationalist, secluded bent to it?

I suppose so. So we circulated it. We sent copies of it to libraries, to some schools.

Will you tell the story of how your husband met A. Philip Randolph?

Well, after Jim graduated from law school, there were no jobs for young black lawyers. So he took every civil service exam and passed. The first one that came up that he passed was for a policeman. And many policemen in those dark days were not very literate, and there were very few ones of color, almost none. Well anyway, he's on the police force and struggling to pay for his uniform and gun.

A. Philip Randolph and Milton Webster, who was the first vice president of the Brotherhood of Sleeping Car Porters, are in their heyday. They are putting together the 1941 March on Washington for jobs for blacks in the defense industries. The only things that blacks were doing, I think, we were sweeping the floor or something like that. Again, you are going to fight a war for democracy and you are faced with this discrimination. There were very few churches, very few places that you could meet. There was one church that was very strong, very supportive of Randolph and Webster and the things that the Brotherhood stood for, equality of opportunity and the war effort.

The police department told Jim to take off his uniform and be a detective. They wanted him to go to these meetings of Randolph's and the Brotherhood and report back what this subversive Randolph is talking about. So Jim put on his only suit (*laughs*), pressed it nicely, he said. Then he went to Randolph and said, "Brother Randolph, I'm a member of the police department. I'm here to find out what you are talking about at these rallies that you will be holding with regard to employment." So they both laughed. And Randolph said (*lowers voice in imitation of him*), "Oh, Brother Kemp, you are most welcome. I will tell you." So Jim would go to the meetings every day, and Randolph knew! There was no secret. Randolph was quite open about what he was about. But Jim wanted to make sure that this great man knew where he stood on this, and that he was being sent by the police department.

This story came out in my home—and I have pictures of them somewhere—in the seventies when Randolph received a doctorate in Chicago from one of the universities, and I was then working for the A. Philip Randolph Institute as the midwest director. After the ceremony, he had some time and, of course, Jim invited him and all of the Brotherhood men to our home until it was time for Randolph to travel. All of the Brotherhood men, the old-timers, were dressed to the nines. So these stories came out and the men talked to one another. Brother Randolph, "Chief" as I called him, and Jim reminisced about this story of when Jim was a skinny, tall young man sent to eavesdrop. It was a wonderful afternoon. The men reminisced about a lot of things about Chicago that I did not know about, things that they had done and shared. Randolph in his gentle way just guffawed as they told stories.

Tell me about your experience in 1962 with the congressional hearings Adam Clayton Powell Jr. was holding on discrimination in the labor movement.

I was supposed to testify when Adam Powell was challenging the union. (*Said with humor.*) I was going to testify on behalf of the union about price settlements for operators. The structure of wages for the majority of workers in this industry is based on the piece-rate system. Herbert Hill, the former labor secretary of the NAACP, was representing Adam Powell. He's a university professor now and very erudite. I knew him and had worked with him to settle a few problems when he was labor secretary. A worker would go to the NAACP and complain about something, and Herbie would tell me about the situation. I would say let me see what I can do about it. Let's see if we can straighten it out. We had that kind of relationship. Our offices were just up and down the street from one another, and we were personal friends. When I appeared at the hearing, they would not let me testify. (*Laughs.*) They closed the hearing down that morning and said enough people had testified.

You think he closed the hearing because he saw you were going to testify?

Well, they ended the hearing. He could not challenge me on the facts of price settlements. What the ILG was up on charges for that morning was an assertion that the ILG settled black and white prices. I'm rephrasing what they said, but in effect this is what they were saying. If a garment was worth $2.00, the ILG settled it for $1.25 for blacks and $2.00 for whites. In a shop with forty machine operators, thirty white and ten black, two price schedules would be almost impossible.

I wasn't working for the ILG then. I was working for the International Affairs Department of the AFL-CIO in Washington. So I called my former office in New York, Local 22, and I just said to them, "Run through settlements

A, B, C" — I named a number of manufacturers — "and have them mimeo-graphed and ready for me, because I have to go to testify." I arrived with a briefcase and Mr. Hill looked at me and I looked at him. They called on everybody, and I was the third or fourth person when they ended the hear-ing. They weren't going to discuss whatever that was anymore. It wasn't rel-evant anymore. But he *couldn't* challenge me on price settlements. There are other practices that could be questionable about the union. But anything that my signature was on, the shops I have settled for . . . no. From that day at the hearing, I've never seen him, I haven't talked to him. They did not know that I was going to testify until he saw me that morning. The last thing he expected was for me to turn up at a hearing for the International Ladies' Garment Workers' Union. They had a vice president from Puerto Rico to testify. They had DD [David Dubinsky] to testify. But I was a surprise, and I think he did not want to go through that.

Not in your case particularly, but the ILG has said that some of the things that were reported to the NAACP about discrimination in the ILG were not correct.

Of course. Of course. Most of it was correct. So you always select what was not correct. (*Laughs.*) The charges that were made of wrongdoing, of discrimination in the union, some of these things were absolutely true! And if I had had to testify and was asked whether there was any discrimination in the ILG, I never would have said no there isn't. Constitutionally, there isn't, but an individual officer can do certain things to you to see that you get only bad shops and a lot of things. So I would *never* go anywhere and say no it isn't true, the ILG is pure and they never do anything wrong. No. I would never say that. I would be like Mr. [Clarence] Thomas.[14] And God knows I don't want to be like him.

Well, concerning those few charges of discrimination against the union that were not true, do you think Herbert Hill was overzealous or out to get the union, as some ILG leaders thought?

I will give him the benefit of the doubt and say that he was overzealous. You see, he comes out of the young radical tradition. Many of his friends were then the leaders — educational directors, political directors. Since I don't know the facts, I can't quote, but there are some who say he was a frustrated person because he had not been an accepted member coming into those early won-derful days of the rebirth of the labor movement. I think he was involved with people in the ILG; all of them came out of the same educational climate.

---

14. During the time of this interview many civil rights and feminist organizations were challenging Clarence Thomas's nomination to the Supreme Court, but the sexual harass-ment charges against him had not yet surfaced.

In the mid to late 1960s, how did you come to work with Martin Morand in the South as a general organizer for the ILG?

Very simple. Dubinsky invited me back to work with the ILG after I had resigned from the AFL-CIO. He had been talking to me about coming back to the ILG before that. He would say it's time for you to come home. Now they had sent me there to Washington. I said to DD, "I've been away from the ILG these years. I don't have a sense of the union around the country." I needed to learn about the union. So he proceeded to write letters to union leaders in many sections of the country, which said Maida Springer will be visiting your area and I want her to see what the processes are, what the progress is, to know what the problems are, and to meet with union members, etc.

There was a whispering campaign going on, I learned later. Some people thought I was coming from the national office to observe their operations and go and tattle on them. In California they all got nervous and jumpy because they thought I was coming to *spy* on them. I thought I was sophisticated and politically aware, but I was very shocked when I learned that a lot of people were feeling anxieties. The assumption was that I was coming there to be a tale bearer. What would I tattle if they were doing what they were supposed to do? I was going to learn something. Our frailties are so great and our insecurities are such that even this limited enterprise threatened people. But I think they got over that. And so I spent some time in California. I spent some time in Chicago. And I spent some time in Pennsylvania.

I had known Marty before. He was then the director of the southeast region. I went to spend some time there, and our chemistry was very good all over again. I liked his staff, and they liked me. So I said this is where I'd like to work for a while. And DD said OK.

The things that Marty Morand did boggles the mind sometimes, in staffing, in organizing, and in working with the community. There were two black men on his staff and the way they were treated just pleased me so much. And the example of his staff, I think, had an effect on the organizing. You could feel the sincerity of the women. We had one husband of a white worker who cooked hush puppies and catfish and the green onions and brought this to the hotel. Oh my, he fed us. And we sat on the bed and (*chuckles*) made that our table. I think he may have been a member of a union. I remark about him because he was a white man and one had all the stereotypes in your head about men and about the South. This man believed that even though we were damn Yankees, we were straight on what we were doing on behalf of the workers.

We had a strike. I wasn't in that particular one. There was an all-white shop [Lake City, South Carolina] and an all-black shop [Florence, South

Carolina]. Marty was attempting to integrate the seniority lists of the shops so black women who were closer to the white shop could transfer there without losing benefits that came with seniority.[15] The policeman told the white women they shouldn't be associating with these black women. What shocked the policeman was that some of these white women were very rude and insisted that they were going to be arrested together and they'd stay in the same rooms together in the jail. We brought a group of women from those plants to Chicago and to New York. There was a Northern employer [Wentworth Manufacturing Company in Falls River, Massachusetts] that these shops in the South were working for. And we did informational picketing.[16]

Marty Morand and the SCLC [the Southern Christian Leadership Conference] worked together to get the women to work together across race lines. But the ILG under Louis Stulburg saw the relationship between Morand and the SCLC as controversial.

Oh, well, Marty got into a lot of trouble about that. I thought that he tried to do a great deal of community work. He tried to work with the Southern Christian Leadership Conference. He would be actively supporting black folks, make sure they register, make sure they vote.

I know that he sent some of the workers to the SCLC Citizenship Education Program run by Dorothy Cotton.

Oh yes, yes. He and Ramelle MaCoy, who was the assistant director of the ILG southeast region. Ramelle is a white Southerner but had lived all over the world working for *Time* and other news media. They were terrific together.[17]

How successful do you think the ILG organizing in the South was during the period you were there?

15. The strikers also wanted to stop Wentworth from opening a plant on the Texas border with Mexico that would be "partnered" with a plant unprotected by union standards on the Mexican side. Yevette Richards, e-mail communication with Martin Morand, April 15, 2003.

16. This picketing was aimed at getting retailers to boycott the products of Wentworth. During the four-month strike groups of strikers attended the Southern Christian Leadership Conference (SCLC) Citizenship Education Program. This educational experience helps explain the behavior of these white females. They spat in the faces of the police to force their arrests along with the black women the police were singling out. However, all the white male workers, who were the cutters for both factories, and many of the white female workers, were strikebreakers. The new contract acceded to the strikers' demands on the two major issues. Yevette Richards, e-mail communication with Martin Morand, April 15, 2003.

17. A Mississippian by birth, Ramelle MaCoy had a racist upbringing which explains his early favorable assessment of Senator Theodore Bilbo. MaCoy overcame his upbringing, however, to become an instructor in the Citizenship Education Program through his connections with Andrew Young, civil rights leader and former UN ambassador under Jimmy Carter. Their wives had first gotten to know each other organizing Atlanta teachers. Yevette Richards, e-mail communication with Martin Morand, April 15, 2003.

Maybe sixty-forty. We were the 40 percent. We had some strikes that we lost badly in the South because the employer could go back and say to workers, "You let these Northerners come down here and do so and so. I knew your father." When we traveled, we'd go to a hotel taking our own mimeograph machine. And in one place, Ahoskie, North Carolina, the switchboard operator got (*chuckles*) on the phone as we were walking to where they were showing us our rooms, and said, "They're here." Didn't say who we were or anything. So we all sat in one hotel room and *howled*. We knew we were in for some difficulty.

We were following one of the *big* firms that was a runaway firm. There were a number of them. Union firms were running away to the South, where they were being offered opportunities, such as the workers could not be organized and the union would be chased out. And they would give firms guarantees, a great many things, years without paying any taxes and other perks like that.

So I came in with another officer of the union, who was not from that part of the South, and we were going to do kind of a big roundup. We needed to talk about organizing. We needed to run leaflets. Do organizing on-site. They had been doing a lot of work, and now you needed to bring it to a climax. People were being threatened. The women who were working there, their men were being threatened, men who were farmers and harvesting their crops. "We're going to call in your loans."

There was a film, I think it was antiunion film about the steelworkers. They had gone to court, and the film was banned because it was a distortion. But the chamber of commerce decided to show the film. The audience would mostly be people of the community. So on the evening that this free film was being shown, we had to figure out who was expendable. I was expendable. (*Laughs.*) I would go to the theater, and somebody else was going to help me. I would distribute leaflets telling the union story. It was agreed that somebody would stay outside; they would sit in the car with the motor running. And if I got chased out or if they were getting ready to attack me, I would run *quickly* to get back in the car and we would hopefully drive off. So that's the story about working out every contingency.

If there had been arrests and they had arrested me, it would not stop the work. If they had arrested some of the others who had been doing the day-to-day meeting with people and going to the homes and getting to know the families, that would make the work more difficult. I couldn't go and visit the families. I didn't know all of the neighborhoods. I tell you, driving around there just when it got dark and you're in and out of those villages with the post office half the size of this room (*chuckles*) was quite something. You knew how carefully you were being watched, and some of our folk had been shot at. I was not, in that Ahoskie deal.

You wrote about working with some white women in Spartanburg, South Carolina, to get them to lobby the local government to extend the bus line at the union's expense so that women living on public assistance would have transportation to the garment factories.

This was a big plant in Spartanburg [Jonathan Logan, Inc. plant] and there was a question of absenteeism. And in one of the contract discussions this high-powered manager spoke about women not coming in on time and other complaints. I was an observer. But since I was the person from the ILG, I simply asked questions. Who was the person who stayed home when the child had colic or the child was sick? The husband doesn't have to stay home. The wife stays home with the child. The long and short of this story was that there was a need for additional employees.

The white women on staff and in the shop who had connections in the community educated me real fast on things that might get done with the local government, and how not to make the wrong step or say the wrong thing. We got in that agreement employment opportunities for people, and we were going to get support from the local government for these new employees. We were going to train black and white women. They were poor women who needed to work somewhere. While they were being trained, they would be paid a certain wage. And then they would get whatever the rate was when they had become proficient. They would have public transportation and the union would underwrite some of that fee. The work was in an industrial park and they would be coming from the city. And they'd be able to bring their children. We thought this was pretty good. The women arranged for two women doctors from two separate hospitals to give free time to the factory for the health of the children. The plant would give certain areas for this work. It was a big plant on a large area of land. The regular union workers would all come in to work on a Saturday and make uniforms, little aprons, so all the little children would have something on that was alike. This way people wouldn't say my child has this and your child doesn't. There are other parts of the agreement that I have forgotten.

So we worked at this and the women were just terrific. Marty then sent me to Washington to see if we were following the labor agreement and to get advice on the legalities of what we were doing. I think I wore out my shoes walking the halls of government buildings. Evelyn Dubrow, who was a lobbyist for the ILGWU, made the arrangements in Washington for me to talk to all the legal people I needed.[18] I didn't know all the offices I needed to see for the health care and other things. The agreement never came to pass, I think because the presidential administration changed from Johnson to Nixon. I was out of the work of it, so I did not see what the end product was. But I was feeling so good about all of that. The experiences I had in the South were tremendous.

I remember you telling me once that you worked undercover as an operator and put a needle through your finger.

Oh, that was in New York. This was around the same period. This was in the area where you had the Chinese workers and the recent arrivals. You had the Hispanic workers and black workers. And there was one employer, this "superior" Spaniard who owned a factory. And this lady with her big comb in her hair was paying miserable wages. I just went and asked for a job as an operator. They made rain garments, rubber garments. And I had never worked on those double needle machines, but I was doing all right. I had a chance to talk to people and we got a delegation to go meet in the union office. And the business agent took over from there. But, I just went into this factory and asked for a job. I didn't go in and say I am an officer of the ILG. No. Is that undercover? (*With humor*).

You wanted to speak to me about a woman you worked with on voter registration while you were working for the A. Philip Randolph Institute.

Ora Lee Malone. She was tops, unequivocally. Meeting her was the most refreshing experience for me in the voter registration program. This woman had her heart in it.

I knew her by name before I met her. She was a union officer in the Amalgamated Clothing Workers. As I was moving around the seven-state area as midwest director, I attended a meeting organized in St. Louis in the offices of the NAACP. There were maybe ten to twenty people from the NAACP, and different labor unions, and people interested in labor unions. This was a cooperative effort concerned with voter registration. Ora Lee Malone and I were attracted to one another in this meeting. And after the meeting we got together and talked about the future of this program. She was very excited about it. She began telling me about the opportunity there was to register

18. Evelyn Dubrow has worked on Capitol Hill as a lobbyist for the ILGWU since 1958. She has served as special assistant to the president of UNITE, as advisory board chair of the Campaign for a Fair Minimum Wage, and as an ILGWU vice president and legislative director. She is a founder of Americans for Democratic Action and CLUW and is a 1999 recipient of the Presidential Medal of Freedom. See Special to the *New York Times*, "Profile: Evelyn Dubrow: A Capitol Hill Lobbyist Everyone Loves," *New York Times*, July 27, 1987, section A, p. 12.

Labor and Civil Rights

people in a variety of places, including supermarkets. We became personal friends. She did personal things with visiting African trade unionists. And I was involved with her family—her sisters, her nieces. One niece became a judge in St. Louis.

I think the sincerity of her work affected other people. They became involved because of her commitment. She did the best organizing and had a talent for putting people together. She would connect with various unions. She included a variety of people outside the labor movement. She is a very religious woman and so involved her church in voter registration. I admired her involvement, her interests. When she would call me at midnight, it was a pleasure to hear from her. (*Laughs.*) She would say, "Maida, I need posters or a printout." I would be at the printers at nine in the morning. The printer was a mutual friend and had the proper union credentials. You have someone work like this, and this is a volunteer activity. My God, I would have gone three extra miles for Ora Lee Malone. She made it a joy to come to St. Louis.

And so I grieved when for various political reasons the program was curtailed. There was a complaint to the ILG. Someone made this challenge and wrote to New York and said this woman is busy working on X, Y, and Z political campaign. Complaints were made about other people's activities also. I know that legally there were some constraints, that the ILG could not do this. And the ILG did not want to have its entire program attacked on the basis of some rumor. That might involve them in a lot of litigation. The accusation made against me was distorted, because I was not campaigning for a particular candidate. What I thought I was doing was working on voter registration. I don't know what I did to go beyond that.

I was irritated enough not to even want to find out who said it. I resigned when I was called and told that it was said that I was doing this, that, and the other. I was asked if I wanted to talk to the president [Louis Stulburg]. I didn't want to talk to anybody else. I said, "No, there's no need for that. You"—the assistant to the president [Gus Tyler]—"are bringing me the message." And I was working my socks off, very pleased with some of the response I was getting. Maybe I wasn't doing all that I could have done. I don't know.

When I told Jim that I had resigned and the program was going to be closed, he said to me, "You didn't even ask my advice. We didn't even discuss it." I said, "No. There are some decisions that are mine." He was very annoyed with me because he respected the Chief greatly. But this was a program that was being underwritten by the ILG.

Were you in the country for the 1963 March on Washington?

Yes. Somebody from *Ebony* showed me pictures of me and the delegation from Guinea I was hosting sitting up on top of the platform. And another picture was of me introducing the delegation to Dr. Ralph Bunche. She may have taken those rather privately. Yes, I had just come back to the country, and I was busy with this delegation, traveling across the country. I was working in the Department of International Affairs for the AFL-CIO. Bayard Rustin, who was handling the march, said to me on the day of the march, "Maida, as part of the warm-up, we'd like you to come and present the delegation."

We were all hesitant. The AFL-CIO did not officially endorse it. I would have hoped that we [the AFL-CIO] could have had a big place where people could come and have a glass of water, a cup of coffee, some tea. But for the unions that participated, there was no question that every union had the right to do what it wanted. Most of the unions, the UAW and the others, were marching abreast and hand in hand and poured hundreds and thousands of dollars into it. And my own union, the ILG, was up front.[19]

No one anticipated the wave of humanity that would come. I was going to introduce the delegation to the audience, but that got twisted up. The crowd was so overwhelming that we were late in getting there. And so when we got there—I'm on the top steps on that platform next to Ralph Bunche, near Mahalia Jackson, and two or three seats away from Dr. King—Bayard said, "Maida, we need to start now." So my delegation and I go and sit down, and they're speechless. They absorbed the atmosphere and their interpreter pointed out who was who. After the rally, they're introduced to Dr. Bunche. They're introduced to Dr. King. I was there. I was there.

Well, you would have been about the only woman to address the marchers.

I wouldn't have been addressing anything. I would have taken two seconds and introduce the delegation. I don't think any woman addressed the audience. Well, Mahalia Jackson sang, but I don't think Dorothy Height or Anna Hedgeman or anybody spoke. It was an all-male affair, I believe.[20]

19. Randolph and Walter Reuther were the only two on the AFL-CIO Executive Council who voted in favor of endorsing the march.

20. Anna Arnold Hedgeman, a dynamic speaker in her own right, was the only woman on the administrative committee of the march movement. She tried behind the scenes to convince the male leaders to have women such as Rosa Parks, Daisy Bates, or Merlie Evers give addresses. She noted that at the march Bates was only "asked to say a few words." See Hedgeman, *The Trumpet Sounds: A Memoir of Negro Leadership* (New York: Holt, Rinehart and Winston, 1964), 172, 178–80.

Labor and Civil Rights

Do you know anything about the involvement of Bayard Rustin, A. Philip Randolph, and Dr. King in putting this march together?

I don't know enough to be factual, and I can't tell you a lot. I only know this secondhand. There would not have been a march if Randolph had not sat down with these high-powered men and suggested this. They didn't believe in the march, really. But Randolph is responsible for being able to put together Roy Wilkins, Martin Luther King, Jim Farmer, and others. I'm leaving out some names, and that's bad. Whitney Young, who was the executive director of the Urban League.[21] They had very fancy meetings, which Randolph wasn't a part of. But there was a select group, and they were talking about the issues of the time. And Randolph went down to talk to them. Of course, he'd be invited. He was a member of the group. And he spoke about the need to dramatize the problem.

With the churches Randolph could do all of this organizing. He had the entrée, but he couldn't do it. Too frail at this point. So he said he wanted "Bayard" Rustin (*imitates Randolph's pronunciation*), who was this tactical genius and the social conscience, to do this work. And they accepted it. There were some misgivings because there were people who did not care for Bayard's lifestyle or politics.[22] But they knew that he had entrée. With Randolph's hands over him, he could get on the phone and call anybody and everybody in the name of A. Philip Randolph. And he was indeed an organizational genius. Bayard put it together, and all of them agreed that they were going to work with and through him. But the drudgery, the day-to-day business of doing the March on Washington in '63 was done by Bayard Rustin.

When did you first meet Dr. King?

Well, I had first met Dr. King in a meeting at the Hotel Theresa in Harlem.

21. Known as the "Big Six," the civil rights leaders heading the march were Randolph, Roy Wilkins (NAACP), Martin Luther King Jr. (Southern Christian Leadership Conference), James Farmer (Congress of Racial Equality), Whitney Young (Urban League), and John Lewis (Student Nonviolent Coordinating Committee).

22. Segregationist senators such as Strom Thurmond and some others active in the civil rights movement tried to deny Rustin a role in the march by intimating that his homosexuality and political associations were liabilities to the movement. Rustin was a Socialist and a former member of the Young Communist League. Earlier, in 1960, Adam Clayton Powell Jr., in an effort to uphold his leadership over Martin Luther King Jr. and gain rank within the Democratic Party reportedly threatened to spread false allegations that Rustin and King were having an affair. See Nancy J. Weiss, "Whitney M. Young, Jr.: Committing the Power Structure to the Cause of Civil Rights," *Black Leaders of the Twentieth Century*, ed. John Hope Franklin and August Meier, 331–58 (Champaign: University of Illinois Press, 1982), 342; Charles V. Hamilton, *Adam Clayton Powell, Jr.: The Political Biography of an American Dilemma* (New York: Macmillan Publishing Co., Inc., 1992), 336–37.

This was after the Montgomery bus boycott. It was during the time that a woman stabbed him [1958]. I had seen him in group meetings before.[23]

Did you know E. D. Nixon?[24]

Yes. The Brotherhood! Of course I knew E. D. Nixon. I was a volunteer member of the Brotherhood. (*Laughing.*) Because of my relationship to the Brotherhood, I think that's why, you see, I got the first Rosina Tucker Award from the A. Philip Randolph Institute last June [1989]. I had been in association with the Brotherhood since 1935. That's a long time ago. I bet your mother wasn't born then. (*Laughter.*) I did not know E. D. Nixon very personally, but I knew him as an officer of the Brotherhood and by way of the conventions and other meetings. I knew him as someone who was committed beyond wages and hours and conditions of service. Before the Montgomery bus boycott I knew him as a strong supporter of A. Philip Randolph's broader commitment to correcting social injustice.

Were you ever in the South during any of the civil rights struggles?

No, I was not. I was mostly out of the country during that period. And I would not count the tangential things that I did. I was making my small contributions in support, but this was during the peak period of my work overseas. If I was in for a month or several weeks, I would be supportive by making small contributions within my trade union movement, speaking on behalf of certain issues, joining with whatever force, whatever committee in some mass thing that we were going to do in Washington. We were going to lobby, talk to congressmen, talk to social groups who believed as we believed. So that's why I say it was tangential.

Have you ever joined the National Council [of Negro Women] in any trips to the South?

Yes. When Pauli Murray was a vice president of Benedict College in South Carolina [1967–1968], I visited her there and we took a trip to rural Georgia where the National Council of Negro Women had a sewing program.[25]

23. The Hotel Theresa located at 125th Street and Seventh Avenue was renowned as a meeting place for various civil rights and political causes. The hotel gained a lot of publicity when Fidel Castro and his Cuban delegation stayed there in 1960 in connection with their UN trip. The building has since been converted into stores and office space.

Later found to be mentally deranged, Izola Curry stabbed King during a book signing for his first book, *Stride Toward Freedom: The Montgomery Story* (New York: Harper and Brothers).

24. As president of the Montgomery branch of the NAACP and regional director of the Brotherhood of Sleeping Car Porters, Edgar Daniel Nixon (c. 1900–1987) helped engineer the Montgomery bus boycott of 1955 and helped to shape Martin Luther King's leadership role in the civil rights movement. Rosa Parks served as Nixon's secretary in the NAACP office.

25. See Murray, *The Autobiography of a Black Activist*, 375–76.

Labor and Civil Rights

Through the National Council and in conjunction with another program by a black man out of Washington, DC—I have forgotten his name and he has since died—I wanted to look at the program and then try to talk to my people in the labor movement in the northeast region about the work that these women were attempting to do. They were training people, doing silk screen printing, they were making jerseys and various things. I was trying to find a way to help them legitimize the work. And trying to legitimize it, of course, could have created a conflict. Here you were way out in this rural area with women with children and no husbands, and the Council was trying to break a cycle of ignorance and incompetence. For me to be able to be supportive in doing this and not break any of the concepts, the tradition of the labor movement, was a fine line, because there was nothing for them to be organized or a part of. It was a training program, a facility for women who had nothing, nothing, nothing, no other way to come up out of the ghetto—can't even call it a ghetto, that's the word that we have borrowed from Europe—out of the plantation mentality. Cotton was not king anymore. And if they asked for the simplest conditions, the employers threatened people by withholding employment on the most *meager* basis. I was able to work within the framework of my own northeast region so that I did not have a conflict. But it was very dicey for a while.

I've been to Mississippi. But during the period when Council was going South on training programs, when they had "Wednesdays in Mississippi," and educational projects, and they challenged so many things, I was in and out of the country and did not to my *regret* have an opportunity to participate in it. I would not bluff and say I did. You know, people rewrite history to suit themselves.[26]

Did you meet Fannie Lou Hamer?

I met her only twice. I went to her house. She was a Council member. We had a pig program in the South, which Fannie Lou Hamer started. This was part of the nutrition program, and one of the Southern universities be-

26. NCNW Board member Polly Cowan was the creator of Wednesdays in Mississippi in response to a call by women in the state capital of Jackson who suggested that the presence of Northern women in the South could help alleviate the violence and provide support for activists in the state. Every week for the summers of 1964 and 1965 an interracial team of notable women of various religious backgrounds flew to the state on Tuesdays, spent Wednesdays there, and flew out on Thursdays. They gave support to voter registration drives and the freedom schools, met with women of diverse backgrounds throughout the state, and gathered information concerning the extreme oppression under which blacks lived. See "Wednesday's Women: About Us," http://www.people.virginia.edu/~hcs8n/WIMS/frame-history.html (accessed March 6, 2003).

came attached to it. You had a big company in the South, Purina or one of those, that was supporting the program by making feed available. In the cooperative project you would start with one pig. You were taught by the university extension program how to care for your animals. Your commitment was that if your sow had a litter in this cooperative venture, then you gave a piglet to everyone who was helping you so they could start their own. This extended to many other community groups, so this was a project I was very proud of being a little bit involved in with the Council.

Fannie Lou Hamer received us. She wasn't feeling well. I think there were four or five of us. It was a glorious day. A couple of hours we spent with her, and we talked of politics and various things. Her spirits were great. She fed us. Her family was there, because, as I say, she was not well. So she was surrounded by people. This was after she was a pretty famous person. This was after the seating fight at the Democratic convention in Atlantic City.

The second time I met her she was also ill. We went to the hospital to see her. I don't know whether this was a year or months later. But she said we could come. I think there were just two or three of us, Dorothy Height and myself and one other person. Both of these times I was vice president of the Council.

What do you think of the legacy of the civil rights movement, of the strategy of integration?

My first answer to you is you don't really want me to answer that in one evening. Now, I have to consider the civil rights movement from where I came from and what I think of all of those generations, the contributions that they have made. It is a misnomer *absolutely* to talk about the civil rights movement as beginning in the sixties. In my view that is sheer nonsense! The struggle for self-respect, for dignity, for an opportunity for a better education, for respect for black women in this country went on since the time of slavery.

Now, what has happened within *my* lifetime of seventy-three years in this country,[27] I have seen change in that the civil rights movement has made revolutions in a number of phases. *Lynching* was almost customary in the United States, and people in the Southern states particularly used to fight over the burned-up remains, the tarred and feathered remains of black people as souvenirs after they were burnt to ashes. The fact that you had a voting rights act passed [1965] in the United States was a change. It is a big change now that you have blacks as congressmen and congresswomen in the United

27. The year of this interview was 1990. Springer immigrated to the United States in 1917 at the age of seven.

States, mayors, a governor, school board directors, black men and women holding positions in universities all over the country. These are the things that those people who did not know anything about what it was like before are too casual about and take for granted. The people who have lost their lives and lost their homes and lost their families in this struggle is a part of the unfinished heroics of the civil rights movement. So that's what I think of the civil rights movement.

What are my evaluations of the strategies that you had? In 1954, for example, when you had the *Brown vs. the Board of Education*—my God!—that was revolutionary. The right to have children go to schools where you had better books, where you had access to libraries was a part of that integration strategy. It may not obtain today. There has to be maybe a different strategy. But for those times, it was absolute. That fight had to be made. From where we came, *every* black man, black woman, and every white person who joined in that fight has something to stand tall and be proud about. Now, it is for the young people to carry that torch and to broaden the equation.

That's as much as I need to say about the civil rights movement. It's unfinished business. Whenever you have bad times, the people who are going to be challenged and shortchanged because we look different are going to be American blacks. This is the home of everybody in the world. The Statue of Liberty says everybody should come here. The American involvement in all kind of wars have placed them in the position of responsibility for rehabilitating people from all parts of the world, whose countries we have been involved in. And so, we have the additional crisis within the black community that feels that perhaps they are ignored and that they are not getting enough of the pie. No! We're not getting enough of it! But we have got to make a further challenge and make a greater investment ourselves. That's where I stand on civil rights.

9

The AFL-CIO and South Africa

Springer chronicles the contacts she had with South Africans through her work with the NAACP and the African-American Labor Center (AALC), an international auxiliary of the AFL-CIO. Her representation in South Africa reflects the contentious nature of AFL-CIO foreign policy in the country as well as resentment of the United States government for its tacit support of the apartheid regime. The AFL-CIO's rejection of the ANC was its major stumbling block in gaining better relations with some of the dominant South African labor unions. The federation's objections to the ANC hinged on the liberation movement's acceptance of Communist members, support for divestment, and advocacy of armed struggle. Against the backdrop of unpopular AFL-CIO policy, Springer met the distrust and hostility of some groups during her NAACP trip to the country, her stint as team coordinator for a 1979 and a 1980 AALC study program for South Africans, and her two-week fact-finding mission to South Africa with AALC deputy director Lester Trachtman.

Springer's remarks on South Africa include comments on the vicious nature of apartheid policies. These policies gave whites some of the highest standards of living in the world while they relegated the black masses to destitution and oppression and with no legal means to challenge apartheid. The 1959 Promotion of Bantu Self-Government Act denied Africans citizenship in the country by providing for the placement of twenty-one million Africans in ten ethnically divided homelands. Over a twenty-year period the government forced more than three million blacks to move to the homelands, which were situated on 13 percent of some of the least arable soil and often lacking in any essential services or employment.[1] South African law also clamped down hard on African workers by main-

---

1. "Ciskei Declared 'Free,'" *African Recorder*, January 1–14, 1982, 5814; "Pan-Africanist Congress of Azania," Encyclopedia Britannica Online, http://search.eb.com/eb/article?eu=59651 (accessed March 13, 2003).

taining abysmally low wages, reserving high-paying skilled jobs for whites, and forbidding blacks to organize in independent labor unions.

Springer speaks of her trip to South Africa in 1977 as a participant in the NAACP's Task Force on Africa. Comprised of sixteen members, the task force was divided into four teams covering different regions of Africa. The group's mission was to gather information that would be used in the development of policy positions and guidelines for NAACP members and the U.S. public. Springer's team met Robert Mangaliso Sobukwe (1924–1978), who helped to found the Pan-Africanist Congress (PAC) and served as its first president. In 1960 the regime banned both liberation movements, the African National Congress (ANC) and the PAC, following the Sharpeville massacre. In this tragedy police killed 69 and wounded 180 unarmed, nonviolent Africans who had responded to the PAC's call for protests against the pass laws that required nonwhites to carry documents giving them permission to be in restricted areas. With the option of nonviolent struggle in South Africa closed off, both liberation groups went underground and into exile and instituted an armed struggle against South Africa. Sobukwe was among the 1,800 arrested following the Sharpeville massacre. He was kept in prison after his initial term under a special amendment to the Suppression of Communism Act, known as the "Sobukwe Clause" because he was the only one detained under it. After nine years in the Robben Island prison, he was put under house arrest until his death. Wanting to put a good face on their policies, the South African government allowed the meeting with the NAACP team.[2]

Springer's task force report outlined the various legal means used to keep African labor voiceless and powerless and disputed the notion that multinational corporations operating in South Africa were effecting gradual change in the country's economic racial policies. The NAACP soon called for a complete economic boycott of South Africa, urging U.S. businesses to pull out and the U.S. government to pressure banks and businesses not to invest in the country.[3]

Eight years later the AFL-CIO came out in favor of "total economic pressure" against South Africa. Before then, the federation joined with those who believed less strident measures than divestment should be taken first to effect the end of apartheid on the premise that divestment would primarily harm Africans. Starting in 1960 the federation began advocating various sanctions against the regime, such as the boycott of South African consumer goods, international embargoes

2. George Houser, *No One Can Stop the Rain: Glimpses of Africa's Liberation Struggle* (New York: Pilgrim Press, 1989), 257–58; "NAACP Task Force Travels to Africa," *AFL-CIO Free Trade Union News*, April–May 1977.

3. Memorandum, MSK to NAACP Task Force—Africa: Labor Relations [1977] (MSK PP); "South Africa: NAACP Asks U.S. Business Withdrawal," *Facts on File World News Digest*, January 20, 1978, http://www.2facts.com (accessed March 13, 2003).

on oil and military imports to the country, and expulsion from the United Nations. In this regard federation policy departed from U.S. foreign policy, which often helped to shield the apartheid regime from the full brunt of international pressure. The United States, Britain, and France vetoed three UN Security Council resolutions dealing with arms embargo and UN expulsion. Bowing to overwhelming public pressure for full economic sanctions the U.S. Congress in 1986 passed the Comprehensive Anti-Apartheid Act over the veto of President Ronald Reagan.[4]

Springer's commentary conveys the difficulties and challenges that the anti-Communist policies of the AFL-CIO posed for working with the emerging black and nonracial unions following changes brought about by the Wiehahn Commission in 1979.[5] The growth of black labor activism in the wake of the 1973 Durban strikes and the need of businesses for an increased pool of skilled labor influenced the white minority regime to accept most of the Wiehahn Commission's recommendations for liberalizing labor law. The changes included allowing blacks to legally form trade unions and join white ones and with some exceptions the abolition of the reserved job categories.[6] At this juncture the AALC was able to deal directly with black and nonracial unions.

In the AFL-CIO's attempt to lend aid to antiapartheid forces outside the ANC framework, the federation supported some labor and political people who did not represent the majority will of African workers or who were seen as political rivals to the ANC. Springer relates how the presence of former PAC executive member (Nelson) Nana Mahomo on the AALC staff as program officer and the federation's support of labor leader Lucy Buyaphi Mvubelo and Zulu leader Mangosuthu Gatsha Buthelezi were factors that heightened the anger and suspicion of pro-ANC trade unionists.

One of the founders of the black nationalist Pan-Africanist Congress, Mahomo had been head of Culture and Youth. The PAC had split from the ANC in 1959 over issues of Communist and white leadership, charging that the ANC was too

4. "AFL-CIO Resolutions," *AALC Reporter* 8 (November 1973); "AFL-CIO Continues to Speak Out Against South African Apartheid," *AALC Reporter* 15 (May–June 1980); "U.S. Worker Delegate Supports Apartheid Policy Adopted at ILO's 67th Conference in Geneva," *AALC Reporter* 16 (July–August 1981); "United Nations: South Africa Expulsion Blocked; Other Developments," Facts on File World News Digest, November 2, 1974; "South Africa: Arms Embargo Vetoed in U.N. Council," Facts on File World News Digest, June 14, 1975; "United Nations: South Africa Arms Ban Vetoed," Facts on File World News Digest, October 23, 1976. All in Facts on File World News Digest, http://www.2facts.com. "South Africa, History of," *Encyclopedia Britannica*, Britannica Online, http://search.eb.com/eb/article?eu=117926 (accessed March 13, 2003).

5. In the South African context, "multiracial" implies that distinctions are made on account of race, whereas "nonracial" implies an absence of distinctions and racial hierarchies.

6. "South Africa: Racial Labor Limits to Be Lifted," Facts on File World News Digest, May 4, 1979, http://www.2facts.com (accessed March 13, 2003).

compromising toward the interests of non-Africans. However, the PAC became hopelessly faction ridden and in 1964 the controversial acting president Potlako Leballo expelled Mahomo. Mahomo's opposition accused him of unexplained use of funds and connections with the CIA.[7]

As Springer reports, some of the South Africans participating in the 1980 AALC program refused to meet with Mahomo. Yet Mahomo did not have a smooth relationship with the AALC, either. He had profound differences with AALC director Patrick J. O'Farrell, charging that he was not knowledgeable enough about South Africa to make effective policy decisions.[8] O'Farrell, who came out of the United Steelworkers, served as AALC executive director from 1973 to 1995. He previously had served as AALC representative to Ghana and then as AALC deputy director (1968–1973). In 1994 he headed a team of U.S. trade unionists to South Africa to participate in the monitoring of the first democratic elections. Although Mahomo and O'Farrell were at odds with one another, Springer seems to have gotten along well with both.

Springer's remarks indicate that the support the AALC gave to Lucy Mvubelo also damaged its ability to garner support from the emerging unions and influenced how some trade unionists perceived her own work. Mvubelo's trade union involvement and antiapartheid activism began in the early 1950s. Her union, the National Union of Clothing Workers, had been one of the separate black unions called "parallel" unions organized within the white-dominated Trade Union Council of South Africa (TUCSA). Bowing to government pressure, TUCSA banned the "parallel" black unions from 1969 to 1972. Labor leaders in the emerging black and nonracial unions viewed Mvubelo as too compromising and conciliatory regarding TUCSA's decision and in other issues dealing with the antiapartheid struggle. Among the many suggestions that came out of their fact-finding mission, Springer and Lester Trachtman urged the AALC to broaden its trade union contacts. Regarding Mvubelo in particular, they remarked that she was not representative of black trade union leaders and that in her time she had been a significant force but had since not done as much as she could have to improve the extremely poor wages of garment workers.[9]

7. Mahomo produced two anti-apartheid films, *End of Dialogue* (1969) and *Last Grave at Dimbaza* (1973), which were shot clandestinely in South Africa. Houser, *No One Can Stop the Rain*, 125–26, 258–59.

8. Mahomo communication with Yevette Richards, June 24, 2000.

9. Denis MacShane et al., *Power! Black Workers, Their Unions and the Struggle for Freedom in South Africa* (Boston: South End Press, 1984), 32; *South African Labour Bulletin* 3 (January–February 1977): 30; "Historic Meeting in Botswana . . . South African Trade Unionists Speak Out," *AALC Reporter* 8 (May 1973); "South Africa Labor Trip Undertaken by Les Trachtman and Maida Springer, 3/31–4/11/80" (Amistad).

The AFL-CIO's decision in 1982 to grant the George Meany Human Rights Award to Gatsha Buthelezi virtually destroyed any potential of working with the pro-ANC nonracial labor unions. The award was jointly conferred upon Buthelezi and posthumously the trade unionist Neil Aggett, who was the first white and the forty-sixth person since 1963 to die in detention under suspicious circumstances. Buthelezi, chief of the Buthelezi clan of Zulus since 1953 and chief minister of KwaZulu (1972–1994), had been a member of the Youth League of the ANC from 1948 to 1950. In 1975 he formed the Inkatha Yenkululeko ye Sizwe (the National Cultural Liberation Movement) as an alternative to the ANC. Since 1990 it has become the Inkatha Freedom Party. In the ceremony for Buthelezi, AFL-CIO President Lane Kirkland described him as "the single most potent force in resisting the onward rush of apartheid" by his refusal to accept South Africa's conference of independence for KwaZulu, one of the ten black homelands designated under apartheid policy.[10]

Buthelezi's support of peaceful change and continued investment and his representation as an alternative to the ANC made him attractive not only to the AFL-CIO but also to some in the South African regime. His detractors viewed him as a collaborator with apartheid. By 1986 critics were charging that Buthelezi's professed belief in "peaceful change" only applied to the struggle to overthrow apartheid, as deadly and prolonged violence erupted between his followers and the United Democratic Front, a coalition of antiapartheid groups supporting the ANC's Freedom Charter. ANC supporters have accused South African defense forces of aiding Inkatha in the fighting in which fourteen thousand were killed. In 1991 the regime admitted providing payments and services to Inkatha on a couple of occasions, clearly as a strategy to undermine the ANC. Buthelezi denied knowledge of the connections.[11] Following the outcry against the AFL-CIO for giving the award to Buthelezi, the federation began to move away from him.

In the interviews, Springer indicates that in hindsight it is understandable why granting the award to Buthelezi was not appropriate. However, at that time and within the context of the foreign policy limitations of the AFL-CIO, she did not

10. "Mangosuthu Buthelezi, Dr.," South Africa Government OnLine, http://www.gov.za/profiles/buthelezi.htm (accessed March 15, 2003); "AFL-CIO Bestows George Meany Human Rights Award on 2 South African Black Rights Leaders," *AALC Reporter* 17 (July–August 1982); and "Two South Africans Receive Human Rights Award," *AALC Reporter* 17 (November–December 1982).

11. "South Africa: Inkatha Funding Scandal Surfaces," Facts on File World News Digest, August 1, 1991; "South Africa: More Inkatha Funding Revealed," Facts on File World News Digest, December 31, 1991, both at http://www.2facts.com; "Truth and Reconciliation Findings: Buthelezi," *BBC News Online*, October 29, 1998, http://news.bbc.co.uk/1/hi/special_report/1998/10/98/truth_and_reconciliation/203978.stm (all accessed March 15, 2003).

think of the award in terms of the differences between Buthelezi and the ANC as much as the common goal in opposing apartheid. Since the electoral victory of the ANC in 1994 the party has seen it as prudent to work with Buthelezi. Under the ANC governments of Nelson Rolihlahla Mandela and Thabo Mbeki, Buthelezi has served as the minister of home affairs.

The AFL-CIO in 1992 was finally legally able to set up an office in South Africa, one of Springer's policy suggestions in 1980. Springer recalls that her friend, African American Barbara Lomax (1940–1997), who became the AALC country program director in 1992, did a stellar job in gaining the respect and trust of the South African labor movement. Lomax came out of the United Food and Commercial Workers and Meatcutters Union. In South Africa she brought together African labor women of different ethnic groups for trade union education programs around the country. Such respect was given to her ability to engender trust and cooperation among the different groups that the Worker's College of Durban named the program after her, The Barbara Lomax School for Trade Union Women of South Africa.[12]

Springer's penchant of looking beyond the limitations of policy differences toward the larger goal of social and political change informed her exultation over the 1990 release of Mandela from twenty-seven years of imprisonment and the triumph of Sam Shafishuna Nujoma, leader of the Marxist-oriented South-West Africa People's Organisation (SWAPO), the resistance movement in South-West Africa (now Namibia) against South Africa's illegal hold on the territory. In 1986 Springer was among those who wrote congressional leaders to pass legislation to force South Africa to free Nelson Mandela and other political prisoners. When Mandela made his first trips outside South Africa after gaining freedom, Springer wrote Julius Nyerere: "When I saw you, Mwalimu, President Kenneth Kaunda, and President Mugabe in the press and on television greeting Mr. Nelson Mandela in your independent countries, I wept unashamedly as I rejoiced in your triumph . . . You may recall that I was in Tanganyika at a time of South Africa's most ruthless repression. TANU gave refuge to the hunted men and women seeking Simple Justice."[13]

12. Before 1992, the AALC field representative for South Africa was stationed in Lesotho after two years of trying unsuccessfully to get a visa entry. See "Trade Unions, Legislation and Civil Rights," AALC Reporter 23, no. 21 (1988); Mary Ann Forbes (AALC) and James B. Parks (AFL-CIO), "Giving Birth to Freedom" (Washington, DC: AALC, 1995), 8 (pamphlet).

13. Springer Kemp letters to Senators John Heinz and Arlen Specter, and Representative William Coyne (dated June 12, 1986). Springer Kemp to U.S. Congressmen Walter E. Fauntroy and William H. Gray (sponsors of the bill), both dated June 12, 1986, and Fauntroy to Springer Kemp, June 27, 1986 (all in MSK PP). Springer to Nyerere, March 21, 1990 (MSK PP). "Mandela Visits Zambia: ANC Plans Strategy," Facts on File World News Digest, March 2, 1990, http://www.2facts.com (accessed March 13, 2003).

Before his engagement in politics, Mandela decided to forgo his claim to the chieftainship of the Xhosa-speaking Tembu people. As a lawyer, he along with Walter Sisulu and Oliver Tambo set up the first black law firm in South Africa. In 1944 they organized the ANC Youth League, and Mandela became its president in 1950. Arrested for treason in 1956, he was acquitted in 1961. Following the ANC banning, Mandela formed the ANC's military wing, Umkhonto we Sizwe (Spear of the Nation). After a second arrest and a sentence of five years for sabotage and attempting to overthrow the government, Mandela faced additional charges of treason. In the famous Rivonia trial of October 1963 he and seven others were given life sentences. Mandela became president of South Africa in 1994. He declined a second term.[14]

In 1959 Sam Nujoma, who had roots in the labor movement as an employee of the South African Railways, became the leader of South-West Africa's long-running struggle for liberation from South Africa. Following a UN-brokered cease-fire, SWAPO won a majority of parliamentary seats and Nujoma became president under UN-supervised elections in 1989. Namibia gained independence on March 21, 1990, a month after Mandela's release.[15] Similar to Springer's assessment of AFL-CIO policy in South Africa, her reflections on Nujoma are framed within the parameters of cold war politics whereby the AFL-CIO was often perceived as reactionary.

Finally, Springer turns sadly reflective in her discussion of the spread of state repression and economic difficulties that led to the electoral defeat of Kenneth David Kaunda in Zambia. Kaunda led his country to independence in 1964. In 1972 Zambia became a one-party state. Kaunda was defeated in multiparty elections in 1991 by trade union leader Frederick Jacob Titus Chiluba. In late 1997 the Chiluba government charged Kaunda with knowing about a coup attempt and placed him under arrest. They released him to house arrest after an international outcry. Six months later charges were dropped. His son Wezi Kaunda was assassinated in 1999.[16]

14. "Facts on Nelson Mandela," Biography, World News Service, 2001 Facts on File News Services.

15. "Namibia," *The Columbia Encyclopedia*, 6th ed. (New York: Columbia University Press, 2002). See http://www.bartleby.com/65/na/Namibia.html, and "Our President," http://www.gmnet.gov.na/Government/Our_President/Background_Hist.htm (accessed March 13, 2003).

16. Human Rights Watch has cited human rights abuses under Chiluba's government. See "Zambia No Model for Democracy; Continuing Human Rights Violations," in Recent Short Country Reports, Human Rights Watch Publications, More, HRW Publications, Human Rights Watch, www.hrw.org/reports98/zambia/ (accessed June 30, 2000).

In 1977 you participated in the NAACP Task Force for Africa.

The NAACP Task Force was divided into five committees. We were going all over Africa. My committee, headed by Dr. Broadus Butler, drew South Africa.[17] I was included among six people to be a member of the South African delegation. Dr. Broadus Butler was an educator and chairman of the NAACP Task Force. Our fare was raised by Margaret Bush Wilson and Dr. Broadus Butler. This South African delegation trip was partly influenced by the contacts in South Africa of Montague Cobb, who was the president of the NAACP and a noted anthropologist and medical doctor.[18] He was a member of the delegation, and had had a history of intellectual exchange. His reputation was such that he had been invited to do some lectures at Witwatersrand University in South Africa, which was the only interracial—I'm not saying integrated (*chuckles*)—college.

We traveled all over the country. The understanding was that we would be able to go anywhere in South Africa and talk to various people. The people who were making some of this possible represented a South African liaison committee, and they were supposed to be an "independent" agency and not a part of the South African government. They were trying to make efforts to show us all of the supposed right things the South African government was doing.

A meeting was arranged very early in the morning to meet Robert Sobukwe. They escorted him to our hotel. Special arrangements were made because he could not leave his house because of the ban. I think some relative of his studying in the United States helped us arrange this meeting. We met with him in a room of our hotel. Knowing his background and what they had

17. Broadus Nathaniel Butler (c. 1920–1996) served as a university administrator, director of the Office of Leadership Development at the American Council on Education in Washington, and president of the East Coast chapter of the acclaimed World War II Tuskegee Airmen. In 1964 he was assistant for special education under the United States Commissioner of Education. Wolfgang Saxon, "Ex-Tuskegee Airman and College Leader," *New York Times*, January 13, 1996, section 1, p. 12.

18. William Montague Cobb (1903–1990) was a renowned physical anthropology professor. He was notable as the only black physical anthropologist with a Ph.D. before the Korean War, and as the first black president of the American Association of Physical Anthropologists. See National Academy of Sciences, "W. Montague Cobb," African Americans in Science, Engineering, and Medicine: A Portrait Collection of the National Academy of Sciences, http://www.nas.edu/aahm/portrait.htm (accessed March 13, 2003); Kyle Melville, "W. Montague Cobb," http://www.anthro.mankato.msus.edu/information/biography/abcde/cobb_w.html (accessed March 13, 2003).

The AFL-CIO and South Africa

done, you had to be full of respect and in awe of him. They had torn up pass books. I was in awe of their courage. And I had read about the history of Robben Island prison. Nelson Mandela had been imprisoned there, too.

When I met with the trade unions, I first met with the garment workers. I went to the office. I was treated very courteously and *learned* a great deal. The garment workers had an old, old history. They had nine thousand members, all black. Another union, a white one, had three thousand members. The black garment workers could be in the same building with the white workers, but they could not be on the same floor and not in the same union. The white workers were downstairs and the black workers were in an office upstairs. But the white workers represented the black workers, who could not negotiate with the employers. There was no other union like that. It was not until after the Wiehahn Commission that you had any semblance of real social change in South Africa. Until 1979 a black person in South Africa was not a person and could not take on the responsibilities that accrue to the leadership of a worker's representative organization. And then I met with some of the other people. For instance, I met some of the technical workers, who were part of the railway union, and a young woman who was leading it. The people were in detention! She was holding the fort and leading the union. So you heard the bad and the good.

This "independent" group was supporting our visit to see South Africa. On these bus trips that we took, a white South African from that group was driving. From where I was sitting on the back of this little minibus, the black South African who was sitting near me would say under his breath as the situation would be described by the white bus driver, "It's not so." (*Laughs.*) "That's not true." We would be told one thing in the day, and we would meet with people at night who would tell us quite the opposite.

The hope was to woo us, so we would write back an extraordinary report. We came back and wrote a report that was *extremely* critical of what was happening. We wrote that the places we were shown were for show. We were shown very modest model housing, and I said to myself, sure this is for Indians or coloreds, not for blacks. There's a different level of what you see. On the labor question, somebody in the American embassy gave me a set of papers (*laughs*) and said, "Here are some facts for you." So our report was not complimentary, and this supposedly nongovernmental group was very annoyed with the NAACP for this. We were not supposed to have seen a lot of the things we saw. There wasn't a hotel room that we were in as we moved across the country that didn't have a basket of fruit, *superb* South African fruit, and fine wine and other things. Really wooing us.

And so I came back to the United States and said with sarcasm that I was a temporary white for three weeks. That used to offend some people who did not feel strongly about apartheid. There were people who really got very ticked off about that, because they thought that I had an axe to grind. I was, you know, Maida Springer; I shouldn't have an axe to grind. Normally I could roll with the punches, but I told a lot of people in the labor movement. A man, he wasn't the head of the AFL-CIO then (*laughs*), but I don't think he ever forgot it.[19] A lot of people got ticked off. But in South Africa when it is politically expedient, they would allow you to become temporarily white and treat you with kid gloves.

The task force, I think, left the African trade unionists I was at the time talking to, with a bad feeling. Lucy Mvubelo of the garment workers had all of the various African groups in the labor movement to arrange a house-warming, a dinner party for me. I don't know what the hotel where I was staying told them when they came for me for the gathering, but I did not hear from them. The hotel never called my room to let me know that friends were waiting for me in the lobby. I sat in my room and waited for them. They thought I had deliberately ignored them and offended them, because the hotel said I wasn't in my room.

Late in the evening I went downstairs to try in this international hotel we were in to get something to eat. That was an awkward situation. I've forgotten the issue, but it was something that offended me. So I had a fight with the maître d' and someone else. I just didn't like their behavior. I decided not to eat there. But you can imagine how those young African men and women felt. First, spending the money to have an event that I never showed for. No water in the world could wash that off. So that was a very bad thing that happened. The hotel just did a job on them and on me.

And again this involved Lucy Mvubelo. She was not considered a proper supporter of the ANC. She was an old-timer and had been in the movement a long time. They couldn't and wouldn't ignore her, but she wasn't by their standards up with the times. So the fact that I didn't show just added to the bad feelings. I was *very* sorry that this happened because it redounded on the African-American Labor Center. Never mind that I was in South Africa on something else. That was bad and left me in very bad odor.

19. In this context it is worth noting that Lane Kirkland's father was a cotton buyer in South Carolina, his great-grandfather signed the Confederate declaration of secession, and Kirkland himself often referred to the Civil War as "that War of Northern Aggression." William Serrin, "Lane Kirkland, Who Led Labor in Difficult Times, Is Dead at 77," *New York Times*, August 15, 1999, section 1, p. 1.

The AFL-CIO and South Africa

How did the ICFTU approach the problems of black labor in South Africa in those early days?

The ICFTU is not a negotiating body for the workers in a given country, but what they *could* do and *did* do was to protest. There were resolutions. When you went to the ILO, there were always statements about the case of black workers in South Africa. The ICFTU kept with the AFL-CIO a drumbeat that this type of organization was not representative of the workers of South Africa. I was considered a not very friendly person at the ICFTU — somewhere (*laughing*) in your work you can indicate that I was not anti-ICFTU. I just thought that there were some things that we were attempting to do that they were too legalistically involved with while Rome was burning. The truth of the matter is my emotional black self kept me on edge and upset.

There has been some criticism by some South African trade unionists of the American labor movement involvement there in the early days.

You had political sharpnesses, divisions, because every African belongs to something politically. The emphasis politically for most of the Africans was the African National Congress. Now the ANC for all of its history and all of the troubles it has had fighting *apartheid* made a number of declarations that were anathema to the government of South Africa. The terrible things they wanted were equality and justice and not to be persecuted and murdered. However, since the ANC allegedly always professed violence, there were those — and I'm talking about people in the United States — who had a very sharp opinion. They wanted to support the workers but thought that the workers should divide their feelings, that they should not be political persons and trade unionists second. When you are under the gun, that's very hard to differentiate. So the majority of the people privately belonged to ANC, but you didn't discuss this when you're doing trade union things. The AFL-CIO policy was to support those unions that were not avowed members of the ANC and who indicated they were interested in building a working-class movement without the political strings.

But everybody belonged to something politically. You had a number of basic divisions. The ANC was a political instrument with all of its trade union components. The Pan-Africanist Congress was an offshoot of the ANC. They divided from the ANC because *they* said it is alleged that the ANC was Communist-dominated. Rightly or wrongly, this was the division. The ANC had a lot of white members, who were avowed Communists, who were receiving funds from the Soviet Union, and who were doing various things to challenge the South African government. So this was a very sharp political movement. You then had all kinds of other developments and groups and an attempted political integration after 1977.

So the charges have been made that the AFL-CIO was a conservative organization and that it was, at its worst, looking with a blind eye at the South African government, and, at its best, wanting to support workers that were not as militant. So if you had that as your history, there is little that you can do that is right.

In a very, very, very loose way, I was involved with the South African labor movement in the eighties. We were trying to be supportive and there were all kinds of issues involved, and everybody mistrusted everyone else. Whatever my assignment in the African-American Labor Center, I would work at the project when they brought over people on a couple occasions. On one occasion a person who was supposed to do it became ill, so they asked me if I would pitch in. I think they had the Cornell program then [New York State School of Industrial and Labor Relations of Cornell University]. I was already retired. But I worked with them and tried to stage some things to make sure that they saw trade union people, moved about. It was not the kind of ongoing relationship I had had in other places in Africa. I had an assignment. I knew a number of the South African women. I tried to help them with certain things. They were trying to do little programs. But I don't think I made either an impact or a contribution in the way I think I was involved in East and West Africa. So that's why I make a difference.

For a brief period Lester Trachtman and I traveled to South Africa together for the African-American Labor Center. Les, I think, was probably one of the oldest employees of the AALC. For a time he was the deputy director, and I knew him long before he even worked for the AALC. I knew him when he graduated from Cornell and worked for the labor department. When I was working for the AFL-CIO, we did a book about the labor movement. I think he did a great deal of research on that. I did not work with him on a day-to-day basis except for when the AALC did a program in Nairobi for women [the 1977 Pan-African Conference on the Role of Trade Union Women].

The trip that we took to South Africa was a follow-up fact-finding trip on the training program the AALC had the year before.[20] We met with the unions that had sent delegates to the United States for this, and asked questions. You know, "Don't be polite to us. Is it useful? Is it necessary? What does it contribute to the challenges you need to make?" We asked what was profitable

20. For participants in this program, see "AALC Holds First Program for Southern Africans; Ten Labor Leaders Come to U.S.," *AALC Reporter* 14 (April–May 1979).

and what was not about the program, and whether in the future they saw fit to continue sending delegations to the United States for X number of months in a course designed to suit whatever their purposes were. We reported what we saw and what we felt and what was said to us and what recommendations there were.

We were not cordially moved around the country as in the NAACP trip. When I was by myself, you had a hell of a time getting a cab to go from wherever I was meeting back to my little hotel. So there was a real difference. Usually some trade unionist, somebody was with me. They knew the lines of demarcation and the ropes. Or you would be in someone's car. If you were with a nonblack person, they would be providing you with transportation. For instance, I went to lunch with someone from a woman's group.[21] They came and picked me up. Remembering this makes me want to scratch.

I wrote in our report that there were some things that I thought we ought to be doing. I never had any illusions about how difficult it would be. But my feeling was there ought to be someone stationed in South Africa. And I believed in the kinds of program they had. I thought with someone stationed in South Africa this would be a great opportunity to work with the women whom I admired so and who were strong. They endured the brutality of the system when many of their husbands and their fathers and other relatives had left. They tortured some of these women to find out where the men had gone. No, I had *great* admiration for them. They liked me, you know, but I had *great* admiration and would have done *anything* humanly possible to move the agenda.

Later, Pat O'Farrell, the director of the African-American Labor Center, sent Barbara Lomax to South Africa as their permanent representative. She went there after the period of the Wiehahn Commission when the tide was turning. The worldwide campaign of divestment in South Africa was having some effect. There was constant publicity about the nefarious policies of the South African government. They began to understand that their policies would become economically costly. Even in conservative cold war politics, it was evident that the ANC had a just cause and was not a tool of the Communist Party.

21. One of the women's groups Springer met on her 1980 AALC trip was the Women's Legal Status Committee, whose members, she noted, could work together on common objectives despite political differences. The members were black and white and included women of wealth and prominence. They presented a report before the Wiehahn Commission critical of white male privileges in employment. Memorandum, Springer to O'Farrell, April 20, 1980 (MSK PP).

Barbara had the kind of personality that made you feel comfortable with her. And I think people saw this as an opportunity to move the agenda. Pat saw that she had all the support system she needed to do programs. So I give the two of them great credit. Barbara worked tirelessly to build trust and to develop projects requested by African trade unions. She did *great* work. Very sad that she died, very sad. I was with her the night before she died. Didn't know that she was going. She was traveling [meaning dying] that night, and Jackie [Mullins] and I were just rubbing her hands, talking to her.[22]

You and Trachtman also stressed in your report the need to work with all unions. I found it curious since the AFL-CIO, officially, was so anti-ANC that your report had little or nothing to say about political differences or the ANC.

That was a waste of time as far as I was concerned. There was no point in going to South Africa, establishing an office, if you were going to have a line of demarcation. There were people who were not going to trust you enough in any case to work with you. But there were enough people who saw it to their advantage that these other folks would come over in due course, because there was something constructive about what you were doing. No. What was the point of having conversation? All the unions were weak. All the unions were in trouble. Those who were getting money from Communist sources and trying to do something were also in trouble. No, I was not going to engage in that. That was not my function. I am sorry. How were you going to help people? How were you going to work with the leadership that has suffered so terribly if you are only going to say, only if you are pure and go to mass every Sunday and confess every Saturday can I work with you? That's crazy! These people are still being underpaid, demoralized. No. Not going that way. And the African-American Labor Center couldn't go that way. And until the Wiehahn Commission you didn't have a chance.

Most of the people we talked to were very positive because they wanted others to come. Whatever criticisms they had, we wrote what could be done better. We were held suspect, the AALC, by some of the groups who were anti-AFL-CIO, anti-AALC. We met with them. But even before we met, the die was cast. They were not going to like us, like what we were saying. A lot of them hated us. No, they were so suspicious, you see. You were walking on eggs all the time. Yes, but my feeling was never mind all of that. You had to move beyond that if you were going to try to work with South Africans. But that was my view.

22. Jackie Mullins works for the collective bargaining unit of the United Steelworkers and served as an observer in South Africa's first democratic elections in 1994.

As part of the Cornell program a second delegation was brought here from South Africa in 1980, whose members were strongly ANC.[23] No matter how good the courses were at Cornell or the labor leaders you met across the country, they were not satisfied. The South African delegation was being supported and feted by many groups. Maybe part of all of the hostility of this group was because the AFL-CIO I do not believe was very active in support of the South African liberation groups that were at the UN.[24] There could have been some support that I don't know about, because after my resignation in '65, I was only working on single issues and projects.[25]

This woman on the Cornell program represented the faction that was considered part of the "left-wing group" in South Africa. While here she worked with the United Food and Commercial Workers. The Food and Commercial Workers had helped the South African counterpart in terms of contract negotiations. The South Africans worked for a subsidiary of this American company. The business leadership could not maneuver these people because the United States' unions were feeding them all of the vital information. And they supported them with money. The *American* union was doing its best to be supportive. So even with that good relationship, I think we were all still held as suspect. There were sharp divisions.[26]

The Food and Commercial Workers took her around the country. She met business agents, learned about contracts, and the rest of it. She disliked on sight anything and anybody that had to do with the AFL-CIO. She went back and wrote a report that said she disliked the program. When they came to New York, I organized some things for them. I had the responsibility of working with the delegation after they had done their university work and after they had been to some degree in the field, so this was a very short period. I think her report said I seemed to know something about unions and people, but what *ticked* her off was that I invited Nana Mahomo to meet with them. He was on the staff of the African-American Labor Center, and he came up to New York at my request. He should have been able to talk to fellow South Africans, I thought. I was wrong. He was a part of the political group

23. For participants in this program, see "South African Unionists Complete Work-Study Program," *AALC Reporter* 15 (November–December 1980).

24. The UN General Assembly established the Special Committee against Apartheid in 1963. This committee had ties with antiapartheid movements around the world.

25. Springer's resignation went into effect January 21, 1966. Springer to Meany, January 5, 1966 (MSK PP).

26. According to the descriptions Springer gives, this trade unionist was most likely Maggie Magubane, general secretary of the Sweet Food and Allied Workers. "South African Unionists Complete Work-Study Program," *AALC Reporter* 15 (November–December 1980).

that she and the others had absolutely no use for. He did not represent the African National Congress. He was a South African refugee; he had had to flee the country. He was one of the officers many years ago when the Pan-Africanist Congress was active. So she didn't like the program. She didn't like the people. I mean strictly around the country. So what can I tell you about her? That's it. She was very negative. And there were the political complications—ANC and anyone who's not ANC.

The delegation spoke their mind to everybody, every level of the American labor movement leadership. They spoke on public platforms. They spoke in private meetings and questioned the reason why. The way the world turns around, in due course, leaders of the American labor movement—this is some years after this particular program—were out picketing the South African embassy. This summer when you were here [1990], you met some women from South Africa from COSATU and SACTU.[27] So they were here even if they were critical. The African-American Labor Center was still making it possible for these people to come to the United States, have a point of view, continue to educate us.

But if there was a great deal of hostility in their approach, I accept that. Because when you are under the gun, you are always mad. I think you saw just recently the picture of Nelson Mandela and Chief Buthelezi embracing one another. So again you see the shifts and the need for people fighting for a change in government to attempt to resolve their political differences and fight for the common cause. I understand why they were mad. And I understand why things that are written are misrepresented. I don't mind. (*Chuckles.*)

I think one of the things that one person in the group said was that they thought that you were the one who knew more or less who they should and should not see.[28]

Whom they should or should not see? I'm sure they never said anywhere that I said that they could not see anyone. The *only* person I said they should see was Nana Mahomo.[29] I would consider it a part of my obligation to have Nana Mahomo speak to South African colleagues. They could be by them-

27. COSATU [Congress of South African Trade Unions] and SACTU [the South African Congress of Trade Unions] are labor federations that supported the ANC. The African women in this delegation expressed respect for Springer and were in awe of her years of service in the labor movement.

28. These criticisms of Springer come from two of the South African trade unionists who took part in the AALC programs. As evidence that the AFL-CIO was trying to restrict their movements, Baskin quotes one of them as commenting, "There was Lester Tractman (*sic*) and Maida Springer. She seemed to know, more or less, the people we could possibly meet." Jeremy Baskin, "AFL-CIO-AALC-CIA," *South African Labour Bulletin* 8 (December 1982): 64 (Braamfontein, South Africa: Institute for Industrial Education).

29. Without noting that Springer served as team coordinator for the delegates, Baskin quoted one of the delegates as saying, "One day this woman (Maida Springer), she was always

selves and speak in familiar ways and speak in a language—even though *all* of them were *very* fluent in English and very well informed—but there would be a homeyness that I certainly could not participate in and would not have wanted to. I had the bad judgment to think that here were all Africans with a common goal, and that they would have some reason for an exchange of views. I was entirely wrong. They were *angry, angry, angry,* as if I had done something very vicious to them. When that was resisted, when there was discomfort about that, I didn't press the point. But this created a lot of tumult.

The article I showed you stated that one of the reasons they didn't want to speak to him was that he's alleged to have worked with the CIA. Do you have any knowledge of any of that controversy?

I know about an allegation. There isn't a member of the (*laughs*) international labor movement, you know, that that is not said about. No. I know about that, and there was a great deal of feeling about that. But speaking to him was not going to change anything. They're South Africans, and he might have contributed to something that they didn't know. But that was their choice. I have no problems with that. I think Nana fought for years a battle to clear his name of those allegations. I haven't talked to Nana or seen him in a long time, so I do not now know where that stands. He's back in London.[30]

Not this group but another group was attending an NAACP convention, and I thought it would be nice if the whole delegation had a picture taken with the director, I think, of the NAACP and some other black leaders. There was someone in the delegation, a woman, who they felt was too reactionary, and after I had made all the arrangements, they did not want her in the picture. They had agreed originally. We all thought it was a fine idea. Then they caucused quickly among themselves. If you have never dealt with the caucusing of any group—not just South Africans—about anything that they felt sensitive about, you have an experience yet to come to, because the positions can shift by seconds. And you are caught in the middle of that, so you can never be right. I wouldn't even take the elevator. I ran down the stairs and canceled all of that. *I* did not try to persuade them. They were strong people

---

with us, said we were supposed to have a meeting with Nana Mahomo. It was an order from Washington that we must meet with this man. I personally objected saying that in Washington we were told to have nothing to do with refugees, why is this one an exception? Three of us refused to see him." Ibid., 63.

30. Mahomo visited with Springer during a trip to the United States a decade after my initial interviews with Springer; they had not seen one another since the early 1980s. Currently, Mahomo is co-owner of a company that has designed a multiuse machine that functions to clear away landmines and afterward can be converted into a tool for irrigation. Mahomo communication with Yevette Richards, June 24, 2000.

who knew what they were about and certainly a great deal more about why they felt as they did. I was sorry I wasn't more effective.

As long as you know that this was a single opportunity for many people who might never have an opportunity to travel to the United States again and you were putting your best effort forward, I can always sleep at night. I was never trying to manipulate. The political struggle in South Africa is too mean and too deep and apartheid is too vicious for anyone to be pro the South African government.

Do you know what the South African trade unionists said to members of the Executive Council of the AFL-CIO?

I wasn't at that discussion. I don't know. Listen. You have a chance to talk to the leadership of the union. You are militant people. Whatever the AFL-CIO was doing or whatever they felt was not satisfactory, they said. But as *awful* as we are, this group could come and go to the Executive Council of the AFL-CIO and say any damn thing they pleased. (*Laughs.*) They gave them audience and were concerned. But they *couldn't* be satisfactory to a delegation from South Africa. They *couldn't* be. The AFL-CIO could not give them the answers that they wanted, the commitment that they wanted. I'm sure they couldn't or wouldn't. Support they gave. Some of the AFL-CIO people were on picket lines and were protesting in Washington in front of the South African embassy. The AFL-CIO made statements against the South African government. But the radical things that they wanted I'm *sure* the AFL-CIO could not give them a commitment on them. And anyone who was getting money for *projects* from the AFL-CIO, that person would be condemned as soon as they agreed that they should accept it. But they agreed that they should come here. So it was a tricky political situation. I am not anti what they did. But what I'm saying is the nature of it. This is what *you* want as a person under the *gun*. And you would associate whatever was not being done with the South African government . . . that the AFL-CIO was close enough and big enough and influential enough to be able to take a punitive stance against the government. I should think that would be their view. In their place that would be my view.

The other thing I am accused of—and I think I read that somewhere in one of those critical articles you showed me—was that I did not want them to meet with other South Africans refugees.[31] This is not true. These men

31. Baskin quoted one of the two delegates as saying, "When we got there we first went to Washington and were told to have nothing to do with refugees, because people from SACTU [a labor federation supportive of the ANC] say this and this. After they told us to have nothing to do with refugees, there was a reception held for us, but a PAC man—Molefi from Atteridgeville, he said—was giving us all material, giving it to everybody there." The nature of this

The AFL-CIO and South Africa

300

and women could go where they wanted with whom they wanted. And after we did whatever it was we were doing for whatever small period of the time—because this was at the end when they were getting ready to go back —they were free to do that. I had one concern. These men and women, and particularly the women—I think there were three women in the group—I did not want to be wandering around a city that is as hectic and sometimes unpleasant as New York City, without having some sense of where they were, how long they might be wherever they were. I never asked to go to a meeting with them. I never asked whom they were meeting with. I thought that that would have been an affront. They were all adults. They were all active, young and not so young, struggling leaders in their unions. I have been to South Africa, and I knew the hardships that they faced. I will have to take whatever criticisms they made, but I am telling you what was the motivation. The distrust begins from the AFL-CIO's top-level position not being as sharply focused as they felt it should have been. And they said it in no uncertain terms from the president of the AFL-CIO on down. They spoke their mind.

What do you think of the controversy surrounding Gatsha Buthelezi receiving the George Meany Award for human rights in 1982?

The award, in retrospect, could be questioned, because it was flying in the face of the ANC. But I did not think then against giving an American award to a political group which advocated some of the things that the ANC advocated. I do not know if the AFL-CIO, whomever made the decision, could have given someone in the ANC an award. Buthelezi was a member of the strongest and largest cohesive tribal group in South Africa. At the time he seemed to have been trying to put together a cohesive group that was concerned about working people. It may have been the wrong judgment. In retrospect, you can always see reasons why it shouldn't have been done.

ANC people have said that the South African government has stood idly by as these people fought, ANC and Inkatha, and let Inkatha do their worst. There has to be some validity in that accusation, in my view. But I did not think that Buthelezi was a supporter of the South African government. In terms of the goals and objectives of the movement of ANC, he differed with their policy. These men, Mandela and Buthelezi, when they were young men were friends. They have gone different ways. No, there has to be some truth in this, that he was getting some advantage from the South African

---

material and the identity of those who counseled against meeting other refugees are unclear. Baskin quoted again a delegate as saying, "I wouldn't say they actually said they were pushing some refugees, but it was just a feeling of all of us that whenever you mentioned the fact that you wanted to meet a particular person, they would question you and find out who these people are, what they wanted, and they'd be protective about the whole thing." Baskin, 63–64.

government. But always his goal was a society in which Africans participated. And he never wanted anything less than that. I'm sure he was playing a game that the ANC resented. And Inkatha is a large, homogeneous group.

You wanted to comment on Sam Nujoma, since he was just elected president of Namibia [1990].

Yes. I remember him as a very young man. I'm someone he could not even remember. But many, many years ago this young man was passionately talking about the problems of workers in the then South-West Africa, which is today Namibia. I met him in those early days in New York City, across from the UN. Around those days, I met a lot of other African people around the UN. The National Council of Negro Women was one of the NGOs [nongovernmental organizations] at the UN, and I would go to the UN for meetings the Council had.

Sam Nujoma was asking labor people to look at the conditions of the workers there, which he was documenting. The Reverend Michael Scott was also in on some of these conversations. I imagine Sam Nujoma was introduced to us through maybe labor friends from Africa, other people from Africa who knew that we were anticolonialist. (*Laughter.*) Nujoma was a young politico and a trade unionist who brought to the attention of people in the AFL-CIO office in New York the working conditions, which were virtually slave labor in South-West Africa. And Irving Brown discussed this with him. Irving, of course, was very interested, and they prepared a document, which could be presented to the United Nations with Sam Nujoma as the petitioner.

However, the way you do this is to have a friendly government formally present your petition. The petitioner would then be able to speak. Their purpose would be heard. I, as a staff member of the AFL-CIO, talked to friends in the Nigerian United Nations office. And Aminu Kano, who was the leader the UN Nigerian delegation, of course immediately said yes. In Aminu Kano's first trip to the States I didn't know him. Someone sent him to my office on Fortieth Street. The UN was just over there and so I met all sorts of people. And we became friends. This man was burning, he was just burning. A very simple man, prepossessing with angelic qualities. A brilliant theoretician. A Northerner who thought that equality meant equality for men and women, who felt education ought to be across the board. This was not a very popular concept in Northern Nigeria. As a matter of fact, he was a member of [Nnamdi] Azikiwe's party. And so I think he liked my interest and approach to African politics. And as a matter of fact, I think you read I was his guest at the independence of Nigeria. So I went to him and asked him to forward this petition. When the discussions went on from there, I was out of it. I had done what I could do, and it went forward.[32]

But those things are forgotten because, you know, I was considered a part of the anti-Communist faction in the world. And what Communist governments were doing in support—challenges at the UN on behalf of Africans, doing training schemes, and underwriting a good deal of what was happening in Africa—put me outside the pale in the view of some of them, no matter what I was trying to do. You know, if you are not with me, you are "agin" me. And all of them so young, so young.

Years later, when Sam Nujoma had developed this political organization and they were fighting and challenging South Africa, I did not have a chance to speak to him, but I had gone to their office in New York and left my greetings just as a recalling, sharing of the past and wishing him well. We didn't have to agree politically, but his cause was justice, his cause was the right of the people of South-West Africa.

When I say that we didn't have to agree politically, there were the stories that Sam Nujoma was supported by the Soviet Union, that they had given training programs. I had a choice. Do I listen to what is happening to the workers of South-West Africa and do I do whatever I can do on behalf of the workers. If we are talking about hard-line AFL-CIO ideology, that's what I mean by that. Now Irving knew as well as anybody or better than I did whatever Sam Nujoma was about. But that statement was prepared on behalf of the workers and was prepared out of Irving's office in New York. It is in *that* context I am saying that I was not concerned with whatever they said his ideology was.

Now, I'm looking at Sam Nujoma with a full gray beard and recalling the youth, passionately talking on behalf of his country, and then going to an or-

32. As a northern Nigerian and a Muslim [a Fulani] Aminu Kano (1926–1983) responded to Nigeria's deep ethnic divisions and hostilities by joining the Igbo-dominated political party of (Benjamin) Nnamdi Azikiwe (1904–1996) during the independence struggles. Azikiwe became the first independence president of Nigeria in 1963 but was overthrown in a 1966 military coup. With Nigeria's history of corruption, bloody military coups and flawed election results, Aminu Kano is remembered as an honest and decent political figure. See "Remembering Malam Aminu Kano," *Daily Trust* (Abuja, Nigeria), April 17, 2003, AllAfrica.com, Africa News, Lexis Nexis (accessed March 13, 2003). Springer is referring to Alan Feinstein, *African Revolutionary: The Life and Times of Nigeria's Aminu Kano* (Boulder: Lynne Rienner Publishers, 1987), 191; diary entries for October 29, 31, and November 6, 1962, document the dates of talks with Anglican priest Michael Scott, Irving Brown, Nujoma, Kano, and Israeli Ehud Avriel about putting the exploitation of Namibian workers before the United Nations. See MSK to Ambassador Donald McHenry, September 3, 1981 (MSK PP), and Houser, *No One Can Stop the Rain*, 111.

ganization [the United Nations] that was challenging the South African government. He now has won that struggle after twenty-three years. It took me back a great deal into history and how things happen, what persistence he had, what international help. And finally, finally . . . South Africa had been illegally holding South-West Africa. The South African government did not consider it a mandated territory. Under the agreement after World War II, they were to report to the UN on this territory. The British government reported to the UN on the territory of Tanganyika. But the South African government —no, no. And we've had this war for many years. So I have looked at a lot of changes and this being the latest, the independence of Namibia. There are a lot of good things under the earth in Namibia. Why the South African government would want to hold on to it. A lot of goodies underneath that soil. (*Laughter*.)[33]

Then other things these last weeks have excited me to the point of tears. I saw Nelson Mandela leaving prison [February 11, 1990] and his being welcomed in Zambia, Tanzania, and Zimbabwe, all countries that had become independent during his years of incarceration. To see him welcomed to these countries had me in tears because I knew these countries very well and knew most of their leaders. I knew something of the history of these countries, having seen them change from colonial territories to independent countries.

Did you know Zambia's independence leader, Kenneth Kaunda?

I knew Kenneth Kaunda. Strange how I met him. Meeting him had nothing to do with the trade union movement, because Kenneth Kaunda wasn't involved in the trade union movement. He was in England and on his way to meet with or study with Gandhi in India. Since we were such a small nucleus of people who were involved in international affairs, we were introduced. And my paint job, this brown skin, and the fact that I'm a woman *always* singled me out. The Anti-Slavery Society of London[34] was very involved with African challenges and the African independence movement, and I used to contribute pennies to them and knew some of their people. They used to write to me and say when you're in London stop in and see this one or that one. So some friends in the Anti-Slavery Society sent a note saying that Kenneth Kaunda is one of the young leaders, and they'd like to make an appointment for us to meet. So I had tea and talked with Kaunda then, noth-

33. In 1967 the United Nations terminated South Africa's hold on the country and in 1971 the International Court of Justice concurred with that decision. South Africa still refused to give up its claim and proceeded to establish bantustans as had been done in South Africa.

34. Founded in 1839, the Anti-Slavery International is the oldest human rights organization in the world.

The AFL-CIO and South Africa

ing about unions, but he was another one of the future leaders of Africa. I knew of him and then knew more directly about him when I was in a working arrangement with some of the Northern Rhodesian trade unions.

I think Kenneth Kaunda had all of the right impulses. He was challenging the Central African Federation for *every* right reason. The independence of his country as a result of Kenneth Kaunda's early leadership was positive. Many of the changes that happened in Africa, including Zambia, were too little. There was not a sufficient spread of highly trained people to run the copper belt and to govern.[35] There were many ills that I think happened as a result of too fast assimilation in the jobs to be done. And a lot of things went wrong. On top of that the market dropped out of copper. And the government's social program of underpinning prices, subsidizing foods when you don't have an economic base for it, created problems. Plus there was the normal human frailty that exists in the rest of the world with people in high places in your government who are not doing what they are suppose to do and who succumb to greed and other things.

So I think this is how the disintegration began in Zambia. Kenneth Kaunda's rule became more concerned with maintaining, holding its leadership than perhaps correcting some of the ills. Anything that would have been done to help the economy would have been strong medicine, and maybe the government would not have endured in any case. But I think Kenneth Kaunda started out with *every* right impulse. A lot of things got lost along the way. So now that he has been defeated after these many years, I will not join the band that says I always knew and I told you so. I didn't know, and I'm saddened that one who fought for independence should wind up almost in ignominious defeat.

35. Commenting on the dearth of qualified Africans to change colonial institutions, Ras Makonnen remarked, "This was the anatomy of our misery, that we had nobody trained to implement our aims." Kenneth King, ed., *Ras Makonnen: Pan-Africanism from Within* (New York: Oxford University Press, 1973), 248.

The AFL-CIO and South Africa

10

Reminiscences

In this final chapter Maida Springer recalls her work with labor women internationally, reflects on the meaning of her work and relationships with U.S. labor leadership, and comments on African friendships and associations and the continued work that helps give drive and reason to her life. At the beginning and end of this chapter Springer reminisces about trips she made to East Africa in 1990 and in 2002, respectively. Of special significance to her is the time she spent with Mwalimu Julius Nyerere in his hometown of Butiama. After leaving government service, Nyerere chaired the South Commission for a three-year term after its founding in 1987. Composed of developing nations in the Southern Hemisphere, the commission looked at how these countries could collectively work together for their mutual development. In addressing the dominance of the Northern Hemispheric countries, the commission stressed the need for a more equitable distribution of the world's technology, trade, and finance. Nyerere led the South Centre, an intergovernmental organization that grew out of the recommendations of the South Commission.[1] At his death in 1999, Nyerere remained a beloved leader among his fellow Tanzanians and his work on behalf of the developing nations was praised around the world. This trip marked the last time Springer saw Nyerere, although she continued to correspond with him.

The cold war was nearing its end during our interviews, and Springer reflected on the AFL-CIO leadership and its policies, changes in U.S.–Soviet relations with the institution of glasnost (openness) and perestroika (restructuring), the changes she witnessed in Africa, and the role she played in the African labor and independence movements. At the time of these early interviews, the Soviet Union had instituted political reforms, Eastern Europe had revolted against Soviet domination, and the Persian Gulf War was on the horizon.

Springer also reviews some of her work with labor women internationally. As a

1. "Introduction, About the Center," South Centre, www.southcentre.org/introindex.htm, last updated November 18, 2003 (accessed July 2, 2000).

consultant for the AFL-CIO's African-American Labor Center (AALC) and Asian-American Free Labor Institute (AAFLI) from 1977 to 1982, she headed projects in Africa, Indonesia, and Turkey to raise the level of women's activism in unions and to give voice to issues that concerned them. Many of the labor unions in these countries wanted to establish or strengthen women's departments in unions and national labor centers in order to provide women the opportunity for leadership development and more direct input in the affairs of labor unions. While cognizant of the progress U.S. labor union women have made, Springer also points out that they still grapple with many of the same issues that concern labor women globally such as child care, maternity leave, equal pay for equal work, and women's representation in unions. It was during this period of Springer's activism that Joyce Miller, the president of CLUW and a vice president of the Amalgamated Clothing and Textile Workers,[2] became the first female to sit on the AFL-CIO Executive Council.

Springer's travels in African countries and in Indonesia have brought up the problem of child labor. The HIV-AIDS pandemic that has ravaged Africa has made the problem of child labor more acute. At the end of this chapter, she discusses in connection with her most recent trip to Africa her commitment to raising money for the Maida Fund. The fund is administered through the Education Fund of the AFL-CIO American Center for International Labor Solidarity (Solidarity Center), the successor organization to the four regional international institutes of the federation. Under the leadership of the ILO's International Program on the Elimination of Child Labor (IPEC), the local office of the Solidarity Center based in Kenya has worked with UNICEF, the ICFTU African Regional Organization (AFRO), and East African governments and labor centers toward the eradication of child labor, particularly in its most abusive forms.

The efforts of the Solidarity Center in Kenya and the Maida Fund are directed toward child labor in commercial agriculture. Worldwide about sixteen out of one hundred children are engaged in child labor. The vast majority of the 250 million child laborers who are between the ages of five and fourteen work in agriculture. These child laborers are primarily located in developing countries but are also in the United States, where agriculture shares with mining and construction the position of being the most dangerous fields of employment. The many hardships agricultural child laborers endure include long working days, exposure to carcinogenic pesticides, extremes of temperature, disease-carrying insects, and poisonous snakes. Workers lack adequate shoes and clothing, access to toilet facilities, and sanitary drinking water. The work results in various illnesses, back and

2. In 1976 the ACWA merged with the Textile Workers Union to form the Amalgamated Clothing and Textile Workers Union.

muscle injuries, exhaustion, and injuries related to heavy lifting and working with dangerous equipment. The Maida Fund continues the work of the Solidarity Center in conjunction with the Kenyan Plantation and Agricultural Workers Union and the national federation, Central Organization of Trade Unions (COTU), to return child laborers to school. It has provided for small grants for over eight hundred of the most needy children.[3]

As president of the Union of Needletrades, Industrial and Textile Employees (UNITE), Jay Mazur was instrumental in beginning the Maida Fund in honor of Springer's work in East Africa. She fondly recalls Mazur's support of international labor solidarity and his helpfulness to her in her programs and projects. Mazur began working with Springer's Local 22 around 1950 doing educational and organizational work. He has served as president of UNITE (1995–2000), ILGWU president (1986–1995) and general secretary-treasurer (1983–1986), and manager of ILGWU Local 23–25, the Blouse, Skirt and Sportswear Workers' Union (1977–1983). Mazur served as an executive board member of the ICFTU and has been a leading advocate for the rights of immigrants, refugees, and undocumented workers.[4]

Finally, Springer speaks of the continuing work of the Institute of Tailoring and Cutting, the small trade school she helped to establish in 1963. The school has graduated about 3,620 students as of the year 2002 and each year has a waiting list of over 200. It, too, has worked with COTU on child labor by providing training to former working children associated with an organization called Streetwise. Springer's reflections demonstrate that the work of Streetwise gives sustenance to her vision of a world free of child labor.

༄

Let's talk about your recent trip to Africa.

That's such an incredible story. I'm still in a state of shock. In May [1990] I became eighty years old and my daughter-in-law, Cecile Springer, and my godchildren, Jan McCray and her husband Melvin, talked about doing some

3. "What Is Child Labor?" http://www.fieldsofhope.com; "Around the World, Country Profiles: Kenya," http://www.fieldsofhope.com; Child Labor Coalition, "Children in the Fields," in Consumer Campaigns, Legislation and Best Practice Solutions, http://www.stopchildlabor.org/ (accessed November 25, 2003); "Of Every 100 Children . . . Child Labour Today," http://www.ilo.org (all accessed April 29, 2003); AFL-CIO Solidarity Center, "Maida Springer: Kenya Tour, March 18–26, 2002" (leaflet).

4. Jay Mazur, president, UNITE, USA, in More about the Labor Leaders, in Labor Leaders @ Davos 2001; World Economic Forum, in Global Unions, http://www.global-unions.org/davos.asp (accessed November 25, 2003).

special thing for my birthday. My godson had something to do in Switzerland, and after Switzerland he planned to go to Tanzania and work on this special project he was doing on Dr. Nyerere. He had previously interviewed Dr. Nyerere, and he was going to show Dr. Nyerere what he had done with the material and do some more interviews with him to complete the project.

And so my godchildren and my daughter-in-law thought that as a birthday surprise they would include me in Melvin's mission. My godchildren communicated with Dr. Nyerere's assistant in Dar es Salaam, so that they would know where in Tanzania to meet him when we arrived. The arrangement was made, and it was too late for me to do anything about it. When I heard this was my birthday gift, we were on the plane and on our way.

Tanzania is one of the countries in Africa that I felt most attuned to and would have, if young and single years ago, wanted to remain, to work there rather than as a person who was doing assignments back and forth through the American labor movement. Dr. Nyerere was the father of the country at independence and now is chairman of the South Commission. The South Commission is a combination of the countries of Latin America, Asia, Africa, and the Caribbean. These countries are seeking ways to develop greater self-reliance and internal country-to-country support for the things they need to do to make their economies more viable rather than strangled, in some instances, by the exigencies of the International Monetary Fund and all of the other grant agencies. So he is a very busy man.

We met Dr. Nyerere in Butiama. On the route to Butiama we had stopped in Arusha where an American expatriate, Pete O'Neal, who was a part of the Black Panthers in the United States, has become a very excellent member of the African community. He has been given land, and he's a farmer and is really an asset to the Meru tribe. So we spent two days with Pete O'Neal, his wife, Charlotte, and their two children, Malcolm, nineteen, and Stormy, fifteen. They have been out of the country for twenty-one years. Malcolm was born in Algeria and Stormy was born in Tanzania. The furthest they had been after that was Nairobi, Kenya, but Charlotte and the children were arriving for a visit to the United States the day we got back from Africa.[5]

But to get back to Butiama, this is the village from which Dr. Nyerere comes. He has built a home close to the spot where he was born, and it's carved out of rock, a four-level edifice. This is high country and cattle-grazing

5. Pete O'Neal is among the many Black Panthers who went into exile instead of facing arrest in the United States. Currently he is founder and managing director of the United African American Community Center. He and his family are honorary members of the Meru.

country. The Wazanakis, Dr. Nyerere's tribe, is one of the smallest in Tanzania. He welcomed us upon arrival very happily and invited us to be overnight guests in his home, all six of us—my goddaughter, her husband, their three children, and myself. (*Laughs.*) The housekeeper was very hospitable and kept coming back to make sure that the girls and I were comfortable. We shared a little suite next to Dr. Nyerere's grandchildren.

We had a late lunch, wonderful fresh African food taken out of their *shamba*, which is a little farm or garden. At mealtime if there is a place at the table, members of the village walk in and sit down to eat, and this is their right. I have seen this done in some other places also with the person who is the leader. It's a familial society so villagers would think it's their due if they want to come to Mwalimu's house. And the conversation was historic. We went around the world. I guess we touched 50 percent of the independent countries of Africa. And you sat there with this great statesman giving you a doctoral dissertation on all of the points of conflict and the problems and the hopes and some disappointments. And the same type of conversation happened at dinner that evening.

In the afternoon he gave us a tour of the village. Dr. Nyerere's family, his uncles and his brothers, share all of that land, which is part of their family tradition. The cows go to pasture on grazing land that's for the community. His younger brother Joseph's home is just walking distance to Dr. Nyerere's. And Dr. Nyerere told us that his brother was the first of the family, you know, who was other educated and out of Dar es Salaam, you know, big politicians, who came back and built his home there. So the cohesiveness of the family and the tribe remains.

We went to see the chief of the village, a Nyerere, I think his uncle. We visited his more than ninety-year-old mother and met his sisters, his sister particularly who has taken care of his mother.[6] We visited the school that is waiting for students as soon as he can get the funds. The sisters, the teaching nuns, are there. A new church is being built in the village, modest like Dr. Nyerere but in every detail quite perfect. He introduced us to the young manager, who's taking care of all of the animals. As we drove around, he would describe his hopes. So the whole afternoon was spent in very precious updating.

I had traveled in the fifties over a large part of the then Tanganyika and in

6. Nyerere's mother died just shy of one hundred in the mid-1990s. "Julius K. Nyerere, Chairman of the South Centre, Dies at the Age of 77," in "Introduction; South Centre Tribute to Mwalimu Julius K. Nyerere," Tributes, Nyerere Memorial Site, South Centre, http://www.southcentre.org/ (accessed November 25, 2003).

the seventies to other parts of Tanzania. But I had never been to the village of Butiama. It is difficult to relate all that went on in those precious hours, a day and a half. He saw us off the next day after breakfast, and again there was conversation. We went into his study, which is high upon the topmost point of the rock on which his home is built. The scenery just boggles the mind. In his study my godson, Melvin McCray, showed him the videotape, the documentary, of the part of the first visit when he interviewed Dr. Nyerere in Dodoma four years ago, and it was beautiful footage. He was able to do a little more at Butiama. History, renewed friendship, a graciousness and a simplicity in a man so overburdened with national and international affairs that it still shakes me, because he is able to make his guests feel that he has all the time in the world. That he is happy to see them when the skies are falling all around him, when he's got a million things to do, is a great tribute to this very uncommon man.

You said Nyerere went around many countries in Africa and discussed the situation of those countries. What were his prospects for Africa?

By his standards much that he had hoped for had fallen short of the mark. His hopes, very positive. Always pointing out how much needed to be done. How far you were from your goal. But what you had then by way of education. How you raised the standard of education. And in speaking about Butiama, the need for educational training facilities for young women. His hopes!

And why did he target this school for women?

Let me tell you my assessment. Here are young women—and this is true all over Africa—who would not be among the talented tenth that will go to the university on full bursaries and the rest of it. There are services in every community in Africa that need attention. We need them here in the United States, but it's more subtle. And in Africa you have a more rural community. You need young women trained in health. Nursing care. Nutrition. Young women trained in computer programming, in the services that a community would need today in this advanced technological age. All of the services that a city has to thrive on in order to grow. And if you are in a rural village, that girl's hope is to some way escape to the city or either your leadership has *vision* enough to train people where they are to improve the community of those people living right there. This is what Dr. Nyerere hopes to do. And this can be an excellent model. It can be replicated all over the country. You know, women's organizations are all over every African country. If it can be developed somewhere and is self-supporting—though education seldom is and cannot be—in some ways it can generate enough economic stability into the community and train people.

Reminiscences

What have you seen happening to young women who aren't trained in any specific skills or who can't make a living and who leave for the city?

That's a terrible question. Ooh, that's really loaded. Let me give you an example of what you see happening to young women in the United States, who drop out of school and have no one . . . no training or discipline to understand that you work eight hours, and you must do this, you must do that. If you are not aware of this and you don't want to do it, you think there's some other way. This is a part of a hopeless generation. We are seeing this in the United States. All the young people who are sleeping on grates. The young people who are busy just having babies, babies having babies, or kids taking dope.

Fortunately, that can be staved off in Tanzania. I can't speak for the rest of Africa. I've been too far away from it. A quick trip five years ago. But I think there is a potential for upgrading the lives of people in the community, so that you are not on a subsistence farm level and so that girls have a greater opportunity for service education. One percent or 2 percent or 5 percent will go on to higher education, but the majority of citizens in any country are not university graduates or Ph.D. candidates. And this big rich country of the United States developed on its industrial might.

What shocks me about Africa is here is a continent, which for the most part has the resources, but the resources have not been used for the benefit of the natives of the countries very much. They're working through that now. Independence is only thirty years old, and they're working through that even given all of the mistakes and excesses. Unfortunately for Africa, every time they breathe hard it's on the news broadcast that night. Years ago you didn't know for three months, six years, or maybe twenty-five years all the terrible mistakes that were made. I have great hopes for the continent of Africa. And if the Almighty allowed them not just droughts and plagues . . . Because this is an agrarian society. You have mineral resources. You need water. And if you can make the desert grow . . . It has been done in Israel. It can be done in Africa. I see great possibility, great potential. I'm fortunate to have lived in the time when there was the beginning of the revolution in Africa. It's not over. And I don't mean the fighting revolution, I mean social change in Africa, political change in Africa, the bad and the good.

And so, we ended our visit and went on our way to Dar es Salaam, which is where I had been based and I had lived. But, of course, as in Africa when we arrived at the airport, the flight had been canceled and there was only that one flight. So we just moved into a hotel in Mwanza for that night. And then we had to make all kinds of arrangements to see whether we would have to go by road to get to Nairobi, because we were leaving Africa on Friday, the next day.

An interesting thing happened to me at the hotel. My godchildren and their little ones had gone off to have a meal, probably at an Indian restaurant. They're vegetarians, and you can get such an arrangement there. I was very tired — my old age was catching up with me — and I said I'm going to stay right here in the hotel, and I think I will have a meal of whatever they are serving. So as I sat there and they brought the meal, a young man walked over to me and said, "Pardon me, madam, you have been to Tanganyika before?" I said, "Yes. Good afternoon." He said, "You are Maida. You are Mama Maida." I said, "Yes." He said, "Do you know me?" I said, "Yes. You are Mbutta Milando." And we both screamed. I could not eat. For the next two hours, we talked.

When I met Mbutta Milando, he was twenty-two years old. He was the publicity secretary of the Tanganyika African National Union, of which Julius Nyerere was the president. Mbutta was brilliant! He sat with the United Nations mission that traveled to East Africa — because Tanganyika was a trust territory for which reports had to be made to the UN — and he discussed the history of Tanganyika, supporting the details that Julius Nyerere would put forward and that elders in Tanganyika were able to put together on the history of Tanganyika when it was a German territory. One of the elders was Chom Wanyewe. Mbutta translated what the elders said to this UN mission. This young man pulled all of that together, and it's a part of the history of the United Nations. Mbutta did this work as one of the services that TANU offered to the mission.

Mason Sears was the American delegate on the UN mission. And he had predicted that Tanganyika would be ready for independence in X years and it happened in five years. And I subsequently wrote him a letter to speak to him on the independence of Tanganyika. Letters like those I guess I threw away, not realizing they're a part of history.[7]

I had a close association with Mbutta for the reason that he was the person that arranged all of my travel and traveled with me across the country in 1957, so that I would see TANU activities and operations, because they wanted me. This was my unofficial activity. My official activity was my day-to-day work with the Tanganyika Federation of Labor. There were things I could have done and there were some things I did do for TANU, because of my strong

7. Philip Mason Sears (1899–1973), who served as the U.S. representative on the UN Trusteeship Council, urged the United States to support self-determination for Africans even at the expense of alienating its European allies. Jonathan E. Helmreich, "U.S. Foreign Policy and the Belgian Congo in the 1950s," *The Historian* 58 (Winter 1996): 318–19; Thomas J. Noer, *Cold War and Black Liberation: The United States and White Rule in Africa, 1948–1968* (Columbia: University of Missouri Press, 1985), 52.

Reminiscences

feeling about what TANU as the political instrument for the independence of Tanganyika meant. I did the small things that I thought I could do to be supportive.

After independence, of course, he was a part of the independent government of Tanganyika. The last time I saw Mbutta he was in the Tanzanian Embassy at Ottawa. I was living in Chicago in 1965 or '66, and he came through Chicago to see me as a minister with portfolio, hmm, mm, mm, mm. (*Laughter.*) And all of that. I don't know when he retired, but he retired very early, left the diplomatic service and thought he was going to go back to farming and writing. He's a first-class writer. Then I lost track of him after that. Now, he's struggling, I guess, to support the education of his children. I think when he went back into farming, he had a terrible period of drought, and that created problems. But Mbutta was one of the bright stars in the 1950s for me.

So he said, "Mama, I am fifty-six years old now. I have seven children, three girls and four boys. Only two of them are here." He told me where the others were—at school and who was doing what. "But I must bring my girls to meet you, and if my wife is off-duty"—who was a nurse—"I will bring her." Before he left, since he lives in Mwanza, people would walk by to speak to him, and he would introduce me. "Do you know who this is? This is Mama Maida!" And then he went on with a lot of very flattering things. That evening at nine o'clock, he returned with his youngest daughters. And as people would walk by to speak to him—one ambassador—and it's too embarrassing to say what he said or what he did. Well, he talked about my being all over Africa and what it meant to a young party and to the labor movement.

The man who was the executive secretary of the Tanganyika Federation of Labor in 1956 has been a minister of every important position you can think of in the government of Tanganyika. At present he is the second in command of the political party in Tanzania. His name is Rashidi Kawawa. I had hoped to see or to speak with Rashidi, but then, of course, we didn't get to Dar es Salaam. The Honorable Rashidi Kawawa has been a whole part of the fabric of the development of his country. This was the young trade unionist whom I worked with first to get trade union scholarships for workers to come to the United States. He was always too busy, too involved in trade union and party affairs to come himself.

And Mbutta reminded me of the time when I had said it was possible that I could get him into a university, I could get him into a Harvard program. In those days there were some things I could do, and he was so bright. Between that and all of the intellectuals and the black colleges, I knew I could do some *thing*. I had been given assurances by educators here. So I raised this question with Dr. Nyerere, and he rejected it at the time. I never questioned that and neither did Mbutta for the reason he was one of the parts needed for the functioning of TANU, and you couldn't send all your people out. There were some who were in England and other places. So I didn't pursue it any further. But he reminded me of it. He said, "Mama, do you remember you wanted to take me to the United States?" But both of us agreed that the work he was doing in the party and for the party toward independence had priority over any ideas I may have had. You know, this was the independence of a country and I was talking some extraneous matter. No. And so I had lost track of Mbutta until he was walking past the restaurant. It was outdoors, you know, you could see anyone eating in an outdoor pavilion. Mbutta—same size, same face, maybe slightly heavier. (*Softly*.) One of the most gentle human beings I ever knew.

So that was the visit to Tanzania. We made a quick visit in Nairobi to the women's organization, which is called Maendeleo Wa Wanawake [Women's Progress]. It's a development organization of women. Since we missed our flight and missed connections, we could not have been in Nairobi early enough to document and to do a videotape of some of the work being done. But the women's organization now has their own building. It is a commercial enterprise. They collect rents from people who live in the building, which pays for their community activities on women's development—whether it's for children, whether it's education, whether it's for farming, or raising the quality of their produce, whether it is for basket weaving and other crafts. One of the bags I have here is one of their products, which was presented to me that afternoon by the women. We were able to meet the president and the members of her staff. And we had promised to come back, because I remember the early history of Maendeleo, and in a very small way we tried to be supportive of the women's organization.

So we were able to happily say good-bye to East Africa, not having done as many of the things that we wanted to do because of time constraints. We had to get on that plane. But I think it was so enriching for me and so soul satisfying that I might even live another year.

I was just looking at your pamphlet on Maendeleo Wa Wanawake. Its funding agencies are the government of Kenya, Conrad Andenower Foundation, Associated Country Women of the World, East Africa Industries, Ford Foundation, GTZ, Multiyeto of Finland, Pathfinder Fund of Boston, CETA, and the USSR Soviet Women's Committee. That's quite a wide variety of groups.

Sure. First of all, some of these small countries, you know, like Sweden and Denmark and Norway, support women's activities in ways that we do not.

And they will go to a country and they will spend time there, work with the organization and then go home and make recommendations. Yes. And since most African countries are nonaligned, whatever that means, they get support. And the U.S. or the organizations can or cannot support them. But they are going to get support from the people who believe in what they are doing. And Maendeleo is doing some very fine things.

Let's talk about your involvement with the 1977 conference entitled "Pan-African Conference on the Role of Trade Union Women: Problem, Prospects, and Programs." You and Lester Trachtman served as co-coordinators of the meeting.

I was a coordinator of the conference, but Lester Trachtman, the assistant director of the AALC, set up this conference. He directly did the day-to-day things. I think this was the first conference of its kind, looking at women's participation in trade unions. The ILO, UN Development Program, and the Economic Commission on Africa sent representatives.

In a 1977 document about the conference, you stated that the influence of Ida Simukwai of the Zambian United Local Authorities Union was a towering figure. Would you comment on her work?

Ida was a very mature woman, with many children and a husband. It was very unusual in the seventies that an African husband would be so supportive of her upward move into activities of the unions. She was the director of activities for the women's department of one of the unions. She sat on the national board of the political party of her country and came to the United States as part of the United Nations delegations for one of the sessions. This was how I first met Mrs. Simukwai.

Before Mrs. Simukwai's responsibilities began at the UN, she was a part of a delegation that I was taking to Houston, where the United States President Jimmy Carter was hosting the discussions, the planning for the United Nations International Women's Year. He had endorsed and the government had paid for the meetings around the country of the members of the International Women's Decade in preparation to going to Kenya in 1985. I took a group of women to Houston—all from Africa—to listen to these deliberations, to listen to American women talk about the things they hoped for in the United Nations International Decade and to hear them breathe fire about the things they thought were wrong in the United States and the role of women.[8]

You had on that rostrum Mrs. Carter and the wives of former presidents,

8. Carter appointed the National Commission for the Observance of International Women's Year. Springer commented on the historical significance of the conference. It marked the first time that a president and Congress "authorized, sponsored and financed a national gathering of women to talk and act upon issues of concern to women." There were

Mrs. Johnson and Mrs. Ford. This was just an experience that boggled the mind for these women. You don't see such things happening. A man is out of office; he's out of sight. The democratic process is not old enough. Independence was still so new that there was no tradition of the former president or his family actively doing something like this. So this was quite an experience. I was happy to have been able to participate and to have been the host of these women in Houston.

I was in Zambia in the seventies. And Mrs. Simukwai and I had a wonderful time sort of recalling. She was very excited. The national union had called her and said Sister Maida is here. She arranged all sorts of meetings for me, and I met people and a lot of very wonderful things happened. A lot of the people I had known were either gone or out of the union. The new group of leaders in the copper belt just welcomed me as an old friend.

In 1979 you spent about three and a half weeks visiting women workers at industrial centers in Indonesia in preparation for a seminar that would look into ways of improving women's participation in unions. What stands out about that trip?

Among the things I observed was a great deal of child labor. The children were working in some factories for ten and twelve hours. Indonesia, I felt, had a great deal of labor organization, so I was surprised that child labor was so acceptable to the union. One of the union officers escorted me to a textile mill to meet the employer of what was said was a good employment situation. The employer was bragging to me that the children who worked in his plant had a regular lunch hour and such amenities. But these are seven and eight year olds. That surprised me. Not that child labor itself surprised me. It is all over the world as it used to be here. Children are working on plantations, farms. Children are among the weavers of the beautiful rugs that get made in certain parts of the world. I just thought that in Indonesia with the labor organization they had that there would at least be some protest, that the union would not be supportive. It was just a different psychology. When you reflect on the economic situation in many parts of the world the thought is the more children you have the more you can set out to work at an early age.

In terms of an electrical factory I visited, I just thought there should have been greater enforcement so young girls did not get pock-marked faces and damage to their nails and the other dangers that can happen when you are working with dangerous materials like acid. I asked the employer about this

twenty thousand people present at the conference. Observer at National Women's Conference, November 18–21, 1977 [Springer Kemp], "American Women on the Move," and "Spirit of Houston: An Official Report to the President, the Congress, and the People of the United States" (MSK PP).

Reminiscences

situation and he told me that he complied with the regulations. He said he had gloves and fulfilled other requirements, but the employees were careless and didn't use them. Since this was a unionized plant, I thought that there should be stricter enforcement, and I said this in my report. I was being so singleminded that I thought the rest of the world, as imperfect as we all are, ought to be doing *more*. Both nonenforcement and child labor are evil. As far as I am concerned wherever it happens child labor undermines the opportunity for adults to earn a decent living. And the children cannot contribute as adults to a society because they will be ignorant. These were my humble opinions on that.

Do you have any recollections of two women you worked with in Indonesia, Ida Pidada, the director of the Women's Bureau, and Stella Marie Angela, vice president of the Women's Bureau?

Of course. Ida Pidada traveled with me to see all the people I wanted to see, and she worked with Don Newsom, who was the Asian-American Free Labor Institute director for Indonesia. The Asian-American Free Labor Institute knew that I would not go unless it was understood by those in Indonesia that I could speak directly to the women. No one else should be telling me about the experiences of these women. There would be meetings organized around the country to meet with the women workers. I would go from plant to plant. We would have a wrap-up meeting and then the women would select delegates to come to Jakarta for a seminar. These women workers would have a chance to state their concerns. The male leaders were very surprised in many places I've been — here in Indonesia, in Turkey and countries in Africa — to see that these quiet women had points of view about a whole lot of things. That came as quite a shock to them.

In your report you described Angela as a "warm and responsive woman" who was also sharp-tongued about injustices.[9]

Well, she spoke her mind about things wherever. She had been to the United States. So she spoke about things she felt strongly about and saw in the United States. The women in Asia, Africa, wherever . . . all feel women should have a wider voice. You go to certain places and the majority of workers are women but they don't have a wide voice. And so these nice, quiet women all thought that women should have more representation. Women had the same point of view in the United States. We are still talking about the same things. But we have moved a long way by world standards. Not enough.

Talk about your experience with the Turkish Confederation of Labor.

9. Seminar at Puncak [Indonesia], February 25, 1979 (MSK PP).

(*Laughs.*) Well. To the credit of some of the very rigid, male-oriented society in Turkey, the leaders of the Turkish Confederation of Labor saw that they needed to make some changes. Women weren't on the executive boards. Women weren't on the staffs. (*Claps hands.*) They were hardly shop stewards. No woman in Turkey held either a paid or unpaid office in the Turkish federation. Look! In the union I came from, 440,000 members, and they had one woman vice president. There was nothing terribly unique about this.

The Turkish federation had the inclusion of women leadership in their current and future plans. The Asian-American Free Labor Institute had an office in Turkey, and they were always bringing over male delegates to the United States. A delegation of Turkish union officials had just had a very fine experience in the United States. So what they did after that was send for the first time a delegation of women. I was asked to be responsible for programming these women across the country. This was my introduction to the Turkish Confederation of Labor.

Jay Mazur, who was then manager of Local 23–25, knew the garment union leaders from Turkey very well. He had been to Turkey as an officer of the International Trade Secretariat [ITS]. So, naturally, I received help from him in planning the New York agenda for the women. Around the country the program went very well. In New York it was spectacular. We had a meeting in Jay's office. In attendance were members of his staff, many of whom were women. I think the chair of the executive board of Local 23–25 was a woman. So it was important that the women from Turkey see women in these positions. Jay entertained them that evening at the Rockefeller Center. We had dinner and danced. The women went home and some of them . . . the slang of some of my colleagues in Washington . . . they said you were the nicest thing since sliced bread. (*Laughs.*)

I was then invited to Turkey to meet with the union leaders and begin to develop a program for women workers in Turkey. I went the first year, traveled across the country. And at the end of whatever number of weeks or a couple of months, we were to end with a seminar in the capital city, Ankara. I insisted that the delegates for the Ankara conference be chosen from the women who attended the meetings that were held across the country with me rather than the personal choices of the top leadership, which was all male. It's a wonderful thing. You come from all over the country as a delegate to come to Ankara, to the headquarters of the union for a conference. We videotaped. The women could see themselves for the first time in a playback presenting their point of view for improving the union. This was very exciting for them.

The president of the garment workers' federation walked in and wondered what was going on. This was the first time anything had been videotaped. He was so pleased with what we were doing that he took the whole delegation to lunch in one of the largest restaurants in town. But he didn't like some of the things the women were saying. The video showed the women to be very articulate. They wanted a greater participation and representation.

My recommendation was that they should use these tapes at every local meeting. We thought that this would be a tool for the women to use to show what they said or what they were doing. It would help in organizing; it would help to stimulate them. Then I went back for another couple of years, moving the agenda forward until the end of the third year we established a Women's Bureau in the Turkish Confederation of Labor.

Your work for the AFL-CIO spanned two different generations of leadership. What is your view of the leadership under George Meany and under Lane Kirkland?

In my later years I was working on single assignments for the African-American Labor Center, for the Asian-American Free Labor Institute. I was not on the staff of the AFL-CIO. The last person I worked with in the Department of International Affairs was Mr. Ernest Lee. He and the rest of the staff in International Affairs gave me a small reception when I resigned in 1965.[10]

Some years after I had resigned, President Meany died, and there was a new leadership in the AFL-CIO. The secretary-treasurer, Thomas Donahue, I had known a long time as a young man when he was out of the New York Service Employees International Union.[11] My husband, Jim Kemp, was an officer of the Service Employees International Union. The present president of the AFL-CIO, Lane Kirkland, was, I think, secretary-treasurer during the time I was on the staff of the Department of International Affairs.[12]

10. Ernest S. Lee was the son-in-law of George Meany. Springer's resignation went into effect January 21, 1966. Springer to Meany, January 5, 1966 (MSK PP).

11. Thomas R. Donahue served as executive assistant to AFL-CIO president George Meany and as AFL-CIO secretary treasurer, and as interim AFL-CIO president following Lane Kirkland's resignation.

12. Coming from the Masters, Mates, and Pilots Union, Joseph Lane Kirkland (1922–1999) attended the School of Foreign Service at Georgetown University, worked as an AFL researcher, a speech writer for politicians, and served the positions of executive assistant to George Meany and AFL-CIO secretary-treasurer before assuming the presidency from 1979 to 1995. While he was instrumental in putting AFL-CIO support behind Solidarity, the labor movement in Poland that led to the downfall of the Communist regime there, he presided over the American union during a period of decline marked by shrinking membership and job loss through plant closings and relocation outside the United States. In 1995 John Joseph Sweeney of the Service Employees International Union was elected as AFL-CIO president after defeating Thomas Donahue by promising reform and an end to the old guard leadership. See William Serrin, "Lane Kirkland, Who Led Labor in Difficult Times, Is Dead at 77," *New York Times*, August 15, 1999, section 1, p. 1.

The past and current leaderships are different in terms of their background and in terms of the organization and operation of the AFL-CIO. The past leadership had to come from further than the younger leadership in terms of an acceptance of black-white working relationships. The men in the labor movement that I knew going back to the late thirties were men of strong prejudices. They were part of the old guard whose traditions dated back to the old guild systems of Europe. They had a commitment to improved hours and conditions of service, but enforcement of equality of opportunity, I think, was a very hard commitment for their times. Yet for the most part they strove toward making that commitment. They were intelligent men and knew that by depriving one segment of workers, the employer would look at the bottom line in due course and determine that if he could pay these workers of a different color less money, then that would be what was important.

The relationship that tied me to the labor movement, to the International Ladies' Garment Workers' Union, was the insistence of the union that in the labor contracts our union did not have double agreements, an agreement for whites and an agreement for blacks. They fought for a unanimity in terms of black and white workers meeting together. This is not to say that all union officers across the country followed this absolutely.

The old leadership of the labor movement came from the warp and woof of the labor movement and was brilliant. They built the unions during a time when there was little protective legislation and employers could weaken the strength of unions at will. Coming from this background, these leaders had to be constantly rough campaigners. So considering where these men had to come from in accepting black-white working relationships and the fact that they built the labor movement, I admired and respected them.

This younger generation of leadership could accept mass organization as a given and work for racial equality and equal opportunity more easily. They had a philosophy. They had better educations and had a current policy. They were more professionally educated men and had the boardroom facade and facility of words.

The leadership of both generations brings something to the labor movement that was needed. And my admiration for those men that I knew as I came up in the labor movement, those men who built the union out of mud and bricks and mortar, should not take anything away from the current leadership of today. The times are different today. The shrinking of the labor movement has a dozen sources, including multinationals, including the American industrialists taking their equipment and taking the materials and pauperizing workers in the Third World.

As a staff member of the International Affairs Department of the AFL-CIO in the 1950s and 1960s, I realized we were cutting new ground. I was a woman, black, and an international representative. Everything was so new. This was post–World War II, and the AFL-CIO's position had always been anticolonialist. A. Philip Randolph was a spokesman in the international circles, particularly in the International Confederation of Free Trade Unions and in all of those international assemblies, for the aspirations of African, Asian, Caribbean, and Latin American representatives. It gave them that extra feeling, because he was so outspoken. Others were, too, of course, many others. But Randolph was significant because he spoke with the voice of authority within the councils of the AFL-CIO and as a champion of black labor in the United States.

In the course of that relationship with the past AFL-CIO leadership, retrospectively, I think I was able to do many things. Some I did not do as well or was not as effective as I needed to be because I was developing my own blueprint as to how you work with your colleagues in Africa. Then, of course, you had political differences, all the cold war business of that period.

Within the AFL-CIO for all of the years that I was on that staff, I was treated as a staff representative with a responsibility. So on that score I had no problems. I am sure I had points of view that did not (*chuckles*) entirely please the leadership of the AFL-CIO because I possibly looked at some of the things I was doing with a different perception. My brown skin would make that so. I would see ways in which things were to be done, look at problems in perhaps a different light.

I was never questioned by President Meany about what I was doing. And any program that I asked to do, I had until the day I resigned from the AFL-CIO the full backing of the AFL-CIO, which means President Meany on down. So in that sense my relationship was a good working one. I come from a generation where I had to have great respect, given the limitations these older leaders came from (*chuckles*), those old-timers came from.

Do you think that sometimes AFL-CIO policy may have been misplaced in any instances in Africa in supporting one faction of a union instead of another?

In the course of things, this always has to happen. But let me tell you where I stood and where some of my colleagues stood. While they were strongly anti-Communist, they worked with anyone whose real concern was on behalf of the workers and not the first priority on behalf of the political party. And that's where the dichotomy happens.

It was a bad time. It was for many years, you know, that you were either Communist or anti-Communist. And then you had the development after

World War II of independence for many countries. They then became the nonaligned, called themselves nonaligned. To be nonaligned, you simply picked people you wanted to be a part of. But the continued hostility, the continued suspicion should have been expected for the reason that you do not come out of a colonial situation without constantly expecting the worst of the formal colonial master. They were the ones who kept you down.

Similarly, while the United States didn't have colonies, they were "a capitalist country" whose vision was the profit motive. So the emphasis of the United States by the standards of the trade union movement was not as committed to the complete general good. We wanted wages, hours, and conditions of service for the workers. The dignity of the worker. But unions overseas and poor unions always talked that the bottom line was profit, that there was no social conscience. The fact that these business unions that were called bottom line were always the ones that people could refer to, to get help with whatever it was they wanted to do in their country, begged the question. There were streams of letters and communiqués asking for help.

Fortunately, unions around Europe, particularly the Scandinavian countries, are superb in their support of what was happening in the Third World countries. I felt what we tried to do was good, but I think they did more socially oriented things. Some of the other European unions were very good, once the suspicion was gotten over that they weren't trying to push you back into colonialism.

I came into the AFL-CIO international affairs with a concept. My view of myself was that I had an international awareness. I knew something about the kinds of struggles. I had a sense of the injustices and the inequities in Africa. I saw my role not as a politicist. I saw my role as finding a way to develop a small nucleus of men and women who could serve their unions more effectively. This came out of my own growing up in the labor movement and being force-fed. I do not have a university degree. I have a basic-type school education. But I've been to a variety of colleges, studied a lot of things, but the focus for me was the training I had received in the labor movement. So I thought with the African unions having so little—they didn't have national headquarters. They couldn't go to conferences freely. They were locked up, put in jail for their trade union activity. And so I saw it as my focus to try to develop educational structures and cadres. That was my approach. I was not unaware of the politics and the social change that was moving these countries to independence. I was close to it! But I continued to see my role as helping to strengthen the future labor leaders, and in turn they could strengthen an independent government that would be trading with the world. I thought that a helping, an infrastructure, a trade union strength in the workers' movement would be supportive. I saw that as an important function, this focus on training and education. I still think that's true.

A lot of things went awry within the policies and politics of independent governments. This is a part of social change, and that will right itself. Maybe not in my lifetime, but it will right itself. But nothing can take away the importance, the greatness of the men and women of Africa, the leaders of their government on the world stage answering to the issues, and in the future the resources of their country being channeled for the citizens. It is not true yet, but it will be. Not in my lifetime. It will be. To see the focus on education all African leaders took on, which can't *pay* for generations, was a positive change. To change the educational potential, to develop it and to see . . . You walk in the United Nations and you see the women who are doing various things. I saw one of the women, Angie Brooks, who was a lawyer and at that point serving her turn as president of the UN, in the position to put forward the motion that would take the South African government to the International Court of Justice for not abiding by the mandate to report on trust territories.[13] And South-West Africa just became independent [1990]. So, these things give one a great deal of hope and charge my batteries. When you are privy to events like this and you're talking to this person, it's enough to make your head swirl.

Since you lived through the height of the cold war period, I'd like to know what you think about the changes in the relationship between the United States and Soviet Union.

I think it's positive. I think it is good. If it does nothing else, we'll have things breaking out in other areas, which is happening right now.[14] But the two largest, aggressive, and powerful nations—if they are finding a way to talk to one another and not always planning destruction, there is some hope. The disparity in our economic systems will continue to irritate and create problems.

The big question mark for me is in the imbalance in the "Third World," because within that Third World there are those *riches* and those things which

---

13. Angie Brooks (Randolph) is from Liberia and was elected president of the UN General Assembly in 1969. She has been touted as the first woman and the first African to hold that position. In 1971 the International Court of Justice concurred with the UN decision on South-West Africa. Ellen Johnson Sirleaf, "Liberia: A Framework for Change and Renewal," *The Perspective*, November 12, 1999, Africa News Service, Global News Wire, Lexis Nexis (accessed November 25, 2003); Bobby Tapson, "No Reason to Abandon Liberia—Opposition Parties Tell International Community," *The News* (Monrovia), June 7, 2002, AllAfrica, Inc., Africa News Service, Global News Wire, Lexis Nexis (accessed November 25, 2003).

14. This portion of the interview took place just before the start of the Persian Gulf War (January–March 1991).

should make those countries stable and more powerful. I think the euphoria and the mistakes of many governments around independence in some of the tiny, tiny countries, which are not viable, I think that's going to take shape, that there will be some changes. The very fact of the matter is that you have countries in not only Africa but in the Americas where some of these countries are older than the United States, with very large populations, and they're in a stranglehold. These countries that belong to the South Commission are looking at their potential and how they can relate to one another internally and not always having to go for financial demands in such large measure to the "great powers," countries which too often strangle them. These countries —and I'm thinking particularly of those in Africa—are trying to correct their mistakes so that they can utilize their resources.

The fact is that through the independence of that continent and Asia, you have men and women trained that would *never* have been trained, never know all of the things they do. The universities have developed. And the travel that these people have done all over the world will make them—not in my lifetime —but *they* will be a force. Because those *wonderful* resources the rest of this consumer-minded Western world will want, and they will have to deal for those resources on a better basis. Unless the rich countries and the nonblack countries do more than they are doing, there will be continued hostilities and real problems.

But the Soviet Union and the United States, I think that's *very* positive. I'm not standing on a pedestal shouting. I think it has to do with the practicality of total world destruction and the disaster of a social system which relied so much on force and—I can't think of the word—obsequiousness. Everyone speaking the same way and *no* possibility for change or opposition. The eruption in the quiet Soviet and Eastern Europe bloc has shown you that people still were seething and demanding a voice in social change. And, of course, the United States has nothing to be too arrogant about. They better mind their manners. (*Laughs.*) We are not the be-all. Like the Hippocratic oath tells the physician that he is practicing, democracy is practicing. The socialist system is practicing. We're going to come to the meeting of the minds where we get the best of each. That's my hope. It may never happen, but that's my hope. I'll never live to see it.

We have spoken about your 1990 trip to Africa. Now it is 2002 and you were again in Africa this year. Will you explain the purpose of your trip?

Well, this was presumably a private trip. Cecile and Eric were going to Africa and they invited me. But of course I wouldn't go to Africa and certainly wouldn't go to Kenya and Tanzania without having some contact with some people there in the labor movement. And so I talked with the AFL-CIO Solidarity Center and told them I was going. I said this is a private trip, but the Solidarity Center then had their local center in Nairobi set up an agenda for me for the many days I was going to be there. It was incredible.

One of the things that the Solidarity Center is involved in is a big program dealing with child labor. Today organizations are looking at child labor more seriously worldwide. World organizations are now getting interested in world health problems like HIV and AIDS and their role in increasing child labor. Such things are happening rather seriously in Africa. One of the worst offenders of child labor in Africa are the plantations. They have schools on the plantations, but there are many orphans who are working on these plantations. So many children who have lost parents are now working on plantations for *nothing*. The Solidarity Center is putting a special emphasis on working with these orphans and with parents whose children are working. The labor unions in Africa, in particular the agricultural workers, are working with parents to keep their children in school and to support training programs. They are attempting to teach parents that the future of the country rests on how they have trained these children. The largest union in Kenya now is the agricultural workers, and with support from the Solidarity Center and the ILO they are looking at ways that we can help to change the child labor situation. And the government is not having a blind eye anymore on child labor. There is a greater sense of cooperation.

Now in my last hurrah, I have been asked to participate in a program that is using my name to raise funds to give additional support to the struggle to eliminate child labor. The Maida Fund developed out of the Pittsburgh event in March 2000 honoring me. Jay Mazur as president made it possible to have UNITE make a ten thousand dollar grant to the Maida Fund. I have known Jay since he was a very young educational director.

The Maida Fund is administered by the Solidarity Center of the AFL-CIO, but it is a broad-based effort, which includes the ILO. The Maida Fund is miniscule but it helps support some of the most extreme cases and it strengthens the labor movement. It helps return orphans to school and helps the preschool ones. It helps to provide medical assistance, to buy school uniforms, shoes, books, to get the pencils and paper, the things that we throw in the trash pail.

I saw the things that are being done on these plantations. The workers have taken in some of these children, including them in a part of their family. The teachers in Kenya are so entranced by this work with the children that they go above and beyond anything that you would consider your teaching responsibility to help keep them in school. About half of them are orphans. A child will open a notebook and show you how important it is to have his or her own notebook, own pencil. Well, the children all wanted to be around you and take pictures with you and tell their story. I met a young girl who wasn't even ten years old yet. She was taking care of younger children. She was a nut picker and an orphan.

When I came back home, I started raising money. I thought some of the organizations and the people I know have got to do some token thing. So we have put the community's face on this. The Presbyterian Black Caucus donated five hundred dollars. My family made a contribution and the Aurora Reading Club made a contribution. I'm hoping for another grant to come through for me. So I am trying hard before I die to raise some more money because I think this is so important.

While in Kenya I visited with labor women. I have seen a lot of movement with women in the labor movement. There's now a women's division of COTU. The opportunity for me to have a meeting with a delegation of women who are now active and who hold staff positions was very heartwarming. Among the things they want is to have exchange programs, to be able to study in the United States.

I also visited the Institute of Tailoring and Cutting. Whenever I could I would try to see to it that they would get help to improve their equipment. And they've got a tough job now, if they want to help the workers in the needle industry. They are going to have to perform on a much higher level. What they do now is old-fashioned; they make the whole garment. The students learn how to do this, but all of them will not be self-employed. Thousands are going to go into the factory where one person does not make a whole garment.

As a matter of fact, I was taken to an American factory with two thousand workers. It had all of the finest equipment and had used time and motion studies for the greater efficiency of the company. It had a minimum of 150 applicants a day beating at the door. This is just outside of Nairobi. And this is going to be a complete unit. There will be a bank and other entities to employ Africans. It's a little city. Industry today is discovering Africa. It is reaching Africa now the way it has done in many parts of what is called the Third World.

They had a picture of me at the Institute of Tailoring and Cutting as the person who started the program for them. They pointed out the picture to the young people who are there now. And they were showing a picture of Oliver Montgomery, a retired person from the steel workers who was also president of the NAACP chapter of Penn Hills in Pennsylvania. When he was in

Kenya, he talked with the government about Social Security in the United States. The school is one of the things the government is showing off, this school started thirty-nine years ago and has a waiting list and is still run by a union. So they showed the school to this trade unionist.

The Institute of Tailoring and Cutting made the COTU T-shirts that the children on the plantations in the pictures I showed you are wearing. They have also helped some of the Streetwise children. At that March 2000 event there were souvenir cups for sale made by the children of Streetwise. All of the money raised from the souvenirs and the proceeds of the event went to the Institute of Tailoring and Cutting. Streetwise is an organization in Nairobi for abandoned children, children without parents. A group of Americans started it. They began to train them in artwork. They began to make table mats and napkin rings, and sell them. As a cooperative effort with Streetwise, the Institute of Tailoring and Cutting gave scholarships to some of these young boys and girls. They learned all the hand sewing and machine sewing techniques for making table mats and little rugs.

Now Streetwise is run by a group of Africans, these kids who are now seventeen and eighteen years old and are heads of families. They're in business on their own. They have a place where they do their work and sell their ware as tourist objects. I went to their place, and some of them graduated from the Institute of Tailoring and Cutting. The artwork they do makes them independent. I tell you, it just made me want to cry.

Abbreviations

AAFLI	Asian-American Free Labor Institute (AFL-CIO)
AALC	African-American Labor Center (AFL-CIO)
AAPC	All-African People's Conference
AATUF	All-African Trade Union Federation
ACWA	Amalgamated Clothing Workers of America
AFL	American Federation of Labor
AFRO	African Regional Organization
AFSCME	American Federation of State, County and Municipal Employees
ANC	African National Congress
APRI	A. Philip Randolph Institute
ATUC	African Trade Union Confederation
CCM	Chama Cha Mapinduzi (Revolutionary Party [Tanzania])
CIO	Congress of Industrial Organizations
CLUW	Coalition of Labor Union Women
COSATU	Congress of South African Trade Unions
COTU	Central Organization of Trade Unions (Kenya)
CP	Communist Party
CPP	Convention People's Party (Ghana)
CWA	Communication Workers of America
DGB	German Federation of Labor
FEPC	Fair Employment Practices Committee
IBEW	International Brotherhood of Electrical Workers
IBT	International Brotherhood of Teamsters
ICFTU	International Confederation of Free Trade Unions
IFCTU	International Federation of Christian Trade Unions
IISH	International Institute for Social History
ILD	International Labor Defense
ILGWU	International Ladies' Garment Workers' Union
ILO	International Labor Organization
IPEC	International Programme on the Elimination of Child Labour
ITS	International Trade Secretariat
KFL	Kenya Federation of Labor
LEGCO	Legislative Council (Colonial Africa)

MFDP	Mississippi Freedom Democratic Party
MP	Member of Parliament
NAACP	National Association for the Advancement of Colored People
NATO	North Atlantic Treaty Organization
NCNW	National Council of Negro Women
NGO	Non-Governmental Organization
NIRA	National Industrial Recovery Act
NLRA	National Labor Relations Act (Wagner Act)
NRA	National Recovery Administration
NUTA	National Union of Tanganyikan Workers
OATUU	Organization of African Trade Union Unity
OAU	Organization of African Unity
ORT	Organization for Rehabilitation and Training
PAC	Pan-Africanist Congress
SACTU	South African Congress of Trade Unions
SCLC	Southern Christian Leadership Conference
SEIU	Service Employees International Union
SNCC	Student Nonviolent Coordinating Committee
SWAPO	South-West Africa People's Organisation
TANU	Tanganyika African National Union
TFL	Tanganyika Federation of Labor
TUC	Trades Union Congress
TUCSA	Trade Union Council of South Africa
UAR	United Arab Republic
UAW	United Auto Workers
UGTAN	Union Générale des Travailleurs d'Afrique Noire
UN	United Nations
UNIA	Universal Negro Improvement Association
UNITE	Union of Needletrades, Industrial and Textile Employees
UNRRA	United Nations Relief and Rehabilitation Administration
WFTU	World Federation of Trade Unions
WTUL	Women's Trade Union League
ZANU	Zimbabwe African National Union
ZAPU	Zimbabwe African People's Union

Chronology

1910	(May 12) born in Panama
1917	(August 4) Immigration to the United States
1917	St. Marks Catholic School
1918	Public School 90
1923–1926	Bordentown Manual Training and Industrial School for Colored Youth
1926	Night school in New York
1927	Receptionist at Poro School
1927	Married Owen Winston Springer
1929	Birth of Eric Springer
1929–1930	Lived in East Orange, New Jersey
1932	Began work in the garment industry
1933	(May) Joined ILGWU Local 22
1935–1936	Variety of training classes
1937–1939	Represented union in union and community work
	Member of Committee on Prices, Local 22
1938	Naturalized a citizen of the United States
1938–1942	Executive Board Member, Local 22
1940	Chair of Education Committee, Local 22
1942	Trained as first aid teacher, ILGWU
1942	American Labor Party candidate for New York State 21st AD (Harlem)
1942–1944	Captain of Women's Health Brigade (ILGWU)
1943–1945	Educational Director, Local 132
1944	Member of the War Price and Rationing Board of the Office of Price Administration
1945	Labor exchange delegate to England
1945–1948	Staff member of the Joint Board of Dress and Waistmakers Union, ILGWU (1945 Complaint Department)
1946	(February 28) Executive Director of Madison Square Garden Rally for a Permanent FEPC
1948–1959	Business Agent for Local 22
1950	(January 16) Local 22 Representative for the NAACP delegation to the Washington, DC, Civil Rights Conference

1951	(August–September) Studied workers' education in Sweden and Denmark
1951–1952	Urban League Fellow, Ruskin College, Oxford University (England)
1952	Observed labor conditions in France and Italy
1953	Local 22 delegate to the 49th Annual Convention of the NAACP
1954	Trade Union Committee member of the New York Branch of the NAACP 1954 Fight for Freedom Campaign
1955	Divorced from Owen Springer
1955	(October–November) AFL Observer to the ICFTU International Seminar (Accra, Ghana)
1956	Among the prime coordinators of Madison Square Garden rally honoring Heroes of Civil Rights
1957	(January 14–18) Observer at the first ICFTU African Regional Conference (Accra, Ghana)
1957	(January–February) Visited East Africa at the invitation of the KFL and TFL, and visited Belgian Congo
1957	(March 6) Independence Celebration of Ghana
1957–1958	(October 18–January 29) Based in Tanganyika for the American Trade Union Scholarship Program for Africa
1958	(December 8–13) All-African People's Conference (Accra, Ghana)
1958–1959	(December and January) Observed trade schools in Israel
1959	Ill for eight months and unable to work
1960–1966	(January 21) International Representative for Africa, AFL-CIO International Affairs Department
1960	Independence Celebration of Nigeria
1961	Independence Celebration of Tanganyika
1963	Independence Celebration of Kenya
1964	Adviser to the U.S. Worker Delegates at the 48th Session of the ILO for Special Commission of Women Workers in a Changing World
1965	(January 27–30) Adviser to the Liberian CIO at the First National Industrial Relations Conference
1965	Independence Celebration of Gambia
1965	(April 29) Married James Horace Kemp
1965–1969	General organizer for the ILGWU, Southeast Region
1969–1973	Midwest Director of the A. Philip Randolph Institute
1970–1974	Vice President of the NCNW
1973–	Consultant to African American Labor History Center
1973–1976	Staff member of the AALC
1975	World Conference on the United Nation's Decade for Women (Mexico City, Mexico)

1977–1981	Consultant for the AALC
1977–1981	Consultant for the AAFLI
1977	(November 18–21) Observer at National Women's Conference, "American Women on the Move" (Houston, Texas)
1977	Member of the NAACP Task Force on Africa
1977	(July 17–27) Pan-African Conference on the Role of Trade Union Women: Problems, Prospects and Programs (Nairobi, Kenya)
1980	AALC Trip to South Africa with Lester Trachtman
1985	(July 15–26) World Conference on the United Nation's Decade for Women (Nairobi, Kenya)
1990–1993	Hosts foreign labor delegations traveling to Pittsburgh
1996	Commentator in the PBS/WETA documentary, A. *Philip Randolph: For Jobs and Freedom*
2000	Honored by National Labor Leaders in a tribute dinner
2000	Solidarity Center of AFL-CIO establishes the Maida Springer Fund
2002	Participates in a Labor Tour in East Africa

Selected Bibliography

Archives

Amistad: MSK Papers, Amistad Research Center, Tulane University, New Orleans, LA.

APR Papers: A. Philip Randolph Papers, Schomburg Center for Research in Black Culture, New York Public Library, New York, NY.

BP: Borochowicz Papers, Wagner Labor Archives, Bobst Library, New York University, New York, NY.

Brown files: Record Group 18-004, International Affairs Department, Irving Brown files, 1943–1989, George Meany Memorial Archives, Silver Spring, MD.

BSP: Bordentown School Papers, Bordentown branch of the Burlington County Library, Bordentown, NJ.

Country Files: Record Group 18-001, International Affairs Department, Country Files, 1945–1971, George Meany Memorial Archives, Silver Spring, MD.

ILGWU Archives: General Collection number 5780, ILGWU Archives, Kheel Center for Labor-Management Documentation and Archives, Cornell University, Ithaca, NY.

Lovestone files: Record Group 18-003, International Affairs Department, Jay Lovestone files, 1939–1974, George Meany Memorial Archives, Silver Spring, MD.

LP: Jay Lovestone Papers, Hoover Institute, Stanford University, Stanford, CA.

Meany files: Record Group 1-027, International Affairs Department, Office of the President, Presidents Files: George Meany, 1944–1960, George Meany Memorial Archives, Silver Spring, MD.

MSK PP: Maida Springer Kemp Private Papers, Pittsburgh, PA. (In 1999 Springer added many of her private papers but not all to a collection of her work already in existence at Tulane University's Amistad Center.)

RP: Microfilm Edition of the A. Philip Randolph Papers, Schomburg Center for Research in Black Culture, New York Public Library, New York, NY

Schlesinger: MSK Papers, Schlesinger Library, Radcliffe College, Cambridge, MA.

Welsh Papers: Welsh Papers, Wagner Labor Archives, Bobst Library, New York University, New York, NY.

Books

Alpern, Sara, et al. *The Challenge of Feminist Biography*. Chicago: University of Illinois Press, 1992.

Ananaba, Wogu. *The Trade Union Movement in Africa, Promise and Performance*. New York: St. Martin's Press, 1979.

Anderson, Jervis. A. *Philip Randolph: A Biographical Portrait*. Berkeley and Los Angeles: University of California Press, 1972.

Aronowitz, Stanley. *False Promises: The Shaping of American Working Class Consciousness*. New York: McGraw-Hill, 1973.

Busby, Margaret, ed. *Daughters of Africa: An International Anthology of Words and Writings by Women of African Descent from the Ancient Egyptian to the Present*. London: Jonathan Cape, 1992.

Chamberlain, Mary, and Paul Thompson, eds. *Narrative and Genre*. New York: Routledge, 1998.

Conniff, Michael L. *Black Labor on a White Canal, Panama, 1904–1981*. Pittsburgh: University of Pittsburgh Press, 1985.

Cooper, Frederick. *Decolonization and African Society: The Labor Question in French and British Africa*. New York: Cambridge University Press, 1996.

Danish, Max D., and Leon Stein, ed. *ILGWU News-History, 1900–1950, the Story of the Ladies' Garment Workers*. Atlantic City: ILGWU Golden Jubilee Convention, 1950.

Dubinsky, David, and A. H. Raskin. *David Dubinsky: A Life with Labor*. New York: Simon & Schuster, 1977.

Dunaway, David K., and Willa K. Baum, eds. *Oral History: An Interdisciplinary Anthology*. 2nd ed. Walnut Creek, CA: AltaMira Press, 1996.

Epstein, Melech. *Jewish Labor in U.S.A.: An Industrial, Political and Cultural History of the Jewish Labor Movement, Two Volumes in One*. Vol. 2, 1914–1952. Jersey City, NJ: Ktav Publishing House, Inc., 1969.

Feinstein, Alan. *African Revolutionary: The Life and Times of Nigeria's Aminu Kano*. Boulder, CO: Lynne Rienner Publishers, 1987.

Foner, Philip S., and Ronald L. Lewis, eds. *Black Workers: A Documentary History from Colonial Times to the Present*. Philadelphia: Temple University Press, 1989.

———. *The Black Worker from the Founding of the CIO to the AFL-CIO Merger, 1936–1955*. Vol. 7, *The Black Worker: A Documentary History from Colonial Times to the Present*. Philadelphia: Temple University Press, 1983.

Franklin, John Hope, and August Meier, eds. *Black Leaders of the Twentieth Century*. Chicago: University of Illinois Press, 1982.

Friedman, Steven. *Building Tomorrow Today: African Workers in Trade Unions, 1970–1984*. Johannesburg: Ravan Press, 1987.

Frisch, Michael. A *Shared Authority: Essays on the Craft and Meaning of Oral and Public History*. Albany: State University of New York, 1990.

Geiger, Susan. *TANU Women: Gender and Culture in the Making of Tanganyikan Nationalism, 1955–1965*. Portsmouth, NH: Heinemann, 1997.

Geiss, Imanuel. *The Pan-African Movement: A History of Pan-Africanism in America, Europe and Africa*. New York: Africana Publishing Co., 1974.

Giddings, Paula. *When and Where I Enter: The Impact of Black Women on Race and Sex in America*. 1984; repr., New York: Bantam Books, 1988.

Gluck, Sherna Berger, and Daphne Patai. *Women's Words: The Feminist Practice of Oral History*. New York: Routledge, 1991.

Goldsworthy, David. *Tom Mboya: The Man Kenya Wanted to Forget*. New York: Africana Publishing Co., 1982.

Gray, Paul. *Unions and Leaders in Ghana: A Model of Labor and Development*. New York: Conch Magazine Ltd., 1981.

Hamilton, Charles V. *Adam Clayton Powell, Jr.: The Political Biography of an American Dilemma*. New York: Macmillan Publishing Co., Inc., 1992.

Haywood, Harry. *Black Bolshevik: Autobiography of an Afro-American Communist*. Chicago: Liberator Press, 1978.

Hedgeman, Anna Arnold. *The Trumpet Sounds: A Memoir of Negro Leadership*. New York: Holt, Rinehart and Winston, 1964.

Hill, Ruth Edmonds, ed. *The Black Women Oral History Project*. 10 vols. New Providence, NJ: K. G. Saur Verlag, 1991.

Houser, George. *No One Can Stop the Rain: Glimpses of Africa's Liberation Struggle*. New York: Pilgrim Press, 1989.

Jarret-Macauley, Delia. *The Life of Una Marson, 1905–1965*. Manchester: Manchester University Press, 1998.

Jeffrey, Jaclyn, and Glenace Edwall, eds. *Memory and History: Essays on Recalling and Interpreting Experience*. Lanham, MD: University Press of America, 1994.

Kelly, Sean. *America's Tyrant: The CIA and Mobutu of Zaire*. Washington, DC: The American University Press, 1993.

King, Kenneth, ed. *Ras Makonnen: Pan-Africanism from Within*. New York: Oxford University Press, 1973.

Kurtz, Laura S. *Historical Dictionary of Tanzania*. African Historical Dictionaries, no. 15. Metuchen, NJ: Scarecrow Press, 1978.

LaFeber, Walter. *The Panama Canal: The Crisis in Historical Perspective*. 2nd ed. New York: Oxford University Press, 1989.

Legum, Colin. *Pan-Africanism: A Short Political Guide*. New York: Praeger, 1965.

Lewis, David Levering. *When Harlem Was in Vogue*. New York: Knopf, 1984.

Leydesdorff, Selma, Luisa Passerini, and Paul Thompson, eds., *International Yearbook of Oral History and Life Stories*. Vol. 4, *Gender and Memory*. New York: Oxford University Press, 1996.

Lynd, G. E. *The Politics of African Trade Unionism*. New York: Praeger, 1968.

MacShane, Denis, et al. *Power! Black Workers, Their Unions and the Struggle for Freedom in South Africa*. Boston: South End Press, 1984.

McFarland, Daniel Miles, ed. *Historical Dictionary of Ghana*. African Historical Dictionaries, no. 39. Metuchen, NJ: Scarecrow Press, 1985.

Morgan, Kathryn. *Children of Strangers: The Stories of a Black Family*. Philadelphia: Temple University Press, 1980.

Morgan, Ted. *A Covert Life: Jay Lovestone, Communist, Anti-Communist, and Spymaster*. New York: Random House, 1999.

Murray, Pauli. *The Autobiography of a Black Activist, Feminist, Lawyer, Priest, and Poet*. Knoxville: University of Tennessee Press, 1987.

Murray, Pauli, and Leslie Rubin. *The Constitution and Government of Ghana*. London: Sweet and Maxwell, 1961.

Naison, Mark. *Communists in Harlem during the Depression*. New York: Grove Press Inc., 1984.

Selected Bibliography

Nasstrom, Kathryn L. *Everybody's Grandmother and Nobody's Fool: Frances Freeborn Pauley and the Struggle for Social Justice* (Ithaca, NY: Cornell University Press, 2000).

Newton, Velma. *The Silver Men, West Indian Labour Migration to Panama.* Kingston, Jamaica: Institute of Social and Economic Research, University of the West Indies, 1984.

Noer, Thomas J. *Cold War and Black Liberation: The United States and White Rule in Africa, 1948–1968.* Columbia: University of Missouri Press, 1985.

Norwood, Stephen H. *Labor's Flaming Youth: Telephone Operators and Worker Militancy, 1878–1923.* Urbana: University of Illinois Press, 1990.

Ojo, Olusola. *Africa and Israel: Relations in Perspective.* Boulder, CO: Westview Press, 1988.

Orlech, Annelise. *Common Sense and a Little Fire: Women and Working-Class Politics in the United States, 1900–1965.* Chapel Hill: University of North Carolina Press, 1995.

Osofsky, Gilbert. *Harlem: The Making of a Ghetto, Negro New York, 1890–1930.* 2nd ed. New York: Harper & Row, 1971.

Padmore, George. *Pan-Africanism or Communism? The Coming Struggle for Africa.* 1956; repr., New York: Doubleday, 1971.

Peters, Joel. *Israel and Africa: The Problematic Friendship.* London: The British Academic Press, 1992.

Proceedings of the AFL-CIO Constitutional Convention. Vol. 1 (1959), 485.

Rasmussen, R. Kent. *Historical Dictionary of Rhodesia/Zimbabwe.* African Historical Dictionaries, no. 18. Metuchen, NJ: Scarecrow Press, 1979.

Ray, Ellen, William Schaap, Karl Van Meter, and Louis Wolf, eds. *Dirty Work 2: The CIA in Africa.* London: Zed Press, 1980.

Richards, Yevette. *Maida Springer: Pan-Africanist and International Labor Leader.* Pittsburgh: University of Pittsburgh Press, 2000.

Smertin, Yuri. *Kwame Nkrumah.* New York: International Publishers, 1987.

Smith, Hilda Worthington. *Opening Vistas in Workers' Education: An Autobiography of Hilda Worthington Smith.* Washington, DC: Privately printed, 1978.

Stein, Leon, ed. *Out of the Sweatshop: The Struggle for Industrial Democracy.* New York: Quadrangle/New York Times Book Co., 1977.

Stevens, Richard P. *Historical Dictionary of Botswana.* African Historical Dictionaries, no. 5. Metuchen, NJ: Scarecrow Press, 1975.

Syme, Adjingboru A., Regional Secretary CPP Northern Ghana. Foreword by J. K. Tettegah, General Secretary, Ghana Trades Union Congress. *Ghanaians Salute to Israel: The Story of the Ghana Youth Delegation to Israel.* Accra, Ghana: Guinea Press Ltd., 1957.

Thelen, David, ed. *Memory and American History.* Bloomington: Indiana University Press, 1990.

Tordoff, William. *Government and Politics in Africa.* 2nd ed. Bloomington: Indiana University Press, 1993.

Vaz, Kim Marie, ed. *Oral Narrative Research with Black Women.* Thousand Oaks, CA: Sage Publications, 1997.

Ware, Susan, ed. *Forgotten Heroes: Inspiring American Portraits from our Leading Historians*. New York: The Free Press, 1998.

Weiler, Peter. *British Labour and the Cold War*. Stanford, CA: Stanford University Press, 1988.

Weisbrot, Robert. *Father Divine and the Struggle for Racial Equality*. Urbana: University of Illinois Press, 1983.

Wolensky, Kenneth C. *Fighting for the Union Label: The Women's Garment Industry and the ILGWU in Pennsylvania*. University Park, PA: The Pennsylvania State University Press, 2002.

Articles and Pamphlets

Baskin, Jeremy. "AFL-CIO-AALC-CIA." *South African Labour Bulletin* 8 (December 1982): 51–67, Braamfontein, South Africa: Institute for Industrial Education.

Blake, Debra J. "Reading Dynamics of Power through Mexican-Origin Women's Oral Histories." *Frontiers* 19 (September–December 1998): 24–41.

Borland, Katherine. "That's Not What I Said": Interpretive Conflict in Oral Narrative Research." In *Women's Words: The Feminist Practice of Oral History*, edited by Sherna Berger Gluck and Daphne Patai, 63–75. New York: Routledge, 1991.

Cohen, Barry. "The CIA and African Trade Unions." In *Dirty Work 2: The CIA in Africa*, ed. Ellen Ray, William Schaap, Karl Van Meter, and Louis Wolf, 70–79. London: Zed Press, 1980.

DuBois, W. E. B. "The Spectator: George Padmore's Life." *National Guardian*, October 12, 1959.

Etter-Lewis, Gwendolyn. "Black Women's Life Stories: Reclaiming Self in Narrative Texts." In *Women's Words: The Feminist Practice of Oral History*, edited by Sherna Berger Gluck and Daphne Patai, 43–58. New York: Routledge, 1991.

Forbes, Mary Ann (AALC), and James B. Parks (AFL-CIO). "Giving Birth to Freedom." Washington, DC: AALC, 1995. Pamphlet.

Frisch, Michael. "Dialogue I." In *Memory and History: Essays on Recalling and Interpreting Experience*, edited by Jaclyn Jeffrey and Glenace Edwall, 59–68. Lanham, MD: University Press of America, 1994.

Geiger, Susan. "Women in Nationalist Struggle: TANU Activists in Dar Es Salaam." *International Journal of African Historical Studies* 20, no. 1 (1987): 1–26.

"Ghana's Descent to Dictatorship." *AFL-CIO Free Trade Union News* 19 (April 1964).

"Gilbert E. Bursley." Biographical information. University of Michigan News Service, January 1965. Ann Arbor: University of Michigan, Bentley Historical Library.

Gluck, Sherna Berger. "Reflections on Oral History in the New Millennium: Roundtable Comments." *Oral History Review* 26 (Summer–Fall 1999).

———. "What's So Special about Women? Women's Oral History." In *Oral History: An Interdisciplinary Anthology*, 2nd ed., edited by David K. Dunaway and Willa K. Baum, 215–30. Walnut Creek, CA: AltaMira Press, 1996.

Grigg, John. "A Very Practical Faith." *The Times* (London), August 14, 1992, features section.

Hale, Sondra. "Feminist Method, Process, and Self-Criticism: Interviewing Sudanese Women." In *Women's Words: The Feminist Practice of Oral History*, edited by Sherna Berger Gluck and Daphne Patai, 121–36. New York: Routledge, 1991.

Helmreich, Jonathan E. "U.S. Foreign Policy and the Belgian Congo in the 1950s." *The Historian* 58 (Winter 1996): 315–29.

"Historic Meeting in Botswana . . . South African Trade Unionists Speak Out." *AALC Reporter* 8 (May 1973).

Hoffman, Alice. "Reliability and Validity in Oral History." In *Oral History: An Interdisciplinary Anthology*, 2nd ed., edited by David K. Dunaway and Willa K. Baum, 87–93. Walnut Creek, CA: AltaMira Press, 1996.

Hoffman, Alice M., and Howard S. Hoffman. "Reliability and Validity in Oral History: The Case for Memory." In *Memory and History: Essays on Recalling and Interpreting Experience*, edited by Jaclyn Jeffrey and Glenace Edwall, 107–30. Lanham, MD: University Press of America, 1994.

Honig, Emily. "Getting to the Source: Striking Lives: Oral History and the Politics of Memory." *Journal of Women's History* 9 (Spring 1997): 139–58.

Marcum, John. "French-Speaking Africa at Accra." *Africa Special Report* 4 (February 1959).

"NAACP Task Force Travels to Africa." *AFL-CIO Free Trade Union News* 12 (April–May 1977).

Portelli, Alessandro. "Oral History as Genre." In *Narrative and Genre*, edited by Mary Chamberlain and Paul Thompson, 23–45. New York: Routledge, 1998.

Schwartz, Jerry. "Labor Leader David Dubinsky Dies at 90." Associated Press, September 17, 1982.

Seraile, William. "Henrietta Vinton Davis and the Garvey Movement." *Afro-Americans in New York Life and History* (July 1983): 7–24.

Solidarity of Labor: The Story of International Worker Organizations. Workers of the World Series, no. 4. Salt River, South Africa: International Labor Research and Information Group, 1984. Pamphlet.

"The Strikes in Ghana: What Are the Facts?" *AFL-CIO Free Trade Union News* 17 (May 1962).

"Support Ghana Strikers." *AFL-CIO Free Trade Union News* 16 (October 1961).

Turner, Diane D. "Reconstructing the History of Musicians' Protective Union Local 274 through Oral Narrative Method." In *Oral Narrative Research with Black Women*, ed. Kim Marie Vaz, 177–96. Thousand Oaks, CA: Sage Publications, 1997.

Velie, Lester. "The Lady and the Gangster." *Reader's Digest* (January 1957).

Watson, Lawrence C. "Understanding Life History as a Subjective Document: Hermeneutical and Phenomenological Perspectives." *Ethos* 4 (Spring 1976): 95–131.

Weiss, Nancy J. "Whitney M. Young, Jr.: Committing the Power Structure to the Cause of Civil Rights." In *Black Leaders of the Twentieth Century*, edited by John Hope Franklin and August Meier, 331–58. Urbana: University of Illinois Press, 1982.

Wilmsen, Carl. "For the Record: Editing and the Production of Meaning in Oral History." *Oral History Review* 28 (Winter–Spring 2001): 65–85.

Williams, Rhonda Y. "'I'm a Keeper of Information': History-Telling and Voice." *Oral History Review* 28 (Winter–Spring 2001): 41–63.

Selected Bibliography

Williams, Stephen. Review of *Guns and Gandhi in Africa*, by Bill Sutherland and Matt Meyer. *African Business* (January 2001): 42.

Oral Histories

Columbia University, New York, NY, Butler Library, Oral History Project.

Granger, Lester. Interview by William Ingersoll, June 1955.

Zimmerman, Charles. Interview by Miles Gavin, May 8, 1979. AFL-CIO Oral History Interview no. 1 (AFL-CIO merger). George Meany Memorial Archives, George Meany Center for Labor Studies Oral History Project, New York.

Hill, Ruth Edmonds, ed. *The Black Women Oral History Project*. 10 vols. New Providence, NJ: K. G. Saur Verlag, 1991.

Greenlee, Marcia M. "Sadie Alexander Interview." Vol. 2, 67–85.

Rothschild, Maurine. "Frances O. Grant Interview." Vol. 4, 361–421.

Balanoff, Elizabeth. "Maida Springer Kemp Interview." Vol. 7, 39–127.

"The Twentieth-Century Trade Union Woman: Vehicle for Social Change." Oral History Project Program on Women and Work. Ann Arbor: Unviersity of Michigan, Bentley Historical Library.

Peterson, Esther. Interview by Martha Ross, 1978.

Robinson, Dollie Lowther. Interview by Bette Craig, 1977.

ILGWU Archives. General Collection number 5780, Kheel Center for Labor-Management Documentation and Archives, Cornell University, Ithaca, NY.

Zimmerman, Charles. Interview by Henoch Mendelsund, 1976.

Interviews by Yevette Richards

Alogo, Joyce, March 21, 1991.

Brombart, David, March 5, 1993.

Chiume, Kanyama, March 20, 1991.

Mohamed, Bibi Titi, March 20, 1991.

Morand, Martin, January 29, 1991.

Mpangala, Maynard, March 9, 1991.

Silverman, Jennie, April 30, 1991.

Organs, Official Journals, and Newspapers

AALC Reporter, AFL-CIO

AFL-CIO Free Trade Union News (also *International Free Trade Union News*)

African Recorder, Asian Recorder, New Delhi, India

Africa Special Report, African-American Institute, Washington, DC

Free Labour World, ICFTU, Brussels, Belgium

Justice, ILGWU

Negro World, UNIA

Online Sources

Africa News. http://www.lexis-nexis.com/.

All Africa News. http://allafrica.com or http://www.lexis-nexis.com/.

Associated Press

The Columbia Encyclopedia. http://www.bartleby.com/65/.

Encyclopedia Britannica Online. http://www.britannica.com.

Facts on File World News Digest. http://www.2facts.com.

Financial Times. http://www.lexis-nexis.com/.

International Press Service. http://www.lexis-nexis.com/.

National Guardian. http://www.lexis-nexis.com/.

New York Times. http://www.lexis-nexis.com/.

The Times (London). http://www.lexis-nexis.com/.

Washington Post. http://www.lexis-nexis.com/.

Xinhua News Agency. http://www.lexis-nexis.com/.

Atkinson, Brooks. "Artful Simplicity of Sholom Aleichem Captured in 'Fiddler on the Roof.'" *New York Times,* October 6, 1964. In "Sholom Aleichem Network on the Worldwide Web, 1997–1999." www.sholom-aleichem.org/fsaws/Memoirs,%20Comentary,%20Reviews/nyt%20fiddler%20review.htm (accessed May 15, 2000).

"Autherine Lucy Foster to Visit, Lecture at UA." University of Alabama home page. http://graduate.ua.edu/news/nov2002/foster20021111.html (accessed May 4, 2003).

Bearden, Romare Howard. "In Black-and-White: Photomontage Projections 1964." Bassett Gallery, August 23–November 16, 1977. http://users.aol.com/MenuBar/bearden/bearden.htm (accessed April 14, 2003).

Beck Cultural Exchange Center, Inc. "William Henry Hastie." www.korrnet.org/beckcec/hastie2.htm (accessed March 18, 2003).

"Bibi Titi and the Treason Trials of 1970." *East African,* November 10–16, 1999, features section. http://www.nationaudio.com/News/EastAfrican/081199/Features/PA3.html (accessed February 24, 2003).

Buffalo Fine Arts Academy. "Bearden." Education Programs, ArtStart Index, Albright Knox Art Gallery, c. 2000. www.albrightknox.org/ArtStart/ASimagesA-I.htm (accessed April 14, 2003).

Bundles, A'Lelia. "Madam C. J. Walker, 1867–1919, Entrepreneur, Philanthropist, Social Activist." 1998–2001, the Lewaro Corporation®. http://www.madamcjwalker.com/ (accessed March 18, 2003).

CLUW mission statement. "Coalition of Labor Union Women." http://www.cluw.org/about.html (accessed April 29, 2003).

"Deaths: Lord Twining." Facts on File World News Digest, August 9, 1967. World News Archive. http://www.2facts.com (accessed November 22, 2003).

Edwards, David, and Mike Callahan. "OKeh Album Discography." www.iconnect.net/home/bsnpubs/okeh.html (accessed March 18, 2003).

Eugene V. Debs Foundation. "Personal History, Eugene V. Debs." http://www.eugenevdebs.com/pages/histry.html (accessed April 14, 2003).

Fellowship of Reconciliation. "History and Supporters." www.forusa.org/about/history.html (accessed March 18, 2003).

Frommer, Harvey. "Remembering the New York Renaissance Five." Travel Watch. www.travel-watch.com/renfive.htm (accessed March 18, 2003).

"Global Unions: Labour Leaders @ Davos 2001: About the Labour Leaders." http://www.union-network.org/Unisite/events/wef/About/Mazur.htm (accessed April 29, 2003).

History Net. "The Tragedy of the S.S. *St. Louis.*" http://history1900s.about.com/library/holocaust/aa103197.htm (accessed April 14, 2003).

Horty Springer, "Legal Services, Attorney Bios, Eric W. Springer." http://www.hortyspringer.com/LS/bios/bio.springer.htm (accessed March 18, 2003).

"Introduction, About the Center." South Centre, www.southcentre.org/introindex.htm. Last updated November 18, 2003 (accessed July 2, 2000).

Johnson, Reginald A. "The Urban League and the A. F. of L.: A Statement on Racial Discrimination." *Opportunity: Journal of Negro Life* 13, no. 8 (August 1935): 247. Posted on the New Deal Network. http://www.newdeal.feri.org/opp/opp35247.htm (accessed April 14, 2003).

Kempton, Murray. "Workers Defense League." *The New York Review of Books*, November 5, 1970. http://www.nybooks.com/articles/10773 (accessed April 14, 2003).

"Kwaku Baah Praises Busia, Danquah . . . Chastises NPP." *Ghanaian Chronicle*, Ghana Web. http://www.ghanaweb.com/GhanaHomePage/NewsArchive/artikel.php?ID=11885 (accessed March 2, 2003).

Lazar, Robert E. "Guide to the International Ladies Garment Workers Union; Local 89; Luigi Antonini, General Secretary; Correspondence, 1919–1968." Collection number 5780/023. Kheel Center for Labor-Management Documentation and Archives, Cornell University Library. http://rmc.library.cornell.edu/EAD/htmldocs/KCL05780-023.html (accessed April 14, 2003).

Library of Congress. "Tenor Roland Hayes." Imagination, American Treasurers of the Library of Congress. www.loc.gov/exhibits/treasures/trio32.html (accessed March 18, 2003).

Melville, Kyle. "W. Montague Cobb." http://www.anthro.mankato.msus.edu/information/biography/abcde/cobb_w.html (accessed March 13, 2003).

National Academy of Sciences. "W. Montague Cobb." African Americans in Science, Engineering, and Medicine: A Portrait Collection of the National Academy of Sciences. http://www.nas.edu/aahm/portrait.htm (accessed March 13, 2003).

"Nkomo, Joshua." Encyclopedia Britannica Online. http://search.eb.com/eb/article?eu=57393 (accessed February 28, 2003).

The Nobel Foundation. Biography, Ralph Bunche, The Nobel Peace Prize—Laureates, Nobel e-Museum. http://www.nobel.se/peace/laureates/ (accessed November 25, 2003).

Park Net, National Park Service. "Florence Mills House, a National Historic Landmark, Places Where Women Made History." A National Register of Historic Places Travel Itinerary. www.cr.nps.gov/nr/travel/pwwmh/ny24.htm (accessed March 18, 2003).

Selected Bibliography

Prince Karim Aga Khan IV (1376/1957), Content 8. "Aga Khans period—Aga Khan I to Aga Khan IV, Ismaili History." First Ismaili Electronic Library and Database. http://ismaili.net/~heritage/histoire/history08/history836.html (accessed May 4, 2003).

"Remembering Malam Aminu Kano." *Daily Trust* (Abuja, Nigeria), April 17, 2003. Africa News Service, copyright 2003, AllAfrica, Inc., Lexis Nexis (accessed March 13, 2003).

Sirleaf, Ellen Johnson. "Liberia: A Framework for Change and Renewal." *The Perspective*, November 12, 1999. Africa News Service, Lexis Nexis (accessed November 25, 2003).

"South Africa: NAACP Asks U.S. Business Withdrawal." Facts on File World News Digest, January 20, 1978. World News Archive. http://www.2facts.com (accessed March 13, 2003).

"South Africa: Racial Labor Limits to Be Lifted." Facts on File World News Digest, May 4, 1979. World News Archive. http://www.2facts.com (accessed March 13, 2003).

Spartacus. "Daily Worker." http://www.spartacus.schoolnet.co.uk/USAworkerD.htm (accessed April 14, 2003).

Tapson, Bobby. "No Reason to Abandon Liberia—Opposition Parties Tell International Community." *The News* (Monrovia), June 7, 2002. Africa News Service, copyright 2003, AllAfrica, Inc., Lexis Nexis (accessed November 25, 2003).

Things Graphics and Fine Arts. "Bearden, Artists Bios," c. 1999. www.thingsgraphics.com/biographs/bearden.htm (accessed April 14, 2003).

Tuskan, Erhan. "Introduction, Historical Background, Inventory of the Archives of the International Confederation of Free Trade Unions, 1949–1993." International Institute of Social History Archives. http://www.iisg.nl/archives/html/i/10751819.html (accessed April 14, 2003).

UNITE. "Women in UNITE History." http://www.uniteunion.org/research/history/womeninunite.html (accessed April 14, 2003)·

Williams, Anthony L. "Annie Turnbo Malone." Black Heritage Day II. http://www.isomedia.com/homes/bhd2/annie_malone.htm (accessed March 18, 2003).

Workmen's Circle/Arbeter Ring, "Workmen's Circle: The Center for Cultural Jewish Life." http://www.circle.org./index.htm (accessed April 14, 2003).

World ORT. "Educating for Life." http://www.ort.org/asp/page.asp?id=1 (accessed April 14, 2003).

"Zambia No Model for Democracy; Continuing Human Rights Violations." In Recent Short Country Reports, Human Rights Watch Publications, More, HRW Publications, Human Rights Watch. www.hrw.org/reports98/zambia/ (accessed June 30, 2000).

Film

Bauman, Suzanne, and Rita Heller. *The Women of Summer: An Unknown Chapter of American Social History*. Filmmakers Library, 1985.

Index

345

American Labor Party, 98–99, 129
Amin, Idi, 136
Anastasia, Albert, 99
Anderson, Elisha, 23
Anderson, Eliza, 11, 19, 23–29, 200
Andrews, Freida Louise, 127
Angela, Stella Maria, 318
Angels, 96, 112–16
Angleton, James Jesus, 16, 63
Angola, 217
anti-apartheid activism, 283–88, 297
anticolonialism, 2, 16, 21, 80, 240, 322–23
anti-Communist policies (AFL-CIO), 133–34, 228, 237, 246–47, 285, 293–94, 322–23
Anti-Slavery Society of London, 304
Antonini, Luigi, 104–5
apartheid, 136, 207, 212, 283–89, 291–94, 297, 300–301
A. Philip Randolph Institute (APRI), 259, 269, 275
Appiah, Anthony, 152
Appiah, Joseph Emmanuel, 152
Arab-Israeli war, 210
Asian-American Free Labor Institute (AAFLI), 307, 318–19
Avriel, Ehud, 303
Azikiwe, Benjamin Nnamdi, 302–3

Baah, Kwaku, 263
Babin, Ms., 264
Banda, Hastings Kamuzu, 236–37
Barbara Lomax School for Trade Union Women of South Africa, The, 288
Barber, Wilfred, 165
Barnett, Ross, 229
Baskin, Jeremy, 298, 300–301
Bates, Daisy, 277
Bearden, Bessie, 125
Bearden, Romare Howard, 125
Beck, Dave, 170
Ben Diner & Schlesinger, 35
Bethune, Mary McLeod, 132, 142–45
Bevin, Ernest, 147
Bilbo, Theodore, 272
Black Cross Nurses, 39
Blackett, Grace Woods, 133
Black Family Reunion, 260
Black Panthers, 309
Blouse, Skirt and Sportswear Workers' Union (Local 23-25), 308, 319
Blumstein, L. M., 19, 40
Bolin, Jane, 125

Bond, Horace Mann, 160
Bond, Julian, 160
Bordentown Industrial School: See Manual Training and Industrial School for Colored Youth
Borha, Lawrence, 252
Botsio, Kojo, 173
Botswana, 152
boycotts, 19, 188, 259, 272, 279, 284–85
Boyer, Arthur, 82–83
Breedlove, Sarah: See Walker, Madame C. J.
British Trade Union Congress, 2
British Trade Union Council (TUC), 169, 174
Brooks, Angie: See Randolph, Angie Brooks
Brotherhood of Sleeping Car Porters, 20, 35–36, 66–67, 74, 127–28, 268–69, 279
Brown, Irving, 162, 207–8, 219, 240–41, 252, 302–3
Brown v. the Board of Education, 282
Bryant, Carolyn, 229
Bryant, Roy, 229
Bryn Mawr Summer School for Women Workers, 64, 78, 136
Building Service Employees' Union (Local 189), 257
Bunche, Ralph Johnson, 259, 277
Bursley, Gilbert E., 214–15
Bush, George H. W., 10
Bush, George W., 210
Busia, Kofi Abrefa, 263
Buthelezi, Mangosuthu Gatsha, 285, 287–88, 298, 301–2
Butler, Broadus Nathaniel, 290

Calera, Marie, 71
Camps and Schools for Unemployed Women, 79
Carey, James B., 129
Carrington, Adina Stewart: activist role, 20, 39–41, 80, 136, 175–76; Back to Africa movement, 43; as beautician, 32–33, 48; childhood, 23–25; cooking skills, 31–32, 41, 59; daughter's wedding, 53–54; employment experiences, 31–33; family stories, 11–12; ill health, 201, 204; immigration to United States, 26; Kubai, Mrs., 166; Mboya, Tom, 162; Mwangi, Kamau, 163; relationship with daughter, 33–35, 42, 47, 131; relationship with mother, 26–28; role models, 22; travels in Africa, 164–67

Hastie, William Henry, 51
Hayes, Helen, 129
Hayes, Mrs. Roland, 98
Hayes, Roland, 51, 98
Haywood, Harry, 62
Hedgeman, Anna Arnold, 128, 277
Height, Dorothy, 259–60, 277, 281
Heinz, John, 288
Helms, Jesse, 229
Hemb, Mzee, 181, 189
Herero people, 207, 213
Hill, Anita, 10
Hill, Herbert, 130, 258, 269–70
Hillman, Bessie Abramowitz, 120
Hillman, Sidney, 64, 98–99, 122
Hitler,Adolph, 96, 104–5
Hoffa, Jimmy, 170
Hooks, Benjamin Lawson, 266
Hoover, Herbert, 90
House Labor Committee, 100, 130
Hudson Shore Labor School, 64, 74, 77–78, 97, 105–7
Humphrey, Hubert, 79
Hyde Park, 97, 116–17

Ibrahim, Fatma Ahmed, 14–15
Ibrahim, Said, 43–44
Igbo people, 253
independence movement: African labor movement, 191–92, 208–9; colonialism, 211–12, 220–21; Congo, 215–16; educated elite, 211–12; ethnic conflicts, 238; Ghana, 135, 158, 211–13; Guinea, 208; market women, 212; Mohamed, Bibi Titi, 191; Namibia, 288–89, 304, 324; Nigeria, 303; Northern Rhodesia, 289, 304–5; Padmore, George, 134, 149–50; political struggles, 323–25; Portuguese colonies, 217; post-World War II, 158–59; repressive regimes, 13; Robeson, Paul Leroy Bustill, 21; South Africa, 284; Southern Africa, 236–38; Southern Rhodesia, 241, 244; Tanzania, 164, 313–15; United States government policies, 206; women as activists, 191, 220–22
Indonesia, 307, 317–18
Industrial Workers of the World (IWW), 62
Inkatha Freedom Party, 287, 301–2
Institute of Tailoring and Cutting, 199, 234, 238, 248–49, 254, 308, 327–28
integration, 36–37, 75, 102–3, 228–29, 229, 321; See also civil rights movement

International Brotherhood of Electrical Workers (IBEW), 133
International Brotherhood of Red Caps, 254
International Brotherhood of Teamsters (IBT), 170
International Confederation of Free Trade Unions (ICFTU): affiliation disputes, 206, 222–25; AFL-CIO, 170; African labor movement, 14, 15, 168, 170–73; African Regional Organization (AFRO), 307; Brown, Irving, 208, 219; formation, 134, 141; international union conference, 172; racial discrimination, 2; resentment towards Maida Springer, 244; South Africa, 293; Welsh, Edward, 62
International Council of Women, 184–87
International Federation of Christian Trade Unions (IFCTU), 244
International Federation of Trade Unions (IFTU), 105
International Labor Defense (ILD), 61
international labor movement, 81, 105, 132, 160–61, 198, 248–52; See also AFL-CIO; International Confederation of Free Trade Unions (ICFTU)
International Labor Organization (ILO), 232, 265, 293, 307
International Ladies' Garment Workers' Union (ILGWU): African labor movement, 203; Broadway play, 72; Cohn, Fannia, 65, 77; Communist Party, 79, 85; Congress of Industrial Organizations (CIO), 133; cooperative housing project, 119; Crosswaith, Frank, 20, 75; Dress Joint Board, 102, 109, 111; Dressmakers' Union (Local 22), 60–61, 72, 79, 85; Dubinsky, David, 63; educational programs, 250; hosting foreign delegations, 161–62; inequality, 17; Institute of Tailoring and Cutting, 248–49; internal fighting, 84–85; Italian Dressmakers' Local (Local 89), 105; labor exchange trip, 137–39, 145–50; Local 10, 63; March on Washington, 277; membership, 1–2, 67; Newman, Pauline, 65; Peterson, Esther, 65; Plastic Button and Novelty Workers' Union (Local 132), 69, 77, 94; rivalries, 98–99; Starr, Mark, 136, 149; training courses, 100; Undergarment Workers' Union (Local 62), 71; Unity House, 162–63; voter registration, 276; war effort, 147; Zimmerman, Charles "Sasha", 62; See also racial discrimination

Index

Index

National Industrial Recovery Act (1933), 68
National Labor Relations Act (1935), 44, 68
National Organization for Women (NOW), 97, 267
National Recovery Administration (NRA), 68
National Union of Clothing Workers, 286
National Union of Tanganyikan Workers (NUTA), 208
National Urban League, 22, 51, 262, 278
Nazi-Soviet Non-Aggression Pact (1939), 85
Neue Heimat, 171, 198–99
New England Telephone Company, 47–48
Newman, Pauline, 65, 78, 144
Newsom, Don, 318
New York City, 19
New York Federation of Labor, 63
New York Renaissance Five (the Rens), 55–56
New York State School of Industrial and Labor Relations of Cornell University, 294, 297
Nigeria, 211, 238–39, 250–53, 302–3
Nigerian-Biafran War, 253
Nixon, Edgar Daniel, 279
Nixon, Richard M., 125
Nkomo, Joshua Mqabuko Nyongolo, 237–38, 244–45
Nkrumah, Kwame, 135, 168, 173, 208–9, 211–13, 223–25, 263
nonviolent protests, 19–20, 168, 284
Norris, Clarence, 61
Northern Rhodesia, 236, 239, 250, 289, 304–5, 316–17
Nujoma, Sam Shafishuna, 288–89, 302–4
Nurse, Malcolm Ivan Meredith: See Padmore, George
Nyasaland, 236–37, 239
Nyerere, Joseph, 310
Nyerere, Julius Kambarage: correspondence with Maida Springer, 11, 288; family, 310; hometown visit, 309–11; independence movement, 136–37, 159–61; interactions with colonial government, 180, 183–84; mission to United Nations, 189, 190–91; rally in Tanganyika, 10; South Commission, 306, 309; Tanganyika African National Union (TANU), 168, 313–15

Obote, Milton, 191
Ochwada, Arthur Aggrey, 189
Odede, Walter, 137
Odeyemi, Ezekiel O. A., 252
O'Farrell, Patrick J., 234, 249, 286, 295–96

Okuku, Alphonse, 164, 203
Oliver, C. Herbert, 29
O'Neal, Charlotte, 309
O'Neal, Pete, 309
Organization for Rehabilitation and Training (ORT), 103
Organization Of African Trade Union Unity (OATUU), 208–9, 223–25
organized labor: African labor movement, 13–16; anti-Communist policies, 17, 63, 80; benefits, 45, 60, 70; black activism, 20–21, 60–62; black leadership, 267–68; equal rights, 321; gender inequality, 17; NAACP, 275; rivalries, 98–99, 122, 132–33; Robeson, Paul Leroy Bustill, 21; runaway businesses, 273; the South, 271–75; standards affecting workers, 272; training courses, 274, 279; women's issues, 274–75, 279–80, 307, 327; See also AFL-CIO; Randolph, Asa Philip; strikes

Padmore, Dorothy, 151, 156
Padmore, George, 1, 134–36, 148–51, 156–57, 173, 178
Palestine, 210
Palmer, J. Mitchell, 41
Pan-African Conference on the Role of Trade Union Women, 294, 316
Pan-African Congress, 134, 149
pan-Africanism, 2, 21, 134–37, 210, 238
Pan-Africanist Congress, 284–86, 293
Panama, 1, 19, 23, 25–27
Parker, Julia O'Connor, 133, 138–40, 146
Parker, Sally, 139
Parks, Rosa, 277, 279
Pasipanodya, Charles Mudundo, 237, 244, 250
Payne, Eugenia (Gene), 55
Perkins, Frances, 64, 132
Persian Gulf War, 9
Peterson, Esther, 64–65, 99, 121, 136, 153–54
Peterson, Oliver, 64, 136, 153–54
picketing, 19, 40, 99, 112–14, 272, 298, 300
Pidada, Ida, 318
Pins and Needles, 72
"Pioneers of Negro Leadership", 267–68
Plastic Button and Novelty Workers' Union (Local 132), 69, 77, 94, 96, 101–16
Poro College, 22, 48–49, 59
Porter, Violet Lewis, 164, 201, 264–65
Powell, Adam Clayton, Jr., 40, 100–101, 129–30, 257–58, 261, 269, 278

Index

Index